Untwisting the Serpent

Untwisting the Serpent

Modernism in Music, Literature, and Other Arts

DANIEL ALBRIGHT

The University of Chicago Press

Chicago and London

DANIEL ALBRIGHT is the Richard L. Turner Professor in the Humanities at the University of Rochester. He is the author, most recently, of *Quantum Poetics: Yeats, Pound, Eliot and the Science of Modernism* and *Stravinsky: The Music-Box and the Nightingale.*

The University of Chicago Press, Chicago 60637
The University of Chicago Press, Ltd., London
© 2000 by The University of Chicago
All rights reserved. Published 2000
Printed in the United States of America
09 08 07 06 05 04 03 02 01 00   5 4 3 2 1

ISBN (cloth): 0-226-01253-0
ISBN (paper): 0-226-01254-9

Library of Congress Cataloging-in-Publication Data

Albright, Daniel, 1945 –
    Untwisting the serpent : modernism in music, literature, and other arts / by Daniel Albright
        p.   cm.
    Includes bibliographical references and index.
    ISBN 0-226-01253-0. — ISBN 0-226-01254-9 (pbk.)
    1. Music—Philosophy and aesthetics.   2. Music and literature.   3. Art and music.   4. Music—20th century—History and criticism.   5. Modernism (Art)   6. Modernism (Literature)   I. Title.
ML3849.A44   2000
700'.4112—dc21
                                                            98-47950
                                                                 CIP
                                                                 MN

Contents

Part Two: Figures of Dissonance among the Arts

Illustrations

Musical Examples

Acknowledgments

This is a book about collaborations, and in many ways it is itself a collaborative act. It grew out of a National Endowment for the Humanities Summer Seminar I directed in 1995, on Modernism in literature and music. I will always treasure my memories of that group, for their intellectual companionship gave me the material and inspiration for much of this study. I owe a great debt to all twelve—especially (for the purposes of this book) to Barbara Tedford, for her translation of Prokofiev and for her research on *Parade;* to Siglind Bruhn, for introducing me to a method for describing the way in which a musical structure can embed a text's changes in point of view; and to Lydia Goehr, for strong intellectual gusts in many different directions. Her hurricane did not spare Pensacola, either.

Two colleagues of mine at the Eastman School of Music gave guest talks at this seminar: Kim Kowalke, on *The Threepenny Opera;* and Ralph Locke, on *Four Saints in Three Acts* and the funding of Modernist music. Both have been kind enough to read parts of this book, and their scholarship and imagination have shaped many a page. It has been a piece of supreme good luck for me to work with two musicologists with such subtle minds and wide culture. I also thank Richard Taruskin, who encouraged me at an early stage in the composition and who suggested one of this book's guiding themes; and Jody Blake, who helped give breadth and detail to the sections on the visual arts. The many gifts I received from these four include a national anthem, an Elizabethan protagonist, a large snake, and a dancing wheel.

In casting about for literary models for a book such as this, I found a great many distinguished precedents, but I was particularly drawn to such narratively gifted critics as Roger Shattuck, Marjorie Perloff, and Carolyn Abbate. All critics tell stories; and if some of the stories I tell are extremely familiar, I can only plead that, in a book written about so many different media, I had to rehearse a number of old tales, since no one (least of all the present writer) is equally familiar with music and literature and the visual arts, and the basic narratives of one medium need retelling to those proficient in other media. The story told in this book is perhaps a bit unusual, in that it concerns itself more with aesthetic philosophy than with political history. This is a book that states a theory of artistic collaboration—though the theory isn't transcendental in character, but an extremely low-flying theory, skimming close to finite art works.

My two research assistants, Marianne Milton and Alyssa O'Brien, not only found for me everything I asked for, but also found for me many things I needed but didn't know I needed, sometimes by a process that can only be explained as clairvoyance.

Kathleen Hansell, the music editor of the University of Chicago Press, gave this book the honor of her devotion, her patience, and her precision of eye and ear; I can scarcely imagine that it would have come into being without her. Nancy Trotic, a superb copy editor, has demonstrated once and for all that God, not the devil, is in the details.

I can hardly express my debt to Su Yin Mak—my student, my teacher, and, in a course on musical semantics that we designed together, my co-worker. She has spent endless hours working with me on the musical analyses in this book, until by now I no longer have the faintest idea where my ideas end and where hers begin: one of the most remarkable acts of intellectual symbiosis I've ever known. If the reader discovers anything valuable in this book, that value pertains to the thread of her wit that is shot through this text.

Finally, I thank two other people. One of them has listened to music with a wholly unprejudiced ear; the other has cast a rigorous but kindly eye on every page of this book. Both have not only shed light on the objects here considered, but have also illustrated and reconfigured the mind of the observer: Christopher and Karin.

Note

Concerning references: these are given at the end of the text, cued by *incipit*. If the title of the reference is in German or French, the translation of the quotation is my responsibility.

Untwisting the Serpent

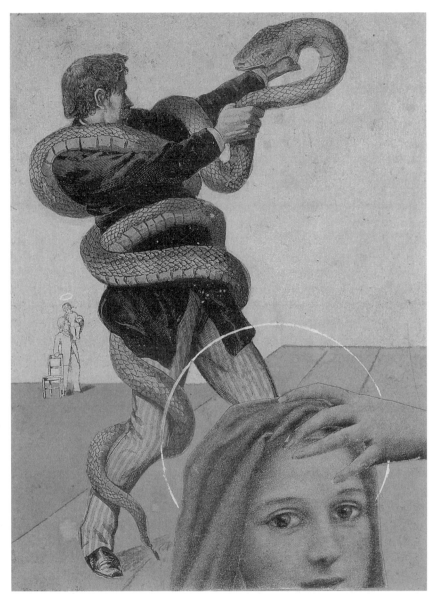

FIG. 1. Max Ernst, untitled, ca. 1920 (© 1999 Artists Rights Society (ARS), New York/ADAGP, Paris)

On the statue base: ⸱LAOCHOON⸱

⸱ROMAE⸱IN⸱PALATI O⸱PONT⸱IN⸱
⸱LOCO⸱QVI⸱VVLGO⸱DICITVR⸱
⸱BELVIDERE⸱

FIG. 2. Nicholas Beatrizet, called Nicola Beatricetto. *Laocoön,* ca. 1570 (*Apollo* 126 [November 1987]: 67)

Laocoön Revisited

A strong theme in the history of music consists of the discovery that counterpoints could be so precisely synchronized and adjusted that the ear could choose to constitute them either horizontally, as independent lines, or vertically, as a succession of chords. And, just like music, the comparative arts have their polyphonies and homophonies.

For a long time, most students of artistic projects involving several media have been contrapuntalists, tracing horizontal lines of development. An opera, for example, may be dissected into a libretto, a series of stage pictures, and a musical score; then the analyst can describe the patterns of reinforcement or weakening generated from the superposition of these three independent media—the words, the décor, the music.

This horizontal approach has often been successful. But this book will examine the possibilities for a more vertical treatment. Perhaps there are chords in which one element is a musical note, another element is a word, and a third element is a picture— chords that compose themselves out of different layers of sensuous reality. Perhaps those artists involved in the collaboration understood the total effect not in terms of the private effects of the separate media, but in terms of progressions, cadences, of these transmediating chords. Certain collaborations seem to possess such an intimate integrity that all consciousness of the constituent arts vanishes. The arts that pertain to time, such as poetry and music, seem to acquire a new dimension in space; the arts that pertain to space, such as painting, seem strangely temporalized.

Recent critics have been wary of speaking of vertical phenomena in the comparative arts, and for good reason. We don't want to appeal to pop-Wagnerian mystical fusions of the arts; we want to be exact and lucid. But I believe that it is possible to be rigorous in the treatment of the hypothetical entities that exist in fringe regions of the aesthetic experience, where time touches space, and music acquires semantic weight. And further, I believe that artists themselves have tried to assist critics by naming and classifying the basic vertical units of the comparative arts. For example, Pound described the *ideogram,* in which a picture takes on the responsibility of writing; and Lessing, Brecht, and Weill described the *gestus,* in which a contortion or movement of the body takes on the responsibility of speech. An ideogram or a *gestus* is not an element within any specific artistic medium; it is not an icon, not a word, but a chord, vibrating between media, abolishing the distinctness of media.

The purpose of this book is to examine a number of highly charged Modernist experiments in discovering how strongly the boundaries separating the various artistic media manage to repel transgression. In some cases, the component media seem to pull apart; in other cases, they seem to draw together. And in the cases where they draw together, the complete art work seems to presuppose the existence of some indivisible center, casting out extensions of itself into the varied realms of music and painting and language, but itself simple and unitary.

This book is in search of the fundamental units of the mixed arts—*figures of consonance,* one might call them, in the sense of presupposing a deep concord among artistic media.

The twentieth century is a particularly fruitful field for this search for figures of consonance, perhaps in part because the physicists of this period refused to separate time from space, but instead regarded time and space as a multidimensional whole. If time and space are part of the same system, then a painting and a poem may be conceived as the same thing, reconstituted on different axes. Similarly, in the domain of the temporal arts, twentieth-century philosophy blurs differences between spoken language and music. The linguistics of Ferdinand de Saussure, the philosophies of Ludwig Wittgenstein and Jacques Derrida, tend to strip language of denotation, to make language a game of arbitrary signifiers; and as words lose connection to the world of hard objects, they become more and more like musical notes. Wittgenstein claimed, "To say that a word has meaning does not imply that it *stands for* or *represents* a thing. . . . The sign plus the rules of grammar applying to it is all we need [to make a language]. We need nothing further to make the connection with reality. If we did we should need something to connect that with reality, which would lead to an infinite regress." For Wittgenstein, the consequence of this disconnection was clear: "Understanding a sentence is much more akin to understanding a theme in music than one may think."

For one stream of Modernism, then, the arts seem endlessly interpermeable, a set of fluid systems of construing and reinterpreting, in which the quest for meaning engages all our senses at once. Thinking is itself looking, hearing, touching— even tasting, since such words as *savoir* and *sapience* are forms of the Latin *sapere,* taste. Of course, other important Modernist collaborations tried to refute this confusion of the senses by insisting strongly on the absolute separateness of the artistic media—an insistence that may have been motivated precisely by a desire to counter the tendency of recent philosophy and science to deny the existence of walls.

The study of these vertical aesthetic units is full of surprises: for example, the more strongly the artists insist that there must be some subsistent transmediating thing beneath the poetry and the music and the pictures, the looser the actual connections among the artistic media often become. To allege that all media are one may serve, paradoxically, to call attention to their recalcitrance, their distinctness, their refusal to cooperate. Artists who rely on figures of consonance may find that those figures are highly radioactive, with short half-lives. A figure of consonance may break down completely into a physical movement and a passage of music or speech, in a state of utter contradiction—a complex partly sympathetic, partly disgusting to the audience. Examples are easy to find in the political operas of Brecht and Weill, where a prostitute's gesture of stretching her hands longingly toward the moon may be accompanied by a song that holds her cramped in a rigid circuit of boredom.

Conversely, artists who deliberately seek divergence among the constituent arts sometimes discover that the impression of realness, *thereness,* is heightened, not diminished. In surrealist spectacles, for example, the systematic misnaming of objects—as when the husband in Apollinaire's *Les mamelles de Tirésias* calls out "The violin" as he picks up a urinal—may ultimately manage to call attention to the solidity, the heft, of what lies beneath the flimsy constructs of language. And artists who relish the discord among artistic media may find that figures of consonance sometimes pop up out of nowhere, when least expected or desired: music, text, and spectacle may seem completely unrelated to one another, but can suddenly achieve moments of bizarre congruence. An example can be found in the recording of Cage's *Europera 5,* when a random collocation of events, a pianist happening to play a lush arrangement of Puccini's *Oh! mio babbino caro* at the same moment that a long-dead soprano sings Verdi's *Caro nome* on an antique gramophone, achieves a strange pathos, a delirious sense of the preciousness and fragility of the operatic medium itself.

The analytical procedures used in this book could be used to describe the artistic collaborations of any age, not just the twentieth century. And so I shall begin by reviewing the history of the problem of coordinating artistic media— what is usually known as the *Laocoön problem.*

Lessing and Horace

The study of comparative arts has two patron saints. One is the old Roman poet Horace, who wrote in his *Ars poetica* that a poem should be like a picture—*ut pictura poesis*. The other is Gotthold Ephraim Lessing, who wrote in his *Laokoon* (1766), in effect, No, it shouldn't. Are the arts all one art, or are the arts fundamentally diverse? Horace and Lessing stated the extremes in this debate.

Horace may not quite deserve his prestige among students of comparative arts. His dictum seems rather casual, even flippant, a restatement of a platitude from the Greek poet Simonides. Why should a poem be like a picture? Because it should appeal to the detailing power of the visual imagination? Because it should be a graduated field where important things are large and central, and unimportant things small and peripheral? These might be thoughtful responses to the question, but they are not Horace's responses: Horace said only that poets and painters are equally free to do anything they please (l. 9), and that poetry is like painting in that some poems, like some paintings, look good up close, whereas others look good from a distance; some look good in the shade, whereas others look good in bright light (ll. 361–64). This innocent and useless argument might almost be taken as a parody of Horace's own catchphrase *ut pictura poesis*—the urbane poet seems to insinuate that there are a good many poems and paintings that would look best of all in total darkness, and from miles away. It fell to Diderot and Wagner and others, long after Horace's time, to devise serious arguments concerning the unity of the arts.

In order to prove the counterargument, that the arts should be considered separately, Lessing told a story. In 1506—Michelangelo's time—an old statue was dug up from the ruins of the Baths of Titus in Rome, showing a large bearded man and two much smaller boys, their arms and legs all tangled in the coils of a gigantic snake. To the Italian Renaissance it seemed a kind of herald from antiquity, as if the classical world were trying to imprint its forms on the modern world, to haul itself into resurrection. The subject matter of the statue was obviously the myth of Laocoön, the Trojan priest who, with his sons, was crushed to death for prophesying that bad luck would befall Troy if the great wooden horse outside the gates were taken into the city—Beware of Greeks bearing gifts, he warned. His loathsome fate seemed to the Trojans a proof of the folly of his counsel; but of course he was right—Poseidon killed him only because Poseidon hated Troy most bitterly. Among other classical authors, Virgil told this tale (*Aeneid* 2.199–224), with some discrepancies from the tale told by the statue. And discrepancies between visual representations and verbal representations interested Lessing enormously.

According to Virgil, Laocoön raised up to the stars a horrible clamor *(Clamores simul horrendos ad sidera tollit),* like the bellowing of a sacrificial bull. But

Lessing noted that the Laocoön of stone was not screaming: his mouth is half-shut, uncontorted. Lessing thought he knew why: the visual arts and the verbal arts are governed by different rules of propriety. It is proper for a poem to represent a man being squeezed to death by a snake as screaming, and it is proper for a statue to represent him as rather calm. For one thing, a statue is obligated to beauty, and a screaming mouth isn't beautiful: "The wide naked opening of the mouth—leaving aside how violently and disgustingly it distorts and shoves aside the rest of the face—becomes in a painting a spot and in sculpture a hollow, making the most repulsive effect." For another thing, Lessing felt that the visual arts must never depict a moment of climax, which inevitably seems ready to slump into a less intense state; the chastity of the medium is violated by the excessive arousal of the subject. But most importantly, Lessing argued that painting and sculpture must observe the decorum of space, while poetry must observe a decorum of time:

> this essential difference between [poetry and the visual arts] is found in that the former is a visible progressive act, the various parts of which take place little by little *[nach und nach]* in the sequence of time; whereas the latter is a visible static act, the various parts of which develop next to one another *[neben einander]* in space. But if painting, by virtue of its signs or its means of imitation, which it can combine in space alone, must completely renounce time, then progressive acts, because progressive, do not belong among its subjects—painting must content itself with acts next to one another, or with mere bodies.

This is the source of Lessing's famous distinction between the spatially juxtapositive arts of *nebeneinander,* such as painting, sculpture, and architecture, and the temporally progressive arts of *nacheinander,* such as poetry and music. For Lessing, time and space are planes of existence that scarcely seem to meet; each defines a domain of art with distinct protocols. In space, Laocoön is stoic, a poised, physically graceful body; his mouth is nearly closed, for the very fixity of stone discords with the evanescence of a scream. In time, Laocoön is psychological, intent, a roar of feeling, a long-drawn convulsion from capture to squeeze to shriek to mute death.

Lessing argued that painting was bad if it resisted its spatiality—for example, if it displayed on one canvas successive stages of the career of one subject. And he argued that poetry was bad if it resisted its temporality—for example, if it piled together long strings of adjectives in static descriptions. Lessing could tolerate certain doubtful cases in which poetry advanced near the margins of the visual, such special stunts as Homer's "round wheels, bronze, eight-spoked"; but he disliked all verbal clutter, all that slowed down the swift trajectory of the action. For Lessing, the right syntax for a poem was verb-oriented, just as the right syntax for a painting was anything that flattened the spectator's sense of temporal progression. Painting should freeze; poetry should move like the wind.

Some of Lessing's contemporaries, such as Herder, disapproved of this rigid segregation of temporal from spatial, this narrowness of taste. But even if Lessing's strictures may seem outmoded by the success of some extreme experiments in crossing the boundaries between time and space—Jackson Pollock's spatters and drips, a painting style that is all verb and no noun, or Gertrude Stein's hermetic prose, bleached, arrested, almost paralyzed—nevertheless Lessing defined the problem with intelligence and resourcefulness. For a long time now, Laocoön's mouth has gaped wide open, despite Lessing's best efforts; and we need a theory of art to explain why this is now permissible—or whether his jaws should snap shut once and for all.

Babbitt and Greenberg

There have been several attempts in the twentieth century to write a successor to Lessing's *Laokoon*, redefining the debate in terms of the radically transgressive art that Lessing didn't live to see. One of the first was Irving Babbitt's *The New Laokoon* (ca. 1910), an erudite book casting a cold eye on many attempts to blur the division between *nacheinander* and *nebeneinander*—from Father Castel's *clavecin oculaire,* a color organ that played silent symphonies with blue and green and red corresponding to *do* and *re* and *sol,* to a concert of perfumes performed at the Carnegie Lyceum in 1902. This is, however, a disappointing book, weak on the philosophy and physiology of cross-sensory appeals, and, though ostensibly broad-minded, actually far fussier and more philistine than Lessing. Babbitt likes rules and discriminations, and considers the advanced artists of his time to be (mostly) a band of freakish synaesthetes and effeminate bad boys. He admires Mozart for his spontaneous obedience to systems of artistic law, and deplores Strauss for laborious and calculated simulations of extramusical phenomena—especially the baby bath in the *Symphonia Domestica* of 1904. Ultimately, Babbitt dismisses many artists, from Hugo and Wagner on, as "eleutheromaniacs"—freedom-crazed; the Harvard humanist prefers an art of firm contour and generic distinction to the flux-ridden, formless art of the modern age.

In 1940 the art historian Clement Greenberg published "Towards a Newer Laocoon," with glances toward both Lessing and Babbitt. Here Greenberg takes one strand of the *Laokoon* argument about as far as it can be taken: both Lessing and Babbitt admit certain *rapprochements* among the artistic media, certain collaborations between time and space, but the puritan Greenberg resists the slightest erasure of the lines that divide one art form from another. Greenberg has a simple criterion for success: a work of art is good to the extent that it displays the substantiality of its medium, without dissembling or fraud. Painting is a thrusting-forth of pigment; sculpture is an extancy of metal, an inertia of stone; music is "the sound beneath the note." As for poetry, Greenberg ridicules the Romantic prevarication that poetry has a celestial status, beyond any finite medium:

> Shelley . . . exalted poetry above the other arts because its medium came closest, as Bosanquet put it, to being no medium at all. In practice this aesthetic encouraged that particular widespread form of artistic dishonesty which consists in the attempt to escape from the problems of the medium of one art by taking refuge in the effects of another. Painting is the most susceptible to evasions of this sort.

> Poetry subsists no longer in the relations between words as meanings, but in the relations between words as personalities composed of sound, history, and possibilities of meaning. Grammatical logic is retained only in so far as it is necessary to set these personalities in motion . . . [the poem's] efficacy . . . is to agitate the consciousness with infinite possibilities by approaching the brink of meaning and yet never falling over it. The poet writes, not so much to *express,* as to create a thing which will . . . produce the emotion of poetry.

To Greenberg, a poem is an open field of acoustic teasing, of ambiguous sounds that engage the reader's mind to grope toward meanings that it will never find. A woodcut should manifest naked wood; a musical composition, naked sound waves; a poem, naked phonemes, trying not to denote anything in particular.

In this essay, Greenberg presents the finest statement I know of Modernist aesthetic purism. Each art should remain inviolate within its own private domain; every act of transmediation is a contamination; space and time are mortal enemies. It seems that painters would do well to be deaf and illiterate, and musicians blind and aphasic.

Babbitt's central motivation behind his new *Laokoon* was to resist confusion and to deride mystic unions of the arts—he found that he could use Lessing's thought as a club to thrash Baudelaire and Wagner. Greenberg, however, had different motives for his newer *Laokoon*. First, he wanted to uphold the dignity of the arts in isolation. For Greenberg, painting was in danger of becoming subsumed in literariness, as if literature were a kind of monster that wanted to eat up all the other arts: "Painting and sculpture in the hands of the lesser talents . . . become nothing more than ghosts and 'stooges' of literature." Second—and this is a crucial advance in formulating the Laocoön problem—Greenberg hated the illusory character of the arts, and thought that by restoring each art to its private medium, he could improve the realness, the ontological self-sufficiency of art: "To restore the identity of an art the opacity of its medium must be emphasized"; "The history of avant-garde painting is that of a progressive surrender to the resistance of its medium; which resistance consists chiefly in the flat picture plane's denial of efforts to 'hole through' it for realistic perspectival space. . . . The motto of the Renaissance artist, *Ars est artem celare* [Art is the concealing of art], is exchanged for *Ars est artem demonstrare* [Art is the manifesting of art]." Greenberg advocated an art that confessed its artificiality, a style of painting that didn't pretend that the canvas was a window, a style of fiction that feigned nothing. Instead of seeing through the medium, we must savor the medium itself: the scarified, slippery feel of metal, the exact sonority of a very high trombone note, the spondaic clumps in a poetic line with few unstressed syllables.

This line of argument suggests that there is a relation between the Laocoön problem—are the arts one or many?—and the problem of mimesis. In a mimetic theory of art, the art work is only a copy, a contingency, not a freestanding, exultant thing: it must always lean for support on the entity in the world of experience on which it is modeled. But an entity in the world of experience generally presents itself as a spatiotemporal whole, and often presents itself to several sense organs at the same time. Therefore, insofar as an art object is focused tightly on some physical thing, it can be sensitive—perhaps *must* be sensitive—to aspects of the thing that extend beyond the range of any one artistic medium. If I am a sculptor, and my goal is to represent a particular man, I can carve a good likeness in stone; but the goal of representation demands that I do more. I might paint the stone with the colors of his skin and eyes and hair; I might spray on a faint fragrance of sweat; I might make the joints and the jawbone flexible; I might even install a little tape player inside the image, uttering some of my subject's characteristic phrases in a simulation of his voice. Soon I will have not a statue, but the talking and hand-shaking Abraham Lincoln at Disneyland. All this seems quite objectionable—an ignominy, a piece of kitsch, not Art with a capital A. But every objection will ultimately reduce itself to some statement that sculpture has some goal other than physical representation; and as soon as the spectator is asked to contemplate the stone itself, not what the stone represents, Greenberg will rise up and say, Aha!—yes, sculpture is about stone, not about modeling.

We all tend to believe that art becomes more deceitful and fraudulent the more mimetic it becomes; it descends to the mere *trompe-l'oeil, trompe-l'oreille*. Nevertheless, mimesis also promotes a friendly affiliation among the arts, a sense of their final oneness. If behind every finite work of art there lies some polysensual complex in the real world, then art should deploy all its resources in space and in time to try to grasp that ambiguous singularity. Painting can suggest temporal movement, and poetry can suggest the static array of objects in space; and each is obliged to do so if it is to present the fullest possible apprehension of reality. But everything changes as soon as the artist or the critic renounces the goal of mimesis. Suddenly the arts fly apart, because there is no common focal point: sculpture recedes into stone, painting into dyestuff, poetry into depictorialized syllables—each regarding the others with suspicion or hostility.

But Greenberg's story of the Modernist movement is biased and partial. In the twentieth century, artists have sought both to deny mimesis altogether, as Greenberg denied it, and also to improve mimesis beyond all bounds—sometimes the same artist has done both in the course of a career. The latter goal will tend to involve the artist with various simulations of secondary media: the poet will play with verbal equivalents of painting and music, and the painter will try to impart a narrative thrust to his images. The former goal will tend to isolate and protect the sanctity of one medium—though, as we'll see later, there have been some fascinating experiments in multiplanar coordinations of diverse arts, not for the sake of mimesis, but for the sake of building abstract mobiles in the space-time continuum. Modernism includes those who seek reality through copying the world of experience, and those who seek reality through the hardness, the heft of the individual artistic medium—itself perhaps at last only a metaphor for the close textures, the thingliness, of the world in which we live.

Greenberg, like Auden and Schoenberg and many others, recommended disillusionment, iconoclasm, as the path to wisdom. How can a painting unprevaricate itself, disentangle itself from the oily artfulnesses and concealments and trickeries of perspective illustration? Greenberg recommends two ways: either "the destruction of realistic pictorial space," by flattening the canvas and making the brushwork obvious; or the emphasizing of "the illusoriness of the illusions which [the artist] pretends to create." The artist may either stop sinning, or confess the sins so publicly that no further penance is needed; in either case the artist is no longer a prestidigitator or clown but someone engaged with the actuality of things. Of such an art we can say not *it imitates,* but *it is;* it is too concrete, or too abstract, to deign to represent. And Greenberg explicitly stated that when art is sufficiently illusionless, the abstract and the concrete converge: "an art . . . is abstract because it is almost nothing except sensuous"; or, as Randall Jarrell put it in 1949, writing of William Carlos Williams, "what is more abstract than a fortuitous collocation of sensations?" A piece of stone that seems carefully cut into no recognizable shape may seem far stonier than, say, Michelangelo's *David* seems; the spectator sees the rockiness of rock. But it may also seem unusually cerebral, since the spectator looks for some principle of geometry or (in Henry Moore's case) topology that guided the sculptor's hand, in the absence of a model in the world of experience. Greenberg liked art in which he felt both the workings of a brain and the roughness of granite, the abstract and the concrete, instead of the blandly modulated, mediated surfaces of conventional art. He felt that where there is no illusion, there must be truth—an attractive conclusion, but not necessarily a correct one.

All the Laocoönists reviewed so far are seekers after clarity and truth. Lessing hated the pretense that time could be like space, or space like time; Babbitt mocked those who saw musical notes as colors, or took the concept of artistic *taste* too literally; Greenberg sought solidity at the unyielding core of the medium itself. But there was another critic still more firmly set against artistic lies, still more gifted at despising: Theodor Adorno, whose *Philosophie der neuen Musik* (Philosophy of the New Music, 1948) is the finest of all modern sequels to *Laokoon,* even though neither Lessing nor the statue explicitly concerned him there. (In other books, Adorno shows he had made a detailed and profound study of Lessing's writings on art.) Adorno wrote the opening parts of the book around 1940, just the year of Greenberg's essay; in fact he cited Greenberg with approval, as a fellow opponent of kitsch. And Adorno's whole project is startlingly similar to that of Greenberg's newer *Laokoon.*

Adorno

How does music fit into the Laocoön problem? Should music isolate itself in a crystalline sphere, or should it attempt to accommodate itself to pictures, landscapes, verbal text? Lessing, Babbitt, and Greenberg had little to say about music—to the detriment of their arguments, since music is the most time-specific of all the arts. Babbitt, by his own admission, was ignorant of music; and music didn't occupy much of Lessing's critical attention, although, in the *Briefwechsel,* he makes the interesting point that we enjoy hearing musical imitations of unpleasant affects, such as sadness, because every affect is pleasurable in the absence of a specific object in the real world. But Adorno knew music—in effect, he created a new discipline, the philosophy of music. He was supremely well equipped to discuss the relation of music to the other arts; and if his conclusions are somewhat unsatisfactory, it is because his arguments are vitiated by the complex of hatreds that empowered them in the first place.

Adorno's book has two parts: praise of Schoenberg, and ridicule of Stravinsky. The intellectual dazzle of Adorno's prose tends to disguise the simplicity of some of his assumptions about art. Adorno is at heart a purist, like Greenberg: art is valuable to the extent that it is disillusioned, authentic. But Greenberg located the reality of music in sounds that impinge on the ear, in the grit of the phonic medium, whereas Adorno locates the reality of music inside the brain, in deep networks shocked into sensation. Why is Schoenberg a progressive force?—because his music is not a simulation of passion, but passion itself:

Dramatic music . . . from Monteverdi to Verdi offered expression as stylized, mediated, the semblance *[Schein]* of the passions. When it went past this and claimed substantiality beyond the semblance of the feelings expressed, this claim scarcely confined itself to the particular musical motions, which were to reflect the motions of the soul. The totality of the form alone, which governed the musical characters and their connection, guaranteed the claim. Completely otherwise with Schoenberg. The truly subversive moment for him lies in the change in the function of musical expression. No longer are passions feigned, but in the medium of music there are registered undissembled the incarnate motions *[leibhafte Regungen]* of the unconscious—shocks, traumata. They assault the taboos of form, because these taboos subject such motions of the unconscious to their censure, rationalize them and transform them into images.

Schoenberg's opera *Moses und Aron* (1930–32) concerns the smashing of a golden calf, in obedience to the commandment against graven images; and for Adorno, and for Greenberg also, every artistic image is a kind of idol, in need of destruction. Greenberg noted that "line . . . is never found in nature as the definition of contour," and he thought that painters tended to coop up their forms inside artificial line-boundaries. Similarly, Adorno wants to decathect music, liberate it from the arbitrary forms that channel expressions into mere images of expression, censored and poised, suitable for family entertainment. For Adorno, the human brain is a kind of touch-tone telephone network, in which the whistling of sounds establishes electrical connections, jolts of meaning; and Schoenberg has discovered the master sound-keys that evoke direct feeling. Monteverdi and Verdi deal in simulacra of shivers; Schoenberg deals in shivers themselves.

Schoenberg shatters idols, but Stravinsky, according to the second part of Adorno's book, manufactures idols: "The completely canny, illusionless *I* exalts the *Not-I* as an idol." In the course of this section, Adorno calls Stravinsky an acrobat, a civil servant, a tailor's dummy, hebephrenic, psychotic, infantile, fascistic, and devoted to making money—Adorno's noble gloom is shot through with a near hysterical spitefulness.

What is Stravinsky's crime? To Adorno, it is fundamentally a kind of fetishism, an endowing of dead musical formalities with a parody of excitement. Adorno noted that Schoenberg, in *Erwartung,* shows a human subject undergoing various shocks and yet still remaining a subject, a coherent human self; but "With Stravinsky there is neither alertness to anxiety nor a resisting *I,* but it is just accepted that the shocks do not allow themselves to be appropriated by anyone. The musical subject renounces any effort to hold out to the end, and is content reflexively to go along with the blows [at the end of *The Rite of Spring*]. He literally behaves like a man badly wounded in an accident that he cannot absorb." Schoenberg's music pertains to the authenticity of feeling, grounded in an actual human subject; Stravinsky's music pertains to disappropriated pseudo-feelings, feelings not felt by anyone in particular, dreams of feeling within a comatose subject. Adorno, like Lessing and Greenberg, had the profoundest horror of the counterfeit; and he thought that Stravinsky's rhythms were hectic but causeless, mere mechanical agitations of the nerves without any filtering through the higher centers of the brain, leading to a general zombification of the listener.

Adorno paid close attention to *Petrushka*, and he conceived Stravinsky along the lines of that ballet's charlatan: a clever manipulator of puppets—the extinct music conventions that he seeks to resuscitate—who attempts to reduce the auditor to a puppet. Stravinsky is shown to be the Thanatos of music, attempting to infect everyone with his own deadness. Adorno claims that Stravinsky's spastic, arbitrary rhythms—rhythms unrelated to the musical content—reduce the conductor to a thing pulled by wires; similarly, Stravinsky's relation to the listener is that of Professor Galvani to the dead frog: "The effect-connection that Stravinsky's music has in view is in fact not the identification of the public with the soul-movements *[Seelenregungen]* supposedly expressed in the dance, but instead a becoming-electrified in the manner of the dancer." This sentence sums up Adorno's differentiation between Schoenberg and Stravinsky: Schoenberg re-creates his subject's nuances of feeling in the listener, in a delicate transference of every spike of the electroencephalogram; but Stravinsky engages in a kind of musical electroconvulsive therapy, burning out the listener's memory, selfhood, jerking the motor nerves. Schoenberg lets you feel another's pain; Stravinsky makes you a robot. Schoenberg widens your field of cognitive sensitivity; Stravinsky unbrains you, makes you "a monad of conditioned reflexes." For Adorno, Stravinsky's music implies a physical body, visibly twisted in ugly spasms, as if Stravinsky were less a musician than a sculptor of grotesques, or a fiendish physiologist.

Part of Stravinsky's failure (as Adorno sees it) is political: it is the proper goal of art to resist the dehumanizing of a late-capitalist society, but Stravinsky, instead of resisting, embodies the dehumanization: today's music displays "the decay of experience, the substitution for 'life' of a process of economic adjustment directed by a concentrated economic force for arranging things." For Adorno, the chill of Stravinsky's music is simply the alienation of the worker from his work, from his whole interior feeling-world, made audible.

But far more of Adorno's study is devoted to criticizing Stravinsky for his aesthetic falseness than for his political incorrectness. And here we return to *Laokoon*: for Adorno thought that Stravinsky's greatest error lay in his refusal to accept the temporal character of music.

Lessing considered a poem that described at length a flower—the striations of the petals, the length of the stalk, the veining-pattern of the leaves—to be an unnatural act, an assault against the nature of the medium, since it performed a labored simulation of something a painter could do swiftly, effortlessly. But Lessing's censure of the flowery poet was nothing compared to the invective of Adorno against Stravinsky, for attempting what Adorno called a *pseudo-morphosis,* an attempt to organize a composition in one medium according to alien principles derived from a wrong medium. Adorno accused Stravinsky of pretending to be a cubist painter: "the spatialization of music is witness to a pseudomorphosis of music to painting, on the innermost level an abdication"; "The trick that defines all of Stravinsky's organizings of form: to let time stand in, as in a circus tableau, and to present time complexes as if spatial—this trick wears off. It loses its power over the consciousness of duration." Adorno's word *Pseudomorphose* is similar to the German word for metamorphosis, *Metamorphose;* and it implies a botched transformation, as if Proteus were caught in the midst of an uncompletable shape change, stuck between eel and tree. Stravinsky's evil reveals itself finally as a resistance to the medium of music—Adorno even found the predilection for ballet symptomatic, for Adorno regarded ballet as an essentially static and pictorial art, in which the music is a kind of standing-in-place to which dancers can wave their arms and legs while moving in circles. Lessing would have smiled to read Adorno's denunciations of juxtapositive musical form: the argument is a simple extension of the *Laokoon* into music.

Adorno almost implies that music constructed from triads (such as *do-mi-sol*) is pseudomorphic. He certainly implies that it's outmoded, rotten, part of the bourgeois domain of relaxed, unchallenging entertainment:

> The more dissonant the chord, the more . . . polyphonic it is . . . each single note, within the simultaneity of the sounding-together, assumes the quality of a "voice." The predominance of dissonance seems to destroy the rational, "logical" connections, the simple triad-relations, within tonality. And yet dissonance is more rational than consonance, insofar as it puts articulately in view the relation of the preceding notes, however complex—instead of purchasing unity through annihilation of the moments comprised in it, through "homogeneous" sound.

For Adorno, dissonant music is tense, articulate in its internal counterpoint, and therefore articulate in the realm of expression; but consonant music is smeary and bleary, its separate notes washed out onto smooth acoustic surfaces. The very familiarity, the commonness of common chord progressions, tends to detemporalize the music: we know what's going to happen before it happens. The unity of consonant music, the production of a shapeless sound-complex in which the constituent notes are annihilated, seems static, rather pictorial; for Adorno, music can best emphasize its temporality, its thrusting-forward, by maximum dissonance. Music that looks like slabs of preexisting music, chopped up and put back together in the wrong order, is for Adorno an affront to the audience and a crime against art—it asks the eye to do the work of hearing. Only music addressed to the ear, music that doesn't soothe but jolts into utter attention, is music worthy of the name. The arts of time must remain pure, distinct from the arts of space—this is the message of Adorno and Lessing and Greenberg alike.

Apollo and Marsyas

We have now examined a few of the windings of Lessing's snake into the world of Modernism. Possibly the book you're reading now will be the last twentieth-century *Laokoon,* since it is published so close to the end of this overwhelmingly sad and exhilarating century.

Lessing based his book on an ancient sculpture's congruence to an ancient poem; and perhaps another classical story, concerning the relation of music to other arts, would be helpful in conveying the argument of my book. There is a Greek parable that seems to state, in terms useful for a general theory of the arts, the antithesis between music that retains its pure apartness and music that impinges on many sensory areas of life: the myth of Apollo and Marsyas. It is a story that develops two kinds of artistic temperaments, the purist and the mimetic, which lead to ease or angst about the composer's role in complicated artistic projects.

Marsyas was a satyr, so pleased with his skill at playing the *aulos,* a reed instrument invented by Minerva, that he challenged Apollo to a music contest, to be judged by the Muses. The god won, and was so enraged by Marsyas's temerity that he roped him to a tree and flayed him alive—his whole body was one wound, his raw nerves and lungs and quivering organs exposed to the air (as Ovid tells the story in the sixth book of the *Metamorphoses*). One of the shocking aspects of this myth is that Apollo seems to act out of character: ever since Nietzsche's *The Birth of Tragedy* (1872), we are used to thinking of Apollo as a lucid, clarifying, beautiful god, the opponent of Dionysus and every sort of ecstasy and riot. If even Apollo can be maddened by a music contest, it suggests how dangerous is the goal of expression in the arts: the expresser may find himself most horribly exhibited, ex-pressed, pressed out.

Some of the force of this myth dwells in Greek assumptions about the superiority of music for strings to wind music. (A useful history of this theme can be found in John Hollander's *The Untuning of the Sky.*) For string players, such as Apollo, music is research, an inquiry into systems of correspondences. Music and astronomy are similar investigations of the proportionality of the cosmos: for the pitch ratios of vibrating strings are direct analogues of the ratios of the crystalline spheres on which the planets and the stars whirl. But for Marsyas, music is wind, breath, *pneuma*—animating spirit, feeling made sound; Marsyas was a satyr, and a satyr's grossness, sexual panting, clings to his music. The flaying of Marsyas can be read as a literalization of the sense-immediacy of expressive music—music that cuts to the quick of the player and the listener. The right response to Apollo's lyre is transcendental calm, for it grasps and re-presents the whole zodiac; the right response to Marsyas's aulos is to convulse in a dance orgy. Marsyas is the genius of *mimesis* in music; his piping evokes pleasure and pain, the fullness of emotional life, and therefore naturally lends itself to intensification through other artistic media, such as singing and dancing. Mimesis, as ever, works against purism in art: it tends to confound the distinctness of media.

Most composers tend either to the Apollonian or to the Marsyan model; and the model helps to determine the kind of collaboration that the composer can enjoy with artists in other media. An Apollonian composer tends to be quite comfortable with other artists: partly because the music dwells on such a lofty and disengaged plane of accomplishment that it has no significant connection to what poets and painters might do and therefore has nothing to lose from cross-media contexts, and partly because the music is conceived as sounding numbers, numbers that can easily be transferred to any other medium. Therefore the later Stravinsky—who claimed to be strictly Apollonian by temperament—wrote text-settings far more attentive to the verbal prosody (if only to contradict it) than to the verbal meaning. Number schemes, such as the ratio of two to one, or the golden section, can effortlessly be translated among words and painting and music; such formalities can be made exactly congruent, or can be counterpointed, as the artists choose. No intercontamination is possible, because where relations are purely formal, asemantic, no misunderstanding is possible.

But the Marsyan composer feels anxiety about collaboration. Here there is a need for semantic precision, for fidelity to feeling; and here there is possibility for betrayal. When Marsyas enters the theatre, he demands that the set designer and the poet and the lighting man all cooperate toward a single devastating effect, the effect intended by the music. Whereas Apollo may be magnanimous to the other artists or may casually flog them for their failings, because he is ultimately indifferent to them, Marsyas is close and crabbed, eager to control everything, fearful that emotional focus will be blurred or displaced. Therefore the earlier Schoenberg—as Marsyan as a composer can be—kept insisting on commonplace, unobtrusive, "realistic" décor for his short operas, so that his musical subjects, skinless and nerve-wracked, could howl without any circumambient distraction. The ideal solution for Marsyas is to attain universal competency in the arts, so that he can write the words, compose the music, paint the stage set, and sing the lead role.

Few artists are capable of putting together an opera single-handedly, but among the Modernists, we find a painter who wrote an opera libretto (Ko-koschka), a poet who composed music (Pound), a poet who sang his own theatre songs on recordings (Brecht), and a composer who painted pictures (Schoen-berg). It is as if artistic talent were a kind of libido, an electricity that could dis-charge itself with equal success in a poem, a sonata, a sculpture, or a tenor solo. This attitude is the opposite of that of the puritan Greenberg: instead of several arts cooped up in separate compartments, we have one art, fluid and dazzling, without internal boundaries.

The ultimate discharge of undifferentiated psychic energy is the scream, and it would seem that this sound belongs properly to Marsyas. But Apollo is also concerned with screaming, as the old fable suggests, and we find among our Apollonian theorists—Lessing, Greenberg, and Adorno, all suspicious of connec-tions among the arts—a certain purist preoccupation with the scream. Lessing ridiculed the excessive decorum of the French theatre of his day: he wanted ges-tures of tremendous intensity, what he called *gestus* (to be discussed in a later chapter); he wanted, in a sense, screams—he insisted that for the old Greek he-roes, wails and streams of tears were not at all ignoble. For Lessing, the purity of Laocoön's scream might be compromised by a plastic representation that made it look silly; in a sense, the whole *Laokoon* creates a theory of aesthetic division in order to maintain the sanctity of the expressive act in the temporal arts. All aestheticians who despise fakery in the arts, who seek authenticity, will tend to be connoisseurs of screams: for a scream is, arguably, the primal human response to the world, a response in no way prevaricated, or dissembled, or embellished. The reality that music seeks to convey, to embody, lies in that noise. To extend Greenberg's argument a little further than Greenberg went, one might say: Sculp-ture is the flaunting of stone; painting is the flaunting of pigment; and so music is the flaunting of shriek.

For Adorno, the most intense music is also the most time-conscious music, the music that most clearly insists on its nonspatial, nontextual, strictly musical character. He claims that the purity of the scream in Schoenberg's *Erwartung* requires a complete surrender to the concrete musical split-second, the intimate texture of discord, synaptic breakdown: every movement into abstract formal-ism, into predictable patterns of recurrence, represents a movement away from reality. Adorno wants music so intent on palpating the instantaneities of its pass-ing that it is completely unconscious of the wholes that it might comprise in space. The more deeply the composer penetrates into the hippocampus, the amygdala, the whole limbic system of emotional response, the less likely it will be that a poet or a painter can assist the surgery.

According to Apollonian purism, a scream is a phonic essence. From the Marsyan perspective, however, a scream isn't an essence, but a representation of some peak feeling that might be represented equally well by a great gash of red pigment, or by a dancer's simulation of an epileptic seizure, or by other artistic means. (Adorno, an Apollonian in wolf's clothes, avoids this conclusion by arguing that a dissonant chord is not a representation of a spasm in the brain, but *is* a spasm in the brain.) For a Marsyan composer, a musical scream may be intensified, not diminished, by finding a way of making music, painting, and text dissolve into a single devastating convulsion.

Kokoschka's Mörder, Hoffnung der Frauen

On occasion a Marsyan composer and a Marsyan painter have succeeded in creating an effective rhythm among vertical coordinations of the component arts. One such example is the opera *Mörder, Hoffnung der Frauen* (Murderer, Hope of Women), with a libretto by Oskar Kokoschka and music by Paul Hindemith. Such a collaboration demands nearly perfect unanimity of expressive aim, a sense that a single phenomenon can extend itself in space and time without becoming two different phenomena, located in different dimensions. Whereas the Apollonian artist is often content with inexact matching of music and pictures, the Marsyan artist tends to demand a unison effect. First we'll see how Kokoschka flays his characters alive in order to screw up the tension level of his art to its peak; then we'll see how Hindemith contributes lashings from his own whip, and thereby creates vertical complexes with Kokoschka's text.

Kokoschka was such a good Marsyan that he even liked to paint satyrs: in the second (1966) of two paintings entitled *The Power of Music,* he showed a laurel-wreathed impish creature playing a little horn, while to the side a naked woman stares forward with fixed, inane gaze, as if hypnotized; and in the first painting (1920) of this title, a woman flees in terror before another horn player. The head god of the satyrs and nymphs was Pan, who gave his name to the ultimate Power of Music: panic. In general, the Marsyan artist has two expressive goals, the goals depicted in these two paintings: seduction, and the sensation evoked by the point of a drill on a raw nerve.

Kokoschka was attracted to the musical world of Austria and Germany, partly because of his tormented sexual relations with Alma Mahler. And he was attracted to the theatre as well: in 1907 he tried his hand at writing a play, which was to be, by many accounts, the first German expressionist drama—*Mörder, Hoffnung der Frauen.* The intended dramatic effect may be seen in a drawing Kokoschka made for the play: a man stands on a fallen woman, his foot half-covered by her fat breast, his hand clenching a dagger; the woman's hand, more lobster claw than hand, seems to be groping for the man's groin. Both large figures, and the scrawny dog behind them, are drawn with vehement cross-

FIG. 3. Oskar Kokoschka, drawing for *Mörder, Hoffnung der Frauen*, ca. 1908 (Dube, *The Expressionists*, p. 181)

hatchings, as if the musculature and nerve structure were popping through the skin. It seems that men and women come together for the sake of flaying one another. Kokoschka explained his occasional predilection for anorexic models in the following way: "because you can see their joints, sinew and muscles so clearly, and because the effect of each movement is modeled more emphatically with them"; and the drawing for *Mörder, Hoffnung der Frauen* shows that the search for the truth (as Kokoschka understood truth) requires a peeling-away of the flesh.

The search for the truth about women requires not only a radical undressing of women's bodies, but a radical undressing of the *idea* of a woman. Kokoschka derived his black fable of human sexuality from Otto Weininger's *Geschlecht und Charakter* (Sex and Character, 1903). Weininger was perhaps the most precocious scholar since Nietzsche, widely read in biology, philosophy, and the literature of several languages, an anti-semitic Jew who, at the age of twenty-three, in 1903, staged his suicide at the house where Beethoven died; his career gives comfort to those who believe that extraordinary intellect is a kind of disease. Weininger's book is a mythology of misogyny, presented along the following lines: Maleness is essentially spiritual, anti-materialistic, pure; but maleness suffered a gnostic Fall when it was tempted by sensuality. This fallen manhood created woman, to embody and express, to revel in, its evil. Femaleness is therefore a contingency and an inauthenticity; a virtuous man will have nothing to do with women, and will certainly never stoop to procreation. Women are fundamentally filthy creatures, who have no interest in anything except phallus worship and sexual intercourse; if experience teaches us that there exist such things as chaste women, it is only because these poor freaks have managed to internalize male ethical values—values that so intimately violate the whole nature of women that they necessarily become hysterical. Weininger concludes his book with a recommendation of universal chastity, in the hope that the biological extinction of the human race will lead to its reunion with the spiritual One, lost so long ago when we descended to coarse material existence.

There are two points in *Geschlecht und Charakter* that touch closely on Kokoschka's play. The first lies in Weininger's sense of the deep ferocity of sex:

Novalis often repeated that all sexual urge is related to cruelty. The "association" has a deep foundation. Everything born of a woman must die. Birth and death stand in an indissoluble relation. In the presence of untimely death the sex drive awakens most violently in every being, as the need to propagate itself. And so coitus, not only psychologically as an act, but also from an ethical and scientific viewpoint, is related to murder: it denies the woman, but also the man; in the ideal case, it robs both of consciousness, in order to give life to the child. . . . Love is murder.

The second lies in Weininger's conclusion concerning the ultimate formlessness and nonentity of women. For Weininger, women aren't even evil, since they lack any sort of decisive interior lives:

Women have no existence and no essence, they *are* not, they are *nothing*. . . . Woman has no relation to idea, she neither affirms it nor denies it: she is neither moral nor anti-moral, she has, mathematically speaking, no sign [*Vor-*

zeichen], she is directionless, neither good nor evil, neither angel nor devil . . . she is as amoral as alogical. . . . Woman is a lie.

The concept of signlessness is intriguing. Weininger was thinking of plus or minus signs in arithmetic, but the thrust of his argument tends to push women into a state of general semiotic vacuum, not only an absence of form but an absence of signifiability—there's nothing there to denote, to point to. Weininger liked to cite Pope's line (from *Moral Essays* II) that women have no characters at all: they are simply wax shaped into prostitute or Madonna according to male whim. Weininger murdered the whole female gender, by proving that women never really existed in the first place.

Kokoschka was an artist committed to skinning his subjects alive. But from the perspective of Weininger's misogyny, it's not quite clear whether women are sufficiently real to be flayed; like the Grishkin of T. S. Eliot (to mention another misogynist), a woman may simply be a rubber skin pumped up with air, full of "pneumatic bliss." And Kokoschka may well have felt that women were hollow creatures, mere hallucinations of depraved male fantasy: he commissioned Hermine Moos to construct a life-sized doll bearing the features of Alma Mahler, as if the doll could be a more satisfactory, more authentic companion than the intolerable woman of flesh and blood. The profound sense that a woman is a sham, an eidolon, connects Weininger and Kokoschka: every bride is the bride of Frankenstein. This fury of dismantling normal notions of the feminine imparts an overwhelming luridness to Kokoschka's play; the whole text is one long scream.

The characters and plot of *Mörder, Hoffnung der Frauen* are spare: Man, Woman, male chorus, female chorus. The scene shows a night sky, and a tower with an iron grille for a door. The Man enters, wounded, in armor, with a band of men. The Woman appears, red dress, loose blond hair, with a certain sexual and metaphysical arrogance: "At my breath the yellow disk of the sun flares. My eye gathers the rejoicings of men. Their stammering desire crawls like a beast around me." But soon the Woman becomes disconcerted by the Man's steady gaze—"Why do you charm me, Man, with your glance? All-devouring light, you confuse my flame!"—and the Man, enraged, orders his followers to seize her and to burn his sign into her flesh. But as soon as the men brand her, she leaps up and stabs the Man with a knife. The Man, bleeding, cramped, moans of the general delirium and emptiness of human life: "Senseless craving from horror to horror, ceaseless circling in the void. Being born without birth, plunge of suns, reeling space." They lock him in the tower; the Woman vamps him by rubbing her body against the lattice door; but, paradoxically, he seems to gather strength while she seems to fail, until she is speaking as if *she* were the prisoner: "You weaken me—

I kill you—you chain me! I captured you—and you hold me! . . . you clasp me—as with iron chains—strangled." Her thighs convulse; the Man stands upright, tears the lattice door open; she screams and falls. The men and the girls—who have been engaging in sexual acts during this scene—all attack the Man; but he "kills them like flies" and strides away in the dark, as a cock crows.

This whole drama is an allegory of coition, from a Weininger-like point of view. Sex is an act in which a man tries to brand a woman, establish ownership, compel her signlessness to accept some sign; and an act in which a woman tries to kill a man, drink his blood, incorporate his force. Sex is also a game of mutual imprisonment, torture, and general cramp of being—as Yeats put it, paraphrasing Blake, "sexual love is founded upon spiritual hate." In sexual intercourse a man confronts the formless horror of biological existence; the murderer is the only hope of women, and the only hope of men too, for the woman must be destroyed if the man is to achieve freedom and purity of being. A man can hope to escape, but a woman, being nothing to begin with, can only hope to be annihilated. Kokoschka regarded human sexual relations as a raw wound; his play attempts not to heal it, but to tear it open further, by using every resource of various arts—painting, speech, and bodily movement—in order to maximize sensation.

Hindemith's Mörder, Hoffnung der Frauen

In 1917 Kokoschka published the revised text of *Mörder, Hoffnung der Frauen,* and in October of that year the magazine *Kunstblatt* devoted a special issue to Kokoschka. When Hindemith read this issue, he wrote to a friend that he took a strong interest in this "ultra-overstressed" *(ultra-überspannte)* artistic direction, though he found it difficult to grasp. In 1919 he set the whole text of Kokoschka's play, and proved resourceful in finding musical figures equivalent to flaying and branding.

For example, the first sound heard in the opera is a prolonged crescendo of a two-note chord, C and D♭, on horns and trombones; soon this fanfare of pain is interrupted by a heavy trudge (scale degrees $\hat{1}-\hat{2}-\hat{3}-\hat{2}-\hat{1}$ in F minor), the principal theme of the work, probably to be associated with the Man. Above a solid harmonic foundation, the semitone chord becomes a sort of elementary expressive particle, a quantum of scream, the sound of fingernails scraping down a blackboard. Above Kokoschka's play there is a kind of free-floating shriek, loosely tethered to the text and the stage action; Hindemith's music imparts an auditory precision to the mood. For another example, we may look at the moment when the sign is burned onto the Woman's flesh (rehearsal figure 27): here, Hindemith superimposes a B♭ chord on an E chord, creating a horrible clash of keys related by a tritone—and the whole subsequent passage is governed by tritonal relations. The tritone (the augmented fourth, known to medieval theory as the devil in music) is, like the minor second, a basic discord in the scale. These root dissonances are Hindemith's scalpels, his tools for cutting to the quick of the ear. In this fashion Hindemith constructs a vertical assemblage, a mixed-media chord in which one element is a tritone and another element is a pantomime of branding: a scream in two different forms of spatiotemporal extension.

EX. 1. Hindemith, *Mörder, Hoffnung der Frauen:* beginning

EX. 2. Hindemith, *Mörder, Hoffnung der Frauen:* branding

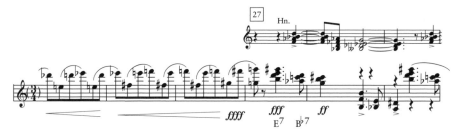

Marsyas sometimes cries out from torture; but at other times, we recall, he tries to seduce. The seduction music in *Mörder, Hoffnung der Frauen* is far flimsier in character than the music of torment: when the Woman, fearfully, longingly, stares at the Man and asks, "Who is this pale man? Hold him back!" the orchestra plays figures of chromatic yearning (ten bars after rehearsal figure 15) straight out of Wagner's *Tristan und Isolde.* Chromaticisms, often associated with the Woman and her cries, tend to corrupt and disable the Man's triadic solidity of being. This music sounds insubstantial, wraithlike, next to the willful and determinate music associated with the Man; perhaps it is an echo in the void, an acoustic image of the nonentity that Weininger, and to some degree Kokoschka, ascribed to the female principle. In the large rhythm of the opera, there is a punctuation of screams with gaps or holes, in which the text and the music cooperate to produce a sort of sounding silence.

EX. 3. Hindemith, *Mörder, Hoffnung der Frauen:* quotation of yearning figure from Wagner's *Tristan und Isolde*

If we imagine what it would be like, at the same time, to stare at Kokoschka's drawing of cut-open muscle and nerve; to witness mutilations enacted on stage; to listen to tonal music that regularly convulses into semitones and tritones and major sevenths; and to feel underneath it all a psychotic philosophy of woman-hating—then we can take *Mörder, Hoffnung der Frauen* as a kind of limit point of the Marsyan aesthetic. Here is flaying at every level of theatre: an ultra-overstress of eye, ear, and mind all pointing toward a single locus of pain.

Aesthetic Paradoxes

In the first half of this book, we will examine the ploys of Marsyas in the domain of the comparative arts. The vertical assemblage, the mixed-media chord—such as the hieroglyph, the Noh play, the *gestus*—is a strategy for trying to defeat the discursiveness, the sequentiality, the temporal extension of language and music; for trying to endow the arts of *nacheinander* with the instantaneity of the eye's grasp of things. If time and space are going to work together to achieve a *single* effect, then time must be spatialized and space temporalized; Laocoön's mouth must show the same shape both in stone and in language. Here the medium is less important than the thing that lies beneath the medium, a thing that is fundamentally *serious.* Here, in the Adorno-like words of Mann's Doktor Faustus, "Art wants to stop being semblance and play, it wants to become knowledge"— the words *Schein und Spiel,* semblance and play, chime through *Philosophie der neuen Musik.*

In the second half, we will examine the ploys of Apollo in the domain of the comparative arts: such structures as the film loop and the cubist's cubes that provide contentless congruities between time and space, formal resemblances that in no way compromise the spatiality of space or the temporality of time. Here art revels in its status as semblance and play, and claims little truth beyond the materiality of its stone or its pigment or its sound waves. Here art is satisfied to remain arithmetical without being expressive, metaphorical without being real.

But in the realm of aesthetics, all extremes tend to converge, and the antithesis of Marsyas and Apollo is somewhat frail. Any work that makes use of several artistic media may be regarded either polyphonically (as Apollo likes) or homophonically (as Marsyas likes); indeed, the two Greek names merely serve to discriminate two points of view. Even a work such as *Mörder, Hoffnung der Frauen*—which seems in every way to ask to be considered as a unity—may collapse into a welter of competing media. To use several arts to reinforce a single point, in the Marsyan manner, may well lead to a kind of overdetermination and overemphasis, which may in turn lead to a kind of ironizing, which may in turn lead to the disaffiliation of the very arts that are trying to cooperate. If one pauses in the midst of *Mörder, Hoffnung der Frauen* and thinks, This is silly—and such a response is by no means impossible—the shrieks turn into smirking caricatures of shrieks, inappropriate to the violent stage action, indeed suitable for a puppet play, such as Hindemith's opera for Burmese marionettes, *Das Nusch-Nuschi* (1921), a kind of sequel to *Mörder, Hoffnung der Frauen*. (Similarly, Schoenberg recoiled from the ecstatic expressionism of *Erwartung* [1909] to the caricature of expressionism in the song *Gemeinheit* from *Pierrot Lunaire* [1912], in which the scream of a clown whose skull has been pierced by a drill is rendered by a piccolo's tiny piping.) Hindemith, of course, grew into one of the most Apollonian composers of his time—his late opera *Die Harmonie der Welt* (1957) concerns Johannes Kepler and the discovery of the true motion of the planets; insofar as Apollo investigated the relations between music and the deep numerical order of things, *Die Harmonie der Welt* is the ideal Apollonian opera. A single composer may have strong tendencies in both directions; and even a fairly pure Apollonian specimen, such as Stravinsky, will on occasion hanker for Marsyas's panpipes— represented, for example, by the bassoon at the beginning of *The Rite of Spring*, a drama of human sacrifice.

Paradox can be found in the region of Apollo as well as that of Marsyas: the planar separation among the arts, in the Apollonian manner, may impart an eerie sense of a subsistent reality that, absurdly, inexplicably, reveals itself to the ear and to the eye in completely different fashion. We sometimes hear thunder but look up to see a cloudless sky; there is a kind of dissociation of sensuous planes built into our apprehension of the world. The very strategy that divorces art from reality, by creating spectacles in which the stage action and the text and the music have nothing to do with one another, may terminate in a kind of seizure of reality.

In a section on surrealism, we'll see how the surrealists used the discrepancies between the spatial and the temporal arts to create a means for intuiting a world that is, on its deepest level, a dissonance.

Dissonance and consonance are terms that will appear everywhere in this book, and not always in the meanings usual in musical harmony. There is a dissonance *within* music, such as the minor second or the tritone; but there is also a dissonance *between* music and painting or poetry—or other arts. The study of Modernist collaborations even suggests that there is a *law of conservation of dissonance:* when the music is dissonant, then the relations (within a given collaboration) between music and painting or poetry tend to be consonant, and vice versa. Schoenberg's *Erwartung* challenges, some would even say punishes, the ear, but Schoenberg wanted a tame, undemanding stage set; Satie's *Parade* isn't harmonically challenging music, and yet the relations between the music and the rest of the spectacle are challenging in the highest degree. And here lies the great paradox of Adorno's *Philosophie der neuen Musik:* Adorno, whose ear was so avid for dissonance, could tolerate no dissonance whatever among artistic media: he demanded that music and poetry and painting cooperate in an obedient, consonant manner. I hope, in this book, to show some of the limits of consonance among the arts, and to help to emancipate the dissonance among the arts.

Modernism, Historical and Transhistorical

Books studying these issues of consonance and dissonance could be written about many different periods, but the Modernist period is especially tantalizing. What sets the art of the twentieth century apart from the art of previous ages? In one sense, the answer must be, Not much; it is a jaded and thrill-seeking age, avid for novelties in the relation of music to the other arts, but the same could be said of the Venetian Baroque and of other times and places. The twentieth century, however, is a particularly useful period for the study of multimedia experiments, because there remains so much evidence of the germinative stages, and because there is so much self-conscious exploration of the ultimates of artistic possibility. The great Modernists are the Pearys and Scotts of art, exploring the arctic and antarctic of the aesthetic phenomenon.

And so, for the purposes of this book, the definition of Modernism is (tentatively) as follows: *the testing of the limits of aesthetic construction.* According to this perspective, the Modernists tried to find the outer bounds of certain artistic traits: volatility of emotion (expressionism); stability and inexpressiveness (the new objectivity); accuracy of representation (hyperrealism); absence of representation (abstractionism); purity of form (neoclassicism); formless energy (neobarbarism); cultivation of the technological present (futurism); cultivation of the prehistoric past (the mythic method). These extremes, of course, have been

arranged in pairs, because aesthetic heresies, like theological ones, come in binary
sets: each limit point presupposes an opposite limit point, a counter-extreme
toward which the artist can push. Furthermore, some of these pairs tend to organize themselves into a Marsyas-Apollo dichotomy, insofar as one side tends to
find its truths in copying, by means of either representation or expression (Marsyas), and the other side tends to find its truths in the medium itself, or in tran-
scendencies of form (Apollo):

Marsyas	*Apollo*
Expressionism	New objectivity
Hyperrealism	Abstractionism
Neobarbarism	Neoclassicism

Much of the strangeness, the stridency, the exhilaration of Modernist art can
be explained by this strong thrust toward the verges of the aesthetic experience:
after certain nineteenth-century artists had established a remarkably safe, intimate center where the artist and the audience could dwell, the twentieth century
reaches out to the freakish circumferences of art. The extremes of the aesthetic
experience tend to converge: in the Modernist movement, the most primitive art
tends to be the most up-to-date and sophisticated. For example, when T. S. Eliot
first heard Stravinsky's *The Rite of Spring,* he wrote that the music seemed to
"transform the rhythm of the steppes into the scream of the motor-horn, the
rattle of machinery, the grind of wheels, the beating of iron and steel, the roar of
the underground railway, and the other barbaric noises of modern life." In the
year that Eliot heard *The Rite of Spring,* 1921, he was assembling *The Waste
Land* according to the same recipe: the world of London, with its grime, boredom, ragtime hits, and abortifacient drugs, overlays the antique world of primal
rites for the rejuvenation of the land through the dismemberment of a god. In
the Modernist movement, things tend to coexist uncomfortably with their exact
opposites.

Although the scope of this book is limited to the art of the first half of the
twentieth century (with the exception of Britten's *Curlew River,* necessary to follow the evolution of the Noh play), it is not necessary to define Modernism in a
historically determinate fashion. I could easily follow an argument, for example,
that the first Modernist experiment in music theatre was the Kotzebue-Beethoven
The Ruins of Athens (1811), in which the goddess Minerva claps her hands over
her ears at hearing the hideous music of the dervishes' chorus (blaring tritones,
Turkish percussion): here is the conscious sensory assault, sensory overload, of
Schoenberg's first operas. There is a sense in which Modernism is confined to the
twentieth century, but there is another sense in which it tends to spill into other

ages. Modernism created its own precursors; it made the past new, as well as the present.

But we use the term Modernism with a certain expectation of historical precision: as a period, the Modernist age needs to be restricted in time. Such a restriction is rarely easy, and becomes immensely difficult for the interdisciplinarian: the Romantic movement, for example, will invariably mean one age for a musicologist, another (perhaps scarcely overlapping) for a student of British poetry. One might say that the Modernist age begins around 1907–9, because in those years Picasso painted *Les demoiselles d'Avignon,* Schoenberg made his "atonal" breakthrough, and the international careers of Stravinsky, Pound, Stein, and Cocteau were just beginning or were about to begin. And one might choose (*very* tentatively) 1951 for a terminus, since in that year John Cage started using the I Ching to compose chance-determined music, and Samuel Beckett's trilogy and *Waiting for Godot* were soon to establish an artistic world that would have partly bewildered the early Modernists. Most Modernists did not (as Cage did) abdicate their artistic responsibilities to a pair of dice; most Modernists did not (as Beckett did) try to cultivate artistic failure. Modernism was a movement associated with scrupulous choice of artistic materials, and with hard work in arranging them. Sometimes the Modernists deflected the domain of artistic selection to unusual states of consciousness (trance, dream, and so forth); but, except for a few dadaist experiments, they didn't abandon artistic selection entirely—and even Tristan Tzara, Kurt Schwitters, and the other dadaists usually attempted a more impudent form of non-sense than aleatory procedures can generate. The Modernists *intended* Modernism—the movement did not come into existence randomly.

But the version of Modernism outlined here—a triumphalist extension of the boundaries of the feasible in art—is only *a* version of Modernism. There exist many Modernisms, and each version is likely to describe a period with different terminal dates. If Modernism were defined as heroic disintegration of object and subject, the movement might begin, say, around 1886 (the year of the last painting exhibition organized by the impressionists, at which Seurat made the first important show of his work)—Nietzsche had privately published *Also sprach Zarathustra* in 1885. And it is possible to construct an argument showing that Modernism has only recently ended, if at all, since Beckett actualized certain potentialities in Joyce (concerning self-regarding language) and Cage actualized certain potentialities in his teacher Schoenberg and his hero Satie: Cage's *Cheap Imitation* (1969) is simply a note-by-note rewriting, with random pitch alterations within a given set of whitish notes, of the vocal line of Satie's *Socrate* (1918). Perhaps the most recent artists are still trying to digest the meal that the Modernists ate—and so post-Modernism hasn't yet begun; perhaps post-

Modernism has not only begun, but is already over. Periodization is subject to endless negotiation of boundaries.

The purpose of this book is not to argue a thesis concerning Modernism, or to delimit Modernism as a period, or to discuss the interaction of the various isms that both organize and perplex the history of twentieth-century art—my tracings of the Laocoön theme will often cut across the usual boundaries of futurism, expressionism, and so forth. The purpose of this book is to develop a method for describing the aesthetic hybrids and chimeras that come into being through artistic collaborations, and to investigate how the artists of one age happened to fight a battle raging through all ages, the warfare among artistic media. Of course, I have space to discuss only a few examples, and my choice to restrict this study to artists involved in significant *musical* experiments in several media has eliminated a number of great figures—such as Rilke and Tatlin—who were profoundly engaged with the questions of the boundaries of aesthetic media but who weren't strongly drawn to collaborations with composers. (The chief exception to this rule is found in my discussion of André Breton, a necessary connection, I think, between the early surrealism of Apollinaire and the mature surrealism of Poulenc.) My other criterion for selecting just which multimedia projects to discuss concerned the issue of ease of interaction among the various media: I chose projects in which the relations among the arts were either unusually tense and hostile, or unusually lax and tolerant. The reader may note many important absences. But I hope that the reader will be struck more by the richness and fullness of the material here considered than by the large number of multimedia projects necessarily omitted from consideration. I assume that the purpose of reading criticism is to intensify intellectual delight in the matter being criticized; and this book tries to please by holding up to the light the fugitive but powerful creatures born from particular unions of music and the other arts.

* * *

I suspect that, in its original form, the Laocoön problem no longer troubles anyone. We have learned to tolerate or love all sorts of transvestism between time and space, from pictures that literally move, in the cinema, to the straightforward recasting of musical surface according to models derived from the visual arts, as in Antheil's *Ballet Mécanique* (1926) or Philip Glass's *The Photographer* (1982). No one is dainty enough these days to be vexed by a statue with a wide-open mouth.

I think that the Laocoön problem, to retain its interest for the twentieth century, needs to be reformulated. Lessing erred when he assumed that sculpture had some general decorum, some purpose separate from the particular purpose of a sculptor. The arts themselves have no powers of resistance, no powers of fusion;

they will open themselves to one another, or clench themselves, close themselves from one another, according to the intentions of the artists involved. The revolution of the Information Age began when physicists discovered that silicon could be used either as a resistor or as a conductor of electricity. Modernist art is also a kind of circuit board, a pattern of yieldings and resistances, in which one art sometimes asserts its distinct, inviolable nature—and sometimes yields itself, tries to imitate some foreign aesthetic. A Modernist *Laokoon* might restate the division of the arts as follows: not as a tension between the temporal arts and the spatial, but as a tension between arts that try to retain the propriety, the apartness, of their private media, and arts that try to lose themselves in some panaesthetic whole. On the one hand, *nacheinander* and *nebeneinander* retain their distinctness; on the other hand, they collapse into a single spatiotemporal continuum, in which both duration and extension are arbitrary aspects. Photographs of pupillary movement have traced the patterns that the eye makes as it scans the parts of a picture, trying to apprehend the whole—a picture not only may suggest motion, but is constructed by the mind acting over time. Similarly, a piece of music may be heard so thoroughly that all the notes coexist in the mind in an instant—as Karajan claimed to know Beethoven's Fifth Symphony.

The arts are an endless semblance, an endless dissembling—and a collaboration among several arts is at once a labyrinth and a thread that needs to be followed.

Part One:
Figures of Consonance
among the Arts

Then your diviner *Hieroglyphicks* tell,
How we may Landskips read, and Pictures spell. . . .
You tell us how we may by Gestures talk;
How Feet are made to speak, as well as walk;
How Eyes discourse, how mystick Nods contrive;
Making our Knowledge, too, *Intuitive.*
A Bell no noise but *Rhetorick* affords;
Our Musick Notes are Speeches, Sounds are Words.
Without a Trope there's Language in a *Flow'r,*
Conceits are smelt without a *Metaphor.*

—Richard West, introduction to John Wilkins's *Mercury,
or The Secret and Swift Messenger,* 1641

Hieroglyph

DEFINITIONS. A *hieroglyph* is a visual sign that speaks—an instantaneous grasp of meaning, defying the division between the pictorial and the linguistic, between space and time.

A *musical epigram* is a short musical phrase that is indissolubly bound to a specific verbal phrase—an assault against the division between two modes of temporal art, music and spoken language. The shorter it is, the more it resembles a *hieroglyph*.

Modernist art often assaults the concept of genre. A genre is a kind of contract between the artist and the consumer, an agreement that certain means will be employed in the pursuit of specific aesthetic pleasures; but in the twentieth century this contract may have disconcertingly open terms. For instance, the score to Igor Stravinsky's *Renard* (1915–16; 1922) identifies its genre as *burlesque*—a contract that may indicate the kind of pleasure the audience may expect, but that specifies little about the dramatic or musical form, the manner of staging (if any), or the sorts of performers. But given the bizarre resources used in *Renard*—acrobats and dancers on stage costumed as animals, with singers who take random turns impersonating the characters—Stravinsky had no simple way of naming his genre. According to Jean Cocteau, the only command that Sergei Diaghilev—the impresario of the Ballets Russes, one of the central engines of the Modernist movement—gave him was: *Astound me*. And *Astound me* is the sort of demand that loosens the genre contract: an audience that wishes astonishment can't ask for any sort of expected delight, only for Something Completely Different.

The astoundingness of Modernist art has many aspects: blurring of genre, flagrancy of theme, disobedience to old artistic rules. But I believe that one of the major sources of Modernist amazement is a peculiarly intense application of an old theory: that art is ultimately one, and that the division of art into poetry, music, painting, and so forth is arbitrary and harmful. At the origin of

FIG. 4. Michel Larionov, set design for Stravinsky's *Renard,* 1929 (© 1999 ARS, New York/ADAGP, Paris)

the work of art lies some aesthetic pre-entity that dwells in a kind of limbo, not yet literary or musical or pictorial—though it may extend itself into any of these domains. Any finite artistic product derives a kind of reverberation through the whole field of the arts by constructing (or implying) concords or discords between two or more different artistic media. This is the Marsyan point of view, to use the term proposed in the introduction to this book—the point of view that understands music and poetry and painting as interchangeable, a set of easy, fluid transforms.

Renard offers a striking example. Stravinsky himself was a publicly confessed Apollonian, devoted to maintaining rigid distinctions among the arts; and yet Stravinsky's music is so strongly informed by techniques derived from the visual arts that Marsyas peeks out, grinning, from many corners of Stravinsky's work. (I take this line of argument from Adorno, who regarded Stravinsky as a confector of pseudomorphoses, confusions of the temporal with the spatial—but, unlike Adorno, I find no reason to disapprove.) Some of Stravinsky's collaborators were extraordinarily sensitive to the pictorial character built into the music. In 1929 Michel Larionov designed the décor for a revival: the backdrop shows a large, unmodeled, naked figure, depicted in a combination of profile and frontal view, with a vaguely bestial head and a squiggle coming out of its mouth; below it are schematic simplifications of a bird, a fox, several pine trees, and several houses—the houses are just defective rectangles with two cross-hatchings each to represent windows; to the right side is scribbled, in Russian, the legend "The tale of the fox and the cock by Igor Stravinsky, choreography by Lifar, set by Larionov, ballet by Diaghilev"—the legend is drawn in alternating groups of light and dark letters, in no way conforming to the boundaries of the individual words. Larionov insisted that "décor is primarily an independent creation, maintaining the spirit of the work to be performed, an autonomous art form with its own particular problems and subject to its own laws"—so he felt that he was not illustrating *Renard,* or locating it in time and space, but adding his own contribution to what Stravinsky and the other artists had done. But what is "the spirit of the work," as Larionov read it? Clearly, something primitive: the childishness and flatness of the drawing, the unrelatedness of the iconographic units to one another, all testify to that. And the combination of frontality and profile suggests advanced cubist art—so the stage set is at once barbaric and *à la mode,* in the (by 1929) standard Modernist way. But the combination of frontality and profile, together with the snaky design near the mouth, the reduction of the small figures to a few telling lines, and the prominent Russian calligraphy difficult to parse into separate words, also suggests something else: Egyptian art. Larionov has interpreted *Renard* as a ballet of *hieroglyphs.*

I think that Larionov interpreted well. The hieroglyphic character of *Renard,* and of much else in Modernist art, seems strong and profound. As we will see, *hieroglyph* is the right name for the unit of equivalence between one artistic medium and another—the core of astonishment. To understand the Modernist adaptation of hieroglyphic thinking, we'll need to trace the evolution of the hieroglyph from Neoplatonic philosophy through Mozart's Egyptian opera; and this will require an excursion to the past, a raid on the lost ark of the old sacred writing.

Plotinus

The prestige of the hieroglyph in Western philosophy is of long standing, and its history is the history of a sustained intellectual assault on the separation between the arts of time and the arts of space—an assault that reached a climax in the twentieth century. In his lovely essay "On the Intellectual Beauty," the third-century Neoplatonic philosopher Plotinus began by discussing sculpture: "the stone thus brought under the artist's hand to the beauty of form is beautiful not as stone—for so the crude block would be as pleasant—but in virtue of the Form or Idea introduced by the art." Later, Plotinus went on to discuss hieroglyphics:

the wise of Egypt—whether in precise knowledge or by a prompting of nature—indicated the truth where, in their effort towards philosophical statement, they left aside the writing-forms that take in the detail of words and
sentences—those characters that represent sounds and convey the propositions of reasoning—and drew pictures instead, engraving in the temple-
inscriptions a separate image for every separate item: thus they exhibited the
absence of discursiveness in the Intellectual Realm.

For each manifestation of knowledge and wisdom is a distinct image, an
object in itself, an immediate unity, not an aggregate of discursive reasoning
and detailed willing. Later from this wisdom there appears, in another form
of being, an image, already less compact, which announces the original in
terms of discourse.

According to Liselotte Dieckmann, Plotinus used the same word (*agalma,* or
form) to refer to (1) the statue, (2) the intelligible form that guided the sculptor's
hand, and (3) Egyptian sacred writing. A transcendental form, then, can manifest
itself indifferently as a statue or as a hieroglyph; in either case, it is the immanence
of a god. It can further manifest itself in a discursive language, such as Greek or
English, but at the expense of its original immediacy and instantaneity: it becomes tangled and distorted into the time-sequence of subject and predicate, a
kind of gnostic Fall into the material world. Hieroglyphic language (in Plotinus's
sense) is the only sort of language that can present wisdom in its full purity and
distinctness. A hieroglyph isn't contaminated by temporality, isn't limited by the
shortcomings of any particular artistic medium; it is as close as the human mind
can come to a kind of art that is neither *nacheinander* nor *nebeneinander,* neither discursive nor juxtapositive, but a direct seizure of transcendental knowledge. The goal of a work of art (for artists susceptible to the lures of an art
that transcends any finite medium) is to approximate the revelation-intensity of
a hieroglyph.

A hieroglyph dwells on the boundary among the artistic media. It is a recognizable picture of a real object, but a picture that is doing the work of language:
signifying, gesturing, acting as a thought medium. According to the *Corpus
Hermeticum,* the original force of a *thing* operates inside its hieroglyph, instead
of being diluted and exhausted, as in other sorts of language; according to Sir
Thomas Browne's *Pseudodoxia* (1646), hieroglyphs undid the curse of Babel,
since anyone can understand a picture—perhaps the Egyptians even recovered
the original names that Adam gave to the things he found in Eden.

There is, of course, an irony in the fact that from late antiquity until the early
nineteenth century, the hieroglyphic language of ancient Egypt was praised for
its rigorous clarity, its luminous apprehension of meaning, when in fact no one
could read it. And attempts to make a language of things rather than words didn't

always have happy results. Many writers on hieroglyphics (including Vico) cite Herodotus's story of how the Scythian king Idanture dispatched to the Persian king Darius a herald, carrying a frog, a mouse, a bird, a plow, and five arrows tied together:

> In vain did the Persians question the bearer. The self-confident Darius therefore proclaimed that the gifts signified that the Scythians gave up land and water, the bird for swift flight, the mouse for land, the frog for water, the arrows as a surrender of arms. But later he found that the intended message was: "Unless, O Persians, ye can turn yourselves into birds and fly through the air, or become mice and burrow under the ground, or be as frogs and take refuge in the fens, ye shall never escape from the land, but die pierced by our arrows."

Things don't come with built-in helping verbs to indicate proper mood; and the pedants of Lagado in Swift's *Gulliver's Travels* (1725), who have forsworn language and converse only by means of gesturing with the objects they carry in a rucksack, will necessarily have trouble with certain subtleties and graces of diction.

And yet, despite the fact that hieroglyphs represented less a language than a dream about language, almost every mixed-medium art form in Europe justified itself by trying to assume the glamour of the hieroglyph. The emblem book of the Renaissance—allegorical pictures captioned with mottoes—claimed superiority to both the art of drawing and the art of poetry; one designer of such devices, Estienne, thought that the Egyptian hieroglyphic walls were properly understood as a mural form of emblem book. And several of Ben Jonson's court extravaganzas, such as the *Masque of Blackness* and the *Masque of Beautie,* contain stage directions instructing the performers to arrange themselves into "a mute Hieroglyphick" or a "hieroglyphick of Splendor." There is a deep feeling in European art that collaborative enterprises among the arts are best understood not with reference to their component arts, but with reference to the hieroglyph: a kind of imaginary limit point where the structures of meaning that govern the separate arts converge.

Mozart's The Magic Flute

In the domains of poetry and the visual arts, the term *hieroglyph* has a specific (though tremendous and obscure) meaning. But does the term have any meaning in the domain of music? Few of the older writers discuss music—though Diderot made the intriguing observation that music's "hieroglyph is so light and so fleeting; it is so easy to lose or misinterpret it, that the most beautiful symphony would not have any great effect if the infallible and sudden pleasure of the pure and simple sensation were not infinitely above that of a frequently equivocal expression." Where might we find an example of a "pure and simple sensation" in music that acts hieroglyphically upon the listener, as sheer atemporal grasp of meaning?

One place to look for musical hieroglyphs might be Mozart's *The Magic Flute* (1791). This is a *Singspiel*—a spoken play comprising substantial musical scenes—set in a vaudeville Egypt, typically outfitted with hieroglyphic stage sets, and partly based on pseudo-Egyptian Masonic rituals. Furthermore, one of its crucial themes is the contrast between discursive language and some more powerful means of communication. Two of the major characters represent errors in speech, or errors in the relation between speech and music. The harmless birdcatcher Papageno—his name is Italian for *parrot,* and he is dressed in a costume of feathers—can't stop talking, boasting, telling lies; he's compulsively expressive, a chatterer. At one point a padlock is fastened to his lips in order to shut him up; at another point, a priest threatens him with the direst punishment by thunder and lightning if he says one word—but of course he can't be quiet for even a minute. When at last the merciful theocrats forgive him his blabbering, and even provide a little wife (Papagena) for him, the parrot-pair bursts out in full crow:

```
pa          pa          pa
pa    pa    pa    pa    pa    pa
pa pa pa pa pa pa pa pa pa pa pa
```

This is language veering into rhythmical nonsense, language at the farthest possible remove from the hieroglyph; Plotinus complained that ordinary language was too lax, too discursive, and Papageno offers a kind of burlesque of discursivity. The role of Papageno was originally played by the librettist Emanuel Schikaneder, and Mozart was careful to keep the *tessitura* of the part within the range of a singing actor, rather than an opera singer. To some extent Papageno represents *words,* verbality with a certain capacity for tunefulness, but not for the highest planes of musical expression.

The other character who represents a rupture—a far more disturbing rupture—in the relation between music and language is the Queen of the Night. She is not an innocent, impulsive blunderer, but an active and subtle force for evil. If Papageno represents a kind of speech that can occasionally become heartfelt, lift itself up into simple melody, the Queen of the Night represents a kind of music that liberates itself dangerously from the inconvenience of language, from the need to signify anything at all. As her great aria *Der Hölle Rache kocht in meinem Herzen* [The vengeance of hell boils in my heart] proceeds, it turns into a florid, overwhelmingly impressive vocalise on the *a* of *Bande* in the phrase *Alle Bande der Natur* [All the bonds of nature (are ruined forever)]. In the world of *The Magic Flute,* this sort of melisma is the exact opposite of chatter: a lash of sound, a pure vehemence of will. In this way Mozart devised an opera in which words and music tend, alarmingly, to separate themselves into distinct planes. For an Apollonian composer, this division would be a blessing; but Mozart, an instinctive Marsyan, resisted it strongly.

Amid these lurches of speech and spasms of song—amid all the incoherence and vivacity of humankind—there arises enforced silence. The act of hushing is a central device in comic opera (the first words sung in Rossini's *The Barber of Seville* [1816] are *piano, pianissimo* [softly, most softly], for Almaviva is in terror, as he prepares the onstage musicians to accompany his serenade to Rosina, that the noise will wake the girl's father); and in *The Magic Flute* a whole world of funny noise has to be quenched before the revelation of truth can proceed. In the first-act finale, for example, Prince Tamino, desperately seeking his beloved Pamina in the house of enchanter Sarastro, comes upon a calm priest, who extols the virtues of quiet: *Ein Weib tut wenig, plaudert viel* [A woman does little, chatters much]; and when Tamino asks him where Pamina is, the priest can only reply that he's not allowed to tell the answer, for oath and duty bind his tongue. It seems, then, that religious silence can lead only to endless frustration. But when Tamino asks when the veil over the truth will disappear, the priest suddenly abandons recitative and breaks into melody:

Sobald dich führt der Freundschaft Hand	When friendship leads you by the hand
ins Heiligtum zum ewgen Band.	to the sanctum for the eternal band.

This oracle is an impressive moment: the opera insisted on hushing its brouhaha in order to provide a background of silence against which such quiet wisdom can be heard.

This couplet offers the audience, I believe, the musical equivalent of a hieroglyph. It is not an aria, not a chorale, not a recitative. It is an utterly self-contained entity, as fully isolated as if an oval bounding-line were drawn around it. Its dotted rhythms are perfectly adjusted to the iambic tetrameter of the couplet. It gives a strong feeling of musical completeness, in that it contains all seven notes of the diatonic scale, parceled out in a symmetrical shape of descending arches. It is nondiscursive, an image of eternity, a piece of harmonic truth: the whole melody-unit is a simple expansion of a cadential formula (i–VI–ii§–V–i). It is, so to speak, an apodictic musical phrase, solemn, uncontradictable—an image of the irrefutability of the Masonic wisdom expressed by the words. It is notable that the word *Band* is prominent here: later, in the second act, the Queen of the Night will announce wickedly, convulsively, that all of nature's bands are shattered; but she's proved wrong, for the priest's *Band,* bound by the compelling musical sense of a spell, will last.

EX. I.I. Mozart, *The Magic Flute:* the priest's oracle

As Tamino hears the priest's resonant, dark words, he wonders whether he will ever find light: and immediately the orchestra repeats the priest's phonoglyph, while an invisible chorus intones "Soon, soon, or never." Then Tamino asks the oracle whether Pamina is still alive, and the chorus replies—as the tune is heard for the third and last time—"She lives." Tamino reacts as if stung by a bee; and, overflowing with joy, he decides to show his gratitude by playing his magic flute. The flute (in the major) begins with three notes rising through a minor third, in dotted rhythm, just like the first three notes of the oracle tune we've just heard; and although it is melodically more florid and harmonically more lively than the oracle tune, the magic of the magic flute seems to grow out of the priest's hieroglyph. The priest has given, it seems, both an ethical lesson and a music lesson to Tamino: Tamino now is enabled to play melodies that can exert irresistible force on those that hear them. A hieroglyph is supposed to be a direct incarnation of wisdom; and a musical hieroglyph acts directly on the nervous system of its auditors. As Tamino says, "Through your playing, dear flute, even the wild beasts have joy."

The oracle tells Tamino that Pamina is alive; the flute seems to conjure her actual presence, for soon Tamino hears Papageno's panpipes—"Maybe the sound will lead me to her"—and he echoes the call with his flute as he runs off in search. But before Tamino can find them, Papageno and Pamina are surprised by the evil henchman Monostatos, who tells his men to tie them up; but the men are paralyzed in their tracks, then forced to dance when Papageno plays his magic glockenspiel. The oracle tune was based on stepwise blocks, in A minor; the flute tune was based on suavely inflected scalar runs, in C; now the glockenspiel gives forth a jingle of arpeggios, in G: each is a self-contained, compelling entity based on extremely simple musical material, compelling *because* extremely simple. And each hieroglyph wields a little more cybernetic control than the one before. *The Magic Flute* is not yet half over by the time Papageno tinkles his very *dominant* bells, but the audience already understands that characters who can deploy such resources of musical gubernation are certain to triumph. Having heard the occult wisdom of Isis and Osiris, Tamino can reecho it, flash it out, at the world around him; and even Papageno inherits the power by some contagion of magic. The priest's hieroglyph is a limit of contraction of an epigram: first (so to speak) *A word to the wise is sufficient;* then *A word to the wise;* then simply a musical equivalent of upraised monitory finger. Tamino's and Papageno's formulae are unpackings, extensions into time and dramatic cogency, of the concentrated, timeless truth of the priest. Music and language are no longer descriptive, but useful, powerful. *Verbum sap.*

The operas of Handel, Gluck, and other early composers are occasionally revived, but Mozart is the oldest composer whose works have been routinely performed in opera houses during the twentieth century; and Mozart's forms of musical discourse are at the root of the Modernist music theatre.

Perlocution and Epigram: Liszt and Wagner

For Mozart, the chord struck by a word and a note and a stage picture suggestive of divine presence could possess extraordinary force, could trace an action. Certain linguists speak of *perlocutions:* that is, verbal formulae that are themselves actions, such as "I baptize you," or "May your liver shrivel!" or "I take this man as my lawfully wedded husband," or "Your privilege to eat at the Faculty Club is hereby revoked," or "Ten bucks on Throwaway in the third race." Just as there are speech acts, there are music acts—for a set of notes can also constitute a command, an oath, a blessing. In music drama, a musical figure may summon up a certain verbal formula, in which case it is an *epigram;* or a musical figure may, like Papageno's bells, possess efficacy in the domain of physical movement, in which case it is a *musical perlocution,* or (as I'll call it later) a *gestus.* Epigram, perlocution, gestus can all be treated as *hieroglyphs,* to the extent that they can be grasped intuitively, without procedures of discursive reasoning or of conscious decoding of signs. These vertical formations make up much of the basic vocabulary of the mixed arts.

The hieroglyphs in *The Magic Flute* represent the end of a long line of prophecies and oracles in Mozart's music, including the voice of the statue of Neptune in *Idomeneo* (1781) and the voice of the statue of the Commendatore in *Don Giovanni* (1787)—the oracles became more terse and more memorable as Mozart matured. Perhaps *The Magic Flute* gave Mozart the opportunity to enclose and perfect such vatic musical epigrams along lines suggested by the hieroglyphic decorations that might serve as part of the appurtenances of Masonic ritual.

From a certain point of view, the progress of music theatre from the eighteenth century to the twentieth can be understood as the slow production of a dictionary of hieroglyphs—cues for various shivers and excitements. The musical gestures that the eighteenth and nineteenth centuries would compile, the twentieth century would classify.

The nineteenth century remained fascinated with the concentrated melodies of Mozart's oracles. Franz Liszt, for example, turned the Commendatore's graveyard warning to Don Giovanni, *Di rider finirai pria dell'aurora* [You shall end your laughing before the dawn], into a whole Halloween of spooky piano figuration in *Réminiscences de Don Juan* (1841)—as if Mozart packed such energy into his lapidary phrase that it needed to discharge itself in a Romantic fantasy. The practice of devising simple epigrams along the lines of the melodic units we've been considering also continued, and Liszt's contributions in this field are well worth investigating. Liszt is better known as a composer of instrumental music than of vocal, but his instrumental music is continually informed by the rhythms of speech—and not just speech in general, but specific sentences. For example, the trumpets in Liszt's *Dante Symphony* (1857) terrify the rest of the orchestra by intoning the Italian rhythm of Dante's motto over the Gate of Hell, *Lasciate ogne speranza, voi ch'entrate* [Abandon any hope, you who enter]; and in the *Gretchen* movement of the *Faust Symphony* (1857) there is a startling modulation from A♭ to A—a kind of musical italicizing—at which the orchestra "quotes" a passage of Goethe's text: solo instruments sing out *Er liebt mich— liebt mich nicht* [He loves me—loves me not], in imitation of Goethe's description of the game of plucking daisy petals.

But Liszt's farthest-reaching experiment in epigram, perhaps, can be found in the second book *(Italy)* of the *Années de pèlerinage* (1858). This collection of piano pieces consists almost entirely of experiments in mixed media: the first piece is based on Raphael's painting of the *Sposalizio,* the last piece is based on Dante, and three other pieces are translations of Petrarch sonnets into florid pianisms. (All three were based on preexisting songs by Liszt, but in the *Années* versions it is not easy to follow the exact contour of the declamation.) The second piece in *Italy,* however, is one of the most hieroglyphically impressive pieces of music ever written: *Il penseroso,* based on Michelangelo's statue for the tomb of Lorenzo de' Medici in the church of San Lorenzo in Florence. We remember that Plotinus used the same word to refer to a statue's form and to Egyptian hieroglyph; and Liszt's *Il penseroso* is simultaneously a musical impression of a statue and a precise rendering, in subdued (indeed almost monotone) trochaic rhythms, of the inscription that Michelangelo wrote for the statue *La notte* (Night):

Grato m'è il sonno, e più l'esser di sasso.	Glad to sleep, gladder to be of stone.
Mentre che il danno e la vergogna dura,	While the hurt lingers, and the shame as well,

Non veder, non sentir m'è gran ventura	Good luck is not to see and not to feel.
Però non mi destar, deh'—parla basso!	Oh do not wake me yet—speak low!

Liszt's music hews to the prosody of Michelangelo's inscription with dogged literalness, but the spareness of melody, the lethargy of texture combined with active harmonic inflection, give a sense not of skimpiness or lack of imagination, but of archaic stone. The word *hieroglyph* is Greek for *sacred carving;* and if music is to feel hieroglyphic, it must feel inscriptive, chiseled—not rhetorically straining, but quietly certain. The first bars of *Il penseroso* are an expansion of a cadential formula (i–vi$^{\natural}$–iv$^{7}_{5}$–V–i), very similar to the formula of the hieratic *Sobald dich führt;* and, as with the priest of *The Magic Flute,* we hear in Liszt's *Il penseroso* a kind of revelation that impinges on silence. Liszt wanted an orchestral expansion of this piece, *La notte,* played at his funeral, and if Liszt's project as a composer was to find a music that verged as closely as possible on poetry, painting, and the other arts, then this piece was a fitting crown to his life's work.

Liszt's son-in-law Richard Wagner was equally sensitive to the possibilities of musical epigram—and Wagner, like Liszt, studied Mozart's procedures with great care. For example, when the Norwegian sailors in the third act of *The Flying Dutchman* (1843) are terrified by the Dutchman's zombie mariners, they sing several verses to a closed, compact, somewhat rigid tune with certain similarities to *Sobald dich führt.*

But Wagner's notion of an epigram differs from Mozart's. The priest in *The Magic Flute* sings something that is musically spruce and clear, but semantically ambiguous: Tamino doesn't immediately know whether he's received good news or bad. An oracle is essentially a riddle—formally exact but so *vieldeutig,* much-meaning, that it's hard to decide which meaning is the right meaning. Insofar as a musical hieroglyph is founded on a kind of riddle, Mozart began composing musical hieroglyphs at the age of thirteen: in the second act of *La finta semplice* (The Woman Who Pretends to Be a Simpleton, 1769), there is a pantomime in which a rich, foolish landowner, Cassandro—who prides himself on his skill at conveying emotion through mime—makes imploring gestures of love at Rosina, the Feigned Simpleton (actually a Hungarian baroness); but crafty Rosina has fun by countering with gestures that mean nothing at all. Eventually Cassandro is so befuddled by her gesticulations that he—bizarrely—falls asleep on stage. To accompany this semantic abyss, Mozart wrote remarkably inert and ambiguous music—it might be construed as a slow, agreeable dance, in which some of the falling semitones might be imagined as stylized sighs; but chiefly the music is an empty slate, a tease, a drowse. It is perhaps the most tensionless, the least meaningful music Mozart ever wrote. In the affectively intense world of Haydn and Mozart, absurdity can best be imaged as a kind of repose—for the proper response to an absence of signs is simply a yawn. But it is not so very far from the fake oracle in *La finta semplice* to the real oracle in *The Magic Flute:* in both cases the audience is treated to sound that is at once well-defined and hard to understand. The calm of the priest, his wisdom tranquilized into a kind of congealed silence, is not far from sleep.

The Wagnerian epigram, on the other hand, is semantically overcharged, and tends to carry a fixed burden of affect. The sailors in *The Flying Dutchman,* seeing that the sweethearts of the Dutchman's crew aren't exactly alive, feel horror, and mean horror, and nothing but horror, by their tune. By the time of *Lohengrin* (1850), Wagner was so adept at inventing musical feeling-aphorisms that he could compress a world of solemn menace into the brief accompaniment to the phrase *Nie sollst du mich befragen* [You are never to question me]—Lohengrin's formula for the oath that Elsa must take in order to marry him. The demand is enigmatic—why should a husband refuse to reveal his name to his wife?—but the emotional tenor is clear, and the musical formula is incisive, emphatic, unforgettable; and whenever the music reappears in the orchestra, it summons up the verbal motto. The words *Nie sollst du mich befragen* take on a life independent of Lohengrin, independent of any human speaker; the whole music drama becomes, at times, a gigantic mouth to utter these words. To some extent this epigram even managed to liberate itself from the confines of its opera, since Tchaikovsky's *Swan Lake* (1877)—another swan-dominated stage piece—uses a motto-theme similar to *Nie sollst du mich befragen.*

As we approach the twentieth century, we see that hieroglyphs and epigrams progressively extricate themselves from any particular musical composition and become part of a fluid system of quotations, a speech in several dimensions at once. Even abstract musical figures, if they are striking enough, acquire a sort of theatrical depth, a mixed-media presence: the famous dot-dot-dot-dash figure in Beethoven's Fifth Symphony (1808) acquires a great deal of semantic and pictorial resonance from its associations with Fate Knocking at the Door, and the Morse code version of V-for-Victory, and the Promethean mythos of Beethoven himself. As for *Lohengrin,* its epigrams—the third-act prelude, the bridal chorus, *Nie sollst du mich befragen*—were destined to become, in the early twentieth century, part of the standard repertoire of emotive gestures for silent film accompanists.

Rapée's Dictionary of Silent Film Music and the Leitmotiv

In 1919 Giuseppe Brecce assembled a *Kinothek,* a library of short, standard music bits correlative to any mood or action, a kind of textbook of musical physiology; and in 1924 Erno Rapée published *Motion Picture Moods for Pianists and Organists,* which classifies a large number of pieces under fifty-two headings, such as "Aëroplane" (Mendelssohn's *Rondo capriccioso*), "Battle" (the third movement of Beethoven's *Moonlight* Sonata), "Horror" (the bride's abduction from Grieg's *Peer Gynt*), "Railroad" (the Spinning Song from Wagner's *The Flying Dutchman*), "Sadness" (the first movement of the *Moonlight* Sonata), and—"for use in situations . . . where *there is neither action,* nor atmosphere, nor the elements of human temperament"—"Neutral" (Schubert's *Moment musical,* Op. 94/3). Most of these bits are stolen from pieces of absolute music: Rapée has *re-created* the music fragment as a hieroglyph, by fastening it to a class of visual action, as a tin can is fastened to a dog's tail.

The concept of a set of frozen musical cues, instantly interpretable as emotion or kinesthesis, attracted the attention of a number of advanced composers: Joseph Matthias Hauer, the dodecaphonic theorist who competed with Schoenberg, wrote a set of twenty-one pieces, *Musik-Film* (1927), with such titles as *Expectation, Resolute Attack, Dying Passion*—oddly winsome pieces, more like parodies of expression than like expression itself. And even Schoenberg composed an *Accompanying Music to a Cinematographic Scene* (1930): the first movement, *Threatening Danger,* begins with a threateningly dangerous tremolo, a stock gesture, and it is uncertain whether Schoenberg intended this as a caricature of film music, or as a caricature of himself, or as a serious exploration of the points of resemblance between movie music (which Schoenberg generally disliked) and the implicit cinema behind his own compositions (around 1913 he drew up a set of instructions for making a film of his short, unperformed opera *Die glückliche Hand*). It may be that Schoenberg found that film images had possibilities for investigating emotional quintessences, just as his own music did; and that something doubly devastating might arise from the conjunction of light-play and sound-play.

But in the real cinema, as opposed to Schoenberg's imaginary or theoretical cinema, the interpretation of cues is much aided by familiarity, and, with some important exceptions, most film music relied on nineteenth-century compositions, or on Modernist imitations of them. It was as if Wagner had managed to find the ultimate musical gesture for a warning, whether the menace came from a grail knight's reluctance to compromise his mission or from a mustached villain tying a heroine to the railroad tracks. The Romantic writer Novalis, whose *Hymns to the Night* influenced Wagner's *Tristan und Isolde,* once wrote that primitive man devised a "hieroglyphical formula [that is, sound and image in one] which contained nothing but the sentence and was so physiognomically expressive that one could not miss its soul." In this sense, *Nie sollst du mich befragen* is a hieroglyph of Threat, a reversion to archaic intensity of meaning, otherwise lost in our abstracted and etiolated forms of discourse.

Of course, after *Lohengrin,* Wagner worked on *The Ring of the Nibelung,* an operatic cycle dominated less by the concept of epigram than by the concept of *Leitmotiv* (or, to use Wagner's own term, *Grundthema,* ground-theme). It is difficult to draw a firm distinction between an epigram and a *Leitmotiv,* but they represent different tendencies in musical discourse. An epigram is a self-contained, fairly rigid unit, associated with (and evocative of) a specific verbal sentence, and typically an expansion of a cadence: for example, *Nie sollst du mich befragen* has, by the end of its quatrain, proceeded through a solid, un-assailable harmonization—a phrase as impregnable as a fortress. On the other hand, a *Leitmotiv* is less a sentence than a name, a memorable shard of music capable of endless combination and recombination with other musical gestures. Most of Wagner's *Leitmotive* either do not terminate in a cadence or can easily be shorn of cadence, in order to facilitate counterpoint and linkages with the tissue of music out of which they rise and into which they sink; an epigram, by contrast, is isolated from the music before it and after it—the oracle develops its private meaning and ends in impressive silence. In order to develop the *Leit-motive* of *The Ring,* Wagner made sure that (with some exceptions) his musical gestures did *not* connect themselves too strongly with particular words. The his-tory of the Valkyrie motive is a case in point: it is a musical phrase that suggests verbal rhythms, and in fact Wagner provided it with a kind of dummy lyric, writ-ten in his pseudo–Old Germanic alliterative verse:

Nach Süden wir ziehen,   Siege zu zeugen,
kämpfenden Heeren   zu kiesen das Los

[We draw toward the south, to bring forth victories, to choose the lot for the fighting armies.] The alliterated stressed syllables in *s* and *k* are the beats of the Valkyrie motive marked with a heavy accent, and the unstressed syllables fit ex-actly into the musical line. But this couplet appears nowhere in the finished score of *The Ring;* indeed, the Valkyrie motive, despite its word-generating structure, is never sung at all, except briefly and distortedly during Wotan's Narration in the second act of *Die Walküre.* By freeing the music from a definitive verbal set-ting, Wagner made it available as a *Leitmotiv.* The most conspicuous exception to this rule is Alberich's Curse, in the fourth scene of *Das Rheingold,* which *is* definitively associated with a verbal phrase:

Wie durch Fluch er mir gerieth, verflucht sei dieser Ring.

[As through a curse it came to me, accursed be this ring.] It is remarkable how at the end of this potent aphorism, a C-major triad unresolves itself, moves backward, into a diminished chord. This is the epigram of *The Ring*, comparable to *Nie sollst du mich befragen* in *Lohengrin*: the oracle that dominates the shape of the whole evolving action. Wotan's spear has magical runes engraved on it, the source of his divine authority; but the chief rune of Wagner's music is Alberich's Curse.

The Wagnerian rhythm, by which *Leitmotive* tend to freeze into epigrams, and epigrams tend to dissolve into *Leitmotive*, is of crucial importance to all later experiments in mixed media. *Leitmotive* are fluid, contrapuntal, the elements of a horizontal discourse in theatre; epigrams are vertical and static, a seizure of an instant in which poetry and music (and perhaps the stage picture) suddenly converge. *Leitmotive* are anticipatory or retrospective, and pertain to becoming, to vagrant meanings that slowly take shape; epigrams dwell in the present tense, and pertain to being. An epigram is attained, clinched. The moments of peak intensity in the Modernist music theatre, when speech and music ravish together—the shriek of *Agamemnon!* in Strauss's *Elektra* (1909), or Britten's unforgettable setting of a line stolen from Yeats, *The ceremony of innocence is drowned*, in *The Turn of the Screw* (1954)—owe more to Wagner's epigrams than to his *Leitmotive*.

Wagner and the Origin of Music

As a transcendental locus of meaning, the hieroglyph tends to propose a mythology about the origin of language. For Plotinus, the hieroglyph is *older* than discursive writing; and most of the later writers on hieroglyphs also tend to regard European languages as corrupt and new, compared to the Egyptian sacred carving. Musicians drawn to the lure of pan-aesthetic art, an art that takes place in all media at once and abolishes the distinctions among them, might well believe that the origin of music lies in some compound of music and poetry and other arts. (Indeed, the etymology of the word *music,* from the Greek *mousikē,* any art over which the Muses presided, gives comfort to this Marsyan point of view.) Wagner bequeathed to the twentieth century a mythology about the origin of music that suggests that the fundamental musical act is the production of epigrams—shards in which speech and music are inextricably one.

Wagner's music dramas propose at least three different theories for the origin of music. Perhaps the most famous is that of *Das Rheingold* (1854; 1869): in the prelude, we hear music beginning primevally, in the depths of the lowest possible E♭—the *ur*-tonic—and slowly heaving itself into a triad, finally rising into a series of buoyant arpeggios. This diapason-oriented theory, however, is contradicted by the expressionist theory of *Tristan und Isolde* (1865), according to which (as Wagner put it in his great essay on Beethoven) every musical act is a weakening of a scream—in a later chapter we'll look at this in more detail. A third theory for the origin of music may be found in *Die Meistersinger von Nürnberg* (1868): music begins shackled to words by a complicated system of rules, and evolves toward harmonic and melodic freedom. This freedom, represented by Walther's Prize Song, is not an assertion of independence from spoken language: it is only an assertion that music can respond to semantic as well as prosodic aspects of language. Walther, the fiery young rebel, so dominates Wagner's drama that it is possible to forget how sympathetic Wagner is toward the old conventional art of the mastersingers, the art that Walther is trying to loosen.

The plot concerns a proud young knight, Walther von Stolzing, who wishes to marry Eva, the daughter of a mastersinger; but her father has pledged her hand in marriage as the prize in a song contest. Walther's only hope is a few quick lessons in the rules of mastersinging—rules at which his native genius often balks. In mastersinging, spontaneity, extempore expression, are little valued; instead, one must conform to an elaborate system of rules:

«Ein jedes Meistergesanges Bar	Each section of a mastersong
stell ordentlich ein Gemäße dar	shall be no more and no less long
aus unterschiedlichen Gesätzen,	than proportion shall dictate,
die keiner soll verletzen.	lest the offense be great.
Ein Gesätz besteht aus zweenen Stollen,	One part consists of just two stanzas,
die gleiche Melodei haben sollen. . . .»	and the law of the same tune commands us. . . .

Walther hears these rules in the third scene of the first act, read by an amiable pedant named Kothner, who sings them to a stiff, foursquare, scalar C-major tune, a sort of endlessly reusable chorale fragment, as dry and conventionally ornamented as the recipe could ordain—the ideal specimen mastersong, in a sense the doxology of their tribe. Nothing could be less like this crabbed, cramped, repetitive list of rules than the ardent and flexible cantilena of Walther's Prize Song, which scandalizes the assembled mastersingers through its daring modulations, its general disobedience to Kothner's quotation of the Laws of Tablature; but of course the emotional intensity of Walther's Prize Song sweeps aside all objection, and Walther is granted Eva's hand. Kothner's aria symbolizes the whole rigid, diatonic world of medieval Nuremberg: tidy, kempt, orderly, achieved, but suspicious of novelty—a world in which the Old Dispensation of the Ten Commandments works pretty well, but a world that could be much improved by loosening the ligatures of the law through Walther's Dispensation of Love.

EX. 1.2. Wagner, *Die Meistersinger:* Kothner's reading of the rules

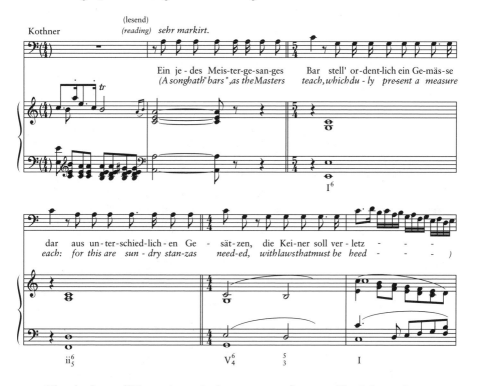

The rhythms of Wagner's music drama ensure that we will rejoice at the structure of liberation achieved in the gaudy pageant, the midsummer revels, the harmonic audacity of Walther's Prize Song. And yet, I wonder whether the debonair Kothner's list of rules is entirely superseded. Kothner's tune appears again at a critical juncture, in the fourth scene of the third act (just before the final scene), when Sachs decides to promote his apprentice David to journeyman: after singing this rule-theme, he boxes David's ear, in a parody of a king's dubbing of a knight with his sword. This is partly a joke, but also partly serious, and as late as this scene Kothner's scalar theme still retains great authority. Perhaps Wagner meant to allude, at the end of the comedy, to some still larger, more liberated order, in which both Kothner's old order and Walther's Romanticism were comprehended. But I may think so because I'm probably the only person on earth who enjoys Kothner's reading of the rules more than Walther's Prize Song.

The difference between *Die Meistersinger* and *Tristan* can be expressed in many ways, such as the contrast between diatonic and chromatic; but perhaps Wagner suggested their fundamental opposition when he wrote in 1870:

next to the world that represents itself visibly . . . a second world, perceivable only through the sense of hearing, announcing itself through sound, truly a *sound world* next to the *light world,* is present to our consciousness, a world of which we can say that it is related to the light world as dream is to waking. . . . As the vivid world of dream can take shape only through a special activity of the brain, so music can take shape through a similar brain activity [*Gehirntätigkeit*].

Tristan is a night-piece, a dream-piece, so perfectly ear-oriented that the actual visible staging is usually an embarrassment. It has little to do with epigrams, or with vertical assemblages of planes of reality; the text simply vanishes into the musical flow, and the *Liebestod* might as well be a vocalise of orgasm. But *Die Meistersinger* is wide awake, pageantlike, and belongs to the world of day: even its musical practice is, in a sense, eye-oriented, especially where the master-singers themselves are concerned. The ear, according to Wagner, is a synthesizing, esemplastic sort of organ, a direct canal to the unconscious; whereas the eye is cool, poised, analytical, judgmental, fault-finding. *Die Meistersinger* belongs to the world of art criticism as much as to the world of art. When the cobbler-mastersinger Hans Sachs hears the song of the incompetent composer Beck-messer, he taps a nail into the shoe he's cobbling each time he notes a fault of scansion; and so Beckmesser's song is accompanied by a steady tap-tap-tap of music criticism. (At one point Wagner thought of calling Beckmesser Veit Hanslick, after the music critic Eduard Hanslick, who persecuted Wagner relent-lessly.) To understand the gulf between *Tristan* and *Die Meistersinger,* one needs only to imagine King Marke and Melot bursting in on the lovers at the end of the great love duet and commenting not on the grief and anger of a betrayed hus-band, but on the faulty modulations of Tristan's singing, the defects of Isolde's grammar. In *Tristan,* Wagner conceived the drama horizontally and acoustically; in *Die Meistersinger,* Wagner conceived the drama in terms of units of total spec-tacle, that is, of epigrams—it is a self-aware sort of theatre, which keeps calling attention to its artifice.

But mastersinging is eye music not only because it is a self-conscious, mechani-cal sort of art, but also in the ease of its apprehension. A mastersong is so stro-phically delimited and melodically hedged that it scarcely has any temporal extension at all; when Kothner sings the rules, he simply repeats his sturdy ca-dential formula (I^6–ii^6_5–V^6_{4-3}–I—this is almost Mozart's oracular *Sobald dich führt* translated into the major), suitable for any short iambic line. Of course, Wagner knew little of the historical practice of real mastersingers—he simply invented an aboriginality that suited him. But Wagner evidently conceived ar-chaic musical practice along the lines of a terse stepwise formula to which each line of poem was sung, a tune-slab without any special expression, a mere device to inflect and push forward a piece of *Stabreim,* alliterative verse. It is interesting that after Wagner's time, Milman Parry discovered similar devices in South Slavic oral epics; John Collins Pope has hypothesized a musical form for *Beowulf* along these same lines; and Leo Treitler has argued that the formulaic structure of Gregorian chant functions like the formulaic structure of the Homeric recitation-tunes, as Parry imagined them. Kothner's rules are discursive, but the discourse is chopped into tough, leathery chunks, so predictable that the ear stops straining to understand, simply waits for the next bit to fall into place. A musical composition that consists of a stringing-together of cadences has no possibility of moving toward a goal, no possibility of genuine discursive development at all. Kothner's rules remain glued to the tablet from which he reads them: isolated commandments, not a fluently organized paragraph.

We should finally note that Kothner's musical formula could be construed as a hieroglyph of authority, but it has no emotional specificity and no semantic content: Wagner used the formula to state the laws of prosody and to dub the apprentice David as a journeyman of song, but he could have used it to endow with emphatic shape anything from the laws of Moses to a recipe for fudge. This fungibility can be seen in the music of the historical Hans Sachs, who invented an insistent, ponderous, somewhat Kothneresque tune (which he called the *kuercer thon*) and used it, in 1520, to set a poem describing Christ at Golgotha, shivering on the cross to expiate our sins; then reused it, in 1536, to set a poem called *Die zwelff Dreck*—The Twelve Piles of Shit. Often the tunes of mastersongs have poetical titles: Sachs gave his tunes such picturesque names as *silber* (silver) or *klingend* (ringing), but these tunes are not signs so much as empty cartouches in which signs might be inscribed.

According to *Die Meistersinger,* music begins in a state of epigram, and must evolve into the state of aria. Modernist music, as we'll see, needed (in part) to reverse that curriculum: to decompose arias back to epigrams. Wagner is so diffusive in tendency that the twentieth-century masters of concentration, such as Schoenberg and Webern, had to (so to speak) play him backward to attain their desired epitomes. But behind Wagner's delirious excesses, the listener can find a few perfect and tidy coordinations of text and music. Wagner is always, and rightly, credited as the father of that sort of Modernist art that strains the boundaries of the tonal system in search of new expressive possibilities; but perhaps Wagner also deserves some credit as a father of neoclassicism: Kothner is one of the very few characters in all opera who argues in favor of strict musical legalities. Kothner is Stravinsky, made gothic, in the only fashion in which the nineteenth century could anticipate him.

Eye Music

Epigrammatic music is music for the eye, insofar as the ear can grasp it instantly and totally, in the way that the eye grasps a simple design. The epigrams we've been studying, from Mozart to Wagner, take only a few seconds to perform; and once the ear is accustomed to their shape, the mind comprehends the whole from only about one second's worth of cue. In an Egyptian hieroglyph, the eye does the work of the ear, reading a series of pictorial forms as language; in a musical epigram, the ear does the work of the eye, apprehending an entire figure in an instant. The term *eye music,* I believe, is often misleading, as when, for example, it is used to relate the music of Debussy to the paintings of the French impressionists:

> When Debussy was new to us, those of us who "heard" him at all found in the "Sunken Cathedral" [*Préludes* 1.10], in "Sails" [*Préludes* 1.2], in "Gold Fish" [*Images* 2.3], in the "Granada" [*Estampes* 2] . . . suggestion of colours, suggestion of visions. . . . And this visionary world was a delight. By his very titles it was hinted to us that the composer wished to suggest scenes and visions and objects, and, to a great extent, he succeeded. He succeeded, I do not wish to be paradoxical, in writing music for the eye, with the result [that] . . . the effect of his music diminishes on repeated hearing.

This is Ezra Pound, writing in 1918. But no music is less visual than Debussy's, insofar as the music consists of what would be subtle transitions—if anything had been definitely established in the first place to be transited from or toward. Debussy's music is typically an art of delicate temporal adjustments, discursive, an artful sequence of instabilities; it seems visual only because of the peculiar evolution of the visual arts in Europe, from the notion that the primary act of drawing is the recognizable depiction of a finite object—as it is in most cultures—to the notion that the primary act of drawing is the recognizable depiction of the eyeball's whole visual field. In Western art, the space in which objects appear is often more vivid than objects themselves: perspective drawing carefully poses and graduates the objects that it treats, to create the illusion that the artist is presenting everything that a certain angle of vision makes available. Debussy's works are like French impressionist painting—or like Renaissance chiaroscuro, for that matter—in that the mind tries to grasp fleeting phenomena from a puzzling density of events. But it is not Debussy who is visual, but Monet and Leonardo who are discursive, in that they require the spectator to apprehend slowly and to work out over time the possibilities inherent in the painted surface.

Truly visual music, it seems to me, is epigrammatic: music that operates by means of instantaneously grasped units, pieced together not according to progressive tonalities, not according to some standard template of evolution (the sonata-allegro, the fugue, the rondo, the three-part song), but according to any principle that can *not* be understood as discursive development. Music becomes visual simply by lacking musically comprehensible connections between its parts, and by having parts that permit rapid apprehension as elementary units. Certain older procedures of form, such as the rondo (a repetitive piece with a pattern of symmetrical digressions, according to a scheme such as ABACABA), can approach the condition of eye music, in that the listener is conscious of the phonic equivalent of charms tallied on a bracelet; and as A and B get shorter and shorter, and as the musical links between A and B grow more unsettled and hard to understand, the composition will increasingly lose any sense of temporal progression and flatten into eye music. It will be noted that this definition of visual music is mostly negative in character; but this is fitting, since the whole history of music has consisted not only of investigating novelties of harmony and structure, but also of discovering what music can do without. Beethoven, for example, was (among other things) a genius of omission, who found that a whole movement of a piano sonata could be constructed out of an arpeggio and a dactyl—or who could, in another case, illustrate how an arietta fines itself down to a simple trill.

Stravinsky's Renard *and Prokofiev's* Semyon Kotko

Now, for an example of Modernist eye music, let's return to Stravinsky's *Renard,* and imagine ourselves at a performance. On stage there cavort dancers dressed as a cock, a fox, a cat, and a goat: the cock has his own elevated platform (clearly visible in Larionov's sketch for the 1929 revival), and twice during the twenty minutes or so of the piece will execute a *salto mortale,* a death-defying leap, as he falls into the clutches of the fox. Among the instrumentalists are two tenors and two basses, each of whom (singly or in concert) may find himself singing the part of any one of the four characters; so the auditor cannot connect a singer with a role. This is one of several disconcerting fractures of the normal theatrical experience. Another source of potential anxiety lies in the fact that some of the sung text is nonsensical, or seems to pertain to some action other than the action being depicted in the dance; and frequently singers simply make animal noises ("Chuck-chuck-chuck-a-dah") or imitate musical instruments ("Plinc, plinc . . . zoum! zoum! patazoum!"). Stravinsky continually challenges the boundaries that separate the singers, the real musical instruments, and the fake zither-like *gusli* carried on stage by the goat. (My quotations in English are from Robert Craft's version, familiar from Stravinsky's recording: in the original Russian text, by Stravinsky, the cock-a-doodle-doo goes *Kudá kudá* and the *gusli* goes *Tyuk tyuk.*) The spectator is accustomed to two distinct but closely related domains: the action on stage perceived by the eye and (if there is speech or song) by the ear, and the sounds from the orchestra pit perceived by the ear alone. But Stravinsky confuses these domains: "the performers, musical and mimetic, should all be together on the stage, with the singers in the center of the instrumental ensemble." So the sound of the onstage actors comes not from the actors themselves but from a little knot of singers standing amid trumpets, flutes, violins, and so forth; and the sound of the onstage *gusli* comes not from the *gusli* but from the nearby cimbalom—or, still more confusingly, from the larynxes of the singers who are the tentative surrogates for the dancers.

Renard is a ballet-cantata with an intelligible plot: a fox twice attempts to persuade a boastful cock to come down from his perch and accompany him (or her—the sex of the fox varies from one language to another in the authorized versions). First the fox wears the costume of a monk (or a nun) and persuades the remorseful cock to come confess his sins; then—after the cat and the goat free the cock from the fox's clutches—the fox repeats the whole seduction, offering food instead of absolution; this trick also succeeds, but the fox is strangled to death by cat and goat; after some celebration, the dancers leave the stage to the same march to which they entered, but not before asking the audience for money. But this action is so oddly cut up, and the pieces so oddly distributed among the performers, that the spectator can't feel caught up in any progressive, seamless theatrical illusion: the jagged edges of the intersecting planes of music, mime, song, and stage enforce a kind of detachment. This is a theatrical experience that is less like engrossment than like *reading*, reading in several artistic media at once.

The audience's effort of deciphering peculiar theatrical events is reflected in Larionov's rebus-like stage set for *Renard*: Stravinsky and his collaborators offer to the audience hieroglyphs in which music, dance, costume, and stage set work together to provide odd temporal-spatial complexes, burlesques of meaning. Stravinsky admired Larionov's set and costumes for *Renard,* and he liked the incongruity of the whole spectacle: "who, alas, now plays the *guzla* [recte: *gusli*]? ('Guzli' means 'string music played by human touch.' Part of the fun of *Renard* is that this extremely nimble-fingered instrument should be played by the cloven-hooved goat. . . .)" Touch—the goat's implied touch of the *gusli*—hearing, sight, are all engaged: but engaged *dissonantly,* in that what is seen doesn't match what is heard. The sound track (so to speak) and the image are deliberately uncoordinated, like a film with errors in synchronization. When Cyril W. Beaumont remembered Larionov's design for Prokofiev's ballet *Chout* in 1921, he wrote that "the colour contrasts, accentuated by the angular shapes composing the design, were so vivid and so dazzling that it was almost painful to look at the stage, and the position was not improved when brilliantly clad figures were set in movement against such a background. I would say that the effect on the eyes was almost as irritating as those flickering streaks of coloured light so characteristic of early colour films." Larionov, especially in his later collaboration with Stravinsky, challenged the sensorium of the spectator by a kind of polyphony of event. *Renard,* then, is a dissonant spectacle *about* figures of consonance. Here we learn what Apollo has to say concerning Marsyas: Stravinsky manufactures hieroglyphs—bits of picture-music—but instead of claiming that these cross-media entities have any prestige or expressive value, he handles them with tweezers, pieces them together like a collage of butterfly wings.

We can study Stravinsky's hieroglyphic, or *faux*-hieroglyphic, method of musical composition by comparing a detail in *Renard* with a similar detail in the music of a composer with a background like Stravinsky's—but whose music has a different aesthetic orientation, tending toward mimesis and expressivity. In *Renard,* after the fox captures the cock for the second time and begins to pluck his feathers, the cat and the goat (both now represented by basses) step forward, with *gusli,* and offer to sing a pretty little song for the fox; they start up with their plinc-plincking, and then, in slightly overlapping fashion, the basses sing: "Are you there, old Brother Fox? Are you there, old Brother Fox?" There is an episode in Sergei Prokofiev's opera *Semyon Kotko* (1940) also constructed on an emphatic movement between two semitones: it looks different in the score, because Prokofiev wrote a descending phrase afterward, to indicate a kind of trailing-off of voice, whereas Stravinsky had his singers remain on the note; but the sounds of the two passages are alike—and it is quite rare for a vocal line to get stuck on a single minor second, as in these two passages. The Prokofiev episode comes from Lyubka's third-act aria, in which she's driven mad by the sight of her dead sweetheart, hanged by the Germans and their Ukrainian collaborators: "No, no, it's not Vassilek, no, not Vassilek . . . but another, another sailor. . . . He hangs like a puppet, from a limb, a rubber doll, a frightful doll, without movement, already stiff." This passage goes on insistently, hysterically, for several tense minutes. Stravinsky's passage, by contrast, is simply one musical event among many; it is soon repeated, but most of the musical events are repeated—the whole fable, with its double temptation of cock, is designed to facilitate repetition. Stravinsky believed (incorrectly, as it happened) that the double temptation was his own idea, not part of the original Russian fable: "my text was too short. I then conceived the idea of repeating the 'salto mortale' episode. In my version, the cock is twice seduced, and he twice jumps into Renard's jaws; this repetition was a most successful accident, for the reprise of the form is a chief element in the fun." Amid these repetitions there is little subordination of one event to another: the canvas of *Renard* is crowded with details of equal interest—all figure, no background. It is repetition for repetition's sake, not for the sake of insistence or highlighting. *Semyon Kotko,* however, is a traditional opera, rising toward and falling away from moments of peak expressivity—and "No, no, it's not Vassilek" is arguably the climax of the whole opera. *Renard* is a "banal moral tale," according to its composer—a kind of étude in the juxtaposition of gestures; *Semyon Kotko,* on the other hand, is a serious patriotic drama, with carefully graduated emotive surfaces.

EX. 1.3. Stravinsky, *Renard:* "Are you there, old Brother Fox?"

It is clear that Stravinsky and Prokofiev are using textures of repeated tiny pattern-units to different ends. Despite the obstinate quality of the vocal line in *Semyon Kotko*—Lyubka repeats the identical bar five times, and then keeps on repeating after a faint alteration, as if she were a kind of human passacaglia, or air-raid siren—this bar-long phrase is not especially static in character: for one thing, the change of harmony after the fifth bar (from C♯ minor to G minor) provides a shifting of weight, keeping the line of the aria unstable, vacillating; and, as it turns out, Lyubka is just as uncomfortable in G minor, for she soon switches back to C♯ minor. Despite its extreme monotony of gesture, Prokofiev's

EX. 1.4. Prokofiev, *Semyon Kotko*: "No, no, it's not Vassilek"

passage is interpretable according to the normal canons of musical semantics, in which tritonally related chords are likely to imply emotional disjunction. Stravinsky's harmony, on the other hand, does not provide a triadic underpinning for the two notes in the vocal line: here the harmony *is* the vocal line, for the orchestra plays A and G♯ together, while the singers keep exchanging A and G♯. Such harmony is functional neither in the musical sense nor in the semantic sense. For Prokofiev, the semitone figure is salient vertically, against the background of a minor triad; for Stravinsky, the semitone figure is salient horizontally, against other music chunks that occur before and after. Prokofiev's figure achieves significance from the queasy harmonic complexities beneath it; Stravinsky's figure, absolutely simple and unitary, backgroundless, is merely a bead strung on a necklace. There is no particular reason for emphatic semitones as the cat and the goat hunt for the fox—other pattern-units plausible for the theme of urgent hailing might have been just as satisfactory. But Prokofiev needed emphatic semitones for the same reason that Monteverdi needed them for *Lasciatemi morire* [Let me die] in his *Lamento d'Arianna* (1608): because the ultimate verges of despair need naked dissonance. In *Renard*, too, horrible things happen: a fox is strangled to death, and we often hear of knives being sharpened for slaughter. But these things happen to clowns, not to men and women—it's play, not life.

Prokofiev's "No, no, it's not Vassilek" is a hieroglyph in the sense that Wagner's *Nie sollst du mich befragen* is a hieroglyph: an affect-icon representing (in this case) helplessly stuck frenzy. On the other hand, Stravinsky's "Are you there, old Brother Fox?" is a turn in a musical circus, taking its place among the other jugglings and acrobatics and zoo noises. It has a hieroglyphic incisiveness of design. But it is in no sense an affect-icon: there is no particular quality of emotion behind it, much less wisdom or transcendental meaning. It is a hieroglyph reduced to the state of a purely decorative element—just as the pictograms on Larionov's curtain are purely decorative elements. The pleasure of "Are you there, old Brother Fox?" lies in the event-rhythm of its insertion among other vivid musical designs.

By the canons of Wagner or Prokofiev or most operatic composers, the pattern-units of *Renard* are denatured, shrunken things. "Are you there, old Brother Fox?" assaults the temporal nature of its medium, in that it doesn't sound like part of an evolution, a development, a progressive continuity, a movement toward or away from climax; in that sense it is hieroglyphic. On the other hand, it doesn't seem to be a word or a character in any sort of language—it doesn't seem to be *saying* anything; in this sense it is only a parody of a hieroglyph, a nonsense hieroglyph. Insofar as it resists deciphering, insofar as it remains at once loud and mute, it anticipates the sorts of entities found in Satie and other composers, which I will be discussing in the chapters on dissonance among the arts: for where the arts diverge most aggressively, insistent musical gestures tend to vitiate meaning, instead of reinforcing it.

Arnold Newman took a series of photographs of the elderly Stravinsky at work with his scissors, snipping out short musical phrases and piecing them in place; he also snapped something that must be unique in the history of photographs of composers, a picture of Stravinsky *erasing* a note—perhaps the most Stravinskian gesture of all. But even in Stravinsky's earlier work, the scissors and the glue make themselves audible: *Renard,* for example, is obviously a collage, in that the music snippets are audibly shoved together without transitions. This procedure was not a Modernist invention; Rossini's overture to *La gazza ladra* (1815) is assembled out of transitionless chunks of hard, shiny musical material, as if the Thieving Magpie had constructed its own overture from gewgaws that caught its eye. But the Modernist taste for ocularity in music, for easily apprehended pattern-units juxtaposed rather than developed, brought the principle of scissors construction to its highest level. It is remarkable how strongly this procedure in sound appeals to the visual imagination: when I hear Stravinsky, I often feel exactly as Pound felt hearing Stravinsky's *Capriccio* in 1935—that a kind of slide projection of the score starts to hover in front of the music: "I had the mirage of seeing the unknown score from the aural stimulæ offered." In one of Newman's photographs, we see Stravinsky poring over his music at a solitary table, in the middle of an empty floor made of large checkerboard tiles; and if Stravinsky there looks like a kind of Mondrian of music, a partitioner of partiturs into bright squares, the music justifies the rigor of the photograph.

Ideogram

DEFINITION. An *ideogram* is a picture of an abstract or complex idea, generated by juxtaposing pieces of pictures of various concrete objects. Like a *hieroglyph*, it inhabits a threshold zone of meaning, neither strictly temporal nor strictly spatial.

The decisive event in the history of the use of Egyptian hieroglyphs as metaphors for Western art was, of course, Champollion's deciphering of the ancient Egyptian language (1819), following the discovery of the Rosetta stone. It turned out to be disappointingly clumsy and—as all languages must be—prosaic. Furthermore, it turned out to be a strange amalgam of alphabet and pictogram. Most of the famous picture elements represented not concepts but, in the most laborious manner imaginable, sounds. For example, to write the word *thirst* in hieroglyphs required the scribe to draw a picture of a reed (an alphabetic sign for the letter *a*) and a picture of the lower part of a human leg (an alphabetic sign for the letter *b*), spelling the word *ab*. But since the word *ab* had some twenty different meanings, ranging from "thirst" to "goat," the scribe added a picture of a goat, and then, to show that the word was *not* intended to mean "goat," a stylized water-ripple, which specified the meaning "thirst." If you added a picture of a man drinking water, after the reed, the leg, the goat, and the water-ripple, the meaning "thirst" would be even clearer. After Champollion, hieroglyphics weakened, lost most of their possibilities for transcendental metaphor in the Plotinian sense; they were perhaps doomed to reduce themselves to decoration in exotic ballets.

Perhaps the solving of the riddle of the hieroglyphs tended to increase the prestige of the Chinese ideogram, for, whereas Chinese had never been tantalizingly insoluble in the manner of Egyptian, many (though not all) of its root words were genuine ideograms, meaning-pictures. Many of the Modernist experiments with *chinoiserie*, such as Schoenberg's *Der Wunsch des*

Liebhabers (1925), Constant Lambert's *Eight Poems of Li-Po* (1929), and Harry Partch's *Seventeen Lyrics of Li Po* (1933), are experiments in concentration, in dislocation of meaning from discursive motion onto a static field. But the Modernist who most ardently took the Chinese ideogram as his artistic ideal was Ezra Pound.

Pound, Fenollosa, and the Chinese Character

The American scholar Ernest Fenollosa, a specialist in Chinese and Japanese literature, died in 1908; in 1918 Pound, who had met Fenollosa's widow and received from her a stack of posthumous notes, edited and published them (with much of his own commentary) as *The Chinese Written Character as a Medium for Poetry*. According to Pound and Fenollosa—and it should be said immediately that modern scholars look askance at this whole set of ideas—Chinese is not a language of artificial discourse, but the language of nature itself. Chinese, like nature, has no parts of speech:

> A true noun, an isolated thing, does not exist in nature. Things are only the terminal points, or rather the meeting points, of actions, cross-sections cut through action, snap-shots. Neither can a pure verb, an abstract motion, exist in nature. The eye sees noun and verb as one: things in motion, motion in things, and so the Chinese conception tends to represent them. . . .
>
> The Chinese have one word, *ming* or *mei*. Its ideograph is the sign of the sun together with the sign of the moon. It serves as verb, noun, adjective. Thus you write literally 'the sun and moon of the cup' for 'the cup's brightness.' Placed as a verb, you write 'the cup sun-and-moons,' actually 'cup sun-and-moon,' or in a weakened thought, 'is like sun,' i.e. shines. 'Sun-and-moon cup' is naturally a bright cup. There is no possible confusion of the real meaning, though a stupid scholar may spend a week trying to decide what 'part of speech' he should use in translating a very simple and direct thought from Chinese to English. . . .
>
> . . . Green is only a certain rapidity of vibration, hardness a degree of tenseness in cohering.

Fenollosa had a particular hatred for grammatical inflection in words: English is superior to German or Latin because it has fewer case endings, and Chinese is unthinkably superior to English because it has no case endings at all. A Chinese word is a naked semamorph, capable of occupying any grammatical slot, because nature has no grammar—only an endless flux of connection.

Fenollosa also hated the notion of a sentence, because nature has no full stops:

no full sentence really completes a thought. . . . The truth is that acts are successive, even continuous; one causes or passes into another. And though we may string ever so many clauses into a single compound sentence, motion leaks everywhere, like electricity from an exposed wire. All processes in nature are interrelated; and thus there could be no complete sentence (according to this definition) save one which it would take all time to pronounce.

The ideal linguistic act, the set of words that would best mirror the universe, would be an infinitely long string of infinitely varied and infinitely permuted signs. The only defect of Chinese, it would seem, is not that it has too many characters, but that it has too few: the student can aspire to learn them all.

Imagism

A work like *Renard* can be called ideogrammatic, in that its music chunks (such as "Chuck-chuck-chuck-a-dah" and "Are you there, old Brother Fox?"), though arranged in a pattern, can't be classified according to the formal grammar of music—one never says, Here is the second theme of the exposition, or Now begins the ritornello. *Renard* is built not through sequential logic, but through juxtaposition, a kind of *nebeneinander* conducted not in space but in time. And much of Pound's poetry plays similar games, with verbal instead of musical entities—as he explains in his famous account of how he composed one of the imagist movement's defining poems, "In a Station of the Metro" (1913):

> Three years ago in Paris I got out of a "Metro" train at La Concorde, and saw suddenly a beautiful face, and then another and another, and then a beautiful child's face, and then another beautiful woman, and I tried all that day to find words for what this had meant to me, and I could not find any words that seemed to me worth, or as lovely as that sudden emotion. And that evening, as I went home along the Rue Raynouard, I was still trying, and I found, suddenly, the expression. I do not mean that I found words, but there came an equation . . . not in speech, but in little splotches of colour. It was just that—a "pattern," or hardly a pattern, if by "pattern" you mean something with a repeat in it. . . . if I had the energy to get paints and brushes and keep at it, I might found a new school of painting, of "non-representative" painting, a painting that would speak only by arrangements of colour.
> And so, when I came to read Kandinsky's chapter on the language of form and colour [from *Über das Geistige in der Kunst*] . . . I found little that was new to me. . . .
> The "one image poem" is a form of super-position, that is to say it is one

idea set on top of another. I found it useful in getting out of the impasse in which I had been left by my Metro emotion. I wrote a thirty-line poem, and destroyed it because it was what we call work "of second intensity." Six months later I made a poem half that length; a year later I made the following *hokku*-like sentence:—

> "The apparition of these faces in the crowd:
> Petals, on a wet, black bough."

Just as the Chinese word *ming* is written by combining the ideograms for sun and moon, so "In a Station of the Metro" is devised by combining terse denotations of collinear faces and collinear petals—but in the hope that this superimposition will yield not a simple concept such as *brightness,* but a complex, polysensuous response. A poem that contains only fourteen words is so severely curtailed that it almost lacks any development in time: it can be grasped as quickly as the painting of the subway platform that Pound would have made if he'd known how to paint. The representation is so spare that it almost seems to belong in a school of "'non-representative' painting"—just as an ideogram is a picture so pared down by the scribe's brushstrokes that it is little more than the dots and lines in a constellation of meaning.

Pound's whole canon during the productive 1910s was dominated by the Fenollosa materials. In 1915 Pound published a series of translations from Chinese, *Cathay,* based on cribs by Fenollosa. The relation of these translations to their Chinese originals—filtered, strangely, through the *Japanese* scholars who tried to teach the material to Fenollosa—makes a fascinating story (told in Wai-lim Yip, *Ezra Pound's Cathay*); but it will suffice for our purposes to examine Pound's practice, not in the light of real Chinese, but in the light of Fenollosa's fantasy Chinese, a language of devastating semantic intensity. Here is the shortest of the *Cathay* poems, "The Jewel Stairs' Grievance":

> The jewelled steps are already quite white with dew,
> It is so late that the dew soaks my gauze stockings,
> And I let down the crystal curtain
> And watch the moon through the clear autumn.   *By Rihaku*

(*Rihaku* is the Japanese form of the name of the eighth-century Chinese poet Li Po.) To this poem Pound appended the following:

Note.—Jewel stairs, therefore a palace. Grievance, therefore there is something to complain of. Gauze stockings, therefore a court lady, not a servant who complains. Clear autumn, therefore he has no excuse on account of weather. Also she has come early, for the dew has not merely whitened the stair, but has soaked her stockings. The poem is especially prized because she utters no direct reproach.

Any sentence, said Fenollosa, is an arbitrarily chopped-off limb of the infinite sentence that takes all time to pronounce: and Pound took care to suggest the long prose romance, the Chinese *Anna Karenina* into which "The Jewel Stairs' Grievance" would decompose if the tension of its internal winding slipped. The poem is picturesque, but this pictoriality is a kind of rendering-immediate of an intricate narrative—not the pictoriality of a single frame, but of a whole film wound up on a reel. The poem is a metaphor for a sequence of ideograms, simultaneously static and discursive, generating discourse through the tense adjacency of stasis to stasis.

By using the Chinese model, Pound discovered a way of writing a very short poem that did the work of a whole novel. The next step was to see whether it was possible to write a piece for the theatre that did the work of a long play in an immensely abbreviated span of time.

Noh

DEFINITION. A *Noh play* is a spare Japanese drama in which all elements co-operate to produce a single intense effect; the limit of contraction of the theatrical experience.

In the Modernist movement there have been many examples of extremely brief poems and musical works. Pound's imagism assigned the highest value to the poem that disextended itself into "an intellectual and emotional complex in an instant of time"; and Schoenberg said in 1924 that each of the *Six Bagatelles* of Anton Webern managed "to convey a novel through a single gesture, or felicity by a single catch of the breath." Furthermore, some of these minuscule compositions were Orientalist in character—hieroglyphic or ideogrammatic. For one example, Pound's "Papyrus" (1916) consists of four words: "Spring....... / Too long...... / Gongula......"; it is more hole than text, a translation of an almost lost poem of Sappho's that the reader must reconstruct from a few flitters of words—and will probably reconstruct rather along the lines of "The Jewel Stairs' Grievance." For another example, Stravinsky's *Three Japanese Lyrics* (1913) scarcely manage to give any impression of existing in time: according to Richard Taruskin's fine description, "the verbal and musical stresses . . . cancel one another out, leaving a dynamically uninflected, stressless line, the musical equivalent of the flat surface . . . of Japanese paintings and prints." Two modes of discursivity—poetry and music—manage to undo one another, collapse into stasis, like two waves that fall together crest to trough and trough to crest. This phenomenon may be the secret of Stravinsky's fondness for text-setting, otherwise so difficult to explain in a composer so devoted to the inexpressive. Just as Picasso and Braque superimposed text-stencils, or actual newsprint, on certain early cubist paintings in order to flatten the surface—nothing is flatter than words on a sheet on paper—so Stravinsky used sung text in order to flatten his acoustic surfaces, to preclude any feeling of development along strictly musical lines.

But composers and poets aren't likely to rest content writing only very brief pieces; even Webern, by the end of his life, managed to compose something lasting over twelve minutes. Is it possible to write a longer piece that has a quality of taciturnity, of visuality, of incisive starkness of being? This matter vexed Pound, for one: he asked himself, what would a long poem look like if it had the shape or attribute of a single image? How could instantaneity be promoted into a lengthy discourse, without losing its purity of being? For an answer to this aesthetic puzzle, he first looked, in 1914, to the Noh theatre of Japan:

> I am often asked whether there can be a long imagiste . . . poem. The Japanese, who evolved the *hokku,* evolved also the Noh plays. In the best "Noh" the whole play may consist of one image. I mean it is gathered about one image. Its unity consists in one image, enforced by movement and music.

A Noh play, according to this unusual theory, is a *magnified version of a single aesthetic particle.* It is a huge ideogram, expanded to the size of the stage, strung out to an evening's entertainment, read through the motions of the actors. And because the example of classical Japanese drama was to yield some of the most striking musical collaborations of the twentieth century, it is worth examining in some detail the origin of the Modernist preoccupation with Noh, in the strange nexus of Ernest Fenollosa, Ezra Pound, and William Butler Yeats. Aristotle devised a theory that divided the Greek tragedy into several elements, including *opsis* (stage spectacle), *melos* (music), *lexis* (diction), and *mythos* (plot). What Aristotle divided, the Japanese theatre seemed to unite: for several of the Modernists, Noh seemed to provide a model for a genuinely transmediated dramaturgy in which *opsis* and *melos* were not simply decorative adjuncts of *mythos,* but integral to the whole—a theatre of parables achieved through an ideogrammatic method, a *Gesamtkunst* without the fatness and laboriousness of Wagnerian theatre.

Pound, Fenollosa, Yeats, and Michio Ito

Some years ago a company of Japanese Noh players visited my home town, and I watched their performances. I was struck by their incisive movements, at once sudden and impossibly slow, neither gesture nor pantomime nor dance in any Western sense, but a kind of studious surrender to vectors outside human agency. I felt sometimes that they were performing a kind of karate designed to injure the air, other times that they aspired, through their deep, rough intonation, to be organ pipes or conduits for wind. Like most of the audience, I left in a state of happy confusion; and yet, though we had seen little and understood less, we had attained a better acquaintance with the theatrical experience of the Noh than Yeats or Pound or any of those early-twentieth-century poets who hoped to find a sort of dramatic salvation through the purity and severity of the Noh. It is possible to learn a good deal about the actual Japanese Noh theatre—a useful primer can be found in *Yeats and the Noh: A Comparative Study,* by Masaru Sekine and Christopher Murray—but to some extent genuine research into Japanese texts and dramatic practice is beside the point: Modernist Noh is a matter of exuberant fantasies bred in considerable ignorance of the Noh theatre. This is a more usual state of affairs than might be thought, for the great renewals in the history of art have often found it convenient to claim the prestige of some extremely remote sanction: when the opera originated in Florence, at the end of the sixteenth century, its inventors claimed to be reviving the musical drama of classical Greece. Of course Peri and Caccini and Vicenzo Galilei knew almost nothing about the actual music of classical Greece; but this pleasant hope of recovery of long-forgotten aesthetic truth allowed their imaginations the necessary freedom for invention. The Greek theatre and the Noh theatre each stood as a settled and elaborate body of conventions existing at a great distance—the Greek theatre in time, the Noh theatre in space—and susceptible to almost any interpretation.

I do not mean that Yeats and Pound did not do everything they could to discover what the reality of the Noh theatre was; it is simply that there was little they could do in England in 1913 to educate themselves properly. When Yeats wrote his 1916 essay on the Noh, "Certain Noble Plays of Japan," he complained that the war had required the closing of the Print Room of the British Museum, so that he had to rely on old memories of the designs of the Japanese theatre; and almost everything that Yeats and Pound knew about the Noh came from two sources. The first was the body of scattered notes left by Fenollosa, who died in 1908, just before Pound could have met him, but who metamorphosed in death into the occult bridge between East and West needed by Pound for his translations of Noh and of Chinese poetry. As Pound presented it, Fenollosa's life

> was the romance par excellence of modern scholarship. He went to Japan as a professor of economics. He ended as Imperial Commissioner of Arts. He had unearthed treasure that no Japanese had heard of. It may be an exaggeration to say that he saved Japanese art for Japan, but it is certain that he had done as much as any one man could have to set the native art in its rightful preeminence and to stop the apeing of Europe. . . . When he died suddenly in England the Japanese government sent a warship for his body, and the priests buried him with the sacred enclosure at Miidera.

Shortly after giving this description of the scholar as swashbuckler—just the sort of scholar Pound liked best—Pound told the story of the famous Noh actor Umewaka Minoru, who lived through the revolution of 1868 and, when it seemed that all the implements of the Noh theatre, the great masks and costumes, would perish, managed to save them by selling the clothes off his back. The story of Minoru's heroism may well have impressed Yeats also: his *The Player Queen* (1907–22) tells a story about a heroic attempt to rescue theatrical props during the collapse of a culture. And Pound evidently wondered whether he, Pound, could become a new Minoru, rescuing the Noh theatre from destruction—though by means of a microphone, not a bag of masks: in 1941, Pound told those listening to his radio broadcasts in support of Mussolini's Italy that

> The Japanese would be truly grateful to us, not for Guam, but for prodding 'em on to make a complete high grade record of these plays before the tradition gets damaged.
> Umewaka Minoru is dead. I have heard discs of Noh music that did NOT seem to me up to the mark. It is never too soon to start on such records.

To Yeats and Pound, Fenollosa and Minoru were both heroes of the highest rank, saviors of the implements of art from destruction; and indeed the life of Fenollosa (as Pound told it) is almost a little Noh play of its own, in which the mild-mannered scholar, a museum collector and a putterer in antiquities, suddenly reveals himself as a transcendental apparition, sage and sacred, given a burial fit for a god.

Fenollosa, whatever the limitations of his linguistic knowledge, had made a serious study of the Noh, and Pound was fortunate to discover his work; Pound's other source was just as exciting, but far more dubious. Somehow Pound managed to find a starving Japanese dancer, Michio Ito, who seemed to know all about the dances that are placed at the climax of every Noh drama; and Yeats was sufficiently intrigued that he appointed Ito to dance the role of the Guardian of the Well in his own pseudo-Noh play *At the Hawk's Well* (1917). In fact, Ito's training had been of a different sort: he had studied with Émile Jaques-Dalcroze, the inventor of a system of motion and gesture called *eurhythmics,* designed to make one's body express the quality of rhythm and melodic phrase that one heard. In D. H. Lawrence's *Women in Love* (1920), Ursula and Gudrun perform a little eurhythmic ballet using Dalcroze gestures. One of Dalcroze's students also became Nijinsky's coach when the Ballets Russes came to Paris. After studying with Dalcroze, Ito left for New York and danced at the Village Follies, where Ruth St. Denis, of the famous Denishawn modern dance company, first worked on her return to the United States. We see that the origins of Ito's dance style lay not in some priestly cult in Japan, but in the confused provenance of modern dance. Ruth St. Denis herself, it is believed, decided to become a dancer when she saw a poster for "Egyptian Goddess" cigarettes and visited Coney Island to see what Egyptian dance was really like; and to some extent this will serve as a parable for what Yeats and Pound did, as they sought to remold modern theatre from the work of a Japanese dancer who was as remote from the austere old Japanese theatre as the Coney Island dancer was from Egyptian antiquity.

Ito's effect on Yeats and Pound was no less striking because of its bastard beginnings. When Yeats saw him dance in a drawing room, he found in him

> the tragic image that has stirred my imagination. There, where no studied lighting, no stage-picture made an artificial world, he was able, as he rose from the floor, where he had been sitting cross-legged, or as he threw out an arm, to recede from us into some more powerful life. Because that separation was achieved by human means alone, he receded but to inhabit as it were the deeps of the mind. One realised anew, at every separating strangeness, that the measure of all arts' greatness can be but in their intimacy.

It is as if Ito were heaven-sent, so perfectly did he embody everything Yeats wanted in his new theatre: gestures immemorially old, both intimate and eerie; a passion wordlessly raised to new pitches of intensity—the anti-self of the talky, realistic, hateful theatre, made manifest. The Noh theatre was appropriated *in toto* to provide a model for the kind of art desired by early Modernism, in order to prove a historical thesis about the perversion of an ancient and devastating theatre—realized in Sophoclean Greece, lost forever in the West, but miraculously preserved in Japan and available today.

In Yeats's essay on the Noh, we find what seems to be a contradiction in his praise of the Japanese theatre: he celebrated it at once for being the art of sheer body and for being a kind of glorified marionette show. This paradox seems to be at the heart of Yeats's hopes for creating a new sort of play. What amazed Yeats about the Noh was that it appeared to be a full-blown version of the theatre he had been struggling to realize, with varying degrees of success, ever since he helped found the Abbey Theatre in 1902; indeed, in his essay he pointed with interest to the many similarities between Irish myth and Japanese. The Noh, then, as far as Yeats was concerned, was less a Japanese invention than a distant echo of what the Irish national theatre ought to be; and when Pound translated certain Noh passages in a kind of Irish dialect ("There never was anybody heard of Mt. Shinobu but had a kindly feeling for it"), he was helping Yeats to perfect his Hiberno-Japanese hybrid drama.

Unnatural Nature: Kleist and Mallarmé

Conventional Western drama is founded on a suspenseful plot about developing characters—it is a time-driven art, a mimesis of temporality. A detemporalized, de-mimeticized theatre will have to look elsewhere for its interest.

The Noh theatre, as Yeats and Pound understood it, does not imitate human beings; it imitates signs. The dramatis personae are not rounded, credible characters to whom the audience might react personally—by loving or hating. Their sensibilities do not deepen. They are masks, ideograms carved in wood and out-fitted with arms and legs. The proper question is not Who are they? but What do they mean?—for they are incarnations of the transcendental. In this sense, the Noh is a sort of treatise on religion carried out by ambulatory pictograms, pointing to truths beyond our world.

The nineteenth century found that Oriental art could be appropriated for almost any Occidental purpose. One of its most useful functions was simply to provide emblems for the other world, the domain of the spirit, which was defined as whatever was least like our ordinary sensible nature. Oriental art was valued, then, for producing a shiver of the unnatural. Hans Christian Andersen, in his fable about the competition of a real nightingale with a wind-up toy nightingale, had the mechanical version imported from the court of the Japanese emperor; and such fables helped to fix a lasting association between the Orient and the world of sheer artifice. It is to this tradition that Yeats appealed when he compared the Noh drama to a sublime puppet show; and it is to the fable of the emperor and the nightingale that Yeats appealed when, ten years later, he wrote "Sailing to Byzantium," in which the poet claims he desires to become a golden bird singing to a drowsy emperor, after he is gathered into the artifice of eternity.

But, as Edward Said and others have told us, the history of Orientalism provides not a coherent mythology, but an odd body of self-contradictory myths. Sometimes descriptions of the Orient, like heresies, come in opposing pairs. Therefore it is not surprising that on the one hand, the Orient is the domain of sheer artifice, while on the other hand the Orient is the domain of physical health. According to this countermyth, modern Europe is decadent, exhausted, withered into abstraction, while the East is the kingdom of bodily vigor, without any dissociation between thought and feeling, soul and body. Yeats was thinking of this countermyth when he praised the Noh for its presentation of the physical body: if modern European drama consists simply of talking heads yammering in the void, then the Noh is the place where the whole body emotes. It is easy to represent a laughing man, unless your face is covered with a mask; then you will have to make your whole self a corporeal projection of laughter.

Igor Stravinsky's attitude toward the Orient parallels Yeats's peculiar hope of a pseudo-Eastern theatre at once extremely physical and extremely disembodied. In *The Rite of Spring* (1913—the year when Pound discovered the Noh), Stravinsky tried to find in his imagination of pagan Russia a prehistorical vitality, the piercing rhythms of nature before humankind severed itself from natural intensities; and when Nijinsky choreographed the ballet, he looked to the Dalcrozean resources of physical expression similar to those in which Michio Ito was trained. This clearly is the myth of the superior physicality of the Orient. But both before and after *The Rite of Spring*, Stravinsky worked on an opera based on Hans Christian Andersen's fable, *The Nightingale;* what is interesting about the opera is that while Andersen's fable and Stravinsky's libretto make it clear that the pathos of the real nightingale is more admirable than the soulless twittering of the mechanical nightingale, Stravinsky's music seems to argue the opposite. The music of the real nightingale is swoony coloratura, in many broken phrases, as if the bird always limped as it flew; while the music of the mechanical nightingale, represented not by a soprano but by an oboe, is taut, clean, implacable. I take this as a sign that Stravinsky felt that the Oriental-mechanical was more fascinating than the organic, and in his later career he again shows this preference—for example, in his opera *The Rake's Progress* (1951), written to a libretto by W. H. Auden and Chester Kallman. In this opera, the theme of *The Nightingale* returns in a different guise: Tom Rakewell is forced to choose between two girls, the pallidly faithful Anne Truelove, a Mozartean soprano, and the bearded lady Baba the Turk, whom the Devil induces Tom to marry in order to show contempt for normal social expectations, for human desire itself. Baba the Turk is another artifact of the Orient, a wind-up toy, who turns into a piece of furniture when a cloth is placed over her chattering head; indeed, the music she sings even sounds like the music of the mechanical nightingale, rigid permutations of scales. Here is another contest between the organic and the inorganic, between the human and the mechanical; and again the artifice seems at least as fascinating as the woman.

The over-physical and the unphysical seem diametrically opposed, and yet the rhythmic ferocity of the human sacrifice in *The Rite of Spring* and that of *The Nightingale*'s procession of Japanese ambassadors (directly following the mechanical bird's song) are similar in Stravinsky's music. It is the same convergence of opposites that we find in Yeats's theory of the Noh theatre; both Stravinsky and Yeats evidently felt that in the deepest part of nature there is something unnatural, uncanny. Overstress of nature, as through ritual murder, leads to a kind of breakthrough into something beyond nature; just as the cross of Christ's crucifixion becomes a pictogram of a transcendental speech, so the music at the end of Stravinsky's *The Rite of Spring* becomes a phonoglyph that seizes the artifice of eternity.

The roots of the conjoining of the natural and the unnatural go far back into nineteenth-century aesthetics. In his essay on the marionette theatre (1810), Kleist hypothesized that every ballet dancer tries—and fails—to imitate the perfection of movement achievable by marionettes whose limbs are weighted with pendulums to ensure an infallible symmetry of motion and countermotion; Kleist went on to discover an approximation of the divine in this sort of puppet-rhythm, so that the automaton and the god converge. Grace, to Kleist, is an attribute not of human beings but of marionettes and of dancing bears: the unnatural and the perfectly natural. Kleist would have known little about the Noh theatre, but its attempt to reduce and stylize human movement into a sacred marionette show could be taken as the culmination of his dream—as in another sense it was the culmination of Mallarmé's dream, later in the nineteenth century, of a theatre of silence, in which, as he wrote in his essay "Ballets" (1886),

> the dancing woman . . . *is not a woman who dances* . . . but a metaphor summing up one of the elementary aspects of our form, sword, cup, flower, etc., and . . . suggesting, through the wonder of abridgements and leaps *[élans]*, with a corporeal scripture what one would need many paragraphs of dialogue as well as descriptive prose to express . . . a poem disengaged from all the apparatus of writing.

Ballet, according to Mallarmé, consists of hieroglyphs inscribed by (and on) the bodies of the dancers. Just as Mallarmé and Yeats and Pound tried to liberate poetry from every discursive, prosaic element, so it became possible to see in the Noh theatre a kind of poetry liberated almost entirely from the verbal, a pure immanence of symbol interspersed with a little hieratic chanting. A human physique can attain powers of denotation more rapid and more deeply cutting than those of language.

Structure of the Noh Play

What did Pound and Yeats find when they inspected the texts of Noh plays? In Fenollosa's notes, Pound discovered a plan for presenting a six-part suite of Noh plays in a single evening's performance: first, a play about the age of the gods; second, a battle piece; third, a "wig piece," or play about women; fourth, the Noh of spirits; fifth, a piece about the moral duties of man; sixth, a panegyrical play about the lords present at the performance. Behind this plan was an elaborate rationalization about the Noh drama as an epitome of human life: the first four parts move from divine prehistory to war and love (the affairs of the world), and then to a superseding of the mundane in the presentation of spiritual reality. Pound thought that the battle pieces were the usual boring martial exploits and considered the chief interest of the Noh to lie in the spirit plays. Most of the Noh plays that Pound translated could be considered the Noh-of-spirits sort; and when we study them we find a few simple dramatic patterns.

In the Noh of spirits, there is rarely anything that could be called a story; the action, which is minimal, is usually accomplished during, and by means of, the climactic dance. In the simplest plays, a traveling priest (called the *waki*), often a folklorist or a connoisseur of landscape, meets a humble old man or woman; after a series of interrogations, it dawns on the priest that what appears to be a vagrant, a beggar, or a leech gatherer is actually a spirit (called the *shite*)—perhaps the ghost of a great man triumphantly remembering the scene of a mighty deed, or a genius loci taking pleasure in the presence of his or her locus. A metamorphosis is accomplished by means of a costume change and a change of mask; there is no scenery, nothing but bridges and potted pines and the painted pine tree that is the backdrop of all Noh plays. The dramatic action, then, is only a movement toward enlightenment: what is surrounded by material illusion at last reveals itself in its true supernatural glory, a glory that reaches its perfection in the characteristic dance of the spirit. It is not the sort of dramatic action that we are accustomed to, but in certain films we find something similar to it. For example, Steven Spielberg's *Close Encounters of the Third Kind* (1977) is Noh-like in that it has neither heroes nor villains, no action except the tantalizing unveiling of a remarkable and nearly incomprehensible spectacle; since we don't like, these days, to speak of spirits, Spielberg substitutes extraterrestrial beings, which are acceptable versions of the otherworldly; and where a Noh play would have a climactic dance, Spielberg substitutes an increasing visual magnificence of unearthly forms. I doubt that Spielberg was influenced by Noh drama, but I believe that this movie and the Noh share a common aesthetic goal—an attempt to provoke a delirium of wonder.

Nishikigi

Yeats's favorite Noh play, and one of the favorites of Fenollosa and Pound as well, was *Nishikigi*. The play—"charm sticks" is the meaning of the title—is about two lovers: a man spends three fruitless years erecting charm sticks to woo a young woman, who disdains him and chooses instead to spend her time weaving a cloth; the spirits of these two implore an itinerant priest to marry them, for in death the young woman wishes she had been less oblivious to the young man's charms; the play ends with the marriage dance of the two shades. Yeats liked many things about this play: the plot was identical to that of a story he had heard in the Aran Islands of Ireland; the sense of the interconnectedness, the mutual dependence, of the quick and the dead was agreeable to him; and most of all he liked the artistic unity of it, the fact that the whole is a playing upon a single metaphor, as deliberate as the echoing rhythm of line in Chinese and Japanese painting. In the *Nishikigi* the ghost of the girl-lover carries the cloth she went on weaving out of grass when she should have opened the chamber door to her lover, and woven grass returns again and again in metaphor and incident. The lovers, now that in an aëry body they must sorrow for unconsummated love, are 'tangled up as the grass patterns are tangled.' Again they are like an unfinished cloth: 'these bodies, having no weft, even now are not come together . . .'

Pound was similarly impressed with its unity:

When a text seems to 'go off into nothing' at the end, the reader must remember 'that the vagueness or paleness of words is made good by the emotion of the final dance,' for the Noh has its unity in emotion. It has also what we may call Unity of Image.

The crucial matter is that the unity of *Nishikigi* is essentially *pictorial* in character—the play is like a Japanese painting, or like a weaving of grass. The play is apprehended in one glance. Pound even saw the play as a single image, viewed in a magnifying glass:

This intensification of the Image, this manner of construction, is very interesting to me personally, as an Imagiste, for we Imagistes knew nothing of these plays when we set out in our own manner. These plays are also an answer to a question that has several times been put to me: 'Could one do a long Imagiste poem?'

As we have seen, Pound defined an image as "an intellectual and emotional complex in an instant of time." This definition would seem, on the face of it, to preclude poems much longer than "In a Station of the Metro." But Noh drama enabled Pound to see that a poem could be a great deal more than two lines long and yet have a quality of instantaneity to it; for the Noh theatre, with its spareness, its anti-discursiveness, was continually working toward an instant of breakthrough, of buckling between the spiritual and the mortal worlds. The beginning of a Noh play, the whole lead-up to the dance, is static, what Fenollosa called sculptural: nothing happens, no action violates the integrity of the composition; then there is a revelation—the old beggar turns out to be the spirit of a celebrated warrior—and an instant of metamorphosis. This is the dramatic equivalent of the superimposition of the brief imagist poem, a sudden perception of the hidden aesthetic content of an ordinary thing.

Pound's Tristan

The best of the four surviving Noh plays that Pound wrote in 1916 is *Tristan,* probably inspired by a performance, conducted by Thomas Beecham, of Wagner's *Tristan und Isolde* that the Pounds attended on 19 June 1916. Wagner's music drama seemed to many to be the climax of all emotional intensity possible to art. In an unpublished poem of November 1909, "Opera," Eliot wrote of the musical paroxysms of *Tristan und Isolde,* in which life flings out to the last limit of self-expression—though the opera leaves the poet oddly indifferent: he feels himself to be "the ghost of youth / At the undertakers' ball." Pound was more personally susceptible to Wagner's effects; as he wrote in a 1917 review, "One felt the man [Tristan] . . . the victim of fate, the immobile mass of humanity, beaten by blow after blow, unable to shield himself."

Wagner's success encouraged a number of playwrights, particularly of the symbolist school, to attempt to translate the aesthetic effect of *Tristan und Isolde*—ecstasy heightening to *Liebestod*—to a purely verbal sort of drama. Just as Webern tried to see whether a full operatic catharsis could be contracted into a few seconds of music, so certain dramatists tried to see whether an opera could be reduced to a musicless text. To discover whether one can accomplish with fewer media what has been done with many media is part of the normal rhythm of cross-media experimentation. Villiers de l'Isle-Adam's *Axël* (1890), in which the lovers commit suicide by drinking poison rather than allow their love to fall from its high pitch back to common life, is one such opera substitute; another is Yeats's *The Shadowy Waters* (1900, 1906). Like Tristan and Isolde, Yeats's Forgael and Dectora are natural enemies compelled by forces beyond themselves to an intolerable love-intensity; the rough, loyal Aibric resembles Wagner's Kurwenal; and passions are wholly governed by the musical modulations of a magical harp. Yeats had little of the musical knowledge or sensitivity of the French symbolist playwrights, but he knew a good many strategies for etherealizing a text, for evacuating it of common denotation. The words are scarcely words at all, but surrogate music; the images point to something beyond images:

> Yet sometimes there's a torch inside my head
> That makes all clear, but when the light is gone
> I have but images, analogies,
> The mystic bread, the sacramental wine,
> The red rose where the two shafts of the cross,
> Body and soul, waking and sleep, death, life,
> Whatever meaning ancient allegorists
> Have settled on, are mixed into one joy.

The Wagnerian chord of yearning infinitely suspended, overwhelmingly liqui-
dated, is unmistakable throughout. Arthur Symons's essay on Wagner helped
Yeats to rewrite *The Shadowy Waters,* as he told Symons; Yeats wanted the costumes for *The Shadowy Waters* to suggest mythical antiquity, "Wagner's period
more or less"—though there should be no winged helmets; and the text remains
a kind of opera of speech.

Pound's odd conflation of Wagner and Noh opens with a Prologue, in which
the audience is asked to imagine a shore and a ruined castle; a Sculptor (the *waki*)
enters, looking for a certain quince tree, a botanical wonder that blossoms in
Cornwall (because of the Gulf Stream, he thinks) before any other quince tree.
This premise is derived from an episode in the life of Pound's friend, the sculptor
Henri Gaudier-Brzeska:

> Gaudier had been through Wales. He had made a particular pilgrimage to a
> certain tree, that blooms on a set day in the year because of the warmth of the
> Gulf-stream. (This might be out of a Japanese "Noh" play, but it isn't.)

In the play, the Sculptor finds an enigmatic woman (the *shite*), who tries to shoo
him away, then vanishes herself; and soon he finds himself witnessing a spectacle
in which the *shite*, now dressed in brilliant medieval costume, performs a series
of slow passes and re-passes with a man, Tristan. Their costumes are gray on one
side, so that when they turn round they become invisible against the gray background; thus, from the Sculptor's and the audience's point of view, they seem
spectral presences, dissolving and reforming in a slow, stately dance. "They flash
and fade through each other," the Sculptor says; and Tristan tells Isolde, who is
herself having trouble seeing him:

> Your eyes . . .
> *(forte, making use of the Sculptor's voice)* like malachite gone
>   transparent. . . .
> My dust is a veil in the wind
> So frail a thing, that you will turn your head,
> And look at any fool in a daze,
> And not hear me.

Without using any of the resources of technological illusion (slide projectors or
transparent scrims), Pound has managed to create a theatre of dematerializa-
tion, ghost-glimpses, passions detached from finite human beings and personified
into visionary presences. At the beginning, Pound's *Tristan* seemed like a normal
Western drama, governed by plot and character: but the plot vanishes into a

pavane, and the characters vanish into ideograms of half-apprehended medieval glory. Their human side is gray, empty; but they manage to *refer* to something gaudy and ceremonious, jeweled.

What would it be like to be *inside* an image? Pound's *Tristan* suggests an answer: it would be a condition where nothing is solid, nothing is determinate—a condition at the knife-edge, at the metamorphic quick, where the subway train is just about to turn into the black bough. Pound's play is a theatrical presentation of life inside Wagner's *Tristan* chord, a chord that demands harmonic resolution yet remains suspended, incapable of resolving, incapable of construing itself, at once creeping upward and diminishing ever further into its own private hypospace—an endless frustration. Because the whole spectacle is one image, every aspect is bi-representational, pertinent (in this case) both to the ceremoniously erotic, jeweled world of Arthurian romance and to the up-to-date world of 1916; and because an image is timeless, instantaneous, the whole action is only the arbitrary spinning-out of a multidimensional stasis into a metamorphosis.

A true climax or resolution or decision is, then, impossible; in a play that aspires to be one huge drama-particle, the plot's knot cannot be untied, only drawn tighter. Near the end, the *shite* seems undecided whether to remain Isolde or to revert to contemporary humanity:

> Oh, there is too much between us,
> We are neither alone, nor together.
> The court moves and is gone,
> The gold trappings and diaspore
> Show bright and then vanish,
> And I am torn between two lives
> Knowing neither.

Finally the vision fades, but the Sculptor finds the amazing quince tree, indeed in bloom—not because of the Gulf Stream, but because of the fructifications of the lovers' eternally recurrent passion. In "The Spring" (1915), a translation of a poem by Ibycus, Pound had written of a "Cydonian spring"—a spring of quince trees—in which the poet's heart grows wild with desire at the apparition of a "clinging tenuous ghost"; and in *Tristan* Pound turned this lyric into a lyric semblance of drama, as if a single imagist poem could be turned into a theatrical experience.

Despite the Sculptor's slightly proletarian roughness—he has worked on road-repair crews—*Tristan* has an antique, aesthetical savor; in the *shite* there is something of the flimsiness and uncomprehendingness of Maeterlinck's Mélisande, though with a tartness that is not Mélisande's. Yeats, of course, was to become a far more successful writer of pseudo-Noh plays, partly because of the greater urgency, the greater painfulness, of the plots he thought suitable for presentation in this form.

The simplest way of describing the Noh-like plays that Yeats wrote from the end of his period of study with Pound in Sussex (during the winters from 1913 to 1916) until just before his death in 1939 is to call them Irish equivalents of Noh plays with unhappy endings tacked on. Almost every Noh play in Pound's collection ends benignly, the spirits happily manifest, the priest fortunate to behold them; but in Yeats's plays there is a quality of desperation foreign to the mysterious calm of the original. The clearest example of Yeats's revision of Noh themes is found in *The Dreaming of the Bones* (1919), which is a rewriting of—once again—*Nishikigi:* but in Yeats's version the dead lovers who beg a passerby to grant them peace, to let them marry, are frustrated, for they are Diarmuid and Dervorgilla, the traitors who brought foreign armies into Ireland in order to pursue their adulterous love, and no one will forgive them their crime. Their final dance is not, as in *Nishikigi,* a solution, a reconciliation, but instead a further display of the tangledness that can never be untangled. Yeats, like Pound, altered the Japanese originals in the direction of plotlessness, imagistic instantaneity. (It is remarkable how closely *The Dreaming of the Bones* resembles, both in its plangent theme and in its concentrated uneventfulness of dramatic method, Rachmaninov's brief opera from Dante, *Francesca da Rimini* [1906].)

In most of the later pseudo-Noh plays, Yeats mingled the Noh themes with the themes of Wilde's *Salomé* (1893), for Yeats came to understand the passage from the earthly to the unearthly almost exclusively as a severing of the head, a literal disembodiment. While the climactic dance occurs, the severed head itself sings, as in *The King of the Great Clock Tower* (1935)—an oracular paroxysm that even the axe can't stop. It sings of transcendental sexual pleasure:

Crossed fingers there in pleasure can
Exceed the nuptial bed of man. . . .
A nuptial bed exceed all that
Boys at puberty have thought,
Or sibyls in a frenzy sought.

The severed head seems to know a form of orgasm unknown to the living; and indeed Yeats's final dances are metaphors for inhumanly intense sexual consummation. But if beheading is a kind of erotic asphyxia, it is also an entry into a hard-edged domain of Modernist graphics. The culmination of the theme of sacred decapitation occurs in Yeats's play *The Death of Cuchulain* (1939), in which Cuchulain's wife Emer dances the final dance in front of the severed head of her husband, represented by a black parallelogram mounted on a stick; this gesture neatly combines the disengagement from terrestrial life with a kind of abstract art, the cubism that Yeats thought the most appropriate representation of the supernatural. The severed head becomes a geometrical form—a hieroglyph of a head.

We are now at the verge of a drama in which human characters are replaced by pictograms, waving around in legible silence; a drama of pure juxtapositivity, in which all temporal progression has disappeared into the immanence of the letters of a translunar alphabet. Giacomo Balla's futurist stage spectacle (1917) for Stravinsky's *Fireworks,* a ballet "danced" by lights flashing onto pieces of colored cloth cut into geometrical designs, a ballet without human presence, suggests one direction for the evolution of a purely hieroglyphic theatre.

The Pisan Cantos as a Noh Play

When something interesting is achieved through a mixture of media, artists are tempted to see whether it can be done in fewer media—or, finally, within the bounds of one medium alone. Can one medium simulate the complicated interplay between media characteristic of the Noh play? I think that Pound, in his Pisan Cantos (1948), tried to see whether he could achieve what the Noh play achieved, but without a stage, without music, without actors—with nothing at all except typewritten text. Pound's dream of the Noh began with a desire to make all aspects of spectacle and text and music and movement cooperant to a single intense effect; in the Pisan Cantos he tried to see whether a poem could build around itself virtual music and a virtual stage set, become a multimedia extravaganza and yet remain only a poem. Pound figured his pages with musical notation and with actual Chinese ideograms, in order to impart a vertical dimension to his horizontal text. In the Pisan Cantos, as in the opera *Le testament,* Pound attempted to avoid the need for collaboration by supplying all the elements of the spectacle himself.

When in 1935 Yeats sent to Pound the manuscript for *The King of the Great Clock Tower,* Pound returned it with one word: putrid. But in one of those odd reversals that literary historians call ironical, Pound himself, ten years later—in the army detention camp at Pisa, imprisoned as a traitor for broadcasting propaganda favorable to Mussolini, in danger of being hanged—found that he was living the script of Yeats's play: like Yeats's strolling beggar-poet, Pound was seized by forces beyond his control, desperate, and yet still trying to see through his present circumstances into the world of divine energies, imperishable art, before (so to speak) the authorities cut off his head. One of Pound's methods in the Pisan Cantos is to try to understand what is around him as a manifestation of dormant forces in the landscape. Thus the mountain in the distance becomes Mt. Taishan, a sacred mountain in China; the Negro soldiers impinge without knowing it upon the sacred mysteries of African tribes; every common thing is invested with a fringe of eeriness. There are Japanese soldiers in Pisa, too, and they introduce into the detention camp the world of the Noh play:

> Says the Japanese sentry : Paaak yu djeep over there,
> some of the best soldiers we have says the captain
>   Dai Nippon Banzai from the Philippines
> remembering Kagekiyo : "how stiff the shaft of your neck is."
>   and they went off each his own way   (74/462)

Kagekiyo was a young man who single-handedly routed an army of thieves and commented, when he tore off the vizard from an enemy's helmet, "how stiff the shaft of your neck is"; then both hero and villain broke into laughter. (In 1941 Pound remarked that *Kagekiyo* contained "the one truly Homeric passage" found in Fenollosa's Noh translations.) He becomes a paragon in the Pisan Cantos of a kind of delirious magnanimity, a temper that dismisses all the pettiness and faction of earthly life, in favor of a superhuman loftiness of spirit. It is a spirit that Pound sought to cultivate in himself, but could not quite attain. It is as though there were a Noh play lurking behind our lives, a Noh play that we botch through our ignorance and false thinking.

Not only does Pound remember scenes of unearthly splendor from Noh plays; his thoughts also keep turning to the time when he translated them, his sojourn with Yeats from 1913 to 1916. He even recollects Michio Ito, living in extreme poverty, sitting in the dark "lacking the gasometer penny" (77/489). But chiefly Pound keeps turning over and over in his mind his memories of Yeats; I think it fair to say that Yeats is the dominant character in the Pisan Cantos besides Pound himself. Pound dwells on Yeats's dreams of nobility (74/453); he remembers how Yeats looked at the sea cliffs near Pound's home at Rapallo and murmured, "Sligo in heaven" (77/493); he thinks of snatches from Yeats's poems and imitates Yeats's Irish accent (80/516); he takes Yeats as an exemplar of fierce devotion to beauty (80/531), just as in other places he took the Noh drama as a stern ideal; and in one of the remarkable passages in the Cantos, it appears that Yeats himself turns into a sort of aesthetic ghost:

> There is fatigue deep as the grave.
> The Kakemono grows in flat land out of mist   [a painted scroll]
>   sun rises lop-sided over the mountain
>   so that I recalled the noise in the chimney
> as it were the wind in the chimney
>   but was in reality Uncle William
> downstairs composing

```
    that had made a great Peeeeacock
        in the proide ov his oiye
        had made a great peeeeeeecock in the...
    made a great peacock
            in the proide of his oyyee


    proide ov his oy-ee
    as indeed he had, and perdurable


    a great peacock aere perennius          [more lasting than bronze]
                                                    (83/553-54)
```

The Pisan landscape here flattens itself into a painted scroll, and the solitary poet finds his cage populated by a ghost—the poem is starting to turn into a drama. The Pisan Cantos are in a sense a huge Noh play, in which Pound plays the role of the priest (the *waki*) seeking enlightenment and Yeats plays the role of the spirit (the *shite*), who once seemed to be little more than a fussy old man but who in death is revealed to be a sort of disengaged spirit of poetical creativity. Pound remarked in his anthology of Noh translations that the only Western equivalent of the Noh play is the séance; and the passage from Canto 83 in which Yeats's nearly disengaged voice resounds like wind in the chimney as he reads his poem "The Peacock" almost verges on a sort of séance: the ghost of Yeats shows itself to Pound in weird splendor. Here Pound provides a terminal dance for the Pisan Cantos, a dance made of words.

But if the Pisan Cantos are a kind of epicized Noh play, and if a Noh play is a prolonged imagist poem, then the Pisan Cantos also make up an image—perhaps the largest image Pound ever discovered, an ideogram the size of a whole library, a meaning-picture of Pound's whole mind.

The Pisan Cantos as an Opera

The Pisan Cantos are also a kind of opera. For one thing, the sound effects are extraordinarily vivid—as in the immensely prolonged vowels of the keening Yeats, or in the "k-lakk.....thuuuuuu" (77/485), the *musique concrète* of the slapping of tent flaps in the wind. Also, Pound provides an actual score: Canto 75 consists of only seven lines of text, followed by two pages of a photoreproduction of handwritten solo violin music:

```
    Out of Phlegethon!
        out of Phlegethon,
            Gerhart
```

> art thou come forth out of Phlegethon?
> with Buxtehude and Klages in your satchel, with the
> Ständebuch of Sachs in yr/ luggage
> —not of one bird but of many (75/470)

"Gerhart" is Gerhart Münch, a Dresden pianist and composer whom Pound admired, a frequent performer at the concerts Pound organized in Rapallo during the 1930s; here he seems to be a kind of pied piper, leading a band of enlightened souls across the flaming river of hell—the Second World War—into a better, more musical, more pertinent and humane kind of life. And Münch also composed the violin piece printed in Canto 75: it is an arrangement of a lute solo by Francesco da Milano, which is in turn an arrangement of Clément Janequin's *Le chant des oyseaulx,* a choral *chanson* from the early sixteenth century. At the end of the photoreproduction, Pound drew the Chinese ideograms for *Make it new.* He liked his novelty fetched up through layers of antiquity, and Münch's solo has just the sort of historical depth that Pound hoped the Cantos as a whole would have: as he wrote in 1938, "Janequin's concept takes a third life in our time, for catgut or patent silver, its first was choral, its second on the wires of Francesco Milano's lute."

But there is a fourth layer, behind Janequin even: the medieval troubadour songs, extremely responsive to the precise emotive rhythms of nature that, according to Pound, Janequin must have known: "Janequin inherited from the troubadours the fine clear cut *representation* of natural sound, the exactitude of birds." And behind this fourth layer lies a fifth layer: the songs of real birds. Janequin's text consists mostly of excited spasms of onomatopoeia:

Qui lara qui lara ferely fy fy
Teo coquin coqui si ti si ti
Oy ty oy ty . . . trr. Tu
Turri turri . . . qui lara
Huit huit . . . oy ty oy ty . . . teo teo teo

In the *chanson,* Janequin has many of these exuberant birds—redwing, starling, nightingale—singing at the same time, an artful interlace of twitter, trill, stutter. (It is a highly erotic piece: amid all the birdsong, the text asks a girl to show her breasts; and the conclusion is a plea for the departure of cuckoos—that word of fear unpleasing to the married ear.) The impression of polyphony is important in Münch's violin version as well: in fact, the line that precedes the musical score— "not of one bird but of many"—is a quotation from the violinist who first played it, Olga Rudge, Pound's companion. In a sense, Canto 75 stands for all the noise of the natural world, as assimilated into elegance by the human imagination. The score of Pound's quasi-opera isn't simply the Janequin *chanson,* or Münch's new arrangement, but the whole sound of living things. Pound not only forces Münch to collaborate with the Cantos, by photoreproducing his score; he also forces flocks of birds to collaborate on this mixed-media project.

The later Cantos are full of Chinese ideograms; and Münch's score in Canto 75 acts as a kind of hieroglyphic, in the sense (dear to the old writers on hieroglyphs, such as John Webster) that Adam before the Fall could understand the language of birds and that birdsongs today are hieroglyphs of forgotten meaning. There is a lovely passage much earlier in the Cantos, where Pound wrote:

> "as the sculptor sees the form in the air . . .
> "as glass seen under water . . .
> and saw the waves taking form as crystal,
> notes as facets of air,
> and the mind there, before them, moving,
> so that notes needed not move. (25/119)

These luminous quarter notes, arrested in air like a set of pendent diamonds, as if the auditor lived inside a chandelier, illustrate a moment of perfect equivalence of *nacheinander* and *nebeneinander:* music is frozen into rows of glassy sound waves, a kind of sculptural presence of cantilena. In Canto 75, Münch's score realizes (though less attractively to the eye) this vision of graphed, static sound, apprehensible in an instant to the moving mind—a sign of the abiding presence of heard beauty.

The Pisan Cantos reecho with antique music. In Canto 81, there is a section marked *Libretto:*

> Has he tempered the viol's wood
> To enforce   both the grave   and the acute?
> Has he curved us the bowl of the lute?
>> *Lawes and Jenkyns guard thy rest*
>> *Dolmetsch ever be thy guest* (81/540)

Here Pound remembers his work with Arnold Dolmetsch, the rebuilder of extinct musical instruments and reviver of old music. Soon this leads to a great chant of self-excoriation and self-praise: "Pull down thy vanity / Thou art a beaten dog beneath the hail" (81/541)—the climactic aria of the whole Pisan sequence. In a sense, the Cantos represent an attempt to construct a musical instrument, and an attempt to sing with it. Pound even considered writing musical settings of certain passages: "ALL typographic disposition, placings of words *on* the page, is intended to facilitate the reader's intonation, whether he be reading silently to self or aloud to friends. Given time and technique I might even put down the musical notation of passages or 'breaks into song.'" To read the Cantos properly, we must imagine that the typographic spacings, and such words as *grave* and *acute*, are hints about melodic shapes, and constitute a sort of vocal score. We might call the Pisan Cantos a heuristic opera, in which we are expected to improvise our own tunes as we read the text.

And the Pisan Cantos continually reecho with birdsong, a whole *Catalogue d'oiseaux*. In Canto 74 the poet hears "two larks in contrappunto" (74/451); and in Canto 82 we are given some actual notation of birdsong:

> 8th day of September
>   f f
>   d
>   g
>   write the birds in their treble scale
> Terreus! Terreus! (82/545)

The birds remind Pound of Philomela, metamorphosed into a bird, forever accusing Tereus of raping her and mutilating her—a burden of mythological significance lies in their song, a burden that Pound tries to summon both by naming the rapist and by incorporating the sound of the notes into the poem. At the beginning of Canto 79, the poet watches the ever-changing distribution of birds on telephone wires:

>   with 8 birds on a wire
> or rather on 3 wires (79/505)

>   5 of 'em now on 2;
>   on 3; 7 on 4
>   thus what's his name
> and the change in writing the song books (79/506)

>   2 on 2
> what's the name of that bastard? D'Arezzo, Gui d'Arezzo
> notation
>   3 on 3 (79/507)

Pound can't remember the name of that bastard until the name d'Arezzo flies into his mind, like one of the birds he's scrutinizing: the alighting of the birds seems as much a psychological process as a natural one. Guido d'Arezzo was the eleventh-century theorist who devised the system of hexachords, basic to medieval music practice, and who invented the five-line stave that musicians still use. Pound's birds not only sing, but also figure forth eye music on telephone wires, as living notation: ornithoglyphs hovering in the air. To the intelligent spectator, music is constantly trying to inscribe itself on the surfaces of things. Perhaps the most remarkable of all the birds in the Pisan Cantos are those of the Empress Dowager of China, Tzu Hsi:

> I wonder what Tzu Tsze's calligraphy looked like
> they say she could draw down birds from the trees   (80/515)

Here are birds so sensitive to the aesthetic features of ideograms that they insist on studying them, as if to learn how to become more notationally potent themselves. Birds seem to have an inherent tendency toward calligraphy: not content to sing, they must also write on the sky. The shape of a bird seems an image of its sound.

Britten's Curlew River *and* Sumidagawa

But of course, if the Pisan Cantos are a kind of Noh opera, most of the music—except for Münch's violin solo—is virtual, not actual; and, as far as I know, no one has yet risen to the challenge of devising from the Pisan Cantos a play presentable on stage. For an actual opera based on Noh theatre, we must look elsewhere, to compositions that try to adapt for the Western stage some of the musical-dramatic features of the Noh.

A Noh play is more like opera than like Western spoken drama—partly due to the pitch inflections of the Japanese language and the studiedness of the actors' rhetoric, but also due to the musical instruments, such as flutes and drums, that punctuate the performance and establish its rhythm and guide the final dance. Yeats's Noh-play imitations contain some musical cues—timidly, for Yeats was the most tone-deaf of poets—and he asked composers to provide music for performances: for example, Pound's favored composer, George Antheil, wrote music in 1929 for Yeats's *Fighting the Waves*—music in which implacabilities out of Stravinsky's *Oedipus Rex* (1927) are mixed with a lilting tune suitable for an Irish reel. And a certain aesthetic of opera underlies all of Yeats's Noh imitations, in that Yeats inherited his notions of décor from the screens and spare geometrical designs that Gordon Craig had devised at the turn of the century for Purcell's *Dido and Aeneas*.

The first Noh opera that we'll consider is Benjamin Britten's *Curlew River* (1964)—a work as obsessive and bird-haunted as the Noh imitations of Yeats and Pound that we've been studying. Pound actually introduced Britten to the Noh theatre in 1938, when Britten produced a gong player to accompany

Pound's recitation at the Mercury Theatre of his English version of a Noh play; but the genesis of *Curlew River* lies in the play *Sumidagawa* (Sumida River), ascribed to Jūrō Motomasa (1395–1459), which Britten saw in Japan during his 1956 travels in the Orient. One of Britten's companions, Prince Ludwig of Hesse, recorded in his diary an account of the Japanese spectacle:

> The ferryman is waiting in his boat, a traveler turns up and tells him about a woman who will soon be coming to the river. The woman is mad, she is looking for her lost child. Then she appears and the ferryman does not wish to take a mad person, but in the end he lets her into his boat. On the way across the river the two passengers sit behind each other on the floor as if in a narrow boat, while the ferryman stands behind them, symbolically punting with a light stick. The ferryman tells the story of a little boy who came this way a year ago this very day. The child was very tired for he had escaped from robbers who had held him. He crossed the river in this boat, but he died from exhaustion on the other side. The woman starts crying. It was her son. The ferryman is sorry for her and takes her to the child's grave. The mother is acted by a tall man in woman's clothing with a small woman's mask on his face. Accessories help you to understand what is going on: a bamboo branch in the hand indicates madness, a long stick is the ferryman's punting pole, a very small gong is beaten for the sorrowing at the graveside. As soon as these props are no longer necessary, stage-hands who have brought them to the actors take them away again. The sorrowful declamations of the mother rising and subsiding in that oddly pressed voice, the movement of her hand to the brim of her hat as if to protect her sadness from the outside world, the small "ping" of the little gong which she beats at the child's grave, become as absorbing as does the sudden foot-stamping which emphasizes important passages. The play ends in the chanting of the chorus.

Britten had long been interested in Oriental poetry and in writing music to Oriental texts with a kind of ideogrammatic simplicity of musical gesture: in 1938 he wrote *The Red Cockatoo* to one of Arthur Waley's Chinese translations—a song only about forty seconds long, little more than a psittasquawk. So when Britten heard *Sumidagawa*, he heard it as one prepared to imagine Western musical analogies: it seemed a kind of opera—or, as he said in his note to the published libretto, "a totally new 'operatic' experience"—and he soon wished to re-create this hieratically intense theatrical experience as an opera of his own, not as a piece of self-conscious *japanaiserie* or pastiche, but as a neomedieval mystery play, suitable for Christian audiences. Perhaps *Curlew River* was not quite a "totally new" kind of opera, for it had a distinguished predecessor in Gustav Holst's *Sāvitri* (1900–1906), a terse opera based on a Hindu parable, composed as a sort of troped melisma—an extraordinary anticipation of the austere sound-world of Noh opera.

Curlew River's systematic disorientalizing and Christianizing of *Sumidagawa* caused some trouble for William Plomer, Britten's librettist; but he did his work skillfully—he knew the Noh theatre well from his years in Japan—and it is remarkable how well Prince Ludwig's summary of *Sumidagawa* will serve as a summary for *Curlew River* (though Britten's musical resources, of course, are larger). Plomer provided a frame in the shape of an Abbot, who announces to the congregation/audience that the monks are going to present a mystery play rehearsing the story of a sign of God's grace to the unfortunate; and Plomer deleted certain un-Christian passages of *Sumidagawa,* such as the Mother's anguished recollection of the Buddhist doctrine that "the bond of parenthood / Cannot survive the grave"—this directly contradicts Plomer's moral for *Curlew River,* announced by the ghost of the dead child: "The dead shall rise again . . . we shall meet in heaven." Plomer made other noteworthy changes. For example, in *Sumidagawa,* the Mother quotes a famous old text: "'O, birds of Miyako, / If you are worthy of your name, / Tell me, does my love still live?'"; but Plomer turned this quotation of a love song into the quotation of a "riddle" posed by "a famous traveler":

'Birds of the Fenland,
though you float or fly,
wild birds, I cannot understand your cry.
Tell me, does the one I love
in this world still live?'

This riddling serves perhaps as a subliminal *re-orientalizing* of the text—since, to the Western imagination, the Orient is a land of riddles, as in Gozzi's *Turandot.* But to a large extent *Curlew River* remains *Sumidagawa,* even though the ghost of the dead boy, comforting his mad mother, sings *Kyrie eleison.*

The Christian aspect *is,* to a degree, the Japanese aspect: the word *religion* has the same root as *ligature,* or bond, and the sense of strict obedience to predetermined ritual forms will give a religious aspect to any work of art, no matter what its culture.

* * *

There is a certain sort of mystery play that might be called the *theatre of the preterite:* such a play is not an imitation of action but a purgation of action, an untying of knots that persist after death, so that souls may attain peace. *Nishikigi* conforms exactly to this pattern; Yeats's *The Dreaming of the Bones* is a perversion of it, in that Diarmuid and Dervorgilla remain unforgiven, damned, forever reenacting the tangled story of their traitorous love, forever seeking to be dismissed from their compulsive theatre. *Sumidagawa* alters the pattern, in that the person who is caught up in the painful knot of action and remorse—the *shite*—isn't the dead boy, but the mad mother who is seeking him: here, as in *Curlew River,* the dead offer peace to the living. In the theatre of the preterite, the goal of the performance is less the presentation of a plot than the dismissal or dissolution of a plot, for the sake of beatitude; so it is appropriate that we see that the actors can easily take off their costumes and masks, rid themselves of their props, for they do not strive to present any illusion of human life. What has happened in *Curlew River* happened long before the story began: the kidnapping and death of the Madwoman's boy, as narrated by the Ferryman. Therefore we see only a rehearsal of a memory of a narrative of an event. The drama is faint, the action only a kind of illusion of forward movement; the parable takes place in eternity, not time. It is not a doing, but an undoing. Britten's music continually seeks for sound-images that express the remote, past-tense quality of the spectacle: a series of phonic gravestones.

There is a distinct geography of life and death, suffering and beatitude, in *Curlew River:*

PILGRIMS. Between two kingdoms, O river, flow!
  On this side the land of the West,
  on the other, dyke and marsh and mere,
  the land of the Eastern fens. . . .
MADWOMAN. Near the Black Mountains there I dwelt,
  there I dwelt far, far in the West,
  there I was living with my child. . . .
  My only child was lost,
  seized as a slave. . . .

Later the Ferryman tells what happened exactly one year ago, when a little Christian boy, abused by the heathen and left to die, asked to be buried in a chapel on the east side of the river; and indeed, after the whole party crosses Curlew River, the Madwoman discovers her boy's consoling ghost at the eastern chapel.

This geography is suggestive of many things, such as the river Styx, or the Egyptian mythology of the two banks of the Nile—burial sites were located on the western bank, in the direction of the setting sun, which was associated with death. But the pilgrims' phrase "Between two kingdoms" may tend to evoke T. S. Eliot, whose poetry is haunted by *betweens* of various sorts—as, for example, in

"Little Gidding" II (1942), where the ghost of Yeats (d. 1939), wavering between purgatory and the blitzed cityscape of Second World War London, describes himself as a "spirit unappeased and peregrine, / Between two worlds." (The ghost of Yeats haunted Eliot as much as Pound.) In Eliot's poetry the two realms are sometimes separated by a river. For example, in "The wind sprang up at four o'clock" (1924), the speaker, resident in "death's dream kingdom," looking across a river at death's other kingdom, asks

> Is it a dream or something else
> When the surface of the blackened river
> Is a face that sweats with tears?

The topography of Eliot's poetry sometimes consists of a region of lucid transcendence, more or less unavailable, on the other side of a river; and a twilight borderland, a domain of uncertainties and indistinctnesses, where the poet actually lives. Eliot was the most influential Christian poet in the Anglophone world, and Plomer's psychogeography follows Eliot's pretty closely: Plomer's pilgrims are also caught in a kind of limbo, and need to attain blessedness, reality, by crossing an infernal river:

> FERRYMAN. The river is glassy,
>   but the devil himself
>   with strong-flowing current
>   can drag the boat aside,
>   and carry away
>   all who are in her.

The Madwoman is obviously unstable; but all the characters dwell in a dangerously unsteady place. The ritualistic stiffness of the opera is everywhere belied by a certain shiftiness and vertigo. Britten's music first had to reflect the seasickness of time; then had to petrify itself into hieroglyphs of eternity.

Britten also was sensitive to the limbo-like quality of *Curlew River;* in fact, in letters to Plomer of 23 October and 10 November 1963, he suggested that the title of the piece should be "The other side of the River," or "Across the River," or "Over the River," as if the main subject of the opera were a state of transit, intermittency of being. And at its deepest level of construction, *Curlew River* is a hovering opera, an opera without settled coordination among its instrumental and vocal elements: as Britten wrote to Donald Mitchell (one of the foremost scholars of his music) on 5 February 1964, complaining of the difficulty of notation, "one of the problems is how to write it down: there being no conductor, & the tempo is kind of 'controlled floating.'" The score of *Curlew River* is a sort of

pedagogical document, designed to teach the singers and the seven instrumentalists how to conduct themselves; Britten even had to invent a new kind of pause
symbol, which he called a "curlew"—a mark consisting of two adjoining semi-
circles, resembling a schematic of a bird's wings—that specifies a waiting and
listening until a moment of intersection arrives amidst the heterophony: the performers are asked to continue to be silent, or to continue playing whatever note
or figure they're playing, until they reach the next bar line or meeting point.
Curlew River does not go so far as, say, Heinz Holliger's *Scardanelli-Zyklus*
(1975–91), in which each performer finds a tempo by taking his or her own
pulse; but Britten's score has, as Imogen Holst points out in her preface, "no
conventional time signatures," and to a degree each performer inhabits a separate
time-world, a private mini-stage, until the curlew mark enforces a moment of
simultaneity. Britten's phrase for this, "controlled floating," seems to echo the
body of Japanese prints called *ukiyo-e,* or floating-world pictures; and we will
soon see just how pictorial, how atemporal, are the effects of Britten's compositional procedures.

The strange appearance of the curlew mark endows it with a certain ideogrammatic or hieroglyphic character. The manuscript of Joyce's *Finnegans Wake*
(1939) is decorated with nonalphabetic signs, such as a ⊓ representing the ultimate male protagonist, and a Δ representing the ultimate female protagonist:
such sigla helped Joyce to specify rhythms of recurrence independent of discursive language. Similarly, a curlew seems to dwell in the visual text of *Curlew
River,* guiding the busy independent lines to still points, moments of grace, outside the private time-sequences of the singers and instrumentalists. Britten was so
fond of Gerard Manley Hopkins's sonnet "God's Grandeur" that he set it twice,
in his radio cantata *The World of the Spirit* (1938) and in his suite of choruses
A.D.M.G. (1939). The poem's last clause is "the Holy Ghost over the bent /
World broods with warm breast and with ah! bright wings"; and I suspect that
the curlew mark is a figure of the Holy Ghost, brooding over the text of *Curlew
River.* The score of the opera is sanctified by the mark of God's presence, like the
stigmata on the hands of St. Francis. Christian art, with its vocabulary of symbols
and icons, can be extremely useful to the artist in search of figures of consonance.

Yeats and Pound were, in a full sense of the word, pagans: Yeats accepted
Nietzsche's thesis that Christianity was a religion of slaves, and affirmed in
"Vacillation" (1932) that "Homer is my example and his unchristened heart";
and Pound even wrote a curious document called "Religio, or, The Child's Guide
to Knowledge" (1918), which urges the gift of incense and flowers to Apollo,
Aphrodite, Koré, Demeter, "also to lares and to oreiads and to certain elementary
creatures." But Britten was a Christian; indeed, his work can be taken as a profound meditation on the theme of original sin. In 1950 Hans Keller described in
print Britten's musical personality as a dialectic between sadism and repression

of sadism; and Britten commended Keller's perspicacity. What is frightening about Britten's many representations of abused children is the feeling that the composer sometimes seems as sympathetic to the child abuser as to the child: Britten's children are often knowing, brutal, beautiful, good to kiss, good to beat. Orthodox Christianity teaches that children are born with a hereditary taint, since all humankind participated in the crime of Adam and Eve. In Britten's *The Turn of the Screw* (1954), the children are intimate with evil, keenly sensitive to it, while most of the adults have grown blunt and forgetful, pious—except for Peter Quint, who retains in death his nasty capacity for child's play. In Britten's *The Rape of Lucretia* (1946), the bad adults are simply children of a larger growth, who have retained the childish capacity to do harm. When the Roman and Etruscan generals mock one another for the unfaithfulness of their wives, they do it to the child's chant *nyah nyah nya-nyah nyah* (sung in my neighborhood as major scale degrees $\hat{5}-\hat{3}-\hat{6}-\hat{5}-\hat{3}$, with the third note very brief—though Britten's version is more chromatically adventurous); it is a strange thing to hear the words "Junius is a cuckold"—an adult sort of insult—sung to a child's chant, but childishness is the domain of much of the imaginative power of Britten's work. It is not that Innocence is violated by Experience, but that Innocence is itself the source of disease—and, as *Curlew River* shows, the source of grace as well. Innocence is a condition of high responsiveness to ultimate moral issues; Madness is another such condition. In both cases humankind is naked before God and the Devil.

Nyah nyah is about as close as one can come to a musical pattern of universal meaning: it is the sound-hieroglyph of Taunt. (But so arbitrary are musical semantics that it is also the tune of a lullaby, *Bye Baby Bunting*.) And just as there are visual hieroglyphs in the score of *Curlew River*, such as the curlew mark, so there are phonic hieroglyphs as well. The first sound we hear in the opera is a chorus singing a Gregorian chant, *Te lucis ante terminum*—the source, according to Britten, of most of the musical material in the opera. Now, such plainchant can be powerfully hieroglyphic, in the context of tonal music; or, more exactly, can be a quarry from which powerful hieroglyphics can be extracted, since a complete chant is generally too diffuse to be pithily epigrammatic. But a fragment of plainchant may well stand out boldly from the rest of the musical texture; because plainchant resists conventional harmonization, or renders conventional harmonization pointless, it can act as a kind of sudden oracle, an arresting textstrip, the musical equivalent of those ribbons inscribed with words that in certain Renaissance paintings come out of the mouths of angels. An example is Mozart's offertorium *Benedictus sit Deus* (1768): in the *Jubilate* movement, Mozart's second subject is a Gregorian psalm tone, decorated with all manner of lively figuration, but still obviously out of place in the context of Mozart's usual musical

language—an irresistible command of *psallite*, Sing! Of course, the most semantically powerful snatch of chant is the opening of the sequence *Dies Irae*, which
has haunted the musical imagination of the West: it figures many compositions
with a *memento mori*—the equivalent in music of a skull in a nineteenth-century
Gothic illustration.

But Britten plays with plainchant in a different fashion: *Te lucis ante terminum*
is first an explicit motto, then a kind of occult underweaving to the rest of the
music, threads of light behind the spare, sober gesture. Late in the opera, as the
Madwoman prays for the soul of her lost child, the Abbot and the chorus sing
another plainchant, *Custodes hominum,* praising the guardian angels. The first
five syllables are simply set to the notes of the Dorian mode rising from D; and
as the chorus chants them, the organist keeps a finger down on each note as it
appears, so that by the end of the first bar (rehearsal figure 88), he or she is
playing all five white notes from D to A. Britten uses similar procedures for the
subsequent bars of the chant—though less rigorously, since the organist is sometimes allowed to omit some of the sung notes from the assembled tone clusters.
It is as if *Custodes hominum* is spun together, gathered up, phrase by phrase, into
eternity. The organ's great clot of notes from D to A is an ideogram or hieroglyph,
a presentation of the words *Custodes hominum* [guardians of men] in a single
instant; perhaps it sums up every diatonic melody that can be devised from the
span of a fifth. It is an epitome, a detemporalization of the whole experience
of music. (The gathering-together of adjacent semitones into cutting chords in
Mörder, Hoffnung der Frauen and *Renard* is a related phenomenon, but far more
nervous, less comprehensive and calm.) This instantaneous apprehension of a
totality is the desired outcome of the Noh drama, at least as its Western imitators
understood it—for example, Yeats's *The King of the Great Clock Tower* begins
with an odd description of heaven:

> There every lover is a happy rogue;
> And should he speak, it is the speech of birds.
> No thought has he, and therefore has no words,
> No thought because no clock, no clock because
> If I consider deeply, lad and lass,
> Nerve touching nerve upon that happy ground,
> Are bobbins where all time is bound and wound.

The notion of heaven as a perpetual orgasm of the whole body is foreign to
Britten's conception; but the rest of Yeats's heavenly attributes fit perfectly. The
chord comprising all the notes from D to A has escaped from clock time into pure
simultaneity of being—in a larger sense, the whole opera has unclocked itself by

its peculiar conductorless time scheme. And Britten's Noh imitation agrees with Yeats's Noh imitation, to an astonishing degree, in another aspect: should someone speak, it is the speech of birds.

The most salient musical figure in Britten's parable is a short theme heard at the Madwoman's first appearance, to the words "You mock me! You ask me!" (rehearsal figure 20); soon thereafter, she—I say she, though the role is played by a male tenor—sings the same notes to the words "Let me in! Let me out!" Each half of the phrase begins on A and continues to D♯, from which it either glides up to G♯ (in the first half) or descends to E (in the second half); one can think of the phrase as a kind of interlocking of fifths from the triads of A and of G♯, so arranged as to emphasize the wide but dissonant intervals of the tritone (from A to D♯) and the major seventh (from D♯ down to E). Amid all the talk of curlews, this phrase sounds like a bird's cry, a keening. As Yeats once wrote in his youth: "wind cry and water cry / And curlew cry: how does the saying go / That calls them the three oldest cries in the world?" And much later, in Yeats's Noh imitation *The Death of Cuchulain* (1939), as the Blind Man gropes with a knife for Cuchulain's neck, the great hero calls out,

> There floats out there
> The shape that I shall take when I am dead,
> My soul's first shape, a soft feathery shape . . .
> I say it is about to sing.

At those words, the Blind Man cuts off his head; we soon see Emer dancing with the image of the head, a parallelogram on a stick, and we hear "a few faint bird notes." The Madwoman of *Curlew River* also seems to have a kind of pre-audition of the soul's state as pure birdsong: her phrases have a continual tendency to lift, sink, chirp, crow.

EX. 3.1. Britten, *Curlew River:* "You mock me!"

Furthermore, the Madwoman's birdsong tends to infiltrate into the voices of all the characters, even the most stolid. After the Madwoman's entrance (just before rehearsal figure 21), the Traveler sings, "The people were amused / When they heard her singing; / They all began laughing": this passage is set to a uniform sequence of detached, monotone sixteenth notes, except for eighth notes on the syllables *mused* and *laugh*—and *laugh* is further broken into a stutter of more sixteenth notes. At first one listens to this and thinks, This is simply a stylized, but not very funny, representation of laughter; but then one comes, later on, to a musically similar passage that has nothing to do with laughing: after the sad story of the death of the brave boy taken into slavery, the Ferryman says, "You must be soft-hearted / To weep at my story, / To weep so bitterly" (rehearsal figure 71). The syllabic, almost monotone delivery (this time in eighth notes), the shattering of the *bit* in *bitterly* into separate accented notes, both recall the protocol for laughter in the earlier passage. Britten alludes to the traditional methods of operatic expression, but only for the sake of ruining the foundations of emotional discrimination by means of music: the listener can't tell joy and sorrow apart. Laughter and weeping are two modes of the same thing, presented indifferently by a *stile concitato* that is little more than a bird's pecking at notes. When Britten wanted to find a representation for extreme emotion suitable for *Curlew River*, he looked to Rameau's hen.

Just as the phrase *Custodes hominum* wraps itself up in a single chord, so does the chief bird-call, the Madwoman's "You mock me! You ask me!": shortly before she faints, overcome by despair and derision, the organ plays a chord consisting of the four notes of her figure, A–D♯–E–G♯ (rehearsal figure 29). As the Madwoman collapses, her musical figure also collapses, contracts into a single,

EX. 3.2. Britten, *Curlew River:* laughing

EX. 3.3. Britten, *Curlew River:* weeping

EX. 3.4. Rameau, *La poule*

EX. 3.5. Britten, *Curlew River:* "You mock me!" figure, collapsed in a chord

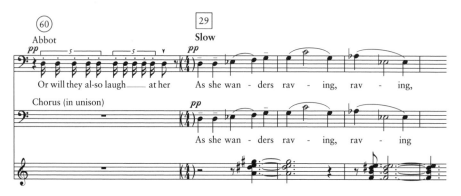

tense chord—another sign of the fragility of the temporal, the difficulty of sustaining any mode of the discursive. To human ears, a bird's song can sound self-
contained, a kind of speech so disinterested and circular that it seems fit for the
kind of discourse to be found in heaven—a completely nonprogressive pattern.
In the second act of Wagner's *Siegfried* (1869; 1876), the young hero touches
a drop of dragon's blood and suddenly can understand the speech of birds: and a
bird tells him exactly what he must do to attain his heart's desire. Wagner's bird
sings a repeated figure, a mechanically descending and reascending arpeggio, like
the birth of tonality at the beginning of *The Ring,* but upside down, beginning
from the heights. This figure is the only example in *The Ring* of the sort of inscription music that Kothner sings in *Die Meistersinger:* a chant-unit to which any
wise, pithy bit of text can be sung. Birdsong tends to exist in music theatre as
acoustic monolith, as static revelation; and when Britten compressed his curlew
cry into a single chord, he offered a kind of proof of this musical theorem.

*   *   *

But *Curlew River* is more than music, more than text: the stage picture is crucial,
too. The last aspect of *Curlew River* that we'll consider is a strange item tucked
into a pocket that is glued onto the inside back cover of the Faber score, a pamphlet entitled *Production Notes and Remarks on the Style of Performing Curlew River* / by Benjamin Britten & William Plomer / Notes by Colin Graham /
Drawings by Alix Stone / Diagrams by Mark Livingstone. This rather Brechtian
pamphlet is an amazingly rigid and detailed set of instructions for the director,
the stage designer, and the performers. It first insists on the building of a three-
layered stage inside the church, and then employs the circular top level—"a special, almost sacred area . . . made of a highly polished redwood"—as a giant

clock, so that the exact position of each performer can be specified at any given moment: for example, the "boat area is always referred to as being at 4 o'clock." I wonder how many performances this pamphlet has managed to abort, by such warnings as this:

> [The audience's] involvement can be shattered by a single uncontrolled, weak, or unnecessary gesture. Every movement of the hand or tilt of the head should assume immense meaning and, although formalized, must be designed and executed with the utmost intensity: this requires enormous concentration on the part of the actor, an almost Yoga-like muscular, as well as physical, control. The cast of the original production underwent a strenuous course of movement instruction and physical education before rehearsals began and this training was maintained throughout the engagement.

Curlew River, then, is as closely choreographed as a ballet; and its body of hieroglyphs includes not only such elements as the curlew mark and the Madwoman's cry "You mock me!" but also such elements as the little drawings that adorn the production notes, specifying certain gestures with the body. (These little drawings follow the example of *Sumidagawa* itself, in the version authorized by the "Publishers' Notes" to the score of *Curlew River*—namely, that in *The Noh Drama: Ten Plays from the Japanese Selected and Translated by the Special Noh Committee, Japanese Translation Committee, Nippon Gakujutsi Shinkō-kai,* 1955, which also figures the texts with line drawings of the posed actors.) Figure 61, for one example, shows the Madwoman almost prone, touching—or not quite touching—her hands to the floor: "She turns and throws herself on ground, sweeping dew off imaginary grass blades with the palm of her hand. (*N.B.* The hand must never touch floor or illusion is destroyed.)" This sort of deliberately incomplete movement is part of the actual repertory of Noh gesture; Yeats remembered it in the battle scene in *The Herne's Egg* (1938), in which a stage direction warns the actors never to allow their weapons to touch—drum

FIG. 5. Alix Stone, *Curlew River* drawing, fig. 158 (Colin Graham, *Production Notes and Remarks* [London: Faber Music, 1965], p. 15)

taps represent the noises of the visibly nonexistent blows. An actor who behaves in this fashion isn't representing an action, but only *feigning* the representation of an action; it is another aspect of the pretendedness, the unreality, of the preterite theatre. By frustrating mimesis, the actor calls attention to the distance between the stage picture and common life: what is obviously not action must be judged by aesthetic criteria. Other examples from the production notes stress the strange combination of monumentality and minuteness in the desired gestures: Figure 158 shows the Madwoman in a cruciform position and comments, "N.B. Throughout the work the fingers of the hand are only separated when the character appears extremely distraught. At all other times the hand should appear as if carved out of one piece of wood"—as if the Madwoman were a barely animate statue, a carved medieval Madonna. The traditional Christian iconography provides a large repertory of frozen gestures, easily read by a Christian audience.

Much of the tension of *Curlew River* is suggested by the reduction of gesture to iconic simplicity—by suppression of movement, not by violence of movement. It could even be said that *Curlew River* is a kind of ritual calisthenics, almost isotonic.

Gestus

DEFINITION. A *gestus* is a bodily pose or gesture that speaks; a hieroglyph corporeally embodied in a human performer; a whole story *(gest)* contracted into a moment. The term *gestus* was popularized by Lessing and was taken up enthusiastically by Weill and Brecht, the main artists that this chapter will discuss.

Dalcroze Exercises

The first advice that Colin Graham gave to apprentice performers of *Curlew River* was to go to an exercise class; and this sort of advice has appeared many times in advanced twentieth-century art. At one point, Diaghilev decided that the new choreography of the Ballets Russes should be based on the rhythmic exercise movements taught by Émile Jaques-Dalcroze, the exercise guru of the Modernist movement; and so the dancers traveled to the Dalcroze institute at Hellerau, near Dresden, to learn the system. In the classes, for example, girls would be taught to walk to the 2/4 beat of a piece of music while gesticulating with one arm to a 3/4 beat and with the other to a 4/4 beat—as Bronislava Nijinska, the original choreographer of Stravinsky's *Renard* and *The Wedding,* explained in her *Early Memoirs.* Dalcroze had little sympathy with traditional ballet: he was interested in physical and psychic fitness and in developing a sense of rhythm; and yet Dalcroze's eurhythmic exercises were a crucial ingredient in the most famous ballet of the Modernist movement, *The Rite of Spring* (1913).

Dalcroze has never been forgotten—indeed, Dalcrozean schools persist to this day—but perhaps he hasn't received the credit he deserves as a Modernist founder. Born in 1865, he was part of the same generation as Yeats, Strauss, and Satie; and far from being an early version of Richard Simmons or Jane Fonda, he was a widely cultured man who devoted his life to promoting the status of kinesthetics—what he called *living plastic*—as an autonomous art capable of interacting with other arts, especially music. He was a composer and a professor of harmony, but his great contribution was to imagine new ways, far outside the traditional province of dance, to conceive physical movement as art.

Dalcroze's published work is a hodgepodge of embarrassing conventionalities combined with eccentric insights. For example, his *Ten Callisthenic Songs* (1915) is a collection of original lyrics and melodies for children's exercise classes—*Faithful Little Legs, The Old Arm-Chair, The Goldenhaired Fairy*—complete with amazingly elaborate instructions for gesture, costume, and lighting. Dalcroze instructed the children to stand still like statues, or to wave their hands in the manner of butterflies. On the other hand, his essays for adults from the mid-1920s show a mind bizarrely alert to the aesthetics of muscle contraction:

> At a gymnastic fête in Geneva, some years ago, a few thousand gymnasts went through *ensemble* movements to musical accompaniment. The space of ground covered was so extensive that the musical rhythms were some time in reaching the most distant rows, the result being that movements involving bodily displacement, gestures and kneeling, were performed in "canon" style, *i.e.* the first rows kept time, those in the centre were half a second and those farther away a full second later than the first, etc. The result was admirable, and this naturally-regulated polymotivity impressed the spectators far more powerfully than an exact synchronism would have done.

This led Dalcroze to imagine a new basis for the Olympic Games, with a fugue of javelins tossed en masse at carefully staggered intervals—as if synchronized swimming should be the model for the whole extravaganza of sports. To Dalcroze, every human movement could be conceived as an element in a spectacle of silent music; and this silent music could be counterpointed (*not,* ideally, performed in unison) with actual music. Dalcroze thought that living plastic could, in the absence of sound, manifest every attribute of music: he dreamed of "a scale of gestures" exactly comparable to the diatonic scale, and thought that the lines traced in space by the twirling or running body could be described as legato or staccato. We limit music, Dalcroze believed, by conceiving it as a merely acoustic phenomenon: "Every man should have *music within himself.* I mean what the Greeks called music, *i.e.* the totality of our sensory and psychic faculties."

Dalcroze read Nietzsche carefully, and he had a certain Nietzschean distaste for Christian disembodiment, rhythmlessness: "Christianity broke the unity between matter and spirit, teaching men to despise the body and to seek after the Beautiful solely in the abstract. . . . Music forgot its origin, which is in the dance, and men lost . . . the instinct for expressive and harmonious movement." An instinctively pagan soul, Dalcroze was part of the Modernist urge to restore corporeality to art. He had nothing but scorn for dance composers who didn't consider the actual physical presence of dancers on stage: "'Sylvia takes flight,' says the text, and, to illustrate this flight, [Delibes] is content to have the orchestra play a simple chromatic scale in demi-semi-quavers, the duration of which might suffice for the scurrying flight of a mouse, but certainly not for that of a *ballerina,* however active." What Dalcroze wanted was a new kind of dance music or gymnastics music, a music attentive to the actual contraction patterns of human muscles and sensitive to the fractions of time and space occupied by any finite gesture:

> This music will have to be wholly inspired by a knowledge of corporal impulses and muscular rhythms. . . . All attempt at picturesque harmony or counterpoint, all search for interest of timbre, must be subordinated to the physical action, or at least directly inspired by it. More than this, the music we need should not constantly accompany the physical manifestations. It should call them forth and sustain them. . . . It should also know how to be silent, to oppose its rhythms to those of the bodily instrument, to counterpoint and unite with them without troubling about any personal effect.

The music of the Ballets Russes was perhaps less self-effacing than this ideal music for living plastic, but Dalcroze was keenly aware of its potential for a kind of kinesthesis far more striking than that of Delibes's *Sylvia.* Dalcroze was not completely swept away by the Ballets Russes: he considered that Diaghilev's company was supreme in the interpretation of "violent or fantastic passages of music," but insufficiently nuanced, deaf to "the *mezzopiano* and *rubato* of tonal phrases." But the futurist in Dalcroze—whose essays are illustrated (by Paulet Thévenaz) with little caricatures of limbs-in-motion in a style derived from Duchamp's *Nude Descending a Staircase* (1911)—responded strongly to certain elements of advanced twentieth-century ballet:

> Canons of lines, files, circles, opposing movements of lines and files, geometrical or pictorial designs, association or dissociation of bending and rising . . . leaps, crouching, etc. All this constitutes a veritable living symphony, a dynamic and spatial art impregnated with moving life. A great field of activity is henceforth open to dramatic and choreographic artists, and already the *mise en scène* of the Russian ballets betrays interesting researches (*e.g. Pas d'Acier,* Prokofieff) in the domain of polyrhythm.
>
> On the other hand, the classical ballet . . . wears threadbare its continual effects of jerky movements, leaps, and voltes.

Prokofiev's *Steel Step* (1927), with its factory setting, its clean intersections of powerfully contrasting rhythmic lines, seemed a good model for the sort of

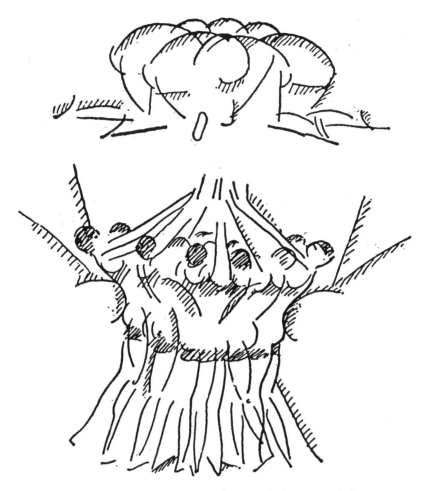

FIG. 6. Paulet Thévenaz, Group Exercise (Jaques-Dalcroze, *Eurhythmics Art and Education*, p. 30)

studiously asymmetrical coordination of moving bodies that Dalcroze desired. But the first major experiment in danced polyrhythm came fourteen years earlier, in *The Rite of Spring*.

Nijinsky, Nijinska, and The Rite of Spring

Dalcroze's essays provide striking evidence of the aesthetic that Vaslav Nijinsky, the choreographer of *The Rite of Spring*, found at the Dalcroze institute. It is not surprising that Nijinsky would emerge from his study fascinated by the notion of musculature as its own private music, to which Stravinsky might give an intriguing assist. Nijinsky wanted an alternative to the pretty, symmetrical motions of classically trained dancers—turned-out, upright, gravity-defying—and so he worked out from Dalcroze movements a kind of anti-ballet: turned-in, bent down, gravity-submitting.

> The men in *Sacre* are primitive. There is something almost bestial in their appearance. Their legs and feet are turned inwards, their fists clenched, their heads held down between hunched shoulders, their walk, on slightly bent knees, is heavy as they laboriously struggle up a winding trail, stamping in the rough, hilly terrain.

What sort of ballet would be credible for such Neanderthals? Not the ultra-elegant Petipa movements, but a set of rain-dance poses (Nijinsky's very first theatrical experience was a childhood visit to an American Indian show) combined with the muscle flexion of a body-building class. Furthermore, this movement was conceived as a powerful spectacle in itself, independent of Stravinsky's music: Nijinsky told his dancers to follow the private count that he called out backstage, not the rhythm of the conductor's baton—partly because the dancers couldn't follow Stravinsky's meters, but also in obeisance to Dalcroze's ideal of the autonomy of living plastic, its refusal to submit to the role of mere accompaniment to music. And yet despite the independence of the choreographic count from the conductor's count, Nijinsky was wholly intent on providing physical movement that would compose a figure of consonance with the musical movement: bodies clenched and clumped when the music was knotted up, or bodies jerked open in deep synchrony with the spasms of the music.

When Nijinsky choreographed Debussy's *L'après-midi d'un faune*, he conceived movements as a kind of Greek frieze set in motion, with poses strictly in profile; and there is a certain sculptural, glyphic aspect to the choreography of *The Rite of Spring* as well: if Rodin's *The Thinker* were asked to walk—elbow still glued to knee—he might walk in just the fashion of these men, with fists balled, shoulders hunched, knees bent. The choreography provides not violence in the warm, angry sense of the word, but abstract definitions, chilly pictograms of violence. As Jann Pasler has noted, in a sketch of the première of *The Rite of Spring* "the dancers look to be an extension of the series of boulders painted on the backdrop." To look at images from the original production is to behold a world in which gravity seems twice normal—as if the mass of the earth had been far greater in pagan Russia, making all movement painful and halting, unusually explicit.

The Dalcroze movements offered a system for the direct translation of musical rhythm into physical gesture:

Nijinsky demonstrated a *pas mouvement* in the choreography to the musical count of 5/4. During his huge leap he counted 5 (3 + 2). On count 1, high in the air, he bent one leg at the knee and stretched his right arm above his head, on count 2 he bent his body towards the left, on count 3 he bent his body towards the right, then on count 1, still high in the air, he stretched his body upwards again and then finally came down lowering his arm on count 2, graphically rendering each note of the uneven measure.

In a work such as *The Rite of Spring,* in which the metrical irregularity defied the traditional *plastique* of ballet, Nijinsky needed to find a new way of embodying music in dance: and through Dalcroze, he found a way of letting the strange meters generate strange gestural icons. Nijinska's phrase for the appearance of her brother's body, "graphically rendering each note of the uneven measure," is telling: Nijinsky thought through his dances by constructing a kind of somato-graph, a stick figure that acted as a corporeal scripture for the music. He made himself a human hieroglyph of Stravinsky's rhythm.

Nijinska herself was assigned the central role in *The Rite of Spring,* the Chosen One, the virgin whose ritual death will rejuvenate the land. She remembered that her brother "wanted me to portray the fanatic strength of the maiden who is ready to sacrifice her life to save the earth by dancing in a frenzied delirium until falling inert to the ground, killed by her own dance." A hieroglyph should be eternal, should represent an epitome of gesture, a sememe decontextualized from human life; and such eternity, such abstraction, can be expressed through the death of the human subject whose body forms the figure.

However, the manner of conceiving ballet hieroglyphically—as spasms of isolated gestures that figure forth the literal rhythms of the music—did not meet universal approval. Jean Cocteau thought that in *The Rite of Spring,*

> The failure consisted in the parallelism of the music and the movement, in their lack of *play,* of counterpoint. We had there a proof that the same often-repeated chord tires the ear less than the frequent repetition of a single gesture tires the eye. The laughter came more from the monotony of automata than from the disruption of poses, and more from the disruption of poses than from the polyphony.

Cocteau, with his love of dissonance among the elements of theatre, such as sound and spectacle, had little sympathy with a breathtakingly humble choreographic style that aspired to be little more than an oscilloscope of the music, traced with human bodies. (Stravinsky, however, made some choreographic notations which show that, far from intending a parallelism of music and movement, he wished in places for a complete asynchrony between the musical meter

FIG. 7. Valentine Hugo, sketch of Maria Piltz in the final scene of *The Rite of Spring,* 1913 (© 1999 ARS, New York/ADAGP, Paris)

and the dance meter.) Even Nijinsky's own sister had great reservations about the usefulness of Dalcroze movements to dancers; and Debussy detested such movements, as is clear from a letter concerning Nijinsky's choreography to *Jeux* (1913):

> Nijinsky has given an odd mathematical twist to his perverse genius. This fellow adds up semiquavers with his feet, proves the result with his arms and then as if suddenly struck by paralysis of one side listens for a while to the music, disapprovingly. This it appears is to be called the stylization of gesture. *How awful! It is in fact Dalcrozian and this is to tell you that I hold Monsieur Dalcroze to be one of the worst enemies of music!*

Debussy wrote the music of *Jeux* to a scenario of a tennis match, and Dalcroze's robust, *al fresco*, physically fit style of movement would seem appropriate to tennis. But Debussy's tennis is no more athletic, sweaty, than Henri Rousseau's rugby: the music is a sort of experiment in prose, shadowy, continuously varying, with few recurrent elements that the ear can grasp. It is not athematic, but it is nearly a-gestural; so Nijinsky's "stylization of gesture" seemed, to Debussy, the wrong sort of choreographic method. To Debussy, Nijinsky was a kind of balletic arithmetician, performing abstract calculations of meter with his arms and legs instead of attending to the subliminal erotic implications of the music. Having devised a choreographic style beautifully suited to the determined, chunky music hieroglyphs of Stravinsky, Nijinsky couldn't easily alter his method to fit the twilit blushings of *Jeux*, its poised wisps of meaning. Debussy was (again) an insufficiently visual composer for the sort of instantaneous, unmodulated, summarizing gestures at which Nijinsky excelled. Debussy required a choreography of clever transition and of ambiguous body shapes; Nijinsky, on the other hand, aspired to be graphic, legible. Nijinsky wanted the eye, the ear, and a third sense—some deep kinesthetic identification between the spectator's muscle tension and the muscle tension of the dancers on stage—to cooperate in producing a series of distinct, intelligible figures.

Lessing's Theory of Gestus

Of all the nine Muses, Polyhymnia, the Muse of legible gesture, has found the fewest worshipers over the centuries: even in our own day, the reputation of Marcel Marceau is nothing like the reputation of Stravinsky or Picasso or Balanchine. But the notion that pantomime is potentially an important sort of artistic expression has never quite died; and Stravinsky paid homage to Polyhymnia by giving her a beautiful variation in *Apollo* (1928). Nijinsky struggled to endow ballet with the gestural precision, the semantic intensity of pantomime, without descending from "pure" dance to "mere" mute storytelling. But in the Modernist age, it is never enough just to do something; one must also have a theory for it, a theory that itself becomes a further form of action.

The theory of the *gestus* came to fill this nearly unoccupied niche in the ecosystem of the art world. It was not in itself a creation of the twentieth century; but I believe the twentieth century extended it beyond its previous domain. Perhaps the first writer to distinguish *Gestus* from *Geste* or *Gebärde*—two established German words meaning "gesture"—was Gotthold Lessing, in an entry from 12 May 1767 in *Hamburgische Dramaturgie*. Lessing hated actors who waved their hands around and stomped about in a prolix, uncontrolled manner: instead, actors should have fewer, and more telling, gestures. Like other writers on pantomime, Lessing imagined that in antiquity there existed a whole language of gesture far more inflamed with significance than anything we know in our present lives:

> We know only very little about the chironomia of the ancients, that is, about the contents of the rules that the ancients had prescribed for the movements of hands; but we know this, that they brought the language of hands to a perfection scarcely possible to conceive from the evidence of what our orators are capable of performing. We seem to have preserved from this whole language nothing but an inarticulate cry; nothing but the power to make movements without knowing how to give these movements a fixed meaning. . . . I only note that among signifying gestures *[bedeutenden Gesten]* there is one kind that the actor has to observe before all things, and with which he alone can impart light and life to the moral. In one word, the individualizing *gestus* *[individualisierenden Gestus]*.

Only by means of the individualizing *gestus* can an actor hope to reconcile a universal truth about human behavior with the particular urgencies of a specific dramatic situation. In the theatre of antiquity (according to Lessing), this happened effortlessly and systematically; but we've forgotten the rules.

Rousseau and Gesticulation

In his *Essai sur l'origine des langues* (1749–55), Jean-Jacques Rousseau dreamed even more intently about the vivacity of old systems of gesture:

> Although the language of gesture and that of the voice are equally natural, still the first is easier and depends less on conventions. For more objects affect our eyes than our ears, and visual figures have more variety than sounds have; also they are more expressive and say more in less time. Love, they say, was the inventor of drawing. . . .

Our gestures signify nothing but our natural disquiet; it is not of those that I want to speak. It is only Europeans who gesticulate when speaking: one would say that all the force of their tongue is in their arms; they still add to it the force of the lungs, and all of that doesn't accomplish much. When a Frenchman made a big fuss, racked his body in order to say a good many words, a Turk removes for a moment his pipe from his mouth, says two words in a low voice, and crushes him with one sentence.

Since we've learned to gesticulate, we've forgotten the art of pantomime, for the same reason that with lots of pretty grammar books we no longer understand the symbols of the Egyptians. What the ancients said in the liveliest way, they expressed not with words but with signs. They didn't say it, they showed it.

And Rousseau, of course, continued by telling the story of how the king of Scythia sent Darius a frog, a bird, a mouse, and five arrows—though in Rousseau's version Darius instantly understood the terrible meaning of the thing-message, and skedaddled. "Substitute a letter for these signs: the more it will threaten, the less it will frighten; it will be no more than a boast that will make Darius laugh." For Rousseau, French and German and English are hopelessly bleached, dull, abstract, distracted: we need a language that will rouse without having to be learned; something archaic, pregrammatical, visual, *true;* a language of pantomime, a language of hieroglyph. Europeans flail their arms about, instead of making the lost acute signs that render mouth-speech superfluous. The letter kills; but semiosis gives life.

Weill's Theory of Gestus

In the Modernist period, the word *gestus* and the notion that communication can be perfected by gestural specificity were revived by Kurt Weill and Bertolt Brecht. Of these two collaborators, Weill was evidently the first to use the word *gestus* in print. Now, the only obvious reason for preferring *gestus* to its established cognates is to have a term free of modern distortion and ill-usage, to return to a Latin purity of expression. *Gestus*—the plural is the same as the singular—is derived from *gerere,* to bear or carry; a gesture, then, is a bearing, a way of carrying oneself, a posture, a habitual bit of behavior. (Incidentally, the word *gist,* sometimes used as an English gloss for *gestus,* comes from a different Latin verb altogether.) The modern European cognates have not deviated far from this old meaning. But *gestus* may imply something not often felt in the modern equivalents: the fact that the Latin root is also the root of various Medieval words meaning "story" or "tale"—as in the archaic English word *gest,* or the *Gesta roma-*

norum (an old collection of tall tales about saints, emperors, and so forth). A *gestus*, then, might be defined as an entity intermediate between a gesture and a narrative; a sort of schematic of a human figure that defines or epitomizes a whole discursive context in which such a contortion might come into play. In other words, a *gestus* is a whole story contracted into a single bodily movement.

A *gestus* can be understood as a hieroglyph or ideogram read from a human body; but the physicality of the *gestus* sets it apart from other entities that join the pictorial and the discursive. A *gestus* is a confrontation, a demand, a political act; it is a pose of a body that breathes, that trembles, that engages the spectator in its humanness. Pound's ideograms, by contrast, were the designs of an extremely literary man much attracted to the shapes of writing—as, for example, in Canto 30 (1930), which ends with an account of the development in 1503 of a cursive typeface. Pound and Brecht both wanted to change the world through extremely distilled forms of expression. But Brecht (and Weill) wanted to write messages that could be understood by the illiterate, messages to change the world; and the most legible messages were written in figures built up from arms and legs and swaying torsos, an alphabet of *gestus*.

In an essay of 1929, "Concerning the Gestic Character of Music," Weill looked back on his recent achievements in music theatre—the *Mahagonny-Songspiel* (1927) and *The Threepenny Opera* (1928)—and tried to show how he and Brecht had reformed the genre, indeed achieved (as he put it in a contemporary letter) a "prototype *[Urform]* of opera." Weill believed that opera had gone astray in the nineteenth century, in that the composer had placed himself in a state of unhealthy subservience to the words of the text: "the task of music consisted of producing moods, underpainting the situations, and underlining the dramatic accents." Weill had no use for this opera in which music aspired only to be a handmaiden of the text, a form of complacent enjoyment, a narcotic; instead, he wanted an opera that stimulated the intelligence, not the pleasure receptors in the nerves *[Genußnerven]*. The new music drama should be antipsychological—not as an act of renunciation, but as an acknowledgment of the fact that music is, and always has been, completely impotent in the field of psychology:

> Now, as you know, music lacks all psychologizing or characterizing capability. Instead, music has a capability that, for the representation of man in the theater, is of decisive significance: it can reproduce the *gestus,* which clarifies the incident on stage; it can even create a sort of fundamental *gestus [Grundgestus],* which prescribes a determined posture for the actor and eliminates any doubt or misunderstanding about the incident in question; it can, in the ideal case, so strongly fix this *gestus* that a false representation of the incident in question is no longer possible.

The *gestus,* then, is the basic unit of music theatre, the new music theatre of rational analysis of human affairs.

The highest goal of the *gestus* is to eliminate all ambiguity of interpretation: it is a hieroglyph, but without oracular fog. The composer strives to create a pattern of sound that specifies a precise bodily movement, a precise inflection of speech: the *gestus* is a multidimensional fixity, in which pantomime, speech, and music cooperate toward a pure flash of meaning. Weill found that generically unsettled music theatre—not opera, not concert, not ballet, but something in the limbo at their common center—was best adapted to the presentation of *gestus.* The spectator of an opera or ballet has developed habited strategies for picking the spectacle apart, for ignoring the dull passages and concentrating on the thrilling chain of high Cs, or thirty-two consecutive *fouettés;* but where the genre is uncertain, the spectator has to attend to everything, and becomes sensitive to multimedia effects. Weill thought that the whole future of music theatre could be seen in Stravinsky's *The Soldier's Tale* (1918), "standing on the boundary between play, pantomime, and opera"; and in a letter to his publisher, Weill noted that such works as the *Mahagonny-Songspiel* needed to be performed "in a new form between concert and theater." *Gestus* can be made visible, audible, tactile where the audience has no ready-made pattern of assimilation and deflection; the inscape, the inflex, of the detail becomes telling where there exist no channels for draining the meaning into familiar theatrical excitements.

In his essay on gestic music, Weill provided three examples of *gestus,* plus some general observations, such as the comment that the recitatives in Bach's passions are often gestic in character. The first example is the second-act duet *Nur hurtig fort, nur frisch gegraben* from Beethoven's *Fidelio* (1805). Weill didn't explain how this duet constituted a *gestus,* but it's not hard to see why Weill chose it. The mood of the duet is hushed urgency: the jailer Rocco and his young assistant must dig a grave for the noble hero, soon to die (they fear) for resisting the tyrant. The *gestus* of the duet is, unmistakably, digging: the most musically memorable element isn't the vocal line but a swelling figure in the low winds and brass, below a restless, continual accompaniment of triads broken into triplets— a representation of a shovel turning earth, all anxious persistence. The orchestra exerts a cybernetic force over the action: it commands, Dig! Insofar as the great theme of *Fidelio* is liberation, it could be argued that digging a pit is one of two fundamental *gestus* in the opera: on the one hand virtue is consigned to the grave; on the other hand virtue must be set free. Digging, then, is not an act that pertains merely to the psychological needs of Leonore (disguised as the jailer's assistant Fidelio), who is willing to go to any length to discover the whereabouts of her heroic husband, but an act that pertains to the social needs of a whole oppressed group. Finally, we should note that the vocal line stays close to the natural speech patterns of the German text, in an arioso-like fashion.

EX. 4.1. Beethoven, *Fidelio:* digging a grave

EX. 4.2. Mozart, *The Magic Flute:* staring at a beautiful picture

Weill's second example is much less kinetic in character:

"Dies Bildnis ist bezaubernd schön"—the posture of a man contemplating a picture is here determined by the music alone. He can hold the picture in his right or left hand, hold it high or low, he can be lit by a spotlight or stand in the dark—his fundamental *gestus* is correct because it is correctly dictated by the music.

This is an aria from *The Magic Flute*—as we've already seen, an opera of hieroglyphs. Here Prince Tamino falls in love with Pamina, a woman he's never seen, as he stares at her picture: the *gestus* is clearly paralysis from concentrated attention, as Tamino, gazing at an icon, turns into a statue. As Weill pointed out, the gestic precision of the music allows the tenor some latitude in his movement on stage: because the raptness, the turning inward, is built into the music, the physical gestures (barring real stupidity in the singer) won't descend into meaningless gesticulation. "This picture is enchantingly beautiful," Tamino begins singing, in simple falling scales in E♭ major; "I feel it, I feel it"—and at each syllable *fühl* (feel), Tamino lands on a B♮ or an A♮, as if ecstasy had shocked him for an instant into a heavy *appoggiatura,* into a richly colored, cherished private fantasy: the *appoggiature* slightly tilt the harmonic plane, as if Tamino, hypnotized by

Pamina's image, were entering into the tilted plane of the picture he holds in front of him. Weill liked to stress the unpsychological aspects of gestic music, and in some ways *Dies Bildnis ist bezaubernd schön,* with its stress on interior feeling— Tamino, for the duration, pays no attention to the other characters on stage—is a poor example; unless perhaps Weill thought of Tamino's love for Pamina as a community-forming sort of love, since it leads to a general liberation from the tyranny of the Queen of the Night. Finally, let's note that, like Beethoven, Mozart carefully adapted his musical rhythms to the cut of the verbal rhythms: the crucial syllable *Bild,* in the first line, is set to a dotted note, in order to lengthen its quantity.

Weill's third example is from his own *Mahagonny-Songspiel,* the *Alabama-Song:*

Oh, moon of Alabama,
We now must say good-bye,
We've lost our good old mamma
And must have whisky,
Oh, you know why.

Weill first gave the tune as Brecht himself wrote it: "Here a fundamental *gestus* has been established rhythmically in the most primitive form, while melodically there is established the quite personal and inimitable way of singing in which Brecht performs his songs." The tune consists of mere bouncings up and down a minor third or a major third, in regular eighth notes except where a strongly stressed syllable suggests a certain lengthening of value. After presenting Brecht's version with a civil leer, Weill then offered *his* version (unforgettable, world-famous) of the melody, with its soaring line, its sophisticated shifts between a G^7 chord with a natural seventh and one with a flattened seventh (as if G were experimenting with the possibility of becoming a kind of dominant to itself), its rich progress to the relative minor ("we now must say good-") and to a walloping operatic diminished chord ("bye"), and at last to the true dominant, D major, while maintaining a steady G in the bass. But Weill insisted that the *gestus*—"the rhythmic fixing of the text," as he defined it—was exactly the same as that of Brecht's music:

In my composition on the same text, the same fundamental *gestus* is fashioned, only here it is for the first time truly "composed" with the much freer means of the musician. With me the song is laid out much more broadly, swings out further melodically, and also, with respect to rhythm, is based *[fundiert]* completely differently because of its accompaniment formula—but the gestic character has been preserved, although it manifests itself in a completely different form of appearance.

This is hard to follow. If a *gestus* is "the rhythmic fixing of the text," how is it possible that "the same *gestus* is expressed in different rhythms"? And how is it possible that two settings of the same text, presenting the same *gestus,* could be based on completely different rhythmic groundwork? It seems that Weill is appealing to some sort of rhythm beyond our ordinary rhythmic notation—not the loose iambic trimeter of the *Alabama-Song,* but some motor or spring underneath it. But this rhythm remains hypothetical, or fictitious, unless it can be specified more closely than Weill specifies it.

EX. 4.3. The *Alabama-Song:* melody for the refrain, as Brecht wrote it

EX. 4.4. The *Alabama-Song:* melody for the refrain, as Weill wrote it (operatic version)

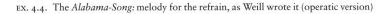

(continued)

EX. 4.4. (Continued)

Just what is the *gestus* of the *Alabama-Song*? We are used to thinking of the song in the context of the opera *Rise and Fall of the City of Mahagonny* (1930), which hadn't yet been finished when Weill wrote his essay on gestic music. In the *Mahagonny-Songspiel* of 1927, the *Alabama-Song* has no context except insofar as the other Mahagonny songs provide a certain shudder of the meaninglessness of luxury, when greed itself is a kind of artifice—as if desire could be as factitious as the object of desire. The text, then, must generate its own *gestus:* perhaps it might be described as the boredom that results when distractions from boredom rotate in a closed circle. It is a song of real loss and unreal yearning—unreal because whisky, boys, and dollars are the objects yearned for, and the singer doesn't seem to question why these objects provide only the illusion of fulfillment. It is a song about incompetent desiring.

As a *gestus* of tedium, the *Alabama-Song* seems better served by Brecht than by Weill; as a *gestus* of desiring, however vague and inept, it seems better served by Weill than by Brecht. But Weill skewed his evidence considerably by citing only the song's refrain. The first stanza goes as follows:

> Oh, show us the way to the next whisky-bar!
> Oh, don't ask why; oh, don't ask why!
> For we must find the next whisky-bar,
> For if we don't find the next whisky-bar,
> I tell you we must die.

Weill's music for this section consists of the same sort of bouncing-between-thirds as Brecht's music for the refrain; and there is a good reason for this, in that Weill's stanza tune is an adaptation of Brecht's own stanza tune (though Weill contributed the accompaniment's abrupt gear-shifts between F minor and F♯ minor as the song lurches up toward G major for the refrain). The score suggests that the

Alabama-Song consists of music by Weill and text by Brecht, but it would be more correct to say that it consists of music by Weill and Brecht and text by Brecht and Elisabeth Hauptmann—Brecht's lover and collaborator, who contributed much to Brecht's work, particularly in situations where knowledge of the English language was helpful. (Hauptmann's contribution to the writing of well-known texts ascribed to Brecht is the subject of John Fuegi's *Brecht and Company,* which may overstate the case.) Brecht, in his youth, made some money as a cabaret singer; and in the mid-1920s he met a young composer, Franz S. Bruinier, who helped him revise the tunes that he wrote for some of his poems. In later life, Brecht claimed that Weill had been "a composer of atonal psychological operas" until Weill learned the right path when he, Brecht, "whistled things to him bar by bar and above all performed them for him." Almost no one accepts this comment as it stands; and yet it should be remembered that Brecht may indeed have made some contributions to the famous tunes that we still sing, hum, and whistle today. When Arthur Sullivan found himself unable to compose Jack Point's song, so central to *The Yeomen of the Guard* (1888), he asked W. S. Gilbert to hum the sea chantey on which Gilbert had modeled his prosody—and Sullivan quickly found his inspiration. Weill had little trouble devising tunes, but collaboration often makes the boundaries of individual contributions difficult to make out.

As a composer, Brecht had two different modes: the first is a kind of speaking to exact pitch, in which a melody oscillates up and down, up to stressed syllables, down to unstressed syllables, until it becomes convenient to redound between two different notes. This is the style we've been examining in the *Alabama-Song*—though this example is atypical, in that the English prosody is so mangled that the stanzas seem generated by a broken wheel in the organ-grinder's organ. In Brecht's original setting (in which the wording is slightly different), the beginning appears as "Oh, lead us [pause] the way to [pause] the next whisky bar," as if singing any three consecutive eighth notes were so exhausting that the singer needed to catch her breath—a jaded parody of breathless anticipation; and it is not until bar 10 that a note appears that is not C, B, or A, so caged is the singer inside the span of a minor third. Weill's setting is only slightly less eccentric in prosody and slightly less straitened in melody. I don't deplore this: the effect of the *Alabama-Song,* as we know it, partly depends on the mechanically off-kilter text-setting—"FOR IF we don't FIND the next whisky BAR"—as if the singer were too deadened, too strung out, to bother to scan the lines properly. Mahagonny is, in any case, a city without native speakers: *everyone* is a foreigner.

But when Brecht wanted melody instead of recitative, he sometimes used a different technique: he stole. For example, Brecht composed a version of another Mahagonny song, the pidgin-English *Benares-Song,* in which the stanzas are sung to an old tune that I know as *There is a tavern in the town,* and the refrain is sung to (of all things) *Un bel dì vedremo,* from Puccini's *Madama Butterfly* (1904). To end the *Benares-Song* with *Un bel dì* was simply to plaster a sign upon the text, reading "Weep here, fools"; Puccini's famous aria must have seemed to Brecht a sort of icon of melody, a blatant numbskull tune made to please the sentimental bourgeoisie. Weill's music for the *Benares-Song* has nothing whatever to do with Brecht's music; but the refrain that Weill provided for the *Alabama-Song* might easily have been conceived along the lines of *Un bel dì,* as it might be understood not by an innocent young woman eagerly waiting for her beloved husband's ship to steam into harbor, but by a prostitute eagerly waiting for a sucker to buy her a drink. (The Pucciniesque effect is much stronger in the opera, where a sextet of women's voices provides a soft cushion on which Jenny can sprawl her tune, than in the *Songspiel,* where Weill provided a canonic duet for Jessie and Bessie.)

Brecht and Weill both liked, as a template for songwriting, a talky, prosodically self-conscious stanza followed by a billowing, melodious refrain. In the case of the *Alabama-Song,* the model provides a stanza pertinent to boredom, followed by a refrain pertinent to hollow yearning—less desire than a parody of desire. And this combination of boredom and yearning is, I take it, the *gestus* of the song. If a *gestus* is both a gest and a gesture—a story and a bodily figure—the *gestus,* the deep internal rhythm, of the *Alabama-Song* is a kind of life-cramp: a constricted circuit of wish-whisky-wish-boy-wish-dollar-wish-whisky, a state of No Exit from the banality of thirst. When Lotte Lenya sang the *Alabama-Song,* Brecht told her, "Not so Egyptian," and coached her to turn her palms upward in a direct appeal to the moon. But perhaps Lenya had the right idea: a certain hieroglyphic rigidity is appropriate to this *gestus* of self-conscious, half-shrugging supplication, performed by a priestess in the cult of money.

Brecht's Theory of Gestus

Brecht was uncomfortable with the extraordinary charm of Weill's music. To Brecht, music should be written with a knife's blade—should be confrontational, aggressive, disturbing; instead, Brecht had the strange experience of hearing the detested bourgeoisie merrily singing his words to Weill's tunes. What is to be done when the tyrant can't stop singing, Down down down with tyranny? when the king gives sacks of gold to the jester who cries, Let the king's head roll?

Brecht resolved this cognitive dissonance by deciding that he and Weill were engaged in two different businesses. The business of Brecht was to display the monstrousness, the untenability, of modern life; the business of Weill was to make this bitter wisdom so adorable that it could be smuggled into a theatre dominated by reactionary forces. As Brecht wrote (with Peter Suhrkamp) in 1930, after *Rise and Fall of the City of Mahagonny* appeared:

> The opera that we have is the *culinary opera*. It was a means of enjoyment long before it was a commodity. . . . Why is *Mahagonny* an opera? The fundamental attitude is that of an opera: namely, culinary. . . . *The opera* Mahagonny *is properly conscious of how nonsensical a thing opera is.*

Brecht did not say explicitly that in the operatic kitchen, Weill was in charge of the sugar and Brecht was in charge of the vinegar—and indeed, each man had some expertise with both ingredients. But Brecht clearly worried that Weill was too little concerned with politics and too much concerned with ingratiation: later on, there was to be a notorious episode in which Brecht threatened that if he saw Weill, he would kick that phony Richard Strauss down a staircase. Even at the height of the collaboration, Brecht proposed a striking division of labor between poet and composer:

> The invasion of the methods of epic theatre into the opera first leads to a radical *division of the elements*. The great fight for primacy among words, music, and production . . . can simply be laid aside by radically dividing the elements. As long as the term "total art work" *[Gesamtkunstwerk]* implies that the totality is a smear *[Aufwaschen],* as long as the arts are to be "fused" together, the separate elements will all be degraded in equal measure, and each can be for the others only a supplier of cues. . . . Such magic is naturally to be fought against. Everything that attempts to hypnotize will produce unworthy intoxications, will make fog, and must be given up.
> *Music, text, and setting must each learn better how to stand by itself. . . .*
> For music, the following shifts in weight are submitted:

DRAMATIC OPERA	EPIC OPERA
The music is deferential *[serviert]*	The music enables *[vermittelt]*
music heightening the text	music explaining the text
music affirming the text	music accepting the text for what it is
music illustrating	music taking a position
music depicting the psychic situation	music giving the demeanor *[Verhalten]*

We see that Brecht conceived the function of music in the old Dramatic Opera according to metaphors derived from painting, and in the new Epic Opera according to metaphors derived from pantomime or sign-making. In the old opera, the text was conceived as *mouth-uttered,* and the music was a system for achieving further saturation in the text's emotional color—the shaking-with-anger or cooing-with-love in the voice; in the new opera, the text is conceived as *written,* and the music is a system for chiseling the inscription more deeply.

But as music is progressively liberated from text, it becomes unclear whether the position given by the music is going to be the same as the position given by the text. Perhaps the text can, in effect, hold up a sign saying, Look at this bad cowering man—he deserves to be kicked; and the music can hold up a sign saying, Pity him. And perhaps the two arts can combine to express something along the lines of, say, Despise yourself for pitying him. Such complexity of attitude generated by dissonance between word-gesture and music-gesture would accord well with Brecht's hope that *Rise and Fall of the City of Mahagonny,* though it was "as culinary as ever," might nevertheless have "a society-changing function; it puts culinary matters to discussion." I think that this means, chiefly, that an unculinary text can make the audience critical of the delightfully culinary music; and that culinary music can provide an incentive for an audience to sit through a play full of challenging and disagreeable insights into social structure.

In these notes on *Mahagonny,* Brecht used the word *gestus* in print—almost for the first time in his career. But Brecht's ideas about *gestus,* though similar to Weill's, were perhaps not identical. Brecht had two sorts of favorite examples for *gestus.* The first example illustrates *gestus* in prosody: the phrases "Pluck out the eye that offends thee" and "If thine eye offends thee: pluck it out" say the same thing; but the first phrase is gestically weak, the second strong, in that its "first clause contains a supposition, and the peculiar aspect, the bizarre aspect of it can be fully expressed by the inflection of voice. Then comes a little pause of helplessness, and only then the amazing advice." The version with the marked *gestus* permits, within the compass of a single sentence, a tiny narrative of moues, grimaces, roughenings of voice—it is a line with a built-in rim shot, a line that clicks shut like the clasp of Mother Courage's purse; the other version permits little attitudinizing, in that the main force of the sentence is spent after the first word, "Pluck." This example is taken from an essay on free verse (1939), in which Brecht claimed that irregular distributions of long and short syllables facilitate strength of *gestus* through unusual, memorable phrase-shapes.

The other major class of *gestus* is found in the analysis not of prosody but of physical gesture: "Not every *gestus* is a social *gestus.* To begin with, the posture of defense against a fly is not a social *gestus,* though the posture of defense against a dog can be one, for example if the fight that a badly dressed man has to wage against watchdogs achieves expression through it." Of course, the raw material of the theatre should consist of social *gestus,* not private *gestus. Shooing* is a *gestus* worthy of meditation only if it arises from some socially rectifiable difficulty; otherwise it is of no interest to anyone except the sufferer. Again, we should note how a piece of behavior becomes a significant *gestus* only when it implies a story: a man exasperated by a mosquito isn't necessarily part of a narrative, but a tramp foraging for food in a garbage can, making a *Scram!* gesture at a rich man's angry watchdog, implies a whole parable of Dives and Lazarus.

As Brecht and Weill became more experienced in the manipulation of *gestus*, they became more conscious of the powerful effects that could be achieved by considering the *gestus* not as a figure of consonance, but as a figure of dissonance between text and music. Originally, both artists conceived a *gestus* as a unit of rhythm: the scansion rhythm of a text or the body rhythm that shapes arms, legs, torso, head into signs. But their shared doctrine (anti-psychological, pro-sociological) that music ought not to be the slave of text, that music must instead exert itself with all the resources acquired over centuries of independent development, tended to split the *gestus* in two. This insight didn't come easily. Even as late as 1929, in "Concerning the Gestic Character of Music," Weill evidently thought that on some level, the *gestus* of the words and the *gestus* of the music should be unanimous—a kind of convergent evolution of separate text and separate music toward the same goal. Weill felt that he hadn't altered in any way the *gestus* of the text of the *Alabama-Song*: he had only brought out the *gestus* in a more skillful, more trenchant, more attractive manner. Furthermore, he claimed that his music for the *Alabama-Song* tended to provoke rational thought, not sensuous enjoyment. On the other hand, Weill was quite aware by then that the *gestus* of his music often functioned differently from the *gestus* of the text: for example, he wrote in 1928 to his publisher that "the appeal [of the *Zuhälter-Ballade*] lies precisely in the fact that a somewhat risqué text . . . is composed in a tender, pleasant manner." By 1933 Weill was noting that "every text I've set looks entirely different once it's been swept through my music." Weill, like Brecht, came to conceive his music drama as a theatre based on a sort of over-*gestus*, a coordination of the distinct *gestus* of the text and of the music into a superior meaning not available to either one separately. Brecht read the *Zuhälter-Ballade* exactly as Weill did—Brecht felt glee at the thought of the audience of *The Threepenny Opera* swooning over a romantic duet: "The tenderest and most intimate love song in the play [the *Zuhälter-Ballade*] described the everlasting, indestructible affection between a pimp and his best girl. Not without feeling, the lovers celebrated in song their little home, the brothel." This is an effect difficult to achieve with either poetry or music alone: it requires a deliberate misapplication of (sentimental) music to (low-life) text. The proper response to the *Zuhälter-Ballade* is not to remain detached and derisive, as the text might suggest; it is not to gush with warm sticky feelings for pimp and whore, as the music might suggest; it is first to gush, then to dislike oneself for being such a gull or ninny— to feel, and then to criticize one's feeling. The bourgeoisie should learn the inadequacy of its own Pavlovian responses to the theatre: to salivate identically over reminiscences of starry-eyed young love in a brothel and in a well-chaperoned middle-class parlor might suggest a certain skepticism concerning the value of saliva. The interior tension between text and music generated a new kind of figure. In this fashion, irony entered the domain of Modernist hieroglyphs.

Theodor Adorno invented modern, intellectually respectable musicology almost as an act of hatred, so that the music he disliked would give the whole world a stomachache. During a period when he considered Weill not too sickening, or perhaps intriguingly sickening, Adorno found it possible to defend Weill as a kind of surrealist: in 1930 Adorno called *Mahagonny* "the first surrealist opera," because of its "head-on confrontation with the dilapidated world of the bourgeoisie"; and in 1928, after seeing *The Threepenny Opera,* Adorno wrote:

> How distant I at first feel from music that does not draw any consequences from the current state of musical material, but rather seeks its effect by transforming old, atrophied material: Weill achieves this effect with such force and originality that, faced with the fact, the objection pales. In Weill there is a regression, one which exposes the demonic traits of dead music and uses them.

Adorno regarded Weill as the Frankenstein of music, stitching together the *membra disjecta* of decayed musical material, jolting them with electricity, and then pointing his zombies at a terrified public. (But if Adorno hoped that an audience exposed to the stench of the corrupt tonal system in *The Threepenny Opera* would suddenly grow queasy at the thought of hearing *La Bohème,* he was mistaken.) Brecht, of course, was himself a master hacker-apart and gluer-together of extinct texts; and Adorno's defense of *The Threepenny Opera* is another version of Brecht's defenses of the epic opera, but framed in the terms not of the kitchen, but of the morgue. Adorno carried to an extreme Brecht's argument that the public must be taught to be suspicious of its outrushes of feeling, its knee-jerks to musical cues. In a later chapter, we'll see that Adorno was correct in using the term *surrealism* to describe this effect; for the present, it will be enough to note that a strange sort of hybrid meaning-gesture can be synthesized by the *wrongness* of relation between music and text.

Farragoes: Mann ist Mann *and* The Threepenny Opera

The reader, scrutinizing Brecht's table listing the differences between dramatic opera and epic opera, may feel that Brecht exaggerated the novelty of the new style. But I believe that in some important ways, Brecht and Weill *underestimated* the strangeness of gestic opera.

To think gestically means to think in terms of a figure or a posture that sums up a narrative, a whole attitude toward life. But this method tends to undermine completely the old notion of character. Dramatists, from long before *Hamlet* to long after *A Doll's House,* have tended to conceive a character as a mask—the literal meaning of the term *persona;* a character might evolve, might grow wiser, might grow more inane, but still bears a habitual grimace. Hamlet smiles and

Falstaff smiles, yet no one would draw their smiles in the same way. Brecht, however, thought not of faces and masks, but of telling twists of the body. A face, though to some degree typifiable, is unique; but a man who shoos away a dog is much like any other man who shoos away a dog. If you try to imitate my facial expression, you are clowning; but if you try to imitate my gesture, you have just as much right to the gesture as I do. My gesture isn't *mine;* it expresses an attitude, a mode of response, valid for anyone in similar circumstances. Brecht's theatre is deeply anti-capitalistic in that by insisting on the primacy of *gestus,* he rid his characters of private property.

Both early and late, Brecht claimed that there is no such thing as character: in 1926 he told an interviewer, "when a character behaves by contradiction that's only because nobody can be identically the same at two unidentical moments. Changes in his exterior continually lead to an inner reshuffling. The continuity of the ego is a myth. A man is an atom that perpetually breaks up and forms anew." And in 1954, Brecht warned an actress, "One should never start out on the basis of a figure's character because a person has no character." A person doesn't have a *gestus,* either, in the sense of a permanent possession: a person *exhibits* a *gestus,* but a change of circumstance will make the strutter cringe, the cringer strut. People have significant existence only in relation to one another, and the unit of relation is the *gestus.* It is little wonder that Brecht was attracted to the theories of the American behaviorist John B. Watson, who believed that personality was infinitely mutable: for Brecht, as for the later behaviorist B. F. Skinner, human beings are basically pigeons of a larger growth. In one of Watson's experiments in instrumental conditioning, babies were rewarded with hugs if they drew back from a rat; soon Watson discovered that such babies would react fearfully not only to rats but to rabbits and other innocent animals. To Brecht, Watson's work must have proved that *gestus* could be easily taught and untaught—that human life was a sort of school of *gestus.*

Brecht, in selecting plays to be published under his name, was attracted to parables; but, left to his own devices, he tended to write not parables but *farragoes.* By this term I mean a drama that, even if it is quite brief, sprawls; a drama without a linear plot, a drama that moves by fits and starts, in a repetitious or zigzag fashion. This sort of shattered dramaturgy could be justified, in all sorts of fancy ways, by the theory of epic theatre; but in many ways it was more intuitive than political or didactic, in that it arose as a theatrical reflex of the discontinuity of the ego, not as a theatrical reflex of the inadequacy of capitalism. The Brechtian farrago reached its high point in *Mann ist Mann* (1926), the story of Galy Gay, a humble Irish packer who leaves home one morning to buy a flounder for his wife and endures a thousand vicissitudes—including impressment into the army, suffering at the hands of a violent, self-castrating sergeant, and a death sentence in connection with the sale of a phony elephant—until he eventually becomes an outstanding gunner in the British army's campaign to seize Tibet. In the fourth scene, the Widow Begbick (not to become a founder of the city of Mahagonny until a few years later) invites the sergeant to visit her in the night "as a human being! as a contradiction"; and the two terms do seem to be synonymous. A man isn't a character, but an occupant of an ecological niche; as the niche changes, so does the shape of the occupant. In the fifth scene, three roguish army buddies enter a pagoda in search of the fourth member of their detail; in the course of their investigation, the bonze, Wang, draws on the wall chalk images of the four criminals: the simplest possible stick figures, three with black circles for heads, one (more innocent) with a white circle. Wang is trying to provide ideograms of guilt, but the spectator might draw a much larger conclusion: that all people are simply stick figures, assigned black or white values in the arbitrary semiotics of morality; virtue and vice are little more than differently colored hats. Brecht's clearest statement of the theme of human malleability comes in the eighth scene, when the three scheming soldiers ask Galy Gay to surrender the name of Galy Gay and become the missing soldier, Jeraiah Jip:

POLLY. What will he say if we transform him into the soldier Jeraiah Jip?
URIA. So someone is transformed into an essentially different person. If you
    fling him in a pool, in two days' time webs will grow between his fingers.
    That's because he has nothing to lose.

The servant Sosias in Kleist's *Amphitryon* has his identity cudgeled out of him when Mercury needs to assume his identity; and Galy Gay also yields to an overwhelming pressure of circumstance, by un-Galy-Gaying himself. The very shape of a man's body will change under stress: in due time, the swimmer will become a frog.

In order to illustrate this somewhat uncomfortable thesis about the plasticity of the human self, Brecht found it convenient to place the hero in a baggy sort of play, as intrinsically formless as Galy Gay himself: the story is a kind of random mutation of event, allowing full scope for the possibilities of random mutation in the protagonist. This way of conceiving the interrelation between character (or characterlessness) and plot (or plotlessness) came in handy when, not long after *Mann ist Mann,* Brecht's co-worker Elisabeth Hauptmann wrote a draft of a translation of Gay's *The Beggar's Opera* (1728).

Brecht seems to have been slow to rouse himself to the project, but he came to see its potential. Frederick Austin's 1920 version of *The Beggar's Opera* had been a hit in London, and the Schott publishing firm even approached Hindemith about composing a jazzy new score for it. But Brecht came to see that he could rewrite—or, perhaps more exactly, unwrite, unstring—*The Beggar's Opera* into a new kind of farrago, a farrago-with-songs. *The Threepenny Opera* turned into something very like *Mann ist Mann,* with the difference that *all* the characters, not just the protagonist, are amphibians in various states of regression, caught in mid-metamorphosis.

The English poet John Gay, a friend of Pope and Swift, was in many ways a sympathetic figure to Brecht: for one thing, they shared a taste for elegant sarcasms; for another, they wrote music in a similar fashion, by theft. We've seen how Brecht patched together *There is a tavern in the town* and *Un bel dì* to make his *Benares-Song;* but Gay, long before, with the help of the musician Pepusch, had cobbled the score for the ballads in *The Beggar's Opera* by appropriating tunes from low drinking songs and from the high art of Purcell and Handel. Gay devised an opera about thieves, to ridicule the extravagances of Handel's Italian operatic stage; but one of the jokes is that Gay himself was as much a thief as Captain Macheath.

Gay enjoyed the *frisson* of hearing a pop song such as the Lillibullero one moment and a lofty melody by Handel the next, because the opera works to undo any distinction between the high and the low; the wild variance in levels of musical diction is a clever reflection of the incoherence of an England where the prime minister is difficult to distinguish from a robber. Near the beginning, Peachum reads a list of villains who are certain to hang: and the last entry on the little list is "Robin of Bagshot, alias Gorgon, alias Bluff Bob, alias Carbuncle, alias Bob Booty"—because it pleased Gay to quote various nicknames of the prime minister, Robert Walpole. Indeed, *The Beggar's Opera* depends on a careful system of reversals between high art and low art, *prime donne* and prostitutes, ministers of state and robbers. Just as Swift's Yahoos systematically parody the lawyers, doctors, bankers, and so forth of England—in one version of the text of *Gulliver's Travels,* Swift even wrote that Yahoos show the physiognomy of degenerate Englishmen—so Gay's thieves mirror the behavior of much more highly placed thieves. Gay's irony depends on an understanding that the comments concerning criminals refer to two domains at once. And this irony everywhere saturates the music: the closest thing to a sentimental love song, *Pretty Polly, say*—in which Macheath and Polly pledge to be true to one another—is sung to an exceptionally coarse, perky tune, *Pretty Parrot, say;* but a noble, glorious melody, Purcell's *If love's a sweet passion,* billows forth to accompany Lucy's explanation of how her father taught her to kiss "the parson, the squire, and the sot," until she learned the art of social kissing so well that she became pregnant out of wedlock. The low tune undercuts the highfalutin words and vice versa: Gay devised *The Beggar's Opera* as a music theatre of destroyed pretensions, to illustrate the Beggar's keen moral that "you may observe such a similitude of manners in high and low life, that it is difficult to determine whether (in the fashionable vices) the fine gentlemen imitate the gentlemen of the road, or the gentlemen of the road the fine gentlemen."

The Threepenny Opera, on the other hand, though it has tremendous political *incisiveness,* has scarcely any political *meaning.* Brecht had barely begun to study Marx by 1928, and the opera is politically incorrect, an embarrassment to Marxists: how can we admire the proletariat if the proletariat consists of beggars involved in a kind of outdoor theatre of false poverty? Peachum—the head of the Beggar's Union—is full of advice along lines that would have made Lenin frown. In the first scene, Filch, an apprentice beggar, comes to get a costume sufficiently pitiable that passersby will throw money at him; Peachum shows him the types of beggar costumes: the cheerful cripple, the spastic mutilated in war, the lamentable blind man, and, finally, the young man who has seen better days. Filch instantly wants the last costume—after all, he *is* a young man who has seen better days. But Peachum says no: "Because a man never believes his own misery. If you have a stomachache and you say so, it seems only repulsive." Peachum preaches universal inauthenticity: life is merely a long dissembling. Not the state, but humankind itself has withered away.

The Threepenny Opera almost foundered before it began, when Harold Paulsen insisted on wearing an especially spiffy suit and necktie—ludicrous on a thief—when he acted the role of Mackie. But Paulsen was right and Brecht and the others wrong, for *The Threepenny Opera* is a story about clothes: the characters are merely dressmaker's dummies supporting various costumes, from Polly's wedding dress to the beggars' duds, with spots carefully crafted from candle wax to avoid the appearance of real dirt. A production centered around couture is more likely to be successful than one centered around Marxist economics. Alexander von Zemlinsky, Schoenberg's teacher, wrote a comic opera called *Clothes Make the Man;* and that's a key proverb for Brecht as well. One of the most revealing details of Brecht's life is his habit of buying expensive simulations of ill-cut proletarian clothes, made from the best wool: it did not take him long to discover the exact costume most appropriate to the beggar he wished to be.

Gestures also make the man. In the sixth scene, Mackie decides to make his friend, the police chief Tiger Brown, feel bad, because Mackie has had to undergo the vexation of being arrested:

> This miserable Brown. Bad conscience personified. And that sort of man is the high police chief in London. It was good that I didn't call him to account. First I thought I'd do that. But then I considered at just the right moment that a deep, punishing look would run up and down his spine. I looked at him, and he wept bitterly. I get this trick from the Bible.

Gestures, like clothes, are borrowed, or stolen. The characters in *The Threepenny Opera* are *programmed* to behave as they do: they are spasmodic assemblages of various tricks of conduct, learned from sources ranging from the Bible to etiquette books (as at Polly's wedding). To live a completely feigned life, one needs skill as an actor; and they are all accomplished mimics. When Mackie's two wives, Polly Peachum and Lucy Brown, start screaming *(Eifersuchts-Duett),* they simply reecho one another's insults—a scene that dimly recalls Gay's satire of the slanging match of two rival sopranos in Handel's company; it might be staged in the manner of Harpo and Groucho Marx in *Duck Soup,* staring at each other in nightgowns through the frame of a nonexistent mirror, trying to discover the limits of aping.

Mackie's cutting stare at Brown is an example of what Brecht would soon start calling a *gestus:* a piece of conduct *quoted* in order to express a certain social situation. Mackie is, in a sense, a kind of human promptbook full of various *gestus,* to be hauled out at the playwright's convenience. But these *gestus* are in no sense private property: in fact, nothing in this promiscuous and thieving opera is private property. The *gestus* of the wronged woman's scolding is equally valid for Lucy and for Polly; indeed, these two characters are, as the *Eifersuchts-Duett* suggests, difficult to distinguish from each other. The most visible distinction between them—Lucy's pregnant belly—turns out to be mere padding, another dissembling, another sample of beggars' duds. In *Mann ist Mann,* the theme of human interchangeability is shown by the fact that no one notices when Galy Gay takes the place of Jeraiah Jip; in *The Threepenny Opera,* it is shown by the fact that *gestus* are effortlessly switched among the characters. Character is simply another aspect of setting (as Brecht wrote in his notes to *Mann ist Mann*): the characters are stage props for the presentation of *gestus.*

Every change from *The Beggar's Opera* is in the direction of farrago: unnecessary reduplication of plot lines, outbreaks of fatuously out-of-place oratory (such as the big speech, lifted out of *Happy End* and shoved into the prison scene in the 1931 version, during which Mackie says that the crime of robbing a bank is nothing compared to the crime of founding a bank), and, most of all, the curiously irrelevant, plot-clogging songs. Some of the songs were preexisting poems—such as the adaptations of Kipling—spliced in wherever they might fit (for example, the *Kanonen-Song,* in which Mackie and Brown remember the joys of serving in the British army in India, making hamburger out of the natives); others were preexisting poems crammed in any which way, even though they didn't fit anywhere. The score's most famous number, *Seeräuber-Jenny* (Pirate Jenny), is an example: originally it is a *divertissement,* sung by Polly to amuse her wedding guests. The song's protagonist, slaving in a bar and dreaming of a pirate ship that would exterminate the populace of London and whisk her away, isn't supposed to be Polly, or the later prostitute Jenny, or any of the characters in the story, but merely some girl working in a really cheap dive in Soho, whom Polly happened to overhear. So Polly's "possession" of the song is weak; and it is perfectly reasonable that it should wind up, in the film version, moved to the second act and sung by the prostitute Jenny, played by Weill's charismatic wife, Lotte Lenya. *Seeräuber-Jenny* is a free-floating song, a bit of poison that could turn up anywhere in order to contradict the happy end—where the Queen grants Mackie not only a stay of execution, but also a hereditary peerage, Castle Marmarel, and a pension of ten thousand pounds. We have seen that a *gestus* is a sort of free radical, independent of character or plot, a sneer or a scold or a submission that might alight anywhere; and the same is true of these extremely gestic songs.

What is the *gestus* of *Seeräuber-Jenny?* It is a song that concerns diseased wishing. German literature is extraordinarily rich in this theme; Goethe's *Faust,* for example, can be understood as a parable about what happens when a genie offers to grant a human being his every wish: as the man wishes and wishes, he seems to expand giddily into all sorts of cosmic apprehensions and fulfillments, dilations of being, but in fact he contracts steadily. As Mephistopheles tells Faust:

> You are in the end—just what you are.
> You can put on a wig with millions of locks,
> you can put your feet in elevator socks,—
> you always remain, just what you are.

By the end of Goethe's first part, Faust has wished for—and received—youth, wine, wisdom, and hot sex; but the man of so many wishes has only one wish left, the wish that he had never been born. Wishing collapses into its own abyss. A couplet of Auden's, from "Death's Echo" (1936), summarizes, from Mephistopheles' point of view, the whole Faustian theme: "The desires of the heart are as crooked as corkscrews, / Not to be born is the best for man." Wishing always contains the seeds of its own destruction, as Brecht wryly noted in a 1920 diary entry concerning the incoherence, the contradictoriness, of what he wanted: "Of course I want Timbuktu and a child and a house and no doors and to be alone in bed and to have a woman in bed, the apple off the tree and the timber too, and not to wield the axe and to have the tree complete with blossom, apples, and foliage." What good is a cake unless you can eat it *and* have it? Wishing tends to terminate in the nonexistence of the wisher, since wishing, logically, pertains to the null set—nowhere and no one. As Auden once wrote, "if the Chinese peasant asks, 'Why cannot I buy a Cadillac?' there are an infinite number of reasons which can only be summed up in the quite irrational answer, 'Because I am I.'" Not only is the whole world a hindrance to the fulfillment of your wishes, but *you* are a hindrance to the fulfillment of your wishes.

Pirate Jenny is also full of crooked desires. Locked in the prison of poverty and ill treatment, she dreams of a great explosion that will release her, will kill her persecutors—namely, everybody. The *gestus* of the song, then, is the progress from a real constriction to an unreal *boom:* in gymnastics, this would be a hunching-up followed by a jump, arms and legs spread wide. The *gestus* of Weill's music follows the same general pattern as the *Alabama-Song,* but with a somewhat different effect: a clattery stanza in which the melody is simply fixated prosody, a repetitive recitation figure, followed by a grand, swooping refrain. The stanza-setting flaunts its limitation: a dead-end melody expressive of Jenny's dead-end job. We even seem to hear the clink of her endless round of wiping glasses; she's trapped in her terse, monotonous speech-unit of complaint. But the refrain-setting escapes into a full statement of her ache of wishing: "And the ship with eight sails, / And with fifty cannons, / Will vanish with me." Critics have noted that this text is reminiscent of Senta's Ballad in Wagner's *The Flying Dutchman,* and I wonder if Weill might not have played a subtle game with Wagner's music as well. Wagner's theme for the Dutchman is a classic example of the hollow fifth: a fifth unsupported by either a major or a minor third and therefore ambiguous, disturbing, since the listener can't tell whether the tune is in a major or a minor key. The Dutchman is a kind of living ghost, condemned to roam the seas forever until he can find forgiveness; and Wagner therefore endowed him with the spectral quality of the hollow fifth. The refrain of *Seeräuber-Jenny* is also a kind of exercise in hollow fifths: it begins clearly in B minor *(Schiff mit acht),* but the following F♯ chord is hollow *(Segeln und mit);* then the harmony proceeds to E minor *(fünfzig Kanonen wird entschwinden mit),* but the final chord is, again, a hollow F♯ *(mir).* This is an ending with great rhetorical force, but with little sense of musical conclusion: after the great B-minor blam, the line droops, tapers off into an eviscerated half-cadence. Pirate Jenny's wish is a hollow wish; and the music's *gestus* reflects the hollowness of her wishing, a striking figure of consonance. The refrain is memorable, but not *achieved,* in the way that the little anapest-iamb figure that governs the stanza is achieved. The inexorability of ta-ta-tump, tump-tump, remains uncompromised by the refrain; and Jenny remains stuck in the Soho dive. You always remain, just what you are.

EX. 4.5. Weill, *The Threepenny Opera: Pirate Jenny,* refrain

Ruined Wishes: Jenny and Lilian

The theatre of Hauptmann, Brecht, and Weill is a theatre of ruined wishes and broken songs. The songs are mostly gests, in that they tell stories; but their stories often have little to do with the story of the play in which they are sung. The stories inside the songs are usually better stories than the general plot of the play: there is no master narrative to connect and justify the random spasms of singing. In 1929, the team attempted to recapture the success of *The Threepenny Opera* with *Happy End*; this time Hauptmann was almost allowed to take credit for writing the play, since the text was ascribed to an imaginary "Dorothy Lane," whose play was "translated" into German by Elisabeth Hauptmann. In every way, *Happy End* is an intensification of the farrago method of *The Threepenny Opera*: the overall plot is still more inept and spasmodic, and the songs are still more narratively concentrated, gestical. The plot is a feeble thing concerning criminals and Salvation Army workers in Chicago; but to think of *Happy End* is not to think of Bill's Ballhaus in Chicago—the ostensible setting—but of Bill's Ballhaus in Bilbao, as described in the *Bilbao-Song,* one of the hit tunes. Underneath Chicago, itself a European hallucination of America derived from gangster movies, there is a still more hallucinatory landscape, a mishmash of exotica ranging from Spain to Burma. This preposterous locale is the domain of wishing—a wishing so thoroughly corrupted that even in the land of Cockaigne, the wisher finds only rejection and despair. It is as if Gauguin went to Tahiti *in order to find* fever, rot, and toothless prostitutes.

Weill's most thorough critique of wishing can be found in *Surabaya-Johnny,* in which Lilian impersonates a sixteen-year-old girl swept off her feet by a sailor arriving from Burma:

> I asked you what your job was:
> you said, sure as I'm standing here,
> you had something to do with the railroad
> and nothing to do with the sea.
> You said a lot, Johnny,
> no word was true, Johnny,
> you have betrayed me, Johnny,
> from the moment we met.
> I hate you so, Johnny,
> as you stand there and grin, Johnny.
> Take your pipe out of your mouth, you dog.
>   Surabaya-Johnny, why treat me so crappy?
>   Surabaya-Johnny, my god, and I love you so!

> Surabaya-Johnny, why can't I be happy?
> You've got no heart, Johnny, and I love you so!

It was nice of Lilian, the Salvation Army worker in Chicago, to entertain the folks at the bar by singing that—even though Bill kept exclaiming, No, don't sing! It has often been noted that the melody of Weill's refrain is based on that of the *Moritat* in *The Threepenny Opera*: both tunes are generated by scale degrees $\hat{3}-\hat{5}-\hat{6}$. In the *Moritat*, however, this figure has the clipped rigidity of an organ-grinder grinding his organ: the *gestus* of the *Moritat* is a kind of pattern-unit of speech, to which any curt, disobliging narrative could be chanted. (We've seen similar icons of talking in Wagner's Kothner and Weill's Pirate Jenny.) But the stories told in the *Moritat*—how Mackie eluded capture after his murders of Schmul Meier, Jenny Towler, seven children in Soho, and so forth and so forth—are extremely short, mere flashes of narrative, almost more pictorial than discursive. In 1930 Weill referred to his *Mahagonny* opera as a "musical picture-sheet *[Bilderbogen]*"; and the *Moritat* could be called a musical comic book, giving glimpses of various plot lines unused in *The Threepenny Opera*. By contrast, the refrain of *Surabaya-Johnny* is expansive, like most of Weill's refrains concerning wishes: the $\hat{3}-\hat{5}-\hat{6}$ pattern is distended, raised, pushed out, as the singer tries to force it into expressive shape; but no amount of struggling can fully conquer the crisp narrowness of the *gestus*. The organ-grinder of the *Moritat* may be replaced by a kind of Hawaiian guitarist, but, just as Pirate Jenny found herself at last in a kind of harmonic collapse, so the singer of *Surabaya-Johnny* finds herself fighting against a static melodic figure that resists the pressure exerted on it. In a sense, the $\hat{3}-\hat{5}-\hat{6}$ figure obstinately belongs to the ballad singer of the *Moritat,* no matter how frantically Lilian tries to abuse it into sentimental expression.

Weill liked to find ways of giving the lie to his dreamers—even the unromantic dreamers of *Happy End,* mooning over creepy and sodden sex in Bilbao, or Burma, or the Mandalay of the *Song von Mandelay,* where impatient customers, lined up at Mother Goddam's brothel, shoot off their guns to encourage those in front of them to hurry up. Weill's hieroglyphs of wishing often contain built-in deflations: the melodies start off with a leaping assertion of will—*SuraBAya-Johnny,* or *Und das SCHIFF*—but quickly sink, compromise themselves with some lower plane of expectation. In the refrain of *Surabaya-Johnny,* Lilian is so flattened by disappointment that she finds herself singing an E♭ in the phrase "You've got no heart." For comparison, one might take Arlen's *Over the Rainbow* from *The Wizard of Oz* (1939), which also begins with a leaping assertion of will—"SomeWHERE"—but which, as it continues, seems to keep strong faith with that initial *gestus;* or does its descending melodic spiral also suggest that Dorothy never left Kansas, just as Pirate Jenny never left the bar?

Inscriptive Tetrachords

Weill thought that gestic music ought to be "naive," and to some extent he sought *gestus* in the very simplest sort of musical formulae. The $\hat{3}$–$\hat{5}$–$\hat{6}$ figure of the *Moritat* is strongly gestic, suggestive of detachment and unstoppable motion; but there is another figure from *The Threepenny Opera* that seems to me the triumph of naïveté in *gestus*. This occurs in the third-act finale, when Peachum steps out of character—not that any of the characters have to step far to step out of character—in order to tell the audience that there's going to be a happy ending: *So wendet alles sich am End zum Glück.* This is accompanied by a descending tetrachord: scale degrees $\hat{1}$–$\hat{7}$–$\hat{6}$–$\hat{5}$ in C minor. It goes on and on, in the manner of an ostinato—but nothing else is happening, except for the Peachums' rhythmic declamation. We have, then, a passacaglia bass in the absence of a passacaglia harmonization: a naked thumping, a *gestus* isolated from any musical context. The descending four-note scalar bass (such as *la-sol-fa-mi*) has an extremely distinguished history; it is the ostinato of Monteverdi's *Lamento della Ninfa,* and it is easy to think of any number of fine old pieces, by Ferrari, Sances, and so on, with similar ground basses. But it may also suggest boogie-woogie. Weill decontextualized the figure: if it can mean lamentation or boogie-woogie, it means everything, or nothing. All the opera's elaboration of drama and music is coming to an end, is fining down to a *gestus* of pure abstract motion—a *gestus* of reality, not to be evaded by the preposterous doings of the plot. As Peachum says over the ground bass, "In real life their end is bad, for royal messengers on horseback seldom come forward." In some sense, the $\hat{1}$–$\hat{7}$–$\hat{6}$–$\hat{5}$ figure is a *gestus* of fundamental being-there, almost beneath semantic construing: it is implacable and immitigable, anti-theatrical, the opposite of pretense and play. The ironical Weill has committed this crime against the *lamento,* against opera itself, within

EX. 4.6. Weill, *The Threepenny Opera*: there's going to be a happy ending

EX. 4.6. (*Continued*)

Glück.
end.
So leicht und
So sweet and
fried - lich wä - re un - ser
peace - ful all our lives would)

an opera—a sign of the anti-operatic nature of *The Threepenny Opera*. As the flimsy play exposes its illusory nature, Weill's musical attention shifts to the frame around the play: the solid $\hat{1}-\hat{7}-\hat{6}-\hat{5}$ figure seems to stand for the proscenium arch itself.

A figure for lamentation has turned into a figure for fate, or for reality. Weill used obstinate four-note basses for many different purposes, but above all this figure is the basic unit of his conception of tragedy. For example, in *Beat! Beat! Drums!* (1942), the second of Weill's *Four Whitman Songs,* Lincoln's funeral dead-marches to the tread of a bass tetrachord. But what is more original is Weill's habit of using this figure to represent the disguised or latent tragedy inside a comedy. In *The Threepenny Opera,* the descending tetrachord is found overtly at the end, but in subtle ways elsewhere. Perhaps we've already examined a hidden version of the tragic tetrachord in the refrain of *Seeräuber-Jenny:* an ordinary harmonization of $\hat{1}-\hat{7}-\hat{6}-\hat{5}$ in the minor would be i–v⁶–iv⁶–V, which would yield, in the B minor of the refrain of *Seeräuber-Jenny,* a fine Phrygian cadence with a bass of B–A–G–F♯. By hollowing out the F♯ chords, Weill provided instead a bass line of B–F♯–G–F♯, but Pirate Jenny's fury of wishing contains a built-in heartache, in that it bears such close musical similarity to a ground bass of lamentation; in Ernst Bloch's brilliant phrase, it is a combination of "*chanson and funeral march.*" The text of *The Threepenny Opera* is often farcical; but the music, with its hand-cranked inexorabilities *(Moritat, Salomon-Song),* its figures of misery and terror, often tends toward semantic zones of remarkable saturation. The farce dreams of tragedy; and the music is the dream of the text.

* * *

The closest approach to *explicit* tragedy in *The Threepenny Opera* is the scene labeled *Grabschrift* (grave inscription), in which Macheath, expecting soon to be hanged, sings a translation of François Villon's *Ballade des pendus:*

You brother men, who live when we are dead,
thinking of us, don't let your hearts grow hard,
watching them hoist us gallows-high, don't laugh;
don't smile a stupid smile behind your beard.

This is accompanied by a steady four-note bass: scale degrees $\hat{5}-\hat{6}-\hat{5}-\hat{2}$, in
E minor, slowly changing into other four-note figures with the same pattern of
rise and fall; but by the end of the stanza, when Macheath begs God's forgiveness,
the figure has reduced itself to a stark two-note figure, $\hat{5}-\hat{6}$ (F#–G, since the implicit key is now B minor)—a figure that becomes the entire musical text of the
next number, the Walk to the Gallows. The *gestus* of these two figures is, kinesthetically, a procession; affectively, a kind of pendulum or chime, marking the
terror of counting out the last few minutes of a man's life. And the two figures are
also hieroglyphs, in that they represent an inscription, an epitaph, the musical
equivalent of something carved in stone—$\hat{5}-\hat{6}-\hat{5}-\hat{2}$ is already quite terse, and
$\hat{5}-\hat{6}$ is still more abbreviated, a mere *r.i.p.* Brecht liked to decorate his epic stage
with captions, slogans, morals, chapter headings; and Weill wrote music that
reinforced the graphological character of Brecht's theatre.

To my mind, Weill was the twentieth century's most gifted composer of musical inscriptions: notably in the *Berliner Requiem* (1928), with a superb text by
Brecht consisting entirely, as Weill noted, of "memorial tablets, epitaphs, and
funeral chants":

Praise the night and the darkness that close you in! . . .
Praise with your hearts the bad memory of Heaven!
And that it knows
Neither your name nor your face
No one knows that you still exist. . . .

Here rests the virgin Johanna Beck.
When she died, already they'd turned her into dreck. . . .

After they had struck him down, we arranged him so that he lost his face
through the dents left by our fists. We made him unrecognizable so that he
might be no person's son. . . . And we buried him under a stone, under an
arch, called Arch of Triumph. Which weighed a thousand tons, so that the
Unknown Soldier might in no circumstances be resurrected on Judgment Day.

Brecht was a poet much concerned with the ways in which faces lose their profile.
In a famous poem of 1920, *Erinnerung an die Marie A.* (which, outfitted with
a stolen French tune, became a cabaret song), the poet, staring up at the clouds,

tries to recollect an old girlfriend; but only the kiss is recalled, not the face that was kissed, and all memory vanishes as the clouds vanish. And the Unknown Soldier in the *Berliner Requiem* is one of several soldiers in Brecht's work whose faces unfeature themselves, discompose, decompose. The *gestus* of a face is perishable, less a memory than an oblivion; but the *gestus* of an inscription is a monument that seems more lasting than the stone in which it is carved—even if the inscription, as in the case of the Unknown Soldier, merely commemorates a forgetting. A *gestus* always struggles to retain its efficacy, its pointedness, its incision, against a general asemic blur, a confusion that tends to swallow up all figures.

Brecht's Photograms

There is an unusual pendent to the story of Brecht's fascination with *gestus* and inscription: his later career as a conscious hieroglypher. During the Second World War, Brecht compiled his *War Primer,* a set of news photographs captioned, in the manner of the old emblem books, with rhyming quatrains: "photograms," Brecht called them. An example will suggest the remarkable semantic power Brecht could achieve by inscribing a short poem on a picture. The photograph shows a series of crosses, on one of which perches a glove, fingers pointing at heaven; a sentence in English, printed on the photo, explains this strange sight:

A line of crude crosses marks American graves near Buna. A grave registrar's glove accidently points toward the sky.

The glove gives a touch of comic pathos to this extremely serious scene: as if a hand were thrust up from underground, waving "Hi!" or "Help!"—even though you can't help a dead man. Brecht saw the glove's implicit *gestus* as a petition to heaven, a sort of manual prayer to God to avenge the wrongs that put these soldiers in their graves; and the quatrain he wrote for this photo suggests that this prayer is misdirected, for it can be answered not by God, but only by the reader:

At school they said that up there in the sky
Lived God, avenger of injustices;
When we rose up to kill, we had to die.
And *you* must punish those who murdered us.

The poem interprets the gesture; the gesture illustrates the poem. A whole dramatic scene about the absurdity of displacing moral responsibility from earth to heaven is compressed into a *tableau mort* and a few words—words that provide a temporary voice for dead soldiers. "The communication / Of the dead is

A LINE OF CRUDE CROSSES MARKS AMERICAN
GRAVES NEAR BUNA. A GRAVE REGISTRAR'S
GLOVE ACCIDENTALLY POINTS TOWARD THE SKY

Wir hörten auf der Schulbank, daß dort oben
Ein Rächer allen Unrechts wohnt und trafen
Den Tod, als wir zum Töten uns erhoben.
Die uns hinaufgeschickt müßt ihr bestrafen.

FIG. 8. Bertolt Brecht, photogram of crosses, 1955 (Reinhold Grimm, "Marxist Emblems: Bertolt Brecht's *War Primer*," *Comparative Literature Studies* 12, no. 3 [1975]: 284)

tongued with fire beyond the language of the living," T. S. Eliot wrote; and in Brecht's quatrain the speech of the dead flashes forth on the margin between *nacheinander* and *nebeneinander,* in a poem that abbreviates itself in time, extends itself in space. In 1957 Hanns Eisler set this quatrain to music, in *Kriegsfibel:* thirty seconds of choral declamation, accompanied by fast, insistent accordion-whiffs. Here a photogram becomes a phonogram—a rare triplet, in which a poem, a musical composition, and a photograph combine to effect a single punch.

Villonaud

DEFINITION. A *villonaud* is a poem imitating the style of François Villon; a term coined by Pound on analogy with *villanelle*. This term is used here to mean an art work that presents the stark essentials of the human condition.

We have seen that a *gestus* is easily detachable from its context: whether a telling act is instinctive, or habitual, or self-consciously adopted, it is still a performance, independent of the performer. It is also surprisingly ahistorical—surprisingly in that Brecht hated such notions as Mankind with a capital M, or Fate, or any doctrine that suggested that human beings were incapable of adaptation and that human circumstances were fixed. And yet, Brecht seemed to conceive history as the slow rotation of *gestus* through various sorts of human agents: the oppressors change, the oppressed change, styles of footwear change, but figures of stomping boots and arms warding off blows remain the same. Modern sociobiologists, such as Edward O. Wilson, regard life on earth as a competition not among species, not among individuals, but among genes; perhaps Brecht could be said to have regarded life as a competition among various *gestus*.

Most of Brecht's best plays—perhaps I should say most of the best plays published under the brand name "Brecht"—are difficult to place historically, and are set in neverland, whatever the stage directions might say. Brecht was never by temperament a chronicler; he offered not construings of history but deconstructions of history. As he noted in the later 1930s, "*Realistic* means: revealing the causal complex of society / unmasking the ruling viewpoint as the viewpoint of the rulers / . . . concrete and making abstraction possible." This closely resembles what we now call post-structuralist modes of thought: Brecht wanted a theatre that depicted not effects, but causes; not actualities, but abstractable potencies.

So, in order to understand modern Germany in *The Threepenny Opera,* Brecht sought a schematic diagram, a flowchart of the passage of money among beggars, whores, and policemen, derived from eighteenth-century London; and in order to understand eighteenth-century London, he roamed as far as Kipling's India (in the *Kanonen-Song*) and Villon's fifteenth-century France *(Zuhälter-Ballade, Ballade vom angenehmen Leben, Salomon-Song, Ballade in der Macheath Jedermann Abbitte leistet).* Brecht wanted to understand the forces that generate the world we know, and so he put pressure on "reality" until it decomposed itself into all sorts of strange, distant places. The "causal complex" behind society seems an infinitely reticulated thing; and when Weill set *The Threepenny Opera* to music, he widened the scope of the web still further, to North and South America, by means of tango rhythms and other echoes of popular music. (The name *Mahagonny* was evidently taken from a recording of a *langsamer Shimmy*—actually a cakewalk.) The Brecht-Weill collaborations tend to illustrate the rickety, mis-synthesized quality of modern civilization by means of patchwork construction and an incoherently vast range of allusion—just like another ambitious work of the 1920s, T. S. Eliot's *The Waste Land* (1922), which, if read properly, is a kind of performance score, full of pop songs (there really *was* a *Shakespearean Rag*) and citations from Wagner. Pound, in *Hugh Selwyn Mauberley* (1920), denounced the "botched civilization" of modern Europe; and when you live in a botched civilization, you show its character by assembling hunks of cultural refuse from the most disparate sources. Gertrude Stein said of Oakland, California, "there is no there there"—and perhaps, for some of the Modernists, there was no there anywhere.

Text-Embezzling in The Threepenny Opera

As culture shatters into jagged decontextualized chunks, so authorship tends to dissolve—not so much into that transcendental anonymity proposed by Barthes, but into an unseemly competition for credit among various plagiarists. Who wrote *The Threepenny Opera?* Brecht, Hauptmann, and Gay are plausible candidates; but, in a sense, the primal author is none of the above but François Villon, the fifteenth-century Parisian scholar, murderer, pimp, carouser, and poet, who narrowly escaped hanging for his thievery. To think of *The Threepenny Opera* is to think of German adaptations of Villon's language:

So we lived, for six months or more,
in the bordello, pimp and whore.

Only he who lives in wealth, lives pleasantly.

The rain will wash us well, wash off our dirt,
and wash the flesh we fed with too much care;
the eyes that saw too much and craved for more,
the ravens see and peck and hack right out.

Ragmen, whores, AND whore-drivers,
idlers, wastrels, and bird-brains,
killers, lady washroom-sweepers,
I pray them all, forgive my sins.

The German version of these lines would rank among Brecht's finest achievements—if Brecht had written them. But they were stolen from a book of Villon translations by a former army officer, K. L. Ammer, whose versions of Villon Brecht had appropriated in his early plays as well. (Brecht often made little changes: for instance, Ammer wrote *Nur wer in Wohlstand schwelgt, lebt angenehm*—Only he who revels in wealth, lives pleasantly—but Brecht altered *schwelgt* to *lebt*.) Eventually, Ammer discovered that *The Threepenny Opera* contained his uncredited work—and so it came to pass that a royalty on every performance of one of the most popular theatrical works ever written went to a militarist and anti-semite. *The Threepenny Opera*, then, isn't only an investigation of the circulation of money; it's also an investigation of the circulation of texts, a study in the embezzlement of poems. Brecht's and Weill's concept of theatre is proto-post-Modernist, not only in its goal of deconstructing the power relations in society, but also in its technique of deliberate *bricolage*, piecing together preexisting material lumpily, without any secure assimilation into a whole. Each *gestus* builds around itself a private landscape, a private society, a private India or Paris. It's little wonder that in *Rise and Fall of the City of Mahagonny*, the characters construct a fake ship out of furniture in order to sing a song about Alaska: in this sort of theatre, each song demands its own locale, its own region of human experience.

In Villon's *Le testament*, Brecht discovered regions of human experience that underlie his whole canon. *Le testament*, with its stark sense that life consists of theft, murder, whoring, and praying, was a trove of *gestus*, a collection of arias waiting for a dramatic context. Many of the famous parts of *Le testament* appear in some corner or other of Brecht's work. For example:

Mais ou sont les neiges d'antan? (Villon, *Ballade des dames du temps jadis*)

But where are the snows of yester-year? (Rossetti, *The Ballad of Dead Ladies*)

Wo ist der Schnee vom vergangenen Jahr? (Brecht, *Die Rundköpfe und die Spitzköpfe*)

(In 1939, Weill set *Nannas Lied,* from which the last example is taken, to complete his personal Brecht-Villon canon.) Villon also appears in some of Brecht's lyric poems: for example, in a sonnet-advertisement for a 1930 reprint of Ammer's translations of Villon—an edition partly provoked by the controversy that arose when Alfred Kerr accused Brecht of plagiarism. In this poem, Brecht suggested that the chief *gestus* in *Le testament* is a flinging of dung:

> From decaying paper, once again in print,
> You have the testament where one bestows
> His excrement on everyone he knows—

Villon tended indeed to think gestically: for Villon, human behavior is all clench, poke, clasp of hands. When we think of the sparest depiction of mankind—mankind *an sich,* mankind unextenuated—we may think of the Preacher's declaration that all is vanity; or of King Lear on naked forked animals; or of Beckett's Molloy, endlessly redistributing stones in his pockets; but Brecht thought of the poetry of Villon. If *realism* is the art of laying bare the causal complex of society, then Villon, the nakedest of poets, is the master of laying bare.

We've already noted the extreme simplicity of some of the music that Weill wrote for the Villon translations: Villon's texts seem to invite passacaglia basses and organ-grinding tunes, popular music, but not music of any special time or locality—ahistorical or prehistorical popular music, the imaginary demotic music of the whole human race. If *The Threepenny Opera* is a drama of costuming and disguise, the Villon sections pertain to the shivering skin that lies beneath all the ingenious and deceptive clothes. Weill attempted to find music appropriate to radical nakedness. If the farce dreams of becoming a tragedy, that tragedy is located precisely in the Paris of *Le testament.*

Pound's Le testament: *Troubadour Imitations*

Some of the Villon songs of *The Threepenny Opera* also appear in a slightly earlier opera, Pound's *Le testament* (written mostly in May 1921, edited and rewritten by George Antheil at "11 o'clock Dec 31, 1923," as the last page of the score notes); and this important work represents an alternate fulfillment of some of the same Modernist aspirations behind the work of Hauptmann, Brecht, and Weill. Pound's musical training was sporadic, unthorough, and his melodies certainly lack the charm of Weill's; but he had gifts as a musician and worked for years as a professional music critic for *The New Age.* Somehow he managed, with some help from Agnes Bedford, Walter Rummel, and Antheil, to write an opera that constructs a remarkably full Modernist vision of the rhyming of an old civilization with a new one: the more closely Pound approached archaic musical material and fifteenth-century Paris, the more exactly he found himself in Modernist Europe. Brecht looted antiquities, to prove that theft was the central attribute of modern life—we live in a stolen culture, *tempo rubato*. Pound carefully borrowed his antiquities from the museum, to provide sturdy cultural underpinnings to a botched civilization—to shore fragments against the ruins, as Pound wrote in Canto 8, borrowing from *The Waste Land*.

In Pound's *Le testament*, it is 1462, and Villon, soon to be hanged, is writing his will within hailing distance of a tavern, and a church, and a brothel. Pound evidently felt that these three establishments take care of most human needs; and so the public squares of modern Europe, sufficiently desophisticated, stripped down, would look exactly the same.

Villon, by bequeathing his poems to his friend Ythier, to his aged mother, to the decayed prostitute La Hëaulmiere, endows his otherwise mute companions with voices; in this way Villon's testament remembers and preserves a whole culture, in fragments of sound. We've seen that iconographically, Stravinsky was properly shown carrying an eraser, as in Arnold Newman's photograph; and the eraser is also Pound's major tool. Pound was by temperament an anthologist: and his books—*ABC of Reading, Guide to Kulchur*—represent human culture in a severely deleted condition, with all the boring and useless parts omitted. In this sense, *Le testament* is the opera of mankind, with all the prose left out. To facilitate a BBC performance of 1931, Pound wrote some spoken dialogue in "hobo language" to connect the musical numbers—thus turning his opera into a "melodrama" to celebrate the quinquecentennial of Villon's birth. The 1931 version begins as follows:

(fade in church bell tolling, hold, and stop; add full echo)
SERGEANT OF POLICE: (pompously) For violence against particular, for violence against the King's officers that he did in the city of Paris . . . .
CAPTAIN OF WATCH: Stt! not so loud, now.
SGT: (softer) . . . . that he did speak with foul language . . . .
PRIVATE OF THE WATCH: A clerk, sir? Do you think he will plead scortum ante?
CAPT: I don't care if he pleads pickled halibut, your job is to run 'em in.
    Twenty of you for the six of 'em, easy takin'.
SGT: Easy takin'?
CAPT: A skirt, that'll fetch him.

Then we hear Villon trying to persuade the barman to give him some wine on credit, even though he's about to be hanged; and the thought of dying segues into the first number, *Et mourut Paris et Helaine* (as the title is given here). But originally—ten years earlier—Pound had conceived very little prose: *Le testament* seemed to be a *Singspiel* without much *Spiel,* abruptly juxtaposed musical numbers with only hints of connective tissue among them.

If *Le testament* is the basic play of the human race, the stark play of desire against coercion, of Eros against Thanatos, it is also the whole musical canon, stripped bare of all that Pound considered the vain excrescences of the art of music as it mis-developed through loss of relation to the sung word. Pound (rather like his hated Wagner) believed that music and poetry were ideally one, and that the fission of the two arts after the time of the troubadours had harmed both; so Pound's new *Gesamtkunst* attempts a radical re-synthesis of word and music, a neomedievalism. Few Modernist artists ever pursued figures of consonance between literature and music with such ferocity; indeed, by choosing as his collaborator a fifteenth-century poet, Pound even attempted to create a kind of consonance between two historical eras, by turning Villon into an honorary Modernist. As we'll see, Villon is a surprisingly engaged and demanding colleague.

We are used to hearing twentieth-century music that's more polyphonic than homophonic, music in which old triadic harmony is emphatically rejected. But we are still not completely used to hearing twentieth-century music that (like *Le testament*) tends to reject the notion of harmony itself as a dangerous perversion of the truth of monody. In this way, Pound is the Arvo Pärt of 1921, writing the Passion of St. Bacchus—a pagan equivalent of recent neomedieval music. Remembering his old theory that the exterminated Albigensian religion wasn't a deviant form of Christianity but an actual efflorescence of the Eleusinian mystery cult, maintained underground from antiquity through the middle ages, Pound wrote in *Credo* (1930):

> Given the material means I would replace the statue of Venus on the cliffs of Terracina. I would erect a temple to Artemis in Park Lane. I believe that a light from Eleusis persisted throughout the middle age and set beauty in the song of Provence and of Italy.

Pound thought that Arnaut Daniel and Guido Cavalcanti were practicing pagans. He didn't make a similar claim for Villon, but Villon's soul may have seemed instinctively pagan: "Villon . . . represents the end of a tradition, the end of the mediaeval dream, the end of a whole body of knowledge, fine, subtle, that had run from Arnaut to Guido Cavalcanti. . . . I personally have been reduced to setting [Villon] to music as I cannot translate [him]." Since he heard an echo of Arnaut's voice in Villon, it is fitting that Pound's Villon music should have a strong troubadour coloring.

In a sense, *Le testament* is the sacred opera of a religion that has never entirely lacked converts, the cult of Venus. The opera's longest number is La Hëaulmiere's

Ha, vieillesse felonne et fiere, in which the old woman, still fiercely carnal, vene-real, laments the shriveling of her sexual organs—as J. M. Synge translated it (1909), in slightly expurgated form:

> my two eyes have died out within my head—those eyes that would be laugh-ing to the men,—my nose has a hook on it, my ears are hanging down, and my lips are sharp and skinny.
>
> That's what's left over from the beauty of a right woman—a bag of bones, and the legs the like of two sausages going beneath it.

Her major regret seems not that she was a whore, but that at the age of eighty, she can no longer be one.

Pound's music is profoundly anachronistic. Not quite all the music was writ-ten by Pound: for example, both the text and the tune for the Priest's hymn to the Virgin, *Mere au sauveur,* were taken from Walter Rummel's 1913 collection of troubadour songs (with translations by Pound). Guillaume li Viniers's tune doesn't seem at all out of place in the musical texture settled by Pound in the preceding numbers—even though the music of the troubadours was several cen-turies out of date in the Paris of 1462, as wrong as the music of Bach would have been. But *Le testament* is an opera about the fundamentals of human experience; and, just as Pound wanted Villon's nakedness of response to life, so he wanted the troubadours' nakedness of musical response to the text. And he wanted pa-ganness, even for his Priest: for even the Priest is a pagan. The pagan associations of the troubadour *melos,* far more than the pious Provençal words, betray the true object of the Priest's devotion—for we soon see him, dressed in lay clothes, trying to slink into the brothel. Throughout the first half of the opera, the char-acters sing monodically, for the most part, and sound rather troubadour-like, in that the secular instrumentation (mandolin, bassoon, cymbal, and so forth) and the strophic organization of the text tend to preclude much Gregorian feeling—plainchant is an art that chiefly pertains to prose, not to poetry.

On the other hand, Pound's method of text-setting would have confused any self-respecting troubadour. Almost all troubadour music (except the *descort,* or irregular song) is strophic: the troubadour didn't invent a new tune for each stanza. But Pound could proceed for long stretches without repeating *any* me-lodic element; and this continuous pitch variation—an endless melody far more interminable than the so-called endless melodies of Wagner—creates a peculiarly disoriented response in the listener. Although there are medieval musical forms that feature a regular change of tune—the *sequence,* the *lai*—the boundaries of the tune are quite well established: in the sequence, for example, the tune is re-peated verbatim, as a rigid couplet, before the composer moves to the next tune.

But in *Le testament,* Pound provided few musical cues to indicate where one stanza ends and the next begins; even the famous refrains—such as *Mais ou sont les neiges d'antan?* and *En ce bordeau ou tenons nostre estat*—usually (but not always) reappear altered in rhythm, altered in melodic shape, extremely varied within a narrow span of four notes, cresting at F and descending to C. Pound's music, for the most part, is resolutely anti-strophic, anti-pattern: the singer's words have an intricate shape, pointedly recollecting what's gone before and anticipating what's to come; but the singer's pitches seem to dwell in a continuous, directionless present tense, in which each note occupies a precisely determined but wholly unpredictable amount of time and then moves (often stepwise) up or down according to no discernable principle.

EX. 5.1. Pound, *Le testament:* three settings of *Mais ou sont les neiges d'antan?*

Furthermore, Pound had an odd habit, on occasion, of working the melody down to a final that's a little lower than most of the notes we've previously heard: for example, *Dictes moy ou* (the *Ballade des dames du temps jadis*) moves in a narrow range in which D seems the lower terminus; but as the first stanza ends, the melody comes to rest first tentatively, then emphatically, on C. (Similar practices are found in some genuine troubadour songs, though there the subfinal is more commonly used as a resting place, a secondary cadential degree, than as the actual last note.) The melody, like a magician's top hat, has a false bottom, providing another aspect of insecurity and deception amid the general patternlessness. Most of the music in the opera's first half is written without sharps or flats, and in the middle range of the singer's voice; and yet I can scarcely imagine music that would be harder for a singer to memorize.

Perhaps this sort of music lacks *gestus*. Since there is so little repetition, the musical phrases don't settle into apprehensible units, but remain in a kind of white-note limbo. Weill thought of his gestic music as a fixing, a nailing-down, of the prosody, the language form; but I find that Pound's music renders the shape of Villon's language *less* clear than it would be if simply read aloud. This is because Pound and Weill had exactly opposite notions of the relation of music to text. Weill, when he looked for a gestic rhythm, looked first to the basic ictus of the line—the pattern of strong beats and weak, of long syllables and short—and then to the ways in which semantic emphasis would tend to grasp this pattern, parcel it out into larger units. Weill conceived poetic meters as musical meters not yet assigned their proper 3/4 or 4/4 or 3/8 value. But Pound had little interest in meters that consisted of a regular alternation of stressed and unstressed syllables; indeed, he believed that Modernist verse should be composed "in the sequence of the musical phrase, not in sequence of a metronome," and he thought that one of the great achievements of the movement was its liberation from predetermined rhythms: "To break the pentameter, that was the first heave." Surely one of the reasons for his decision to write an opera entirely in French and Provençal stemmed from his desire to write music to words that lacked a stress-generated rhythmic pattern, free words open to free music.

Le testament: *Speech as Music*

Pound considered, correctly, that he had an extremely subtle ear for rhythm. As he wrote in 1917:

> there is vers libre with accent heavily marked as a drum-beat . . . and on the other hand I think I have gone as far as can profitably be gone in the other direction (and perhaps too far). I mean I do not think one can use to any advantage rhythms much more tenuous and imperceptible than some I have used.

But when, four years later, he began *Le testament,* he found ways of using to advantage rhythms much more tenuous and imperceptible than any rhythm available without musical notation. Indeed, *Le testament* does not use time signatures in the ordinary sense; the time signatures (evidently devised by Antheil) appear in parentheses beneath the bars when necessary—which is often after every bar. Thus in the first five bars of the first number, we have 11/16, 3/4, 5/8, 7/8, and 2/4, along with a note in Antheil's handwriting with a little box drawn around it: "mechanically ♪ = ♪ always"—a useful piece of advice amid these incoherently fluctuating meters. Eventually we come to some metrical notation of a complexity that was, as far as I know, unprecedented: in *Dame du ciel,* for example, there is a sequence of three bars in 33/16, 21/8, and 36/32; but I speak only of the soprano line, for the orchestra plays beneath this in 8/4, 8/4, and 5/4. Such notation has nothing to do with prosody, if prosody implies regularity or recurrence; far from being sensitive to the fixed eight- or ten-syllable count of Villon's lines, Pound has done everything to erase the stable boundaries of the line. This is not because he wanted to turn Villon's poetry into prose, but because Pound regarded a line of verse as poetical not to the degree that it *conforms* to a fixed pattern, but to the degree that it *deviates* from a fixed pattern. A good line of traditional verse, to Pound, is a line in which the reader is aware of the hesitations and accelerations, the counterpoint between the real rhythm of the words and the imaginary rhythm of the verse template. So, in *Le testament,* Pound imagined, beneath the song, a steady syllabic motion of (say) an eight-syllable line, chanted to uniform eighth notes; but what Pound notated was an unsteady, almost seasick motion of hesitations and accelerations, as the line presented itself as a concretion of phonemes and sememes instead of an arithmetical count of neutral syllables. Occasionally, as in *Dame du ciel,* the orchestra seems aware of the mechanical prosody-beat, of which the singer never seems aware; but for the most part, Pound's rhythm is less rhythm (in the ordinary sense) than *departure* from rhythm. The concreteness of the text is made conspicuous through a species of music that overstresses the bumps and gnarls of speech. The music provides an icon of the deviance of the text from pattern.

EX. 5.2. Pound, *Le testament:* beginning

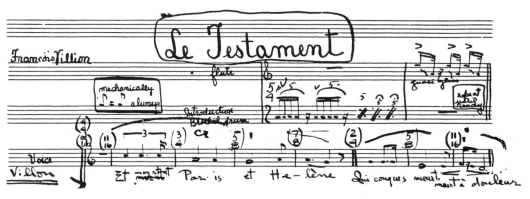

Pound wanted *Le testament* to be speechlike—a quintessence of speech, more profoundly garrulous than anything else on earth. He once described how the Abbé Rousselot "had made a machine for measuring the duration of verbal components. A quill or tube held in the nostril, a less shaved quill or other tube in the mouth, and your consonants signed as you spoke them." The score of *Le testament* behaves almost on this level of phonogram: it is a machine for the exact reproduction of faint inflections of rhythm. And in this sense it is gestic after all: the *gestus* is located not at the coarse level of prosody, still less at the level of the arm movements of the actors on stage, but at the level of the nostrils, the lips, the tongue. The music is an intensifying of pronunciation, a way of feeling more strongly how muscles move within the organs of speech: "The HOLE point of my moozik bein that the moozik fits the WORDS and not some OTHER WORDS." The feel of the mouth muscles becomes a tactile sign that arrests the meaning of the text.

Not long after he worked with Pound on the score to *Le testament*, Antheil began an operatic collaboration with Joyce, *Mr. Bloom and the Cyclops* (based on the "Cyclops" chapter of *Ulysses*), of which nothing seems to remain but the setting of the chapter's first sentence, "I was just passing the time of day with old Troy of the D.M.P at the corner of Arbour hill . . ." Antheil set Joyce's prose syllabically, with a different meter in each bar (4/4, 7/4, 11/4). The few pages of score look like a cross between *Le testament* and *Ballet Mécanique:* if the opera had been finished, it might have been the vehicle through which Pound's bizarre ideas of text-setting entered the repertoire of musical Modernism.

Schoenberg's Erwartung *and the Rejection of Sequence*

Where in music do we find text-setting similar to Pound's? Ceaseless but unrepeating melodic movement, within rhythmic units that are derived simply from counting the number of sixteenth notes and rests within a phrase, isn't a feature of troubadour songs, or of the ballades and rondeaux familiar to musicians contemporary with Villon, or of operatic recitative, even of the loosest, driest sort. The *seconda prattica* of Monteverdi comes a little closer; but melodic repetition is present, or latent, in Monteverdi's ariosi: a line of repeated text will often turn into a ritornello, and an exclamation (such as Ottavia's command to Ottone to kill Poppea in *L'incoronazione di Poppea* [1642] 2.9: *Precipita gli indugi*—Away with your hesitations!) can easily harden into a peremptory *gestus*. But the closest approach to Pound's style that I know is found in a work contemporary with Pound's opera, Schoenberg's *Erwartung* (1909; 1924).

There are critics of Schoenberg who regard *Erwartung* as profoundly speech-driven music, in the same tradition as the reform works of Monteverdi and

Gluck: a style of music that abolishes structures of musical development generated by preexisting musical forms, in order to respond to the text with a kind of
instantaneous immediacy; a style of music without any ballast of expectation, so
that the listener never knows what will happen next. (The German word *Erwartung* means expectation, but since the music provides the listener with no predic-
tive structure, expectation becomes a free-floating anxiety.) A woman, haunted
by the moon, haunted by the memory of her faithless lover, strolls alone in a
forest close to an inhabited street; she comes upon a corpse, perhaps the corpse
of her lover, and utters a long, psychiatrically detailed complaint; but the audience never knows if she mistakes a log for a corpse, or if she really finds a corpse,
or if she killed her lover and has forgotten she did it, or if the whole monodrama
is stark hallucination. The text—by an Austrian medical student, Marie Pappenheim—was evidently a rough draft that Schoenberg decided to set without further polishing; its rawness, its unevenness, its lack of syntactical control may have
seemed the literary equivalent of the encephalographically lurching music that
he wanted to write. For Pound, the poetry of Villon represented naked language;
for Schoenberg, the monologue of Pappenheim represented a halting speech so
naked it had scarcely roused itself to the level of language.

The nearly prelinguistic character of the text makes it hard to argue for
Erwartung what Christopher Butler has argued for Schoenberg's *Entrückung*,
that "Schoenberg has escaped the logic of traditional tonality, by following
another logic, that of the spoken language." In *Erwartung*, Schoenberg has not
surrendered the authority of musical form to the authority of literary form: he
has instead employed a shattered, splintery sort of diction in order to help
him investigate form at a level of improvisation almost unprecedented in the
history of the arts. Pound made his music consonant with Villon's text through
an act of perfect acquiescence to a masterpiece: the music savors every detail
of consonant and vowel. But Schoenberg chose a text so maimed that it seems
already the victim of some ghastly avant-garde surgery, too debilitated to offer
any resistance to the music. The text of *Erwartung* is all ellipsis; and the music of
Erwartung is even more elliptical, in that it omits all the transitions that might
soften or condone the strange successions of chords full of major sevenths, or the
melodic spikes that seem to represent pathological contractions of the heart
through pathological contractions of the larynx. The music isn't entirely nonre-
petitive—as Carl Dahlhaus has noted, there is a figure of Db–C–A woven
through parts of the musical texture; but this figure, if the ear notices it at all, is
likely to be noticed unconsciously, as only the faintest of constraints amid the
general anomie of the flow; it certainly is not a *gestus*. For the most part, Schoenberg was faithful to his extraordinary, all-compassing hatred of repetition in
music.

In Schoenberg's late essay "Criteria for the Evaluation of Music" (1946), it turns out that a central criterion for the evaluation of music is the presence or absence of that godsend to lazy composers, the sequence (in its modern, not medieval, meaning): "Wagner, in order to make his themes suitable for memorability, had to use sequences and semi-sequences, that is, unvaried or slightly varied repetitions differing in nothing essential from first appearances, except that they are exactly transposed to other degrees"; Schoenberg illustrated this with two quotations from *Tristan* (*Befehlen liess dem Eigenholde* and the opening of the prelude), and then claimed that Wagner's practice led to the ruin of Bruckner, Strauss, Debussy, and Puccini. Instead of sequential repetition, Schoenberg advocated "what I call *developing variation*"—that is (very roughly), repetition through an evolving set of differences.

In this passage Schoenberg identified, I believe, the most strongly anti-Wagnerian aspect of his creative personality. Why did Wagner use sequences?— because of their *memorability*. A sequence is an assertion that a figure exists independently of the particular pitches that specify it: it retains its individuality despite transposition. A sequence is a defiance of time, a persistence of an element that may be part of a tissue of recollection and anticipation, but that stands apart from that tissue. A sequence is a useful device for gestic music, in that its ease of grasp can sometimes lead to an effect of atemporal immutability: a gesture is isolated and protected from the encroachment of contexts. Indeed, many of the musical hieroglyphs we've noted so far have been strongly sequential in nature; for example, the priest's *Sobald dich führt* in *The Magic Flute* is a sequential droop of terse ascending phrases.

But for Schoenberg—at least for the "atonal" Schoenberg of 1908–13— music is not exempt from time; music *is* time, time given a voice. Music does not set itself the task of constructing memorable units; music instead sets itself the task of rendering the contours and discontinuities of a shifting subjectivity. *Erwartung* has, of course, few sequences, but Schoenberg did provide a memorable near-sequence, which allows us to measure exactly Schoenberg's distance from Wagner. It occurs as a setting of the words *Ist hier jemand? Ist hier jemand?* in the second scene (after rehearsal figure 70), in which the repetition of the text— "Anybody here? Anybody here?"—led Schoenberg not to an exact transposition, but to a clear echo of the phrase-shape. But this is the only moment in *Erwartung* when the woman enters a potential world of discourse with other singers: no one answers her, no one is within shouting distance, but for an instant, as she calls out, we enter the world of opera, not monodrama. Soon she will discover, or will think she discovers, a corpse, and will become lost for good in the forests of her private night; but first she utters this unique outcry, a *gestus* of fearful hailing, before she abandons all pretense of living in a community.

EX. 5.3. Schoenberg, *Erwartung:* "Anybody here?"

Wagner on Schopenhauer

But of course Wagner's art had other resources beyond the construction of memorable musical gestures; and although Schoenberg repudiated the art of the Wagnerian sequence, he carried to its highest development the art of the Wagnerian scream. In his remarkable centennial essay on Beethoven (1870), Wagner (partly following Schopenhauer) divided human experience into a *light world*—a domain defined by the eye, vigilant, alert, prosaic—and a *sound world*—a domain defined by the ear, inward-turned, unconscious, so far outside the boundaries of time and space as to permit telepathy and prophecy:

> next to the world that represents itself visibly . . . a second world, perceivable only through the sense of hearing, announcing itself through sound, truly a *sound world [Schallwelt]* next to the *light world,* is present to our consciousness, a world of which we can say that it is related to the light world as dream is to waking. . . . now, it is this inner life through which we are immediately related to all nature; consequently we share, in a way, in the essence of things, for in our relations to the inner life we can no longer make use of the forms of outer knowledge, time and space; from this Schopenhauer so convincingly draws conclusions concerning the origin of fatidic dreams, dreams that prophesy, dreams that make distant things visible, even in rare and extreme cases the incidence of somnambulistic clairvoyance. From the most terrifying of such dreams we wake with a *scream [Schrei],* in which the anguished will expresses itself immediately, which thus enters directly, with clear definition, into the sound world, in order to make its presence known on the outside. If we wish to consider the scream, in all the weakenings *[Abschwächungen]* of its violence down to the tenderer lament of longing, as the ground element of every human announcement to the sense of hearing, . . . we find that the scream is the most immediate utterance of the will.

Music, then, is a sort of dreaming with the ear; an endless, subtly readjusting refinement of a shriek. At the beginning of any finite musical act there is pandemonium, a vast, omni-expressive noise in which are located all the sounds that the ear can hear; the musician simply selects a few possibilities out of this confusion of all frequencies and all amplitudes. What is yearning?—weakened terror. What is exhilaration?—weakened terror. What is the soft cooing of lovers?—weakened terror. A chord, a timbre, a snatch of song, is moving to the degree that it can allude to the primal scream that lurks behind it. Wagner wrote this passage five years after the première of *Tristan,* and it is likely that he conceived the *Tristan* chord as a kind of intense secondary shudder of the sublime noise described here. Because the notes of the *Tristan* chord don't seem (according to traditional harmonic procedures) to belong together, the chord seems to be generated by omission. Its notes seem to be a selection from the chord that has *all* the notes in it, a softening of some grand violence.

The Semantics of Erwartung

One of the tasks that Wagner set for subsequent composers was to allude still more fully to the primal scream at the origin of music. One possibility occurs at the climax of the *adagio* of Mahler's Tenth Symphony (left unfinished at his death in 1911): a huge, lacerating chord in which appear nine of the twelve notes of the chromatic scale. (It is a powerful stimulus to fantasy: in Ken Russell's film *Mahler,* this chord illustrates the bursting-into-flames of the little hut in which Mahler wrote his music; and I once had a dream in which this chord sounded during the ripping-loose of a giant curtain covering a whole cross-section of a bombed-out cathedral.) Schoenberg, too, evidently conceived of expressivity as being intense to the degree that it approximated the fullness of the chord in which all notes are sounded. Not every musicologist agrees with Charles Rosen, who argues (following Adorno) that the "atonal" Schoenberg redefined consonance as *chromatic saturation,* so that the chords of *Erwartung* tend to succeed one another complementarily—consecutive chords will contain all twelve notes of the chromatic scale. But as a mythology of Schoenberg's music, Rosen's argument is nearly irresistible; and the famous ending of *Erwartung,* in which various glides up and down the chromatic scale get faster and quieter until they vanish into silence, seems to allude to Wagner's nightmare scream through sheer absence of sound. Perhaps the ultimate weakening of violence and the ultimate violence converge.

A music that dwells in the immediate present of screams, moans, gurgles, and the trilling of blood in the ears is not necessarily a text-driven music. György Ligeti's *Aventures* (1962) has no text at all, only a collection of yelps, chuckles, and other expressive noises; this is not expressionism but a spoof of expressionism, and yet it nevertheless shows how little *Erwartung* needed to have been tied to a text, except insofar as a person on stage making various sorts of sobs,

EX. 5.4. Mahler, Tenth Symphony, Adagio: saturated cry

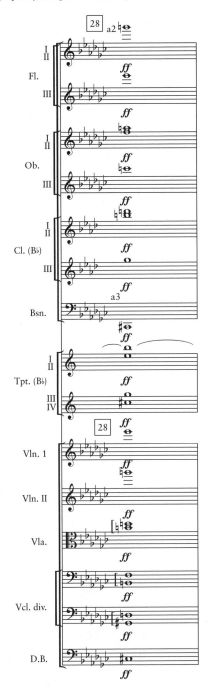

whimpers, and shrieks might look silly in the absence of any explanation of motive. (A fascinating anticipation of Ligeti's procedure can be found in the expression-vocalises in a pantomime from Weill's *Der Protagonist, 1926.*) In *Erwartung,* the music is less an expression of the text than a dismantling of the already disjointed text into a collection of cues for stresses and relaxations of pitch; the words are less like the words of a traditional aria or *scena* than like a set of stage directions cried aloud by the performer, to help her understand and shape her croonings, her wailings. Near the beginning, the woman says, "Oh, always the crickets with their love song . . . don't talk . . . it is so sweet"; and in a sense, her whole monodrama is less an act of talking than an act of listening to a voice not quite her own, uttering something that is not quite language. We speak of conscience as a voice, but it is rare actually to hear the words "Thou shalt not steal" when we are tempted to crime: the contest between impulse and restraint may be a dialogue, but it is a subvocal dialogue, conducted as a mental simulacrum of physical gesture, the reaching out and drawing back of the hand to and from the object of desire. *Erwartung* is an opera in which the subvocal processes of elucidation of madness, or further maddening of madness, are roused into a parody of a human voice. Theodor Adorno conceived *Erwartung* less as text-setting than as an operatic paroxysm or stroke:

> The first atonal works are session notes in the sense of a psychoanalyst's session notes on a patient's dreams. In the first book published on Schoenberg, Kandinsky called Schoenberg's paintings brain-acts *[Gehirnakte]*. The scars of that revolution of expression, however, are the blots that have fixed themselves, in the music as well as on the paintings, as the messengers of the id against the composer's will—blots that disturb the surface and can no more be wiped away by subsequent correction than the traces of blood in the fairy tale.

If Adorno was right, *Erwartung* has little to do with the voluntary, the conscious, the discursive; what counts is not the fairy tale (the plot, the speech) but the leakage of blood from the arteries in the brain. *Erwartung* offers us not musical or verbal discourse in the traditional sense, but hieroglyphs of blood spatters, direct clots of feeling, liquefying in the listener's skull.

And yet, Adorno's vampirish systems of metaphor are misleading in that the experience of hearing *Erwartung* is less like watching a slasher movie than like hearing the music of an exotic and enigmatic culture: the sheer disruptedness of the verbal and musical discourse tends to interfere with semantic construction, to de-expressionize the piece, to soften the sting of dissonance, to make the monodrama abstract, lyrical. It is the old-fashioned Wagnerian or Straussian parts of *Erwartung* that retain the power to horrify—for example, when the woman cuts loose a scream derived from Kundry's *und lachte,* or when the orchestra recalls the trills and deep whomps from the final scene of *Salome.* (Even the vanishing glissandi in the last bar of *Erwartung* seem to recall the instant of death in Strauss's *Death and Transfiguration* [1890], just before the long *moderato* of the Transfiguration.) But the most novel parts of Schoenberg's music have nearly passed beyond the range of our systems of interpreting music as emotional response or stimulus. John Cage was not the least of Schoenberg's pupils, and it is possible to hear *Erwartung* as Cage would have written it, as an exercise in the liquid pleasure of patternlessness.

EX. 5.5. Strauss, *Death and Transfiguration:* moment of death

molto dim.

When I was young, I once spent a summer in which I listened to *Erwartung* every day, often two or three times, without paying attention to the text; I wanted to assimilate its wonders, to understand its discontinuities as occult forms of continuity. As with any repeated succession of sounds, *Erwartung* ultimately became fully predictable; and, slowly, the text started to seem an arbitrary melodrama, a silly hoo-ha uncomfortably fastened to the exquisite music. In 1959 Hermann Scherchen recorded a fine-lined, fiery performance of *Erwartung* entirely omitting the soloist; and a superb concerto for orchestra comes to light when *Erwartung* is liberated from its text. In preparation for performances of *Erwartung* and *Die glückliche Hand* in 1930, Schoenberg wrote to the Intendant of the Opera:

> [Concerning *Erwartung*] It is necessary that one always sees the woman *in the forest,* in order to grasp that she *fears it!!* Then the whole play *can* be comprehended as a nightmare. But on that account it must be a *real* forest and no mere "gist" *["sachlicher"],* for one may shudder at such a thing, but not fear it. . . . [Concerning *Die glückliche Hand*] I am no friend of so-called 'stylized' decorations (what style?) and like to see in the décor the good, practiced hand of a painter who can make a straight line and who does not take his example from children's drawings or the art of savage peoples. The objects and settings in my pieces *play along* with the characters, and therefore one should be able to recognize them as clearly as the pitches of the notes. If the spectator has to ask what the décor means, as in a picture puzzle ("Where is the hunter"?), he hears only a part of the music.

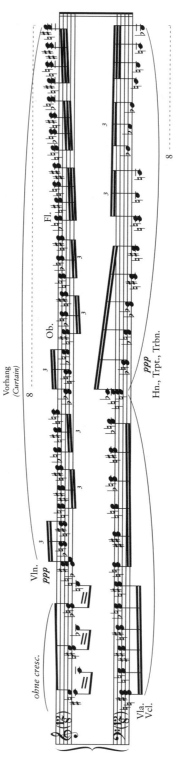

EX. 5.6. Schoenberg, *Erwartung*: ending

Stravinsky, we remember, enjoyed the set designs of Larionov, whose work indeed imitated "children's drawings or the art of savage peoples"; but Schoenberg wanted *Erwartung* to be shown not as a witty adaptation of a dream, but as an actual induction into nightmare. (The modern computer simulation of "virtual reality," which blocks out external stimuli and fully engages the eyes and ears in fictitious experiences, might have been much to Schoenberg's taste.) And yet, I wonder whether Schoenberg's recommended stage set—a forest with recognizable oaks or elms in conventional perspective—might not seem an embarrassment, insofar as the challenging music became confined to an all-too-commonplace spectacle. But Schoenberg perhaps wished to create such a narrow channel for his music precisely because he feared that it would lose all semantic specificity in the absence of a doggedly literal representation of Pappenheim's text. In a sense, the music of *Erwartung* is more entertaining than the emotions that it purports to embody. A roller coaster provides a sufficient simulation of terror to provoke a scream; and yet no one regards the designer of a roller coaster as a great expressionist artist. *Erwartung* aspires to be a correlation to profound psychic shocks, an investigation of the basic vocabulary of feeling in the human brain; but the music is, finally, so self-engrossed, so loosely connected to the text and scenery that it expresses, that Schoenberg had to go to great lengths to establish literal meanings at a level of theatrical ordinariness where misinterpretation would be impossible. The music could not be the subconscious of the text without a continual superimposition of the text onto the music. Schoenberg wasn't quite confident that his scurries, razzes, sforzandi, and sudden silences would be icons of fear, or eagerness, or vague dread; he needed to affix unmistakable captions. By denying himself the possibility of repetition, Schoenberg put more semantic pressure on each gesture than it could bear. Hieroglyphs tend to lose precision of meaning through either too much or too little repetition.

Le testament: *Rhythmic Complexity, Melodic Simplicity*

Pound's *Le testament* also shows how music can disassemble verbal structures, but only the formal structures of prosody, not the larger rhetorical structures of language itself. Pound's opera in no sense denies speech, or looks underneath speech (in the way that *Erwartung* seeks to peer into the textual subconscious); indeed, it is one of the greatest affirmations of discourse ever conceived. The text-driven quality of Monteverdi's and Schoenberg's music is slightly factitious, in that for Monteverdi the shape of the text easily generated new (or fell into old) potentially autonomous musical structures, and for Schoenberg the text was systemically deformed, broken up, into something that would provide no impedance to the self-conscious and brilliant amorphosities of the music. But for Pound, music disrupts the settled shapes of Villon's stanzas only to affirm the power of the speaking voice.

We've seen how Pound's overwrought rhythmic practices were a means for fixing the *gestus* of a speech pattern to a degree impossible without musical notation. And Pound's orchestrational practice has exactly the same goal. His intentions were quite modest:

> I have a vague suspicion that cello ought to be about three notes lower than voice to sustain it, and that bass viol ought to be about an octave below (below voice), running onto nine below on occasion. BUTT this is extremely vague, possibly it shd. be two octaves, save that I want to use that cellarage for definite purposes.

> [I am] encouraged to tear up the whole bloomin' era of harmony and do the thing if necessary on two tins and wash-board.

The instruments are present only to prop up the voice, and might be reduced to a hillbilly simplicity. And yet the combination of extreme spareness and extreme variety in Pound's orchestration imparts a highfalutin, almost Webernesque sound-tint: for example, the first song in *Le testament* employs (among other things) a saxophone, a cymbal, a tambourine, a drum, a bassoon, and a cello, but these instruments do little except occasionally repeat a note or a series of notes from the vocal line, usually on the same pitch. The instruments seem less to accompany the monody than to alter the typeface of the monody, so to speak. The first song begins (I cite Villon's French in a more normal old-time spelling than Pound's):

Et meure Paris ou Helaine	Paris dies or Helen dies
Quiconques meurt meurt a douleur	Who dies, must die in pains of hell
Celui qui pert vent et alaine,	He loses wind and cannot breathe,
Son fiel se creve sur son cueur. . . .	His heart is sopped in his own gall. . . .

The cello underlines the words *Paris ou Helaine . . . meurt meurt a douleur Celui qui pert;* then the saxophone takes over, underlining the words *vent et alaine:* the instruments provide a tissue of insinuation, the cello coloring the most pathetic words with a certain grave urgency, then the saxophone coloring the words for wind and breath with its own windiness. The instruments are devices for roughening or softening the vocal line, for controlling its overtones with rasp or croon; Pound's medievalism, despite its austerity, has a certain fondness for Technicolor.

As Pound wrote at the beginning of the manuscript (in Yale University's Pound collection):

> The "orchestration" in the first part of the opera is not in the usual sense "musical." It is simply an emphasis on the consonantal & vowel sounds of the words. I doubt if the instrumentalist will get much help from "counting the measures." Let him learn the words & make his noises when the singer reaches the syllable the instrument is to emphasize. In the latter part of the opera, secondary melodies are introduced, but looking for harmonies will help no one. . . . There is counter rhythm in Pere Noe to counter line.

In a world where bars may consist of odd counts of thirty-second notes, the advice to listen to the words is probably good—*Le testament* is as much a system of performers listening to one another, cuing one another, as Britten's *Curlew River*.

But, as Pound noted, the opera's musical style changes as it progresses. By the time of La Hëaulmiere's song, the vocal line has started to become increasingly chromatic—as if Pound were permitting himself to use more and more of the resources of musical expressivity. The line *A maint homme l'ay reffusé* [Lots of guys got nothing off me] wavers in semitones from D♯ to C, as if the thought of her stupid abstinence from sex had shocked the old woman out of the realm of troubadour songs and *chansons de toile* and into a new, more chromatically dense and compelling musical world. Later, at an especially giddy moment (marked *jaunty* in the score), La Hëaulmiere sings *Que tous mes maulx oubliasse* [I'd have forgotten all my miseries, if only he'd asked me to kiss him]. The vocal line here is unexceptional: white notes moving stepwise from C to F and then back down, underlined by a saxophone in unison. But when she reaches the word *maulx,* suddenly a flute breaks out with the identical phrase in an irregular diminution—as if the imagined pleasure of the kiss that didn't happen had startled the flute into *forgetting* its place in the opera's decorum. For that moment, we are no longer in the continuous discursive present of most of the opera to this point; discourse is starting to achieve a thickness in time, layers of memory and fantasy suggested by purely musical means. The flute-squawk, detaching itself from the even flow of the text and the rest of the music, turns into a figure, something memorable, part of a pattern of retrospection and anticipation; for an instant, *Le testament* becomes gestic in the Wagnerian sense.

The first part of *Le testament* is given to purity of regret: beautiful women are dead, and the poet too must die. The white-note monody is a pure style appropriate to this narrow but immaculate field of emotion. But as the opera falls into social complexities—as La Hëaulmiere discusses the economic and emotional tangles of a prostitute's life, as Villon's mother ("very cracked & sarcastic, as it were out of tune") joins into La Hëaulmiere's song to the other whores advising them to make money while they're still young—the music more and more falls out of the ideal medieval past and into the asperities and knots of the modern world—both Villon's modern world and ours.

The turning point of the opera occurs when Villon's mother sings her prayer to the Virgin, *Dame du ciel*. This text meant a great deal to Pound, especially the third stanza, where the poor old woman describes her little church with

> Paradis paint ou sont harpes   Heaven's harps and lutes on a painted
>   et lus   wall
> Et ung enfer ou dampnez sont   And there, devils boil the damned in
>   boullus. . . .   hell. . . .

Phrases from this passage figure the Pisan Cantos; and Pound's setting of this text seems to me his highest accomplishment, by far, as a musician.

Pound was not the first to set *Dame du ciel*: Debussy, for one, had set it just a few years before, in 1910, as the second of *Trois ballades de François Villon*. Debussy's old woman keeps her eyes fixed firmly on the mural of paradise, in that Debussy's music is a subtly inflected chorale, *art nouveau* Gothic. But Pound's old woman never stops gazing at hell: if earlier passages in the opera could seem faint or aimless, here Pound composed with rigor and power. Pound regarded *Le testament* as the antidote to Debussy's *Pelléas et Mélisande*—"ignorance having no further terrors if that DAMN thing is the result of what is called musical knowledge"—and *Dame du ciel* is his best vindication of this doubtful thesis. The vocal line has far less motion than previous songs in the opera have, as if Villon's mother were stunned into a kind of static chant: during the first four (long) bars, every note she sings, with two brief exceptions, is an F or a G; and the cello plays a slightly unsteady drone on C. But while voice and cello are working their medieval-sounding perfect consonances, low bells, doubled by the bottom octave of the piano, play a deep, erratic figure, A–A–G♯–A–F–D♯–F. This is difficult to construe as a bass; it moves (and continues to move, after the opening bars) in ways that have little to do with the vocal line. But it is possible to hear it as a distorted version of the *Dies Irae*; and I wonder whether Pound was not remembering the last movement of Berlioz's *Symphonie fantastique* (1830), in which tubular bells and the *Dies Irae* make up the sonorities of a witches' sabbath.

Here Pound's music becomes expressive not in the manner of troubadour song, but in the Modernist way, a convergence of the archaic and the sophisticated, in which the terror of the old chant is heightened through melodic

EX. 5.7. Pound, *Le testament:* Villon's Mother's Song

misshapening and through the manipulation of a rhythm so pulled apart by the non-uniform bar structure that it is almost a rhythmlessness. I know of no other piece of music that seems at once so random and so inexorable. The singer's words come quickly, almost breathlessly, above the huge bass: she seems frantic with *timor mortis*. At several points in the song, Pound extracted from his *Dies Irae* variant a D♯–A tritone, as if his bells and piano, by playing a *diabolus in musica*, were feigning the presence of the Devil himself.

Pound's song-setting for Villon's mother is an unintelligible act of blasphemy by the canons of medieval or Renaissance music; it is a Modernist evocation of the archaic, not an imitation of it. And most of the subsequent numbers also deviate far from the ambit of the troubadours. Just after the mother's ballade, the Priest, in lay costume, tries to slip into the brothel, singing a tune from a collection of old French songs; but the brothel's drunken bouncer, Bozo, shoves him back. Bozo's song, *Si j'ayme et sers la belle de bon hait,* is the same Villon text that Hauptmann and Brecht adapted for the *Zuhälter-Ballade* in *The Three-penny Opera,* where Macheath sings nostalgically over the brothel where he and

Jenny lived for six happy months. But Villon's original text is unsentimental, in fact brutal: when Margot objects to whoring,

j'empoigne ung esclat,   I seize a club,
Dessus son nez lui en fais ung escript   And write a pretty text above her nose

—another kind of inscriptive and performative *gestus*. Pound's music is also unsentimental, brutal. The vocal line is similar to the white-note monody of the earlier part of the opera, but with much wider leaps, and with long rests in odd places and an unsteady punctuation of notated hiccups. But the trombone (the major accompanying instrument) seems to take no account of the sung pitches: most of its notes are flat, often producing tritones and other nasty dissonances against the vocal line. The trombone is rhythmically disordered in almost exactly the same way that the singer is rhythmically disordered; like all Pound's instruments, it is less an accompaniment to the voice than a second version of the voice, now in a state of extreme internal discord. Pound's note instructs the trombonist to play "as rowdily & boozily as possible . . . hiccoughing DRUNK as also the voice." Sometimes the trombone's hiccups seem to make it lose its place—for example, to take up the musical thread a minor ninth above the place where it left off. When a second trombone enters, the possibilities for galumphing become all the greater.

EX. 5.8. Pound, *Le testament*: Bozo's Song

According to Pound's music theory, eccentric rhythm and dissonant intervals must exist together: to have one without the other would be an error of musical grammar. Pound thought that pitch and rhythm were not independent entities, for rhythm is simply a pitch too low for the human ear to hear:

> Certain sounds we accept as "pitch", we say that a certain note is do, re, mi, or B flat in the treble scale, meaning that it has a certain frequency of vibration.
>
> Down below the lowest note synthesized by the ear and "heard" there are slower vibrations. The ratio between these frequencies and those written to be executed by instruments is OBVIOUS in mathematics. The whole question of tempo, and of a main base in all musical structures resides in use of these frequencies.

> The 60, 72, or 84, or 120 per minute is a BASS, or basis. It is the bottom note of the harmony.
>
> If the ear isn't true in its sense of this time-division the whole playing is bound to be molten, and doughy. . . .
>
> Failing to hit the proper great bass, the deficient musician fumbles about OFF the gt. bass key as a poor singer fumbles about a little flat or a ¼ tone too high.

When the oboe sounds the A to which the modern orchestra tunes, it emits a note vibrating at 440 cycles per second. Under that there is another A, an octave lower, vibrating at 220 cycles per second; and under that an A at 110; and under that an A at 55; and under that an A at 27.5; and under that an A at 13.75 — but now we are under the threshold of hearing, for such a slow frequency is simply a series of discrete pulses, like the whuffs and chugs from a deep organ pipe, not a true sound. Eventually the concert A can be divided into something measured not in cycles per second, but in cycles per minute; and then it becomes a rhythm, a ticktick on a metronome, not a sound. (Karlheinz Stockhausen devised a similar analysis of the relation of pitch to rhythm while composing *Gruppen* [1958].) The pitch structure of a musical composition *implies* its rhythm, and vice versa: for Pound, every piece of music has a unique tempo, a tempo derived in some sense from its key. To play a piece at the wrong tempo is to render it viscid, sloppy.

Similarly, a melodic interval of two pitches implies an interval of time between those two pitches:

> the simplest consideration of the physics of the matter . . . should lead to equations showing that A SOUND OF ANY PITCH . . . MAY BE FOLLOWED BY A SOUND

OF ANY OTHER PITCH . . . providing the time interval between them is properly gauged.

Bozo's song is an exercise in coordinating unusual intervals through weird displacements of rhythm. In the early part of the opera, the rhythm was text-driven, a function of deviations from prosody; but now the rhythm is governed by musical considerations: how long should the trombone pause before climbing from a low G to a high A♭? Bozo is presumably too drunk to attend to subtleties of text-patterning, to hear the meter of his own song; and so, since the text has abdicated its control, the musical line is liberated. A hiccup isn't a caesura, but an accident, an interruption; and such textual burps entail various pratfalls and spasms in the melodic line, the jerks from one pitch to the next. The trombone enacts Bozo's clowning for him; or, to put it another way, Bozo's own voice is just another trombone, for this number is less a song than a piece of instrumental polyphony.

But still more surprises are in store. After Bozo passes out, the Gallant renounces love and, "either wounded or dying," collapses with Bozo; and the Parisians, amused by the spectacle of pimp and customer in a drunken heap, start to dance, while singing a jolly song in honor of Noah, responsible for cultivating the grape, and the late Jean Cotard, a noteworthy lover of wine. (In the 1931 radio broadcast, the policemen use this song as a diversion in order to sneak up on Villon: at its end, a voice cries, "Gawd, they've pinched him.") This song, *Pere Noé*, is, in the opera's context, bizarrely un-bizarre: most of it is in a regular 3/8 meter, with plenty of repetition of musical phrases, and arguably in C major, with a tendency toward the note D giving a certain Dorian flavor. Eventually the three syllables of the name *Jean Cotard* establish a regular dactylic beat, falling first a fourth (F–C–C), then a minor third (F–D–D). And in the second bar of this phrase, Pound crossed out the name *Cotard* and replaced it with *Cocteau,* winking at a modern Parisian whose work Pound sometimes praised—though Cocteau's continual giggling when Pound (in January 1922) sang for him passages of *Le testament* may have caused Pound to add the name to the text as a kind of riposte.

Pound liked anachronisms: in Pound's great *Homage to Sextus Propertius* (1917), the first-century Roman poet discusses frigidaire patents. The allusion to Cocteau fits in perfectly with the systematic destabilizing of any temporal focus: the text turns its attention to a Modernist author in order to connive for a moment at the music's radical polystylism, ranging from imitations (and quotations) of twelfth-century monody to experiments with dissonance, rhythm, and timbre of a distinctly twentieth-century character. *Pere Noé* is about as close as Pound came to writing music of Villon's time. The figure for *Jean Cocteau* is a kind of cuckoo call, perhaps in homage to one of Janequin's birds—though Janequin's music came about seventy years after Villon's time.

EX. 5.9. Pound, *Le testament*: Jean Cocteau

Le testament ends with a chorus of the hanged—an eerie effect, as the dead Villon and his comrades sing *Freres humains* in subdued, quietly dissonant four-part harmony. This same poem appears near the end of *The Threepenny Opera;* but instead of Weill's anger and insistence, Pound heard in it resignation, almost empty wind. An opera that began in a relentlessly monodic fashion has at last achieved if not harmony, at least a fully coordinated counterpoint—an ending that gives a sense of completeness. One of Pound's tasks in 1920, just before beginning *Le testament,* was to edit part of the "Oxen of the Sun" chapter of Joyce's *Ulysses* for *The Little Review.* In this chapter Joyce aped, in turn, all the major prose styles of English literature, ranging from pseudo–Old English ("Before born babe bliss had") to the difficult modish slang of the 1910s ("Golly, whatten tunket's yon guy in the mackintosh? . . . Peep at his wearables"). "Oxen of the Sun" is a *Gesamtkunstwerk* in a sense other than Wagner's: it is a total art work in that it gathers up all previous art works in its single medium, instead of gathering up all the different media. *Le testament* is confected according to a similar recipe, in which the ripening of the musical style from troubadour monody to four-part harmony represents a fall into psychological and social complication. It is a grave comedy, in which styles are themselves dramatis personae.

Le testament has connections with other advanced trends in Modernist art as well. Before the opening of the first song, there are two bars for drum and flute: the drum taps out four sixteenth notes, which, with a final sixteenth-note rest, are gathered into a quintuplet; after five of these quintuplets, the flute plays three glissandi down the span of a fifth, from E to A. This odd figure appears at several places in the score: for example, after the *Ballade des dames du temps jadis*, where it is labeled "Inside brothel" and we are told that the flute is a "nose flute" and the drumbeat is to be played by "small African drums." Why *African* drums? One answer might be that the sonority was exactly what Pound wanted; but another answer might be that for Pound, brothel music seemed to imply Africa— just as for Picasso, in *Demoiselles d'Avignon* (1907), brothel imagery seemed to imply African masks, according to a familiar racist model of sexual squalor. The noses of two of Picasso's figures have, so to speak, turned into nose flutes; and perhaps the distance from the Barcelona brothel on Avignon Street celebrated by Picasso and the brothel in Pound's version of fifteenth-century Paris is not great. Pound was no great admirer of Picasso, though he did write in 1921 (the year of *Le testament*) that "The strength of Picasso is largely in his having chewed through and chewed up a great mass of classicism; which . . . the flabby cubists have not." Much later, in 1956, Pound denounced Picasso's work for "showing

EX. 5.10. Pound, *Le testament:* nose flute and African drums

marvellous technique and total lack of human value; in fact it shows only depravity," and Pound congratulated those who refused to follow the "African fad." But Picasso the chewer and spitter, Picasso the depraved, Picasso the Africanist, might be just the right sort of illustrator for the brothel scenes of *Le testament,* as Pound understood them. The chaste monody of the first songs in the opera is regularly interrupted by a satyr's drums and flute, playing a mocking ideogram of sexual arousal—the only music in the opera independent of any verbal text. It is possible that the imitations of American dance rhythms in Weill's *The Threepenny Opera* are, similarly, distant reflections of a common caricature, the black Dionysus.

Pound conceived *Le testament* as a stylized opera, almost a drama of puppets, or of singers in masks, as he noted in a typescript at the end of the score:

> Such gestures as are ma[d]e are *not* to be puppet gestures, though the general convention is very nearly that of puppet play. But there are to be no superfluous gestures. The actors stand STILL save when specifically moving. All save the figity ones, at given moments, the friend getting more worried about V[illon]'s not clearing out. As contrast to V's intense immobility, and the taverner's effacement.

> Lacking masks the make up can be stylized to the utmost. Costuming as the stage man[a]ger likes, either realist rags or utmost stylization (possibly cheaper). The only expensive costumes w/ be the Gallant, his attendants (optional . . . he cd/ save on his servants clothes); and the halbardiers (Beef=eaterish).
> Heaulmiere vivid henna/ Mother tow white.
> Beauté not masked in any case, but no change of expression save in eyes.
> Maximum of non=attention and observation.

The fixity and fidgets, the stylization, the deletion of all superfluity—we have seen all this before. It is Noh drama: although the texts of *Le testament* are derived from Villon, the dramaturgy is straight from Japan. *Pere Noé* is half a drunken orgy, and half the carefully measured climactic dance of a Noh play; and when the corpse of Villon starts to sing, the protagonist reveals himself as the *shite,* the holy spirit, of his drama. It is not far from a singing hanged man to the singing severed heads of Yeats's Noh imitations of the 1930s. *Le testament* has the same preterite quality as many Western imitations of Noh theatre: nothing happens in the course of the play except a rehearsal of long-extinct actions in a composite past tense—a revivification of dead texts, pseudo-voices made to speak in a pseudo-present. The characters are not independent agents, but *personae,* masks, derived from Villon's imaginative use of the word *I* in certain ballads and dramatic lyrics. Pound's opera is an exercise in a theatre of ghosts and figments.

It may seem odd to speak of Villon as a *shite,* a wise ghost; but Pound had long associated Villon with a kind of postmortem state. In a very early poem, "Villonaud for the Yule" (1908)—the word *villonaud* is a neologism, a cross between *Villon* and *villanelle,* as if the poet had himself turned into a genre of poem—Pound adapted *ou sont les neiges* into a refrain, "Wining the ghosts of yester-year," in the course of a Christmas meditation on "the ghosts of dead loves everyone." When Pound thought of Villon, he thought of howling wind, keen regret, and bodies swinging from gibbets. In a sense, the initial stirrings of *Le testament* date from this same year: for the project of *Le testament* is the resurrection of Villon, and the recipe for this resuscitation can be found in another poem of 1908, "Histrion":

> No man hath dared to write this thing as yet,
> And yet I know, how that the souls of all men great
> At times pass through us,
> And we are melted into them, and are not
> Save reflexions of their souls.
> Thus am I Dante for a space and am
> One François Villon, ballad-lord and thief. . . .

Pound's opera is a cultivation of trance, an experiment in mediumship. The hieratic rigidity of the characters on the stage, the masks or mask-like makeup, are all part of this aspect of séance. In *Le testament,* Pound tried to *become* Villon, to animate Villon's complete social world, to use the whole of music history to embody Villon's persistence in time. Villon is hauled out of hell, in order to make certain fundamental sounds about the nature of human life.

Pound completed *Le testament* in a state of supreme confidence: "It is probably the best thing I have done. At any rate the only opera with great verse as a libretto," he wrote in 1922. But by 1954 the poet, long confined to a mental hospital after his trial for treason, had far less sense of the opera's value: "AND my doin muzik is vurry elephant climbing tree / again mere theory / but believe third note in a chord is often horse-feathers, a cushion." But even in dismissing his own work, Pound provided a clue about what he achieved in his musical testament: an opera in agile monody, uncushioned by the normal harmonic props; a music drama of naked voices, in which all the instruments of the orchestra are changed from musical devices into talking devices, contributing nuances and inflections to the singers' speech.

Noh, Again

Le testament, as we've seen, has a number of occult connections to Brecht's and Weill's *The Threepenny Opera:* both works can be seen as Villonesque experiments in finding the naked roots of music theatre, the basic forms of expressivity itself—the prototype of opera, in Weill's phrase. But there is a further important connection between Pound's operatic practice and that of Brecht and Weill: *Le testament* is a derivative of Noh; and Brecht and Weill wrote an explicit Noh opera, *Der Jasager* (The Yes-Sayer, 1930). I regard this as one of the high points of twentieth-century art, in which the collaborators achieved astonishingly powerful figures of consonance by synthesizing the method of the *gestus* and the method of the Noh play. As such, it is the culmination of the techniques described in the first half of this book.

To speak of Brecht in connection with *Der Jasager* is slightly embarrassing, since the text is almost entirely the work of Elisabeth Hauptmann, who translated it from Arthur Waley's English translation of the Noh play *Tanikō* (The Valley-Hurling). Hauptmann consulted some sources independent of Waley, but *Der Jasager* is nevertheless quite close to Waley's English, even to the point of observing Waley's cuttings and condensations of Zenchiku's Japanese text. Brecht's contribution was basically limited to deleting phrases such as *in einem Tempel* [in a temple] from certain passages, in order to secularize the text. (Brecht, too, might be included in our gallery of twentieth-century masters depicted with eraser in hand.) Despite Waley's and Brecht's alterations, *Der Jasager* is the closest approximation in Western music to a literal setting of a Noh play—and this very literalness may offer another point of comparison with *Le testament,* which also seeks to resurrect and dramatize an ancient text with few verbal changes. For the Modernists, quotation was a mode of power—not an abnegation of the ego, but an affirmation of it.

Der Jasager: *Teaching Acquiescence*

The plot of *Der Jasager* was nicely summarized by Weill:

> The main character in it is a boy. That already gave me the idea to let this play be performed by students. The content, briefly, is: the boy would like to go with the teacher on a journey, in order to fetch medicine from the city for his sick mother. The travel is dangerous; on that account, the mother doesn't want to let the boy go. Also the teacher advises against it. The boy goes, however, in order to help the mother. On the way, when they've come to the most dangerous place, he becomes weak and therefore endangers the whole band of travelers. They put to him the decision: should they turn back or should they follow the old rite *[Brauch]*, which commands that the sick must be thrown down into the valley? The boy decides for the valley-hurling. "He has said Yes," sings the chorus. Some of the text is motivated differently by Brecht, compared to what is offered in the original Japanese text. . . . we've considered that students should also *learn* something from a didactic play *[Lehrstück]*. For that reason, we've brought in the sentence about acquiescence *[Einverständnis]*, namely: "The important thing to learn is acquiescence." Students should learn that. They should know that a community to which one is joined demands that one actually bears the consequences. The boy goes the way of the community to the end, when he says Yes to the valley-hurling.

Brecht, then, contributed to *Der Jasager* not a text but a context, an interpretation of a text: by writing a number of plays on the *Einverständnis* theme, such as *Das Badener Lehrstück vom Einverständnis* and *Die Maßnahme*—plays that advocate total submission of the individual will to the governing needs of the socialist community—Brecht specified a particular contemporary meaning for the open Japanese parable. The word *Einverständnis* is usually translated as "acquiescence," but this English word may have a shade suggesting grudging acceptance or biting one's tongue; this connotation is foreign to Brecht's use of the German word, which literally means something like "in-understanding," or full incorporation *[Einverleibung]* of the public good into the private system of desire. In Brecht's sense, to say yes is to consent utterly; to declare to the community, In your will is my peace.

To say yes, of course, raises the possibility that one might also say no; a decision to sacrifice one's life for the commonweal implies a whole complicated moral universe, anguished choice. To some extent, Brecht became sensitive to such potentially Shakespearean complexities, especially after he found, to his dismay, that *Der Jasager* was condemned by some Communist intellectuals and applauded by some Roman Catholic organizations. Brecht then rewrote the ending to make a new play, *Der Neinsager,* in which the boy refuses to be hurled over the precipice, and the teacher and the other boys, shrugging their shoulders, abandon their expedition and go home; this new play was published together with the old play, so that schools could choose which version they wished to perform.

But Weill took no notice of *Der Neinsager,* and indeed the whole musical style of *Der Jasager* forecloses all paths except the path of saying yes. Far from being sensitive to the psychic torment of a boy faced with an unbearable decision, Weill composed the most unpsychological music of his life, music written exclusively from the point of view of the community, not the individual. There is no fork in *Der Jasager*'s road: it is a study in inexorability, in a forced simplicity that precludes alternate behavior of any sort. It is Weill's supreme work of *gestus,* in that the motor rhythms, the inflexible melodic shapes, fix the domain of doing and feeling so precisely that the characters are mere puppets driven, so to speak, by the mechanical tracker action of the music. The *Ja*-hieroglyph in the music is deeply incised, unmistakable; it can't mean *Nein,* for it has no ambiguity whatsoever.

For a number of years, Weill considered *Der Jasager* to be his masterpiece; and so it is, if Weill's project as a composer was to strip theatre music of every ornament, to reduce it to its starkest and most potent gestures. Weill noted that *Der Jasager* was different from the rest of his canon, and yet an extrapolation of his previous method:

> I'd like no longer to bring out explicit *songs,* but rather closed musical forms. By such means I want to take up everything that I've known up to now to be right, for instance, what I once named the *gestus* in music. Through the melody the *gestus* should already be unequivocally expressed. Clarity, not obscurity, should govern what the composer would like to express. . . . Certainly, in the new school opera I don't renounce [motorically] rhythmic effects, but they are no longer explicit dance rhythms; rather, these rhythms are transformed, are "digested" *[verdaut].*

Modernist composers have used "closed musical forms" for many different purposes; but here, I believe, Weill used closed musical forms to symbolize a closed moral realm, where a pathway once taken must be followed to the end. *Der Jasager* is a profoundly fated work: as we've seen, Brecht hated the notion of fate, and rebelled against the potential fatedness of *Der Jasager* by publishing *Der Neinsager;* but in Weill's music, fate seems inescapable. The "digested"-ness of all the musical phenomena is remarkable: nothing is extraneous, nothing is suggestive of dance or lowbrow music or highbrow music. *The Threepenny Opera* was a fascinating sprawl of semi-digested *gestus,* ranging from sexy tango to despairing passacaglia; but *Der Jasager* is tight, "strict in simplicity"—if there are allusions to old musical forms, they work chiefly on the plane of the musical subconscious. It is an opera for schoolchildren, built around a teacher's notion of a single master *gestus:* acquiescence.

This work is spare on every level. The photographs of early performances show children in ordinary school costume, as if it were a perfectly normal thing for uncooperative children to be thrown off Bavarian alps—I wonder whether the commonplace dress might not have heightened the eeriness of the ritual sacrifice, as in Shirley Jackson's "The Lottery." Furthermore, the stage set was as spartan as possible:

> It can be played in the school auditorium. In front, on the platform, is the stage. The chorus sits on or in front of the platform. In the middle of the platform a circle is drawn; in the middle of the circle is a door (the mother's room). In the second act the door is taken away, off to one side of the circle there's set up a platform with a staircase, which represents the mountain. You see, simplicity is the principle of this school opera. Also in the musical part. The orchestral and vocal parts are performed by students.

A play, any play, requires a series of entrances and exits, and a plot, any plot, entails some difficulty that must be overcome. In this sense, the bare essentials of theatre are (1) a door, and (2) a mountain. Samuel Beckett's stage settings—a pair of garbage cans, a tree in various states of blossom, an ash heap—are Zefirellian extravagances compared to this economical sort of drama. But Beckett's plays, like *Der Jasager,* are investigations of nakedness, *théâtre pur,* the kind of drama that is left when everything nondramatic has been rigorously pared away.

Der Jasager is an opera intended for schools, but Brecht hoped that all his plays would be staged as recitation lessons. After the first run of the revised version of *Mann ist Mann,* in 1931, Brecht congratulated the lead actor, Peter Lorre, for his performance of the trial scene, in which his character is condemned to death:

> The "arguments against the verdict" were, as in a poem, divided by caesuras into separate verses, in order to emphasize the way in which various arguments keep following one another . . . without logical progression. . . . There

should arise an impression that here a man was merely reading a script for the defense prepared at some other point in time, without understanding at the present moment what it meant.

Acquiescence is not only the theme of *Der Jasager,* but its whole dramatic mode: just as a child acquiesces in a text read aloud without thinking, so *Der Jasager* is a rote opera, a prolonged exercise in behaviorist narration. In this sense, the ordinary clothes of the singers stress not the contemporaneity of the parable, but its distance, its pastness: the performance is simply a rehearsal of itself. The characters, played by children, don't emote or inflect, but simply read their assigned lines—it is the preterite theatre taken to its farthest bounds. The word *play* is misleading for this sort of extremely disciplined theatrical experience; *Der Jasager* is a most unplayful play, no more fun than rising from one's chair and trying to recall from memory Caesar's account of his battles. Every opportunity for spontaneity has been carefully removed from the text and the music alike. In the Noh play of Japan, the characters wear masks; and in 1930 Weill got excited at the idea of performing *Mahagonny* "with masks, completely rigid ones made to fit the facial form of each performer. . . . they will really hamstring those over-emoting singers." The children in *Der Jasager* didn't wear masks, but the style of the music enforces a performance face as stiff and simple as any mask.

The music of *Der Jasager* is as close as Weill got to Schoenberg, not because of any particular dissonance—the score is an exercise in euphony—but because of the mathematical rigor, the almost total absence of *Durchführung* (development) or any improvisatory element. As we have seen, the sound of organ-grinding lies behind some of Weill's earlier hit tunes, such as the *Moritat;* but *Der Jasager* is an entire cranked-out opera, composed according to an amazingly rigid method. It is an experiment in construction by pattern-unit, a mosaic of discrete pieces—some as short as a single bar—tessellated painstakingly together. In this sense, it is also Weill's most Stravinskian opera, in that such pieces as *Renard* are also constructed piecemeal. But Weill doesn't attempt to startle or amuse, in Stravinsky's fashion, by abrupt juxtaposition of incongruous music bits; instead, Weill offers a continuous, deliberate exposition, a lesson, a whole *Harmonielehre* in working toward a common social good. In 1930—the year of *Der Jasager*—Schoenberg himself wrote a chorus, *Verbundenheit* (Connectedness, or Obligation), in which musical consonance and inversional symmetry are metaphors for the spirit of cooperation in the human race: for the sake of the general welfare, we put out the fires of burning buildings, and pull the drowning out of the water, and stop the runaway horse; *bleibst nicht allein,* you are not alone (as the text says), and the concinnity of the voices of the male chorus demonstrates that the moral is correct. Schoenberg, who thought that music ought ideally to be financed by princes, was repelled by Weill's populism; but *Verbundenheit* and *Der Jasager* both seek musical structures that embody a moral of risking the individual for the betterment of the community. *Gestus* is often a depersonalizing, disappropriating technique; and in both these compositions the individual is caught up, subsumed into musical figures that represent a social good beyond any single person.

Icons of Trudge and Gluck's Hell

Weill's musical methods can be profitably studied in the eighth of the ten numbers of the score, near the beginning of the second act. Here the expedition reaches a way station on the mountain climb and decides to rest; the boy announces that he feels unwell; the other children tell the teacher, who says that he's probably just exhausted from climbing; but everyone knows that the path above the hut follows a ledge too narrow for carrying anyone, and it is possible that the sick boy will have to be flung down the cliffside. This number is pieced together from a handful of pattern-units, of which the most important is that of the opening two bars: the notes D–F–D, followed by a chord with G in the bass and D♭ and E♭ in the treble—that is, a sketch of D minor, followed by a 6/5 chord on E♭, a kind of Neapolitan. In the following two-bar sequences, the first bar keeps steadily tromping its D–F–D, but this figure terminates in other chords: A⁷, then E♭⁷; after this, the figure of the first bar opens outward to D–A–D, and still wider to B♭–A–B♭. The figure keeps straining toward cadence, but never achieves such gratification in a meaningful way; and finally it returns to exactly the same form it took in the first two bars. This pattern-unit is, I believe, a representation of a determined, laborious ascent, an icon of trudge. It has a certain melodic and harmonic flexibility, but flexibility within narrow limits; Weill has constructed its changes not to illustrate a particular harmonic direction, but simply to illustrate a kind of pushing and pulling within the figure itself, a kind of interior tension. The figure dilates itself without developing, then contracts to its original shape: monotony is evaded without compromising the purity and isolation of the gesture.

This is what gestic music looks like when freed from all non-gestic elements. At the beginning of the piece, the resolute figure (scale degrees $\hat{1}$–$\hat{3}$–$\hat{1}$–♭$\hat{2}$ in the minor) doesn't extricate itself from the rest of the music: it *is* the music. What exactly is the *gestus* here, besides the physical motion of making your way over difficult terrain, taking three steps forward ($\hat{1}$–$\hat{3}$–$\hat{1}$), then planting your right foot on a stone that gives way, flattens beneath your weight (♭$\hat{2}$)? Perhaps the figure itself contains a clue to its own meaning. In Gluck's *Orfeo ed Euridice* (1762)— the great reform opera, itself a "prototype of opera"—the chorus of the Furies blocks Orpheus's way through Hades and attempts to terrify him with the darkness, the mists, the howling of Cerebus. This chorus, in C minor, begins with a bar in which the chorus, in unison, sings the notes C–E♭–C; then, moving to the dominant, G major, their first note in the second bar is D—yielding a striking î–ĝ–î–♮2̂ figure. Although Gluck's harmony is more conventional than Weill's, the Furies' figure and Weill's figure bear several strong points of relation: a near-identical melodic shape in 3/4 tempo, a hell-waltz.

EX. 6.1. Weill, *Der Jasager:* trudge

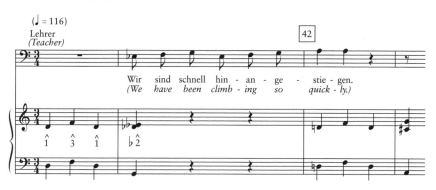

EX. 6.2. Gluck, *Orfeo ed Euridice:* Furies

Tragedy in Music: Plaint vs. Wall

In the infernal scene of *Orfeo*, Gluck discovered an important—perhaps the most important—way of creating a musical form for tragedy. For Gluck, and arguably for Sophocles and Euripides as well, tragedy is ultimately a matter of fists beating against walls: mankind struggling with and crying against the limits of the human condition. Gluck's scene in hell offers an extremely powerful musical representation of both the wall and the cry, as Orpheus pleads, with the simplest, most elegant pathos, against the barrier of the iron-hearted Furies—until at last they weep, the gate swings open, and Orpheus is allowed to proceed. Gluck's discovery that a tragedy could be conceived as a huge ritornello, in which a savage and implacable refrain was interrupted by the miseries of a solo voice, has had incalculable consequences in subsequent opera. To give a few examples: the Fate motive in Verdi's *La forza del destino* (1869) increasingly constricts Leonora's freedom of action, until even a hermit's cave is no longer large enough to let her live in peace; her great lament and curse, *Pace, pace,* is her last attempt to find space to exist in a moral universe in which the walls keep moving closer together. Later, Stravinsky patterned the "mortuary tarantella" at the end of *Oedipus Rex* (1927) after the Gluckian model, but reversed it, so that the solo voice delivers the inexorable refrain (*Divum Jocastae caput mortuum,* the divine head of Jocasta is dead), and the chorus of Thebans whimpers a tune that seems first to push slightly against immobile fate, then to push a little harder—but fate at last drives the Thebans down. In the world of music for Brecht's plays, similar phenomena are easy to find: Paul Dessau's Brecht setting *Die Verurteilung des Lukullus* (1951) provides a strong musical image of a wall (the hammering verdict *Ins Nichts mit ihm* [Annihilate him] at the end of the opera, when the shades of the dead condemn the emperor, that is, the Führer, to hell); this contrasts with the almost naked monody of the Fishwife's moving aria, as she calls out her son's name—a cry answered only by a flute's echo of her own voice, since her son died in Lucullus's bloody wars. As in Gluck, the plaint is hemmed in by a great choral wall: but here the complainer herself becomes part of the wall, since she consigns her tormenter to the void.

But Dessau was only imitating Weill's usage in *his* Brecht settings: Dessau's *Ins Nichts mit ihm* follows the pattern of Anna's vision of the Last Judgment in *The Seven Deadly Sins* (1933)—*Zitternd im Nichts vor verschlossenem Tor* [Trembling in the void, in front of the locked gate]—with its controlled delirium of hatred for all human pleasure. *Rise and Fall of the City of Mahagonny* (1930) also manifests the extended ritornello structure that Gluck discovered: Orpheus's fervent supplication becomes the condemned Jimmy's prayer that the day will never dawn; and the Furies are impersonated by a variety of ritornelli, such as the chorus that keeps announcing the four rules of life in Mahagonny—swilling food, whoring, boxing, swilling drink—and finally the chorus *Können einem toten Mann nicht helfen* [You can't help a dead man], which pounds the end of the opera flat. A man buried under such a heavy gravestone as this chorus will never be able to rise.

The $\hat{1}$–$\hat{3}$–$\hat{1}$–$\flat\hat{2}$ figure in *Der Jasager* is a spare sketch of just such a musical wall. Its *gestus* isn't simply walking, but also the necessity to walk or else be thrown down the side of the mountain. This figure is the musical equivalent both of the impulse that pushes the expedition forward, and of the old rite that demands that those unable to proceed must be killed. The harmonic frustration keeps dilating, without resolving: it thrusts the boy forward onto the path too narrow for him to walk. If there is a subliminal allusion here to Gluck, it is perfectly appropriate, for the boy's teacher and the boy's classmates are, for him— even if they have the best will in the world—Furies.

But in the Gluckian tragic structure, every wall must be balanced by a plaint. The plaint in *Der Jasager* is the controlling pattern-unit of the first part of the tenth number. Over incessant repetitions of this figure, the teacher gives to the boy a formal and explicit reading of the law: one who gets sick on a mountain journey must be thrown into the valley; his companions must ask him if he wants them to abandon the journey and return home on his account; and he must answer, You shall not return. And the boy does indeed cry out, You shall not return. The two-bar musical figure underneath most of this lecture and response consists of two chordal suspensions that (in the case of the first appearance) might be understood as a kind of frustrated i–V half-cadence from A minor to E: in the first bar, a chord of the notes (reading from the bottom up) A, D, and E, a 4–3 suspension over A—but for an instant the D dips down to C, producing a glimpse at exactly the sort of clear, root-position triad that this figure is never going to rest upon. The second bar consists of a static chord of the very widely spaced notes E, B, and A—a complicated version of yet another 4–3 suspension, this time over E. It would be easy to make this chord cadence solidly on E, but that is exactly what Weill didn't do; instead, the figure keeps repeating itself, with various spread-out harmonies in the second bar. I speak of suspensions, but harmony suspended in such a manner is clearly never going to fall: the sonority is cool,

EX. 6.3. Weill, *Der Jasager:* pathos

spare, detached, a set of pure acoustic objects generated from fifths. The figure is not an expression of pain, but a hieroglyph of pain. We've seen many examples of musical hieroglyphs that are simply cadences writ large, from the priest's *So-bald dich führt* in *The Magic Flute* on; but here is an isolated bit of naked expressivity—a succession of 4–3 suspensions that not only don't cadence, but that *mean* the absence of cadence, a state of permanent, unhappy irresolution.

The Chill of Hieroglyphs

I think of this double-suspension figure as a freeze-dried lamentation. A lamentation is, by nature, expansive: overwhelming wretchedness wishes to expatiate on itself. But this is a clipped, truncated lamentation, a lamentation with little blood in it. The more the figure is repeated, the less pathetic it becomes: all semantics depend on systems of differentiation, and in the absence of a context, any figure, no matter how potently charged, will become drained, a kind of fossil of meaning, or a pickled embryo presented coolly with forceps. (This is a potential danger with all musical hieroglyphs: it is impossible for any acoustic object to retain a steady significance, for the mere act of repetition tends to alter or remove the context that provided the meaning in the first place—the hope for a reliable dictionary of music figures can never be fulfilled.) The double-suspension figure in *Der Jasager* is less a lamentation than a kind of semaphore for a lamentation that isn't taking place; a stand-in for an uncomplained complaint. The boy is not so self-indulgent as to protest his fate, so the music indicates what he might have said but didn't. If musical tragedy tends to comprise a wall and a plaint, this strange figure might be conceived as both wall and plaint in one: suitable both for the teacher's reading of the law and for the boy's consent to it. It is the ideal hieroglyph of acquiescence: quietly implacable and coldly sad.

In Weill's American musical plays, we sometimes find similarly chilly figures, musical ghosts of figures that might have once been expressive. For example, the central character in *Lady in the Dark* (1941, with lyrics by Ira Gershwin) is Liza Elliott, a magazine editor who tells her analyst her fears of personal inadequacy; in a dream scene, set in a circus, she justifies her indecisiveness by singing *The Saga of Jenny*, concerning a cheerful, self-indulgent woman who creates havoc by making quick decisions:

> Jenny made her mind up at twenty-two
> to get herself a husband was the thing to do.
> She got herself all dolled up in her satins and furs
> and she got herself a husband but he wasn't hers.

Poor Jenny, bright as a penny!
Her equal would be hard to find.
Deserved a bed of roses,
but history discloses
that she would make up her mind.

The choral refrain, "Poor Jenny, bright as a penny," is sung to a figure of mock lamentation—the term "poor" is obviously inappropriate for this brassy dame, but Weill's music is full of stylized sighs, organized around harmonic scrunches (produced by the simple means of stressing the seventh in dominant-seventh chords). One of the most remarkable features of Weill's whole career is the quality of musical irony in his later works, the way in which his ear remapped the stock figures of American popular music as elements of a sophisticated European semantics. The eighteenth-century satirist Jonathan Swift sometimes used a rhetorical figure that corresponds to irony in the same way that irony corresponds to normal speech: that is, he would say exactly what he meant, but in such a way that the reader would suspect that he meant something completely different—for instance, when he recommended that the Court should make virtuous conduct a matter of good manners, so that courtiers would behave honestly under the same pressure of etiquette that compelled them to use the right fork at the table. Weill, too, developed a manner of expressing what he believed in a way so literal that it's hard to take him seriously. I believe that "Poor Jenny" is, finally, less a mock lamentation than a mock mock lamentation, an expression of Weill's sense of the emptiness of the life of a rich, amoral hedonist such as Jenny. This Jenny might be conceived as Pirate Jenny's great-granddaughter, a far more successful pirate, triumphantly rapacious. "The Saga of Jenny," like *Seeräuber-Jenny* but in a far lighter manner, exposes the desolation at the heart of her wishing. But this simple meaning is so feathered with a fringe of ironic possibilities that Weill evaded all responsibility for it.

Weill's Epitaph

Weill died in 1950, and Adorno, perhaps ashamed because he had once defended Weill's music, wrote a venomous obituary:

> Weill considered himself a kind of Offenbach of his century, and with respect to speed of social-aesthetic reaction and to sketchiness, the analogy is not unreasonable. But the model is not to be repeated. The horror of reality has become too overwhelming for a parody to reach up to it. . . . Indeed, he had something of the genius of the great milliner. The capacity was given him

to find the proper melodies for the year's display, and this completely transitory thing may last.

We have seen that *The Threepenny Opera* is a story about clothes; so perhaps Adorno was in a sense right in conceiving Weill as a musical Chanel or Balenciaga. But I think of Weill as a composer who was able to put on any clothes—ranging from Protestant chorale to Jewish melisma to Euro-tango to Schoenbergian atonality to Richard Rodgers's popcorn—precisely because he was so confident that he had centered his art on the fundamentals of expression: on hieroglyphs. He was not a fake, but a serious composer adept at wearing any sort of frivolous musical drag. Perhaps the simplicity of *Der Jasager* is as much an artifice as any of his other styles, but I'm tempted to see it as the closest approximation of Weill *in sich,* Weill without his dazzling polystylisms, Weill examining the basic tool-kit of his art: *Der Jasager* is music expression performed with flint axe and blade of horn, not much like such gorgeous, glossy devices as *The Threepenny Opera* and *Lady in the Dark.* And yet, even when Weill pretended to be Offenbach, or worse, his music relies on the old semantics as stated and refined by Monteverdi and other great figures. The sometimes fashionable cut of Weill's clothes masks the extraordinary historical force of his language—as responsive to the whole tradition of Western music as the language of Stravinsky or of Adorno's beloved Schoenberg. Weill, like Joyce in *Ulysses,* made his art a total art, by appropriating every resource that history provided: behind any of Weill's stage pieces there lies a nest of other stage pieces, opening out onto everything from *The Play of Daniel* to Rodgers's *Carousel.* To learn what is the common property of all music theatre, listen to Weill.

In chapter 21 of Mann's *Dr. Faustus*—so profoundly informed by the aesthetics of Adorno—the composer-hero opines:

> "The work of art! It's deceit. It's the sort of thing the bourgeois would like to see still existing. It opposes truth, opposes seriousness. Only the very short thing, the highly consistent musical instant, is valid and serious. . . . Today semblance and play [*Schein und Spiel*] have the conscience of art against them. Art wants to stop being semblance and play, it wants to become knowledge [*Erkenntnis*]."
>
> . . . how will art live as knowledge? I remembered what he had written . . . about the expansion of the kingdom of the banal.

Many versions of Weill's life are told from this Faustian point of view: Weill sold his soul to the devil of fame, the devil of money, through relentless expansion of the kingdom of the banal. But Weill faced the same dilemma that Schoenberg and Webern and Mann's Leverkühn faced: after one had concentrated one's art to the limits of sobriety, without development or fancifulness of any sort, what did one do next? That didactic masterpiece, *Der Jasager,* shows a musical art that has stopped being pretense and play and has aspired to become knowledge. But the world cannot subsist on professorial lessons alone; and it is a testament to Weill's richness of imagination that he could use every resource of musical art, from Bach to the most meretricious *chanson,* to convey his strangely urgent critiques of expression.

For the musical hieroglypher, the kingdom of the banal is likely to be vast, since hieroglyphs are concentrated to the point of scarcely possessing temporal extension; and so the whole universe of discourse seems a dilution or a coarsening of the intense instant of meaning. Those composers who seek an irreducible unit of musical expression—the equivalent of a *word* in the language of music— must live with the consequences of their decision. As Stravinsky wrote at the end of *Renard:* You must pay for your fun.

Part Two:
Figures of Dissonance
among the Arts

But instead of limiting these dissonances to the orbit of a single sense, we shall cause them to overlap from the one sense to the other, from a color to a noise, a word to a light, a fluttering gesture to a flat tonality of sound. . .

—Artaud, "The Theatre of Cruelty (Second Manifesto)"

Loop

The great Modernist collaborations all survive as fragments. Diaghilev's ballets are mostly concert scores, sketches for backdrops, reconstructions of dimly remembered choreography, stills of Nijinsky, and fading gaudy costumes worn only by mannequins. Even where a great deal of information remains, as with *The Rite of Spring*, the project is enclosed in a certain glamour of the unrecoverable.

Therefore, imagination is required in order to ponder vertical phenomena in the comparative arts: the critic has to imagine the simultaneity of a musical figure, a twirling body, and a looming backdrop, long since separated, often partly lost. But some Modernist collaborations were always intended to be understood horizontally—and perhaps can even be read better in retrospect, as sets of isolated components. In Diaghilev's world, the preeminent specimen of horizontal theatre, of spectacle in which the constituent arts refuse to fit together into transmediating chords, is *Parade*. Any project that involves several arts can be read either horizontally or vertically; but vertical readings of *Parade* are likely to yield only confusion and various sorts of lexical outrage. It is an abyss of ismlessness: parts of it are expressionist, parts are cubist, parts are futurist, and the whole is contrived to make the parts weaken one another.

What is *Parade* today? Picasso's sketches now belong to the world of Picasso studies; Satie's score is an artifact of musicology; Cocteau's scenario, which seemed so dispensable to Satie and Picasso, has been fully dispensed with. But I don't lament this postmortem cleavage, for the components of *Parade* always belonged apart: it was, from beginning to end, an exercise in coordinated incongruity. The music can't be reintegrated with the plot, nor can the plot be reintegrated with the costumes and the stage designs,

FIG. 9 Pablo Picasso,
Parade, study for the
Chinese Conjuror's cos-
tume, 1917 (© 1999 Es-
tate of Pablo Picasso/ARS,
New York)

because they were never truly together in the first place. *Parade*'s charm is a function of the dissonance among the arts that constitute it. Far from finding ways in
which one art could reinforce or intensify or more deeply instill the meaning of
another art, the confectioners of *Parade* created a theatrical experiment in interference patterns among artistic media.

Parade: *Whorls in Picasso's Designs*

Visual aids can help us to discern the attitude of *Parade*'s collaborators toward
the audience. Besides Satie's music, perhaps the most memorable part of *Parade*
is the costume design for the Chinese Conjuror, one of the most haunting images
of the whole Ballets Russes. Picasso dressed the Conjuror in a red tunic with
widening yellow rays that emanate from his solar plexus; but most of the front is

covered by four large, pale, brocaded whorls, like elephant trunks tightly wound or half-extended. These whorls are tantalizing, enigmatic; and I'll argue that the whorl is the master emblem of the whole ballet, a veiled impudence.

These whorls might be interpreted in a number of ways. Since conjurors are masters of the elements, the whorls might represent stylized waves—though their distinctness is unwatery, and their direction is inconsistent: three of them curve to the left, but one curves to the right. Deborah Menaker Rothschild—in *Picasso's "Parade,"* one of the best books ever written for the student of Modernist collaboration—has noted that the variety-theatre Chinese conjurors whose costumes Picasso took as models sometimes wore the yin/yang insigne; and possibly the whorls are based on that. On the other hand, Picasso's whorls don't interlock within a single circle, or behave complementarily in any manner: they are more like isolated paisley fish than like universal principles of reciprocity.

Other visual material associated with *Parade* suggests different lines of interpretation. In one of Picasso's discarded studies for the stage set, a mermaid's tail

FIG. 10. Pablo Picasso, *Parade,* set design with mermaid's tail, 1917 (© 1999 Estate of Pablo Picasso/ARS, New York; reprinted from Rothschild, *Picasso's "Parade,"* p. 200)

peeks out from behind the tilted edge of an out-of-perspective painted building; it looks exactly like one of the Conjuror's whorls, outfitted with a few scales and a frayed terminus. And Picasso's design for the male Acrobat's costume is a blue leotard decorated with stars and giant white apostrophes: one apostrophe curls directly above the Acrobat's groin. Both the mermaid's tail and the groin-apostrophe might suggest a certain sexual force behind the whorl. The case for the erotic interpretation is, I believe, supported by a page from Cocteau's Italian notebook—Cocteau and Picasso traveled to Italy in 1917 in order to rehearse *Parade* before its première in Paris; and they seem to have spent a good deal of time there drawing penises, evidently imitating each other's designs. One of Cocteau's penises is so erect that it is impossibly recurved—twisted back into the shape of the Chinese Conjuror's whorls. Perhaps the subliminal message of

FIG. 11. *Pablo Picasso, Parade,* project for the male Acrobat's costume, 1917 (© 1999 Estate of Pablo Picasso/ARS, New York; Courtesy of Girau-don/Art Resource, NY)

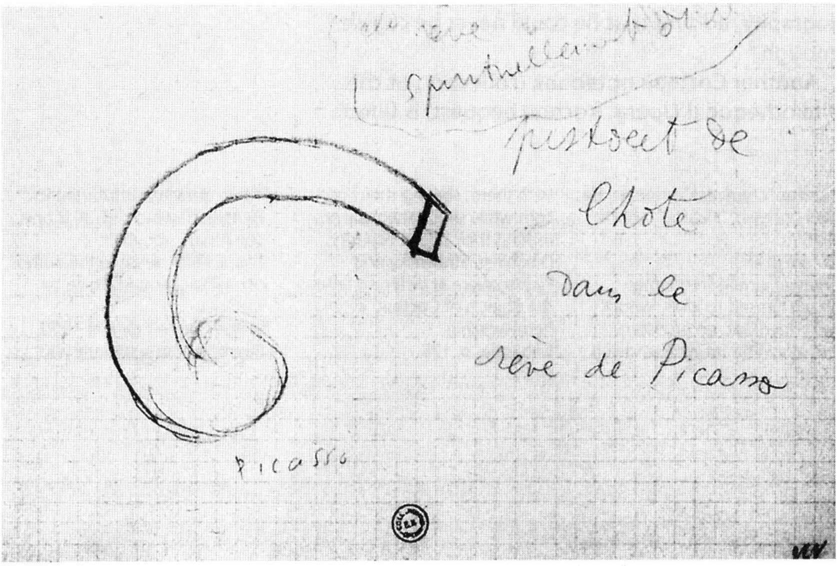

FIG. 12. Jean Cocteau, illustration of penis, 1917 (© 1999 Estate of Pablo Picasso/ARS, New York/ ADAGP, Paris; reprinted from Rothschild, *Picasso's "Parade,"* p. 62)

Parade is the same as that of Marcel Duchamp's grinding machines and other Modernist *blagues:* Go have sexual intercourse with yourself.

Circular Skits

The whorl motif suggests other sorts of loops besides the famous autoerotic one. The plot, the music—everything about *Parade* is dependent on sequences of loops, as Cocteau's synopsis for the theatre program will reveal:

At Country Fairs it is usual for a dancer or acrobat to give a performance in front of the booth in order to attract people to the turnstiles. The same idea, brought up-to-date and treated with accentuated realism, underlies the Ballet "Parade."

The scene represents a Sunday Fair in Paris. There is a traveling Theatre, and three Music Hall turns are employed as Parade. There are the Chinese Conjuror, an American Girl, and a pair of Acrobats.

Three Managers are occupied in advertising the show. They tell each other that the crowd in front is confusing the outside performance with the show which is about to take place within, and they try, in the crudest fashion, to induce the public to come and see the entertainment within, but the crowd remains unconvinced. After the last performance the Managers make another effort, but the Theatre remains empty. The Chinaman, the Acrobats, and the American Girl, seeing that the Managers have failed, make a last appeal on their own account. But it is too late.

One of the meanings of the French word *parade* is a kind of ante-theatre to a carnival show: a sample of the merchandise designed to lure paying customers. The ballet *Parade* is constructed entirely around rhythms of advertising—and, as a sometime copywriter, James Joyce, noted in *Ulysses,* "for an advertisement you must have repetition. That's the whole secret." *Parade* is a parade in vain: the lack of success drives the performers to increasingly frenzied repetitions in order to attract the onlookers, but no one will bite. The ballet is a series of instant replays of itself.

Furthermore, there is a strongly circular quality to the individual turns. Léonide Massine—who wore Picasso's pretty costume while pantomiming the Chinese Conjuror—left this account of his act:

> Cocteau . . . suggested that I should go through the motions of swallowing an egg. The idea appealed to me. With an elaborate flourish I pretended to produce an egg from my sleeve and put it in my mouth. When I had mimed the action of swallowing it, I stretched out my arms, slid my left leg sideways till I was almost sitting down, and with my left hand pretended to pull the egg from the toe of my shoe.

The egg's journey is a remarkable one, but it ends where it began—the trick is as round as the egg itself. This is, of course, typical of magicians' tricks: they depend on the reversibility of irreversible things, such as the digestion of food, or the cutting-up of paper into thousands of pieces, or the sawing-in-half of a lady. Such a trick is less an event than a parody of an event: a complicated demonstration that nothing whatever has happened. The egg trick is a kind of whorl in time, a nonprogressive action. And *Parade* as a whole is nothing but a sum of such zeroes.

Satie's Furniture Music as a Barrier against Expression

For writing music appropriate to *Parade,* Cocteau and Diaghilev found the right man in Erik Satie—that lover of paradoxes and *parapluies,* threadbare dandy, high aesthete of lowbrow art, irritable ascetic, the snowman of lyric. What has struck many listeners about Satie's music is the "anti-teleological" quality (in Leonard Meyer's phrase): it takes up time without seeming to move forward in time. Even when the chords are not strange, even when the chord progressions are not strange, Satie's music is conspicuously lacking in the outward thrust typical of Western tonal music. The sonorities seem to exist for their own sake, rather than pointing toward any sort of grand harmonic culmination outside their brief local context.

For Satie, music was not expression, but a barrier against expression. His famous titles—*Pièces froides, Effronterie, Aperçues désagréables, Préludes flasques (pour un chien), Embryons desséchés*—often suggest that his music should be regarded as profoundly unappetizing, chilly, a naked lunch well past its expiration date. But such music is no more an expression of disgust than of any other emotion, except insofar as the auditor is disgusted not to find any conventional reflexes of sentiment. In some sense, his music even aspired to be a barrier against sound itself, as Satie remarked in describing his 1920 project for *musique d'ameublement,* music-as-furniture:

> You know, there's a need to create furniture music, that is to say, music that would be a part of the surrounding noises and that would take them into account. I see it as melodious, as masking the clatter of knives and forks without drowning it out completely, without imposing itself. It would fill up the awkward silences . . . it would neutralize the street noises.

As Alan Gillmor notes, Satie's only public performance of furniture music—endlessly repeated commonplace figures from Saint-Saëns's *Danse macabre* and Thomas's *Mignon,* played by a small band at the intermission of a play—turned out to be a fiasco when those within earshot insisted on listening to it instead of proceeding about their normal business, even though Satie kept shouting, "Don't listen!"

Satie's effrontery was to challenge the role that music played in human life. Instead of a Wagnerian semantically dense, emotionally quickening music, a music that heightened the vivacity of the listener's responses to the world, Satie intended to produce music that receded into the background, an unobtrusive continuo to daily action. It is possible to speak of this as wallpaper music—Satie himself gave to one of his *musiques d'ameublement* the title *Tapisserie en fer forgé*—and the term is appropriate, in that the music provides a kind of sonorous grid on which the mind superimposes the patterns of its own ambulant musings; the ultrasimple harmonic motion and rhythm provide coordinate axes for the listener's tracing of private mental music. Satie thought of his furniture music as serving a social function; but perhaps it better serves to invite the listener to a kind of autism.

Music as environment is the exact opposite of music as hieroglyph: for Satie, music doesn't aspire toward an instant of devastating apprehension of meaning, but instead aspires toward a pleasant diffusion, a letting-go of meaning. Satie did write pieces that are like hieroglyphs, in that they present brief figures with clear kinesthetic relations to a referent in the exterior world; indeed, he wrote a whole book of them, *Sports et divertissements,* in which musical miniatures, reproduced in Satie's quirky, beautiful handwriting, are juxtaposed with *moderne* illustrations by Charles Martin. In one of these pieces, *Le water-chute* (1914), Martin shows a stylish couple peering doubtfully over the edge of the carnival boat, waiting for the sudden fall; and Satie obliges with a five-octave plunge of an F-major scale, after which he wrote the words *Ne changez pas de couleur—Je me sens mal à l'aise* [Don't turn green—I'm feeling sick]. These words might pertain to the acrophobes on top of the chute, or they might pertain to the composer's own chagrin at providing such an obvious gesture. This is a parody of a hieroglyph, a bit of musical nausea.

Phonometrography

Satie was the first great materialist of music. After a century in which music was conceived according to models derived from psychology and idealist philosophy, Satie conceived music according to models derived from physics. What is the chief property of music?—to Satie, the answer was inertia:

> Everyone will tell you that I am not a musician. It's true.
>
> Since the beginning of my career, I have classified myself among the phonometrographers. My labors are pure phonometrics. Take the *Fils des Étoiles* or the *Morceaux en forme de poire, En habit de Cheval* or the *Sarabandes:* one sees that no musical idea presided in the creation of these works. It is scientific thought that dominates.
>
> Besides, I have more pleasure in measuring a sound than in hearing it. Phonometer in hand, I labor joyously and confidently. . . . The first time I provided myself with a phonoscope, I examined a B flat of middle size. I assure you, I have never seen anything more repugnant. I called my servant to make him see it.
>
> With the phono-weigher *[phono-peseur],* a very common, ordinary F sharp attained 93 kilograms. It emanated from a fat tenor whose weight I took. . . . The future lies with philophony.

This is from Satie's *Memoirs of an Amnesiac* (1912), and it is possible to regard it as a piece of frivolity—it is impossible *not* to regard it as a piece of frivolity. But it is a caricature of Satie's real method of stressing the self-containment and heft of sounds, the acoustic substrate that doesn't develop, doesn't cue emotions, but just lies there, furnishing the ear. Satie's music has a disconcertingly high specific gravity, a strange leadenness; filled with fatuous and illegible mood-indications, it resists semantic construction, remains on its private Franco-lunar planet.

Property Trees That Don't Convulse

When translated to the domain of theatre, Satie's music, with its repugnant B♭s and its F♯s too heavy to lift, makes a flagrant show of its asemantic nature. In 1917—the year of *Parade*—Cocteau quoted with glee Satie's squib against Wagner: "Look, a property tree doesn't go into convulsions when a character enters the stage." Behind that remark lies a whole philosophy of music theatre: the music ought to be a rigid, immiscible background for the stage action, simply a sonorous equivalent to the cutout trees and two-dimensional houses. Theatre music should exercise discretion and tact, like any good piece of furniture.

And yet, the music of *Parade* isn't exactly *musique d'ameublement;* it is memorable, even disturbing. All traditional music, perhaps all traditional art, consists of the binding-together of variable elements by fixed elements—or, to put it another way, the disruption of fixed elements by variable elements. But in *Parade* the fixed elements are so profoundly fixed, as if pounded in with a pile driver, that it's impossible for the variable elements to make them budge, no matter how frenzied they become. The musical fascination derives from the conflict between the immobile and the irresistible: whirling centrifugal figures keep struggling in vain to dislodge a motionless center.

The first turn—the Chinese Conjuror—offers a clear demonstration. The fixed elements here are scale degrees $\hat{7}$–$\hat{2}$–$\hat{3}$—that is, B–D–E in C major, a pentatonic sound suitable for China. This is the striking motive played by trumpet and trombone, where (as Gillmor has noticed) it sounds like an anticipation of the melodically identical $\hat{3}$–$\hat{5}$–$\hat{6}$ figure of the *Moritat* in *The Threepenny Opera*. But this stiff three-note pattern governs the music long before the brass motive appears: the opening bars of *Prestidigitateur chinois,* and much of the subsequent music, consist of an unsettled, repetitious scamper of scale degrees $\hat{1}$, $\hat{4}$–$\hat{3}$–$\hat{7}$, $\hat{4}$–$\hat{3}$–$\hat{2}$, $\hat{4}$–$\hat{3}$–$\hat{3}$, $\hat{4}$–$\hat{3}$–$\hat{7}$, and so forth, in which all the $\hat{4}$–$\hat{3}$ figures are sixteenth notes and the other notes are eighth notes. (I give the figure as it appears for the oboes at rehearsal figure 3.) If all the brief $\hat{4}$–$\hat{3}$ figures are deleted, the scamper reduces to $\hat{1}$–$\hat{7}$–$\hat{2}$–$\hat{3}$; it is simply a disguised version of the basic $\hat{7}$–$\hat{2}$–$\hat{3}$ motive of this scene. The scamper keeps shifting its instrumentation and shifting its meter (between 3/8 and 2/4); but these tuggings, recolorings, and dislocations do little to hide the essential monotony of the scamper—one of the main pattern-units of the piece.

EX. 7.1. Satie, *Parade:* Chinese Conjuror, brass figure

EX. 7.2. Satie, *Parade:* Chinese Conjuror, scamper

The scamper, despite its slight eccentricities, is a music loop, exactly comparable to such action loops as the Conjuror's swallowing the egg and pulling it from the toe of his shoe; and the insistent $\hat{7}$–$\hat{2}$–$\hat{3}$ brass figure is simply a balder presentation of the same loop. It could be argued that Satie has devised a musical strategy for imitating the action—that the music is an active participant in the circularity of the conjuring, rather than an inert backdrop to it. But I find it hard to imagine a performance of *Parade* in which the music would seem to reinforce the events, to mark them more deeply in the listener's mind. The music loop inhabits its self-engrossed domain of sound, and the conjuring loop inhabits its self-engrossed domain of action; their forms are congruent, but they occupy separate theatrical spaces. Neither the music nor the action is going anywhere; they resemble one another in the way that an absence of apples resembles an absence of oranges.

Cocteau's Unspoken Text

In addition to the plane of music and the plane of action, there is a third, wholly imaginary plane, the plane of the spoken text that Cocteau prepared and never heard performed. If the author had not been disappointed, the spectator would have heard Satie's music and watched Massine's pantomime while a carnival barker was saying:

A—WELL-INFORMED—MAN—IS—WORTH—TWO!

IF—you—want—to become—rich. IF—you—feel—sick—IF—you—feel—tired

Enter—see—the—Chinese—wisdom—the missionaries—the dentists—the plague—the gold—the gongs.

The—pigs—that—eat—little—children—the emperor—of—China—in—his—armchair.

The—people—who—did—not—participate—at—the beginning—of—
the—show—can—remain—seated
Enter—see THE KING OF DRAMAS—THE GREAT SUCCESS OF LAUGHTER
AND FEAR

In other words, You ain't seen nothin' yet. The parade, the theatre in front of
the real theatre, dismisses its own entertainment value; in the unseen (and nonexistent) inner theatre lie unimaginable wonders and terrors. The empty loops of
music and conjuring are signs of the emptiness of a liminal realm of advertising,
a no man's land between common life (where you're sick, you're tired, and you'd
like more money) and the monstrous exhilarations of the freak show within.

Furthermore, Cocteau hoped that certain muffled sounds from the occult invisible theatre would penetrate the parade and tease the audience. In Satie's auto-
graph of the score, at a point where clarinets enter (corresponding to five bars after
rehearsal number [15] in the published score), some *Paroles supprimées* [sup-
pressed words] are written: *Ils lui crevèrent les yeux lui arrachèrent la langue* [They
gouge out his eyes, tear out his tongue]; and then, after the double bar, above some
particularly mild, unthreatening, and monotonous music—true furniture music—Satie wrote *bruit*, the howl of the tortured missionary. This section is accompanied by an unusual musical instrument, a spinning lottery wheel; and perhaps all
the loops in *Parade* are in some sense versions of the Wheel of Fortune, inscribing
its arbitrary circles in human space. *O fortuna, velut luna, statu variabilis!*

Parade is, then, a buffer between the audience and an expressionist spectacle.
Perhaps Cocteau heard in his inner ear, when he thought of missionaries tortured
by the Chinese, something like the torture scene in Puccini's *Tosca* (1900), where
Cavaradossi's offstage screams punctuate the extremely tense music. Cocteau
(who often enjoyed comparing the scandalous première of *Parade* to that of *The
Rite of Spring* four years earlier) may also have conceived *Parade* as a kind of de-
construction of a Stravinsky ballet:

> For most artists, a work wouldn't know how to be beautiful without an
> intrigue of mysticism, of love, or of annoyance. The short, the gay, the sad
> without any idyllic quality, are suspect. The hypocritical elegance of the Chi-
> nese Conjuror, the melancholy of the Little Girl's steamboats, the touching
> silliness of the Acrobats, everything that has remained a dead letter for *Pa-
> rade*'s audience, would have pleased it if the Acrobat had loved the Little Girl
> and had been killed by the jealous Conjuror, killed in turn by the Acrobat's
> wife, or any of thirty-six other dramatic combinations.

Lurking behind *Parade* is an undramatized drama along the lines of *I pagliacci*—
or of *Petrushka* (1911), which, like *Parade,* has a conjuror, an Oriental enter-

tainer (in this case a Moor), and several other carnival performers. In *Petrushka* the characters are caught up in a conventional melodrama of amorous intrigue, jealousy, and murder; but in *Parade* the performers inhabit separate performing spaces, like window displays in a department store. Cocteau thought of Satie's score as

> a masterpiece of architecture; that's what ears accustomed to vagueness and thrills can't understand. . . . The numerous *motifs,* each distinct from the others, like objects, follow one another without development and don't get tangled together *[ne s'enchevêtrent pas]*. . . . Never any sortileges, reprises, sleazy caresses, fevers, miasmas. Never does Satie "stir up the swamp."

But Cocteau also was an architect, displaying distinct theatrical objects in carefully immured areas. It isn't far from the dramatic method of *Parade* to the dramatic method that Stravinsky and Cocteau toyed with (but discarded) for *Oedipus Rex* (1927): let each character occupy an individual mini-stage, and draw back his or her private curtain before starting to sing. Just as Satie pulled apart the constituents of his music into pattern-units that take no notice of one another, so Cocteau pulled apart the constituents of his scenario into a series of blackout sketches—the circus equivalent of soliloquy, soliloquy, duet.

But today we may hear other things in the unheard theatre behind *Parade,* beyond *Tosca* or *Petrushka* or anything else that *Parade*'s creators might have known. In 1917, Schoenberg's *Erwartung* was already eight years old, though it would have to wait seven more years until its first performance. *Erwartung* is a long musical scream—perhaps not quite the same sort of scream that a missionary tortured by the Chinese would have screamed; but, on the other hand, how much does one scream differ from another? When Satie ridiculed Wagner for making the property trees go into convulsions, he was ridiculing the "atonal" Schoenberg without having heard him, for *Erwartung* is a continuous convulsion of music in sympathy with the character's psychic torment. In the whole context of the twentieth century, *Parade* looks like a kind of machine for neutralizing *Erwartung,* for demoting its expressive extremities to suppressed backstage cries: Satie found music that regards torture with urbane aplomb. *Erwartung* aspires to catharsis, to exhaustion through emotional saturation; but *Parade* is precatharized, evacuated of troubling material before it begins. *Erwartung* is willing to contemplate any combination of notes, any sequence of chords; *Parade* is a stringently self-limiting domain, in which smooth, impenetrable sound-hunks disengage themselves from all need to evolve or to fit into models of cognitive or perceptual activity. It is a theatre-city walled up against unwanted feelings, so completely sealed that the missionary's shrieks were deleted from the text before the first performance. Perhaps *Parade* is what *Erwartung* sounds like with its tongue torn out: a sort of gesturing—mute, but not silent—at zones of human experience that defy expression. In 1917 the noises of war were never far from the ears of Paris, and *Parade*'s method of dealing with terror through cultivated apathy makes it one of the profoundest artistic responses to the Great War.

Cube

Parade is a profound response not only to the Great War, but also to avant-garde art, from within avant-garde art: an act of self-scrutiny by its creators, an attempt to find the meaning of their previous work. As Jeffrey Weiss has shown, Picasso had by 1917 seen the cubist painter—sometimes dressed in a costume made up of cubes—become a figure of fun on the popular stage, in fashion shows, and so forth; and cubist drawing methods become a stock element of cartoons and even advertising. *Parade* is an attempt to create a totally cubist reality—as if the universe had been swallowed up by a simulacrum of itself, in the manner of Borges's imaginary country where a 1:1 scale map was unfurled over the entire area. This cubist land of feigning can be understood as a displacement of pain, a reconstruction of life rendered hard, safe, and witty by art. Indeed, *Parade* is far too safe—the sharp edges of the cubes no longer have any cutting force. In some ways it is remarkable that Picasso would cooperate in constructing such a monstrous expansion and neutering of cubism, the Pee-wee's Playhouse version of high art. But Picasso, too, could enjoy weightlessness and frivolity.

Rimbaud's "Parade"

Cocteau's main intent in writing *Parade*'s scenario was to devise a vaudeville in which the appurtenances of high art—cubism, symbolism, futurism—would try to cope with all manner of kitsch and dreck. What would happen if one of Picasso's sad clowns—so noble, so flexible, so emaciated—were hired (so to speak) by the Ringling Brothers' Circus, and forced to play gags with whoopee cushions? If Cocteau's scenario had been obeyed, the

American Girl's dance would have been accompanied by the following spiel from the American Manager:

> IT IS A CRIME to kill—the—curiosity—in—yourself—
> What—does—it—take—to—make—a—decision? ONE MINUTE!
> It—takes—A LIFETIME—of—regret—for—not—having—made it!
> Are you dead? NO? Then—you—must—*LIVE*!
>   *Get—this—clear—in—your—head*!
> A / timid / man / is / a / DEAD man.
> Enter—to learn—about—American—life—the trepidations—short circuits—
> detectives—the Hudson—Ragtimes—factories—trains that derail—ocean liners that sink!
>   I was pale—sullen—puny. I was poor—bald—alone.
> Let—me—become—a—RED—Negro—if—you—do not—leave—here—healed!
> Hesitation—can—make—you—lose everything.
> Enter! Enter! DEMAND THE K! (drum-roll)

Rothschild has noted that the American Girl's act is based on such silent film serials as *The Perils of Pauline* and *The Exploits of Elaine,* so popular in wartime France that soldiers on leave demanded to see all the episodes at once, since they couldn't be sure of being in Paris (or being alive) to see the next episode. *The Perils of Pauline* wasn't considered high art, and the art of inducing yokels to pay money to see a dancer is about as low as art can get.

But there is a joke here. The snake-oil barker seems to be stringing together impressive-sounding bits of nonsense vaguely pertinent to America, but his rhetoric is derived from highfalutin art, the prose poetry of Rimbaud—in particular, the section of *Les illuminations* (1875; 1886) entitled (not coincidentally) "Parade":

> O the most violent Paradise of the enraged smile! No comparison with your Fakirs and the other stage buffooneries. In costumes improvised with the taste of bad dreams, they present lamentations, present tragedies of marauders and spiritual demigods such as have never been in history or religions. Chinese, Hottentots, gypsies, silly folk, hyenas, Molochs, old dementias, sinister demons, they all mingle their popular, maternal circus-acts with bestial poses and caresses. They would interpret new plays, and "good girl" songs. Master jugglers, they transform the place and the characters and make use of mag-

netic comedy. Eyes flame, blood sings, bones grow big, tears and red trickles stream down. Their joking or their terror lasts a minute, or whole months.

I alone have the key to this savage parade.

(Britten set this text in his 1939 *Les illuminations,* using the last line as the refrain of the whole piece.) Both the Manager's come-on and the Rimbaud passage tease with an absurd profusion of hair-raising spectacles, pouring out asyndetically, randomly; and Cocteau's line about the foundering of the steamship may recall Rimbaud's *Le bateau ivre,* in which the poet imagines himself as a ship that wishes to sink—its *Peaux-rouges* (redskins) are not so far from the *Nègre rouge* of the Manager's spiel. Even Cocteau's derailing trains seem to recall Rimbaud's hope, in the *lettre du voyant,* that the poet will become like a locomotive no longer compelled to run on a fixed track: perhaps the dream-inconsequential disasters of the early silent films could be understood as a visual realization of *symboliste* dissolving untenable worlds—which would mean that D. W. Griffith was the man who really held the key to this savage parade.

For Cocteau, *Parade* had two parts: the fore-spectacles, including the Acrobats and the American Girl, and the acts inside the tent, never seen by the audience. The hidden interior spectacle of *Parade* contains atrocities derived from *symbolisme,* as well as from other sources: Cocteau's flimsy ante-theatre advertises an unseen theatre of dismemberment, human sacrifice, and bestiality, for which Rimbaud would have been a fine impresario. Cocteau took Rimbaud's Chinese, his jugglers, his "good girl" songs, and put them in the foreground; Cocteau suppressed Rimbaud's hyenas, his Moloch, his bleeding faces, which bulge out from behind a curtain that is never opened.

(Not only *Parade,* but other parts of Cocteau's work can be understood as an attempt to transform recontextualized pieces of *symboliste* poetry into ironic theatrical spectacles. What Cocteau did to Rimbaud in *Parade,* he did, far more grossly, to Mallarmé in *Le gendarme incompris* [The Misunderstood Policeman, 1921], a skit, with music by Poulenc, in which a policeman arrests an old marquise for picking flowers in a park; his description of the crime is a long, incomprehensible speech, maddening to all the other characters. Cocteau was delighted that no one in the audience noticed that the whole speech was a steal of the text of Mallarmé's *L'ecclésiastique.*)

Rimbaud, Picasso, and other advanced artists continually take matter from low art, such as provincial carnivals, and re-present that low art in an abstracted, elated manner; but Cocteau insists on re-imagining, re-immersing their stylized figures back into the original humble context. Cocteau's most delicious joke is that this humiliating of high art takes place within the most elevated venue of all, Diaghilev's Ballets Russes. Cocteau didn't want to erase the distinction between high art and low: he simply wanted to relish the clash between the highbrow and the lowbrow by bringing them face-to-face. Cocteau enjoyed dissonance within spectacles; and the dissonance between brow levels served his purpose well.

Cubism and the Letter K

The most puzzling aspect of the Manager's ballyhoo for the American Girl is his final cry, "Demand the K!"—which also appears in the desperate attempt by all three Managers, at the end of the ballet, to coax or bully the audience into paying for their entertainment:

> IF you want to be loved!
> MADAME! IF you want to have a beautiful bosom!
> MONSIEUR! IF you want to have a more important position!
> DEMAND THE K! YES! YES! YES!

Rothschild speculates that since *K* is far more a feature of the German than the French alphabet, Cocteau was trying to align his vulgar Managers with the enemy; and she further notes that during the Great War, *cubism* was sometimes spelled with a *K* in order to dismiss the style as a vile foreign imposition. This may be so, but Weiss prints some humorous drawings from 1912 that might suggest a different interpretation of the significance of the letter *K*. One shows a *plein-air* artist, himself drawn entirely in straight lines, painting a billboard with a picture of a cube on it, with the legend "Bouillon des 3 dimensions": an allusion to the bouillon "kub," the ideal—perhaps the only—subject for an artist who dwells in a fully cubified world. The other drawing, *Style cubique, la vie parisienne* by Louis Marcoussis, is a satire of cubist fads in interior decoration: a woman, whose box-hat is adorned with square peacock feathers, inhabits a room in which all the furniture seems to be made out of large dice; on her wall are two identical pictures of a square violin, one signed "Pikasso," the other signed "Brak." Marcoussis was himself a cubist painter, and I doubt that he used *k* in order to suggest the style was a Teutonic decadence; more likely, he thought that *k*—a letter made up of straight lines—was a more cubist sort of typography than the rather circular letter *c*. If Cocteau was thinking similarly, "Demand the K!" appeals not to German *caca* but to cubist chic. Learn to love a linear, modern style, and you will get a better-paying job, or your breasts will grow beautiful.

From Kokteau's point of view, *Parade* was an exercise in recontextualizing high art by reversing planes: instead of a world where normal men and women contemplate pictures assembled out of cubes, we have a world in which walking cubes—the Managers—introduce artifices in the form of normal male and female dancers. If people like to look at cubes, cubes seem to like to look at people.

FIG. 13. J. Hemard, *Les vacances du maître cube*, 1912 (Weiss, *The Popular Culture of Modern Art*, p. 65)

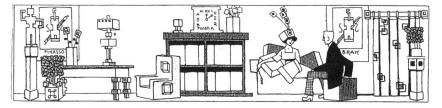

FIG. 14. Louis Marcoussis, *Style cubique, la vie parisienne*, 1912 (Weiss, *The Popular Culture of Modern Art*, p. 65)

Picasso's Managers: Life inside a Cubist Painting

The evolution of the Managers during the development of *Parade* was the most conspicuous cubifying of the spectacle. What became *Parade* started as a piece called *David*, for which Cocteau tried to coax Stravinsky into writing music: the *parade* was to be a come-on to a Biblical story, and a clown hidden in a box would, through a loudspeaker, urge the public to enter the booth. Cocteau at first hoped that *Parade* would have a similar premise:

> In the first version the Managers didn't exist. After each Music-Hall number, an anonymous voice, coming through an amplifying box (a theatrical imitation of the fairground gramophone, an antique mask in the modern fashion), sang out a type-phrase, summing up the perspectives of the character, opening a breach on the dream.

But in the finished *Parade,* the *masque antique à la mode moderne* was no longer a hidden surface for projecting a loud voice, but a silent and extremely conspicuous thing; indeed, it is the strongest evidence of Cocteau's demotion in favor of Picasso, of the demotion of text in favor of visual spectacle. (I know of no other collaboration in the history of art in which the component artistic media seem so bent on annihilating one another.) The French Manager, who introduced the Chinese Conjuror, became a dancer encased in a huge cardboard caricature of Diaghilev, smoking a pipe the size of a trombone, with a row of cutout trees nonchalantly glued to the side, as if he were both a stroller and a perambulating landscape. The American Manager, who introduced the American Girl, became a dancer trying to move within a great cubist reconstruction of a skyscraper. The Manager who introduced the Acrobats was intended to be a dummy astride a pantomime horse, but when the dummy kept falling off, the pantomime horse performed the role bareback, and became a general object of displeasure for audience and performers alike—the audience complained, understandably, that such cheap tricks could be seen elsewhere for far less money.

In *Parade,* Picasso found a way of producing a theatrical reproduction of how we would live if we could live inside a cubist painting. To some extent, the whole cubist revolution consists of the discovery that objects and the space around objects could be treated in a uniform manner: objects made up of facets inhabit a faceted space, as if there were no distinction between foreground and background, between solid bodies and air. Braque said that he tried to paint the "visual space" that "separates objects from each other": "This in-between space *[entre-deux]* seems to me just as important as the objects themselves." In "analytical" cubism, crumpled objects take shape amid a crumpled sky. Picasso himself suggested that his cubist paintings were like flattened-out sculptures, or like instructions for folding paper into a three-dimensional shape: the spectator should feel able to "cut up" the canvas and put it back together and "find oneself confronted with a sculpture." A cubist drawing, then, is more like a set of instructions for folding a paper doll or a paper airplane than like a traditional perspective drawing in which the parallel lines of objects in three-dimensional space are represented as toed-in lines receding to a single vanishing point.

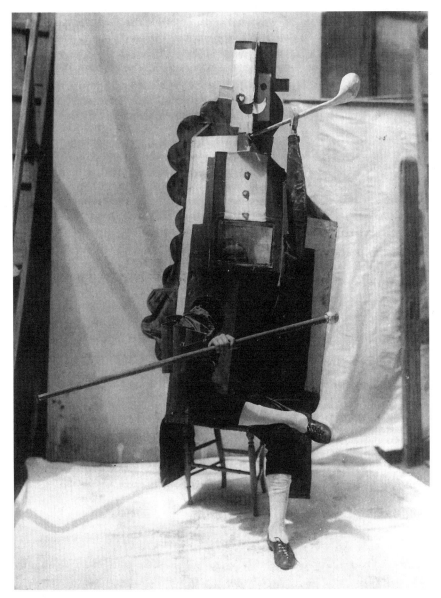

FIG. 15. Pablo Picasso, *Parade,* French Manager, 1917 (© 1999 Estate of Pablo Picasso/ ARS, New York; reprinted from Rothschild, *Picasso's "Parade,"* p. 134)

And yet, it is a mistake to believe that cubist drawing is entirely liberated from the conventions of perspective drawing: Braque and Picasso simply insisted that these conventions must operate not on the whole plane of the picture field, but on the individual facets exclusively. If you take a cross-hatched trapezoid, suspend it against a black background, and display it through a peephole to anyone raised in the conventions of Western art, the spectator will describe it as a rectangle seen obliquely; but a spectator not raised in the conventions of Western art will describe it as what it is, a trapezoid. The facets of a cubist painting depend on the elementary (but not universal) apprehension that a square with slanty lines sticking out of its corners is a representation of a cube; without that understanding the picture is meaningless, but with that understanding the spectator can discover images that constitute themselves volumetrically in an amorphous space made up out of a vast heap of tiny individual spaces—for each facet occupies its own miniature continuum. For the cubist, the cube is an atom of space, susceptible to arbitrary recombination with other atoms of space. And this cubist multi-spatiality entails an altered physiology of perception: the spectator apprehends the drawing with fifty different eyes, projecting outward on stalks and curving around the object, the object seen full-face and three-quarter-face and profile all at the same time. Cubist art may seem somewhat static, passive, but only because the activity has been transferred from the (tranquilized) object depicted to the (vehemently darting) gaze of the onlooker. To study a cubist picture is to become a lobster.

This peculiar intimacy of thing and atmosphere and eyeball makes *Parade* a disturbing spectacle. Picasso's backdrop shows buildings leaning outward at crazy angles over a proscenium arch, itself tilted; when the American Manager ambles out, he is a strange combination of a man and a building—an *homme-décor,* in Cocteau's phrase—as if the stage set has popped itself out into three dimensions and started to dance. Furthermore, in the lower right of the backdrop, Picasso painted stippled silhouettes of figures wearing top hats, fashionable clothes—that is, the imaginary shadows of the audience itself. Instead of the normal three-plane theatrical model, according to which (1) the audience, safe in its seats, contemplates (2) human actors, performing in front of (3) immobile scenery, *Parade* shatters all three planes into fragments, each of which is an odd jumble of décor, performer, and spectator. The French Manager, with trees growing from his back, is a personification of the whole theatrical environment, a stage-fragment moving through a puzzling space constituted by other stage-fragments. The only proper conclusion to such a piece is a scandal, for the audience must surely involve itself in the dramatic action, even if only by throwing things at the performers.

FIG. 16. Pablo Picasso, *Parade,* study for the set, 1917 (© 1999 Estate of Pablo Picasso/ ARS, New York; reprinted from Rothschild, *Picasso's "Parade,"* p. 195)

Metaphors for Cubes in Satie's Music

Of course, the previous paragraph should have begun, This peculiar intimacy of thing and atmosphere and eyeball *and ear:* Satie's music, with its texture of varied or unvaried self-quotation, has a cubist rhythm as well. If the noteheads of the Chinese Conjuror's î, 4̂–3̂–7̂, 4̂–3̂–2̂, 4̂–3̂–3̂, 4̂–3̂–7̂ figure were connected, they would trace a zigzag line starting up in predictable directions from the stable 4–3 unit, like slant lines proceeding from the corners of a square; and there are many places where extremely repetitive two-note bass ostinati seem to figure Satie's score with little rhombs. Darius Milhaud noted that the vocal line of Satie's *Socrate* "is of such absolute purity that, if, just for fun, one followed its ascending and descending, or even static, movement, the result would be a drawing incorporating the pure lines of ancient Greek masterpieces"; but the connect-the-dots game, if played with *Parade,* seems to yield something far more up-to-date. In the Acrobats' scene—which Cocteau intended to represent manned flight and other sorts of technological progress—there is a foghorn-like organ pipe (rehearsal figure 39), above which appear two slow, strongly accented, up-down-up string figures: the first consists of scale degrees (in C major) $\hat{6}$–$\hat{7}$–$\hat{3}$, repeated twelve times; then, as the diapason shifts from $\hat{3}$ to $\hat{2}$, the second figure appears, $\flat\hat{7}$–$\hat{1}$–$\hat{4}$, repeated four times; then the first figure and the first bass reappear, repeated eight times. In the cubist context of *Parade*, these two figures seem to constitute a single acoustic object, carefully examined from two different points of view. The mere fact that the figures are repeated in groups of four gives a strong rectilinearity to this section. This music is not acrobatic, not lithe, not airy, but heavily incised, immobile: Satie felt that his true collaborator on *Parade* was Picasso, not Cocteau.

EX. 8.1. Satie, *Parade:* cubes in music

Satie paid little attention to the content of *Parade,* as Cocteau imagined it: the Chinese Conjuror's music is no more Oriental than the Acrobats' music (the Acrobats, for example, perform to pentatonic xylophones); the scenario of *Parade* did lead Satie to quote Irving Berlin's *That Mysterious Rag* for the American Girl (as Ornella Volta has noticed), but the syncopated tune is oddly de-Americanized, denatured, in the antiseptic context of *Parade*. Satie, however, paid close attention to the style of *Parade,* as Picasso imagined it; and the music can be heard as a kind of academic exercise for a Schola Cuborum. Some critics of *Parade,* such as Richard Axsom, feel that Satie's music is no more cubist than any other piece of music devised according to a principle of pattern-unit construction; but I believe that the angled three-note figures so common in the score of *Parade* are metaphors for cubes as plausible as the individual facets of Picasso's drawing—facets which, as we've seen, are themselves only metaphors for cubes.

Ballet réaliste *and Visual Collage*

In addition to this sound-spectacle derived from "analytical" cubist drawing—the reconstruction of the smooth, continuous volumes of objects in the visible world with big jerky pixels—*Parade* also offers a sound-spectacle derived from

"synthetic" cubist design, that is, the piecing-together of imaginary fields of reality through odd collages of ready-made objects, or artful counterfeits of ready-
made objects. Cocteau thought that this appropriation of "synthetic" cubism
was far more important than such "analytical" artifacts as the American Manager's skyscraper costume:

> Contrary to what the public imagines, [the Chinese Conjuror, the Ameri-
> can Girl, and the two Acrobats] are more relevant to the cubist school than
> our Managers are. The Managers are prop-humans [hommes-décor], Picasso
> pictures that move, and their structure itself imposes a certain choreographic
> style. For the four main characters, it was a question of taking a collection of
> real gestures [gestes réels] and of metamorphosing them into dance, without
> losing their realistic force, as the modern painter is inspired by real objects to
> metamorphose them into pure painting, without, however, losing sight of the
> power of their volumes, their materials, their colors, and their shadows.

Massine, and others involved in the dance aspects of Parade, gave Cocteau
considerable credit for the choreography of the piece: Cocteau would model
commonplace gestures, and Massine and the others would find ways of building
a pantomime around those gestures. In this fashion, Parade translated into the
formal and ceremonious world of ballet the gestural equivalent of slang: for
example, there is a well-known photograph of Marie Chabelska in her vaguely
nautical American schoolgirl costume, with flat, turned-out feet, with her legs
bowed out in an innocent but extremely unladylike fashion, and with her fore-
arms sticking forward, fingers curled and thumbs pointing right and left—a
what-me-worry shrug with her whole body. This gesture never turns into anything like a gestus, because the pose, while striking, has little meaning (except to
confirm French stereotypes about American women), and no purpose within the
larger spectacle; furthermore, the music refuses to shrug in any way that would
confirm or reinforce what the dancer is doing. But as an element in a transmedia
collage, Chabelska's gesture of strenuous casualness takes an important place.

The subtitle of Parade is Ballet réaliste, and it is realistic not only in its visual
gestures but in its sounds. Just as Cocteau hunted for odd moderne bits of body
deportment, Satie hunted for odd moderne noises—though in the absence of a
coherent scenario to connect the sound effects with the gestures, the realism of
the sound only reinforces the dissonance, the uncoordinatedness of the sound
world and the sight world. Satie's score has cues for a typewriter, a pistol, a high
siren, a low siren, a lottery wheel, and something called flaques sonores, sound-
puddles, evidently made by dropping a cymbal on a hard floor; Cocteau also
wanted Morse code apparatus and a variety of other sounds: "The score of
Parade ought to serve as the musical base for suggestive noises, such as sirens,

FIG. 17. *Parade,* photograph of Marie Chabelska as the American Girl, 1917 (© 1999 Estate of Pablo Picasso/ ARS, New York; reprinted from Rothschild, *Picasso's "Parade,"* p. 74)

typewriters, airplanes, dynamos, put there as what Georges Braque so justly calls 'facts' *[faits].*" Just as Braque and Picasso glued real cards or snippets of newsprint or fragments of musical score onto their cubist collages, so Satie created percussion parts, or a background of continuous, indeterminately pitched sound, out of the technological innovations of the age. John Cage considered that the background sounds of a performance were part of the performance itself; Satie, on the other hand, invented the background sounds and scored them into the performance. For proper *musique d'ameublement,* one needs to find talking furniture.

In many ways this technique was derived from Italian futurism, even more than from French cubism. The futurists pursued, more vehemently than the cubists, an assault on the distinction between foreground and background, between object and environment. For example, Umberto Boccioni's *The Street Enters the House* (1911) attempts a complete representation of a city environment from all sides at once, as if a 180-degree (or more) panoramic scan were crinkled together into a single yawning square canvas. As the catalogue for a 1912 futurist exhibition explains:

The dominating sensation is that which one would experience on opening a window: all life, and the noises of the street rush in at the same time as the movement and the reality of the objects outside. The painter does not limit himself to what he sees in the square frame of the window as would a mere photographer, but he also reproduces what he would see by looking out on every side from the window.

This painting suggests what the world would look like if the ear, not the eye, were the organ of vision, capable of assimilating a spatially organized field of perception in all directions at once. William Blake thought that the Fall of Man occurred when the eye, once capable of seeing 360 degrees, became recessed in a socket of bone, trained on a narrow slice of reality right in front of the skull;

FIG. 18. Umberto Boccioni, *The Street Enters the House,* 1911 (Pontus Hulten, *Futurism & Futurisms* [New York: Abbeville Press, 1986], p. 123)

in that sense, Boccioni managed to undo the Fall. And in many other works Boccioni labored to incorporate the environment around objects into the objects themselves: in his astonishing *Development of a Bottle in Space* (1912–13), he sculpted a process of rotating vacuum that will eventually turn itself into a bottle; and in *Unique Forms of Continuity in Space* (1913), he sculpted the displacement of air trailing out behind the muscles of a violently striding human figure, as if a man were a boat that left a visible wake, a trace in the medium through which he moves. *Parade*, too, can be understood as a work that tries to enclose within itself the whole context of wildly centrifugal sight and sound in which any twentieth-century work takes place; *Parade*, too, aspires to wrap itself in tissues of air, tissues of self-interpretation.

Intonarumori: *Russolo and Boccioni*

But *Parade*'s most obvious debt to the futurists lies in its noise-making devices. The futurist Luigi Russolo—more a painter than a musician—devised a series of *intonarumori*, noise-intoners, all enclosed in black boxes, as if a cubist's cubes had been taught to speak. These included *Ululatori, Rombatori, Crepitatori, Gorgogliatori,* and *Sibilatori* (howlers, rumblers, cracklers, gurglers, hissers); and Russolo devised concert pieces for them, such as the 1913 *Veglio di una città* (Awakening of a City), the score to which is a fine piece of futurist graphic, with its normal bars, clefs, time signatures, and staves all decorated with thick black lines holding steadily horizontal, or ascending up and down in slow glides, or proceeding in fast jerks from one flat line to the next—a visual anticipation of the later Mondrian.

It is difficult to know what the *intonarumori* sounded like. The instruments themselves seem no longer to exist; in 1977 Mario Abate and Pietro Verardo reconstructed them and recorded *Veglio di una città*—which seems a disappointingly lackadaisical succession of borborygms and distant airplanes. Still more disappointing is the one surviving recording of the original *intonarumori,* unfortunately used as underlay to a conventional *Corale & Serenata,* composed by Russolo's brother Antonio and scored for normal instruments: one hears insipid tunes faintly disrupted by various growls, like a radio broadcast with low-pitched electric interference. Still, the premise of *Parade* is there, in embryo, in this old futurist record: unpitched contrivances that interject into the domain of tonal art music a collection of sub-artistic noises, a new repertoire in acoustic semantics. Here music tries to cope with the random urgencies of urban sirens, with the information overload of a frantic typewriter and a Morse code apparatus, signaling in the void from no one in particular to no one in particular. *Parade* brought into the theatre a simulation of the general background static of the twentieth century.

It could be said that the Managers are *intonarumori* outfitted with arms and legs: they even look like accordions—buildings and avenues squashed together and pulled apart. But from Cocteau's point of view, the futurist aspect of *Parade* was concentrated in the Acrobats' turn, as the ballyhoo written for the unhorsed and canceled Negro Manager mildly suggests:

PUT / YOUR / LEGS / TO / YOUR / NECK [that is, run]—and—flee—the
    boredom—that—ambushes—you!
The most beautiful spectacle in the world
The past!—the present!—the future!
The film—of—fifty—thousand—meters!
The / great / success / of / laughter / and / fear /
A MAN OFFERS
The remedy—for—all the ailments of the heart—the brain—the spleen
This—is—the—consequence—of a—wish!
MODERN MAN—enters—at—OUR—place.

But the futurist aspect of the Acrobats is far more strongly present in a note that Cocteau wrote for Satie:

Médrano—Orion—two biplanes in the morning . . . the archangel Gabriel balancing himself on the edge of the window . . . the diver's lantern . . . Sodom and Gomorrah at the bottom of the sea . . . the meteorologist—the telescope . . . the parachutist who killed himself on the Eiffel Tower—the sadness of gravity—soles of lead—the sun—man slave of the sun.

Cocteau clearly conceived the Acrobats as personifications of technological adventure, investigating the ultimate verges of human experience in airplanes and diving devices; but Cocteau was sensitive to the danger of such explorations, particularly since his friend the aviator Roland Garros was shot down by the Germans in 1915. Of course, no spectator would leave *Parade* either exhilarated or frightened at the possibilities of technology—the futurist passion for the machine is fully anesthetized by the spectacle as a whole. But various stereotypes of the machine, and of the acrobat, are important components of *Parade*'s style of elated child's play.

The humble pathos of the acrobat, the clown of thin air—a pathos caught in various ways by Picasso in *Family of Saltimbanques* (1905) and by Apollinaire in *Les saltimbanques* (published in 1909 but sent in manuscript to Picasso in 1905, and set to elegant, Golliwoggesque music by Honegger in 1917, the year of *Parade*)—could easily mutate into a strange aesthetic-metaphysical-mechanistical pathos: the pathos of mankind fighting the restrictions of the gravity-ridden, sense-defined lower world. Why are acrobats sad?—because they can escape from the materiality of things for a moment, through death-defying leaps into space, but they must return to prosaic life. In 1922 Franz Kafka wrote *Erstes Leid,* a story of a trapeze artist who refuses to descend from his trapeze, who evolves to such extraordinary *contemptus mundi* that when his circus travels by train, he insists on sleeping on the overhead luggage rack; this parable shares a theme with another parable published in the same volume, *Ein Hungerkünstler,* Kafka's famous tale of the artist whose art is self-starvation. Also in 1922, Rainer Maria Rilke wrote his fifth Duino elegy, based on Picasso's *Family of Saltimbanques:* it describes acrobats as failed angels, tumbling through "oiled, smoother air," intimate with the *Dastehn* of things, only to land once again on the shabby carpet of the earth, where their act is a sham and a bore. Shortly before his death, Rilke wrote a note thanking Cocteau for his *Orphée* (1927), in which the wings of the angel Heurtebise are represented by panes of glass on a glazier's back; and most of the angels of Modernist art have extremely fragile wings, liable to shatter in mid-flight. The angels of our age have a strong aspect of Icarus. If *Parade* had evolved according to Cocteau's wishes, the audience would have been conscious not only of scenes of backstage torture, but of the keen possibility that the Acrobats would crash to their deaths, like Roland Garros in his airplane, or "the parachutist who killed himself on the Eiffel Tower." Acrophobia and the fear of being crushed in a machine were banished to the far margins of *Parade,* where they linger as virtual, not actual, terrors.

Cocteau's note to Satie is fascinating in that the angel Gabriel seems to be hovering over Sodom and Gomorrah—what are the Biblical Cities of the Plain doing in the Acrobats' turn in *Parade?* The answer lies, I believe, in certain connotations of acrobats that lie outside the world of Picasso and the world of theatrical metaphysics. Perhaps the most important precursor of Satie among French composers was Emmanuel Chabrier, who collaborated in 1873 with Paul Verlaine, the symbolist poet, on a remarkable operetta concerning circus life, *Fisch-Ton-Kan.* This spectacle, which was performed only in private, anticipates *Parade,* and not only in its *chinoiserie:* to self-consciously frivolous, clean, dry music, the characters present themselves not as human beings but as objects:

J'engraisse	I swell,
Mon front brille d'allégresse	Happiness shines on my brow,
C'est moi de tous les Poussahs	I am of all the Poussahs
Le plus gras Poussah! . . .	The fattest Poussah! . . .
Bien souvent je fléchis, mais	I admit I often bend,
J'obéis à la secousse,	Readily yield to your push,
Comme ce magot qu'on pousse	Like the tumbler that you bash
Et qui ne tombe jamais!	But that never stays down!

A *poussah* is a toy that, when pushed over, instantly bobs upright; the singer of this aria is, in effect, an *homme-décor*. The acrobats in *Fisch-Ton-Kan* bring us to the Sodom and Gomorrah that lurks, disguised, on the fringes of *Parade:* the very first number that survives from Chabrier's score concerns an acrobat fallen from a trapeze, over whom the other circus performers sing this curious lament:

Adieu le trapèze,	Goodbye, goodbye trapeze,
Ce pitre joli, si joli	This funny, so pretty lad
N'aura plus pour chaise	Will no more put his seat
Un bâton poli.	On polished rod.

Chabrier's music is somewhat elegiac, but accompanied by a treble whirligig— almost like the music loops in Satie's *Parade*—as if to mock the dirge as it is sung. Why should Verlaine want to emphasize the contact between the trapeze and the fallen acrobat's buttocks? The answer lies in a still more outrageous song, the *Couplets du pal;* it concerns the Armchair of Death, the seat of which contains a spring-loaded stake:

Le pal! Le pal!	For the sharp stick
Est de tous les supplices	Gives, of all known means of torture,
Le principal	The biggest prick,
Et le plus fécond en délices.	And is most conducive to pleasure.

This paean to the delights of impalement was yanked out of the suppressed *Fisch-Ton-Kan* and placed in the publicly performed operetta *L'étoile* (1877), where, of course, the unacceptable last line was changed to *Et le moins rempli de délices* [And is least conducive to pleasure]. The homosexual subtext of trapeze art was entirely excluded from the finished *Parade,* except insofar as the French Manager's Diaghilev-like mask might have excited knowing smiles; even the phallic apostrophe on the groin of the male Acrobat's costume has no specifically homosexual suggestion. But Cocteau kept a photograph near his desk of an agile man committing auto-fellatio—and in some sense the various loops that circle around *Parade* are futuro-cubist reimaginings of a compact sexual knot.

One of the principal features of futurism was its systematic confusion of the sexual and the metallurgical—a confusion that persists to this day in the domain of advertising whenever a beautiful woman is used to sell a car. Filippo Tommaso Marinetti, the theorist and organizer of the movement, wrote in "Technical Manifesto of Futurist Literature" (1912) that the goal was "To capture the breath, the sensibility, and the instincts of metals, stones, wood, and so on, through the medium of free objects and whimsical motors. To substitute for human psychology, now exhausted, the lyric obsession with matter. . . . The warmth of a piece of iron or wood is in our opinion more impassioned than the smile or tears of a woman." In his *Battle of Tripoli,* Marinetti showed how this could be accomplished, by writing a loving ode to his *signora* the machine gun. Furthermore, Marinetti dreamed (just around the time of *Parade*) of a cinema that might show a "Discussion between a foot, a hammer, and an umbrella"— or a scene in which the painter "[Giacomo] Balla falls in love with and marries a settee, and a footstool is born." In a sense, *Parade* itself is the giggling offspring of the human race and inanimate objects.

From a futurist point of view, the achievement of *Parade* was its discovery that the theatre could be converted into a playhouse of objects, where revolvers and lottery wheels and sirens carried on an ardent palaver, where skyscrapers tripped around the stage, a triumph of machine erotics over human erotics. Or, to put it another way: the achievement of *Parade* was its discovery that the artistic *medium,* the sheer materiality of sound, of paint, of cardboard, could become a stage spectacle independent of any psychological expressivity. The *Gesamtkunst* of Wagner is predicated on the notion that the stage spectacle is a unified reflex of human sensibility, in several artistic modes of extension through space and time; but the *Gesamtkunst* of *Parade* lacks any intelligible correlation to a human subject—no one is the *auteur* of *Parade*—and thus falls apart into various congruent but independent art-forms, each stressing its own materiality, its own blocked, chunked adequacy to itself. In this sense, *Parade* is Clement Greenberg's dream spectacle: each artistic medium revels in its isolation, its unrelatedness to all others. Sound dramatizes its ninety-three-kilogram phonicality; wood dramatizes its woodenness. Marie Chabelska makes her unforgettable shimmy and the typewriter makes its clatter in the orchestra, but the striking sight-image may have no intelligible connection to the striking sound-image. As if glad to be liberated from the burden of venting and decorating human feeling, objects clap, and property trees dance.

Loop, Again

Parade is a representation of cubist detail work come alive, individual facets moving around on stage and in the orchestra, groping frantically in search of the complete image they might constitute but never do. *Parade* is also, in places, a representation of what people might look like and how people might behave if a strip of motion picture film could come to life. We've seen *Parade*'s debt to cubist painting; now we'll examine *Parade*'s debt to the movies.

Non-synchronicity in Silent Films

The cinema had not long existed before certain critics noticed a discrepancy between its expressive resources and its expressive goals. How could the cinema depict anger? The obvious way was to show a man moving his lips ominously, a man whose whole face, growing darker each second, was drawn up into one clench of fury, and then to interrupt this image with a caption reading something like, "Get out and never darken my door again!" But to see such a sequence is to become all too aware of the extreme artificiality of such expressivity—an artificiality only heightened by the cinema's pretensions to naturalness, its claim that it shows *real* people in (sometimes) *real* surroundings. But in real life, an angry man doesn't express his anger by indulging in a silent pantomime and then holding up a sign on which one can read what he's saying; and this peculiar disjunction of *lexis* from *opsis* is only one of many obviously unreal and conventional aspects of the cinematic expression of anger by means of a human actor. It is possible that a great many Modernist experiments in the misalignment or counterpoint of planes of meaning—including Stravinsky's *Renard* and Weill's *Mahagonny* (as interpreted by

Brecht)—owe something to the non-synchronicity of pantomime and text in silent film.

When Virginia Woolf saw Wiene's *The Cabinet of Dr. Caligari* in 1924, she thought she glimpsed a means by which the cinema could attain a visual expressiveness beyond the capacity of human actors:

> at a performance of *Dr. Caligari* the other day a shadow shaped like a tadpole suddenly appeared at one corner of the screen. It swelled to an immense size, quivered, bulged, and sank back into nonentity. For a moment it seemed to embody some monstrous diseased imagination of the lunatic's brain. For a moment it seemed as if thought could be conveyed by shape more effectively than by words. The monstrous quivering tadpole seemed to be fear itself, and not the statement 'I am afraid'. In fact, the shadow was accidental and the effect unintentional. But if a shadow at a certain moment can suggest so much more than the actual gestures and words of men and women in a state of fear, it seems plain that the cinema has within its grasp innumerable symbols for emotions that have so far failed to find expression. Terror has besides it ordinary forms the shape of a tadpole; it burgeons, bulges, quivers, disappears. Anger is not merely rant and rhetoric, red faces and clenched fists. It is perhaps a black line wriggling upon a white sheet.

A piece of lint on the projector lens is a better expressionist than Wiene. Woolf dreamed of a cinematic vocabulary of abstract images, a continuous electro-encephalography of feeling-traces in the brain, wriggling black lines, or ink blots deleting the visual field like giant moth wings that blot out the sun. It is a recipe for a Kandinskian/Schoenbergian cinema of *Gehirnakte,* brain-acts.

But if expression is better pursued by Disney than by Murnau, what role is left for human actors? They are themselves demoted to captions—other versions of the dialogue placards that interrupt the spectacle: the actors only provide a kind of context, ballast for the feeling-arousal that must be pursued by other cinematic means. They have become *hommes-décor.* In 1929 D. H. Lawrence published a poem concerning the nullity, the anesthesia, the parody of human emotion that he found at the center of the silent film:

> When I went to the film, and saw all the black-and-white feelings that
>   nobody felt,
> and heard the audience sighing and sobbing with all the emotions they none
>   of them felt,
> and saw them cuddling with rising passions they none of them for a moment
>   felt,

and caught them moaning from close-up kisses, black-and-white kisses that
   could not be felt,
It was like being in heaven, which I am sure has a white atmosphere
upon which shadows of people, pure personalities
are cast in black and white, and move
in flat ecstasy, supremely unfelt,
and heavenly.

But a different sensibility might enjoy movies precisely for the sake of this
squashed, sterilized, thinned-out domain of affect—this virtuality of being.

The American Girl's Spoof of The Perils of Pauline

Lawrence hated the filminess of films, the sense of kisses isolated from any rich
human context and turned into objects of visual contemplation; but this sort of
abstraction of gesture was exactly what Cocteau wanted for *Parade*. Films are
réaliste in the sense that *Parade* is a *Ballet réaliste;* films offer a suite of gestures
at once familiar and defamiliarized, gestures liberated from human flesh, gestures disembodied into a pure semiosis. The horror of Pauline tied to the railroad
track, waiting for the train to slice her in three parts, is a distilled, bottled horror,
horror pickled in formaldehyde—pure acting, acting that freely confesses its
feigned character. This is why Cocteau and Massine devised a spectacle in which
almost every action performed by Marie Chabelska, the dancer who played the
American Girl—"riding a horse, jumping on a train, cranking up a Model T
Ford, pedaling a bicycle, swimming, playing cowboys and indians, acting in a
movie . . . dancing a ragtime, imitating Charlie Chaplin, getting seasick, almost
sinking with the *Titanic*"—was a quotation from an actual scene in American
movie serials.

The American Girl, then, was conceived as an artifact derived from cinema, a
copy of a copy of life, or, more exactly, a reversion from two dimensions back to
three dimensions accomplished in such a way that the ludicrous unreality of the
two-dimensional image was heightened. It is telling that the American Girl's only
pantomime (besides the Chaplin walk) *not* based on Pauline or on spunky characters played by Mary Pickford was the snapping of a Kodak camera—an act
that tends to enclose the photographer in the world of the photographed, to seal
up a self-contained universe of images. In many ways the *réalisme* of *Parade* is
simply a technique for being unusually frank about the unreality of art. To the
Apollonian artist, art can never embody reality, can never tell the truth, except
by the backward expedient of telling lies that confess their status as lies: as Stra-

vinsky said in 1912, "Opera is falsehood pretending to be truth, while I need falsehood that pretends to be falsehood."

Cocteau's most remarkable instruction to Chabelska was this: "The little girl . . . vibrates [*trépide*] like the imagery of films." Elsewhere Cocteau wrote, "One day they won't believe what the press said about *Parade*. A newspaper even accused me of 'erotic hysteria.' In general, they took the shipwreck scene and the cinematographic trembling [*tremblement*] of the American dance for the spasms of delirium tremens." If I read these sentences properly, Cocteau asked Chabelska to shake in the way that a film image shakes when the projector wobbles—that is, she was asked to imitate the technical *errors* associated with the film medium, so profoundly was the ballerina to be immersed, shipwrecked, in an alien domain of art. That a newspaper would misunderstand her trembling as "erotic hysteria" is a delightful proof of the tenacity of systems of interpretation based on feeling-expression, even in the excitingly apathetic and technical world of *Parade,* where the medium is the message. Sometimes a wriggling line is just a wriggling line, not sexual excitement or anger or terror.

Film Loops in Saint-Saëns's L'assassinat du duc de Guise

The indebtedness of *Parade* to the silent film extends beyond the American Girl's turn into the basic rhythm of the whole ballet. We've seen how much of *Parade* is predicated on loops: the Chinese Conjuror's trick with the egg that remains whole through the whole circuit of his digestive tract; and the continual whirr of rotating music figures, as if Satie's score were itself a kind of siren slowed down and restricted to finite pitches. But the notion of creating a spectacle based on loops arose first in the world of moving pictures.

Before the twentieth century, there existed many ingenious contrivances, such as the zoetrope, that allowed the spectator to behold continuous pictorial action: cut slits in a drum; paint the inside with a succession of images showing a horse approaching a hurdle, beginning its leap, clearing the hurdle, descending, regaining its footing; spin the drum and peer through the outer slits: you see the horse jumping over the hurdle, jumping over the hurdle, jumping over the hurdle, caught forever in heaven's endless steeplechase.

The notion of the loop as the default mode of action haunted the early cinema. For example, in André Calmettes's film *L'assassinat du duc de Guise* (1908), the murderers stealthily walk up behind the duke; he turns around; they perform deep, unctuous bows; he turns his back; then the scene is repeated; and repeated; and repeated; and at last they kill him. The attractive, very *moderne* and gestic score to this film was written by the seventy-three-year-old Camille Saint-Saëns, amazingly open to the peculiar musical requirements of such a scene: he found an endlessly rewindable pair of figures, first a tiptoeing staccato, then some graphical glissandi to represent the assassins' deep bows. Indeed, all this is quite similar to the sneaky-Pete figure heard in scores of cartoons: scale degrees in the minor

$$\hat{1} \qquad \hat{3} \qquad \hat{5} \qquad \hat{1}' \qquad \hat{6} \text{ (loud trill)} \quad \hat{5}\hat{4}\hat{3}\hat{2}\hat{1},$$

in which the first four staccato notes slowly, quietly, sidle up an octave; then, after the moment of panic (the heavy razz at $\hat{6}$), the last five notes scuttle away as quickly as possible. Ending where it begins, on $\hat{1}$, the whole loop can be replayed as often as the taste for mechanical repetition desires.

Relâche: *Clair's* Entr'acte cinématographique *as a Film Loop*

Satie was a composer born to score film loops. Long before he became involved in theatre work, around 1895, he wrote *Vexations,* a brief piano piece accompanied by instructions asking the pianist to remain immobile for a long time as an act of self-discipline, in case he or she wishes to play the piece 840 times in a row. (In 1963 John Cage organized a concert in which several pianists spent eighteen hours and forty minutes playing the entire *Vexations.*) *Parade* gave Satie some room to display his talent for quasi-cinematic repetition, but it was not until near the end of his life, in 1924, when he received from Rolf de Maré's Ballets Suédois (a rival company to Diaghilev's) a commission for *Relâche* (No Performance Tonight), that Satie had an opportunity to write true film music, for an *Entr'acte cinématographique* directed by René Clair and shown between the ballet's two acts. The outline for the film was written by the ballet's scenarist, Francis Picabia:

> *Rise of the curtain.* Satie and Picabia loading a cannon in slow motion; the explosion should be as loud as possible. . . .
> *During the entr'acte.* 1. Boxing match by white gloves on a black screen. . . . 2. Game of chess between Duchamp and Man Ray. Jet of water directed over the game by Picabia. . . . 3. Juggler. . . . 4. Sportsman shooting an ostrich egg balancing on Jet of water directed by Picabia. A pigeon flies out and settles on the sportsman's head; a second sportsman, aiming at the bird, kills the first sportsman: he falls to the ground; the bird flies off. . . . 5. 21 people lying on their backs, showing us the soles of their feet. . . . 6. Dancer on a transparent plate of glass, filmed from below. . . . 7. Inflation of rubber balloons. . . . 8. A funeral: hearse drawn by a camel. . . .

(Those wishing further information on *Relâche* should consult Bengt Häger's beautiful book *Ballets Suédois,* which cites the full text of this scenario and much

FIG. 19. René Clair, *Relâche: Entr'acte cinématographique:* resurrection, 1924

other information.) Clair didn't hew closely to this outline: he made the sportsman, dressed in a spiffy Tyrol hat, the center of a coherent though preposterous narrative, in which the sportsman's funeral procession picks up speed until it becomes a crazy chase involving bicycles, airplanes, and boats; finally the coffin falls to the ground, and the sportsman, alive, in a magician's formal costume, steps out; he waves his wand, and his pursuers vanish; then, with another flourish, he vanishes as well.

Clair may have transformed Picabia's sportsman into a magician because he noticed that Picabia's outline is an inflation of magician's buffoonery into an elaborate visual spectacle. Even the japing with jets of water suggests a larger version of the clown's squirty flower. And for Clair, as for the Chinese Conjuror in *Parade,* the most notable feature of a magician's act is its loopiness, its fascination with the reversibility of irreversible things. The film is a series of circular displacements: a hunter wishes to shoot not a bird, but an egg, as if he were a little confused about the right moment in the circuit of a bird's life at which one may shoot it; then his attempt to shoot the bird leads not to the bird's death, but to its hatching. Then, out of nowhere, the sportsman is shot by a second sportsman, aiming at the bird: we seem to have entered a hall of mirrors, a backward world in which hunting is an act that kills hunters and brings birds to life. (Mirrors are important to Clair's cinematography: at one point in the film, a street bordered by rows of trees is photographed in such a way that it seems to flex in the middle, the right side and the left side each rising about ten degrees from the center.) When the sportsman resurrects himself from the coffin, the loop is complete, the irreversible is fully reversed, for undying is as easy as dying. No wonder that the film ends with a general poof of disappearance, for nothing has happened, nothing can happen in this *perpetuum mobile,* this unspooling of inconsequential frenzies.

Clair had trouble making this film, especially with the camel, which smelled so bad that no one wanted to give overnight shelter to the carriage to which it had been harnessed. But in the end he and Picabia were both highly pleased with their work. Clair even added a prologue, along the lines Picabia devised, which showed "an unforgettable vision of Satie, with white goatee, pince-nez, bowler and umbrella—descending from the heavens in slow motion and firing a cannonball to announce the start of the show." And Satie, with his dangerous aplomb, was indeed the right Muse for *Relâche:* the whole spectacle—ballet and film alike—struggles to realize visual and kinesthetic effects comparable to the tensionless and directionless pleasure long characteristic of his music.

Relâche: *Segment Construction and Master Bars in Satie's Score*

Clair thought that Satie had laboriously contrived a film score to fit, frame by frame, the images of the film: "As for Satie, the old master of the young music, he lavished meticulous care on each minute of each sequence, thus preparing the first musical composition written for the cinema 'image by image' at a time when film was still silent. Conscientious in the extreme, he was afraid he might not complete the work by the appointed date." But Clair gave Satie both too much and too little credit. What Satie devised was not a continuous underscoring to the action, modulating second by second to accommodate the music-text to the picture-text, in the Wagnerian convulsive-property-tree manner. Instead, Satie devised an ingenious method to spare himself any real work in the counterpoint of ear to eye.

The score of the *Entr'acte cinématographique* consists of an introduction and twenty-six numbered sections; and the score can be further subdivided into segments, with typically one or two segments to each numbered section. But a given segment may recur in several numbered sections. For example, the eight-bar introduction ("chimneys; exploding balloons") reappears as the first half of number 3 ("boxing gloves and kindling-matches"); the second half of number 5; the second half of number 9 ("hunter, and beginning of the burial"); the first half of number 11; the second half of number 13 ("cortège in slow motion"); the first half of number 16; and the second half of number 25 ("split screen and end"). Also, the first half of number 26 is a variation of this segment. Formally, the music can be considered a madly atomized and distended rondo in which the dry, vivacious, snappy introduction anchors a multiplicity of simple but unrelated musical events. Another structural oddity lies in the fact that many of the segments are composed of only one or two different bars, strung together eight times or even more; and furthermore, each bar may consist of only one or two different chords—imparting an obsessively minimalist texture to the score, for the method of pattern-unit construction is reduced to absurdity.

Let us return to the introduction: after the anacrusis and the first bar, which function as a lead-in, the other seven bars are identical to one another; and this repeated bar contains only two chords, a B⁹ (without a third, with the note B on top, and, as it first appears, with the note A on the bottom) and an A minor (in which the C is spelled, in accordance with Satie's often weird notation, as a B♯). The B⁹ chord is a petrified instability: its failure to close itself is glaringly demonstrated by the contrasting A-minor chord, into which it might resolve if only the painful B could learn to consider itself a sort of 9–8 suspension and move down a step to A (and if the F♯ could learn to consider itself a sort of 6–5 suspension and move down a step to E); but instead the B⁹ chord is like an acrobat frozen in an off-balance position, an eternal ache of the muscles. So, by arraying two chords, Satie generated a single master bar that could be repeated as often as desired: in the score it appears, strictly unchanged, fifty-eight times, though no more than eleven times in a row.

EX. 9.1. Satie, *Entr'acte cinématographique* from *Relâche*: introduction, the master bar

It is a bar with no semantic content whatsoever: an imperturbable property tree in the orchestra. It is suitable to accompany exploding balloons, or boxing gloves, or a funeral. Satie conceived the music scenically, in that the duration of a visual scene is matched to the duration of a segment; but there is little attempt to match mood or atmosphere, only an attempt to match visual surprises with mu-

sical novelties and visual stasis with musical tedium. The only major exception
to this rule is the segment for the *Marche funèbre,* the second half of number 11,
which is a severe simplification of the main theme of the funeral march in Chopin's second sonata—but the famous theme is so hamstrung by Satie's consoli-
dation of the last two quarter notes of each bar into a half note that its solemn
tread dwindles into an amusing amble; the mighty march becomes a near-blank
signboard figured with the word "funeral" in thin sans-serif lettering. The *Edri-
ophthalma* movement from Satie's *Embryons desséchés* (1913) borrows a theme,
according to Satie, "from a celebrated mazurka by SCHUBERT"—actually the
second theme of Chopin's funeral march; and the first theme of the funeral
march, as it appears in the *Entr'acte cinématographique,* is also a kind of pickled
embryo. But most of the film music isn't even a stillbirth of meaning, but instead
a calm or frantic simulation of movement by means of patterns generated by
xerography rather than harmonic direction. For example, the single bar that,
repeated eight times, generates the segment of the second part of number 1 consists of a single figure in dactylic rhythm, a chipper V_3^4–I^6–V_3^4 chord progression. But it's hard to speak of chord progression where there is no conceivable
destination, simply a mechanical stutter of V and I chords. Such rigidity tends to
disable the whole tonic-dominant function of harmony: the *oom* loses all interest
in the *pah.*

EX. 9.2. Satie, *Entr'acte cinématographique* from *Relâche:* second part of number 1

EX. 9.3. Satie, *Entr'acte cinématographique* from *Relâche:* second part of number 11, funeral march

FIG. 20. Francis Picabia, *Relâche,* stage set, 1924 (© 1999 ARS, New York/ADAGP, Paris)

Satie's music is right for Clair's film precisely because it has nothing to do with the film: it is simply a time-hanging, a backdrop that occupies the correct number of minutes. If the music is too short, the generative bar—the pattern-unit—can be repeated sixteen or ten times instead of eight. The score is a machine for creating furniture music cut to fit the empty images of Clair's film. In both film and music, big loops are pieced together out of little loops. It is appropriate that the backdrop of the ballet section of *Relâche* consisted of enormous gramophone records flattened against the whole rear of the stage, for the spectacle is a mechanical rotation of film reels and twirling dancers, set to a score that simulates a record consisting entirely of broken grooves. And it is appropriate that the props of the two main dances of the ballet are, first, a revolving door and, second, a wheelbarrow.

Antheil's Ballet Mécanique: *The Big Foot*

In the same year (1923–24) that Satie was working on *Relâche* and its film interlude, George Antheil was working on the score for *Ballet Mécanique,* the apotheosis of the loop. In fact, Antheil took credit for inspiring Satie:

I announced to the press that I was working on a new piece, to be called "Ballet Mécanique." I said that I also sought a motion-picture accompaniment to this piece. The newspapers and art magazines seemed only too happy to publish this request, which interested a young American cameraman, Dudley Murphy. He had really been flushed by Ezra Pound, who convinced him.

Murphy said that he would make the move, providing the French painter Fernand Leger consented to collaborate.

Leger did.

Whereupon Erik Satie immediately announced that he too would write a mechanical ballet, to be called "Relâche."

(Actually, Antheil's claim to have invented mechanical ballet was flawed, since the notion of a ballet of wind-up, life-sized automata extends as far back as Delibes's *Coppélia* [1870], based on an 1817 short story by E. T. A. Hoffmann.)

George Antheil—virtuoso pianist who kept a revolver on the piano during his concerts; writer of a manual on forensic endocrinology; advice-to-the-lovelorn columnist; co-holder, with the actress Hedy Lamarr, of U.S. patent 2,292,387 for a device to aim torpedoes by radio waves—was a man with many opinions. One of his opinions (from a typescript of 1927 or 1928, cited in the book by the indispensable scholar of Antheil, Linda Whitesitt) concerned the feasibility of a new sort of music, composed entirely without contrasts:

When I wrote the *Ballet Mécanique,* near the end of the second part some madness within myself . . . compelled me to start a series of extensions to a gigantism to heretofore unheard-of length; I portrayed, in my theatre, a foot so large that the rest of the body must be imagined as extending beyond and out of the picture. . . . I knew that every dolt believes himself to be a superb critic of musical form; the sole knowledge contained in this unexplainable credo lies in the easy and quick comprehension of the well-known musical formula:—ABA. This is probably his sole anchor which if he knew dragged would explode his understanding, believe me!. Consequently, this formula: AAAAAAAAAAAAAAAAAAAAAAAAAAAA—makes him uneasy: it throws him *into the air.*

Instead of judiciously balanced musical members, Antheil wished to experiment with a music that consisted entirely of a single foot, made up of an interminable row of toes. In fact, I know of no Antheil movement that consists of only one pattern-unit; but there are places where Antheil comes quite close to this puritan ideal. Like Anton Webern, Antheil was an atomist of music: if the virtue of a

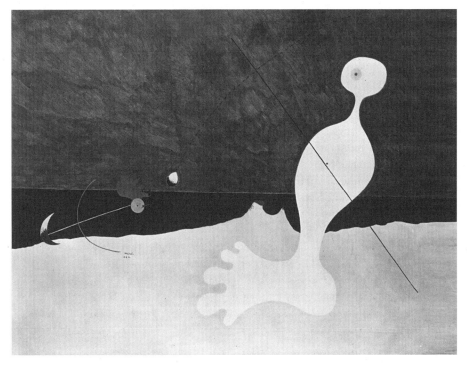

FIG. 21. Joan Miró, *Person Throwing a Stone at a Bird*, 1926 (© 1999 ARS, New York/ADAGP, Paris)

musical composition lies in a tiny, hair-raising, perfect moment, there are two methods of presenting this elementary particle without dilution or compromise: play it once, and be silent (Webern); or play it over and over and over, until it drowns out all consciousness of the rest of reality (Antheil).

Antheil was capable of writing intelligent theoretical defenses of his art, but his self-defenses were overwhelmed by the panegyrics of Ezra Pound, who adopted him not long after the precocious New Jerseyite Antheil appeared on the European music scene, in 1922, at the age of twenty-two. Pound's loud declarations that Antheil was the greatest composer of the century came to embarrass Antheil—no small feat, since Antheil was not a man easily embarrassed by praise; but he was also grateful for Pound's incomparable service in the field of public relations. Pound conceived Antheil as a kind of subatomic physicist in music:

> Strawinsky's merit lies very largely in taking hard bits of rhythm, and noting [i.e., notating] them with great care. Antheil continues this; and these two

composers mark a definite break with the "atmospheric" school; they both write horizontal music.

> this Sonata [Antheil's third violin sonata] thinks in time's razor edge. . . . It means that, via Stravinsky and Antheil . . . we are brought to a closer conception of time, to a faster beat, to a closer realisation or, shall we say, "decomposition" of the musical atom.
>
> The mind, even the musician's mind, is conditioned by contemporary things, our minimum, in a time when the old atom is "bombarded" by electricity, when chemical atoms and elements are more strictly considered, is no longer the minimum of the sixteenth century pre-chemists. Both this composer and this executant [the violinist Olga Rudge, Pound's companion] . . . have acquired—perhaps only half-consciously—a new precision.

> Musical moralists have damned in my presence that very tough baby George Antheil. . . . He was imperfectly schooled, in music, in letters, in all things, but he nevertheless did once demand bits of SOLIDITY, he demanded short hard bits of rhythm hammered down, worn down so that they were indestructible and unbendable. He wanted these gristly and undeformable "monads."

Pound thought that Antheil had discovered what we nowadays might call a *musiceme*, if we could imagine how to spell or pronounce this word: an elementary particle of rhythmic energy. And once this particle is isolated, it can't be developed, or extenuated, or intensified; it can only be repeated.

It is remarkable to think that music, so easily conceived as an art governed only by ratios, by stable relations among unstable acoustic phenomena, might have lurking within it something like a proton; but that is exactly what Pound thought. Pound's attitude is particularly hard to understand, in that many of Antheil's most powerful rhythmic effects derive from erratic pounding, from irregularities and displacements that manifest themselves slowly, through continuous changes of meter within a constant tempo. For example, the relentless hammering of a single clotted chord in eighth notes at the beginning *(allegro feroce)* of the *Ballet Mécanique* derives its excitement from the syncopations across bar lines, as the meter changes, bar by bar, from 3/4 to 5/8 to 3/4 to 2/4, and so forth. This complexity makes for a clumsy hieroglyph or an uncertain proton. And yet, we can see Pound's point: the technique of endless repetition of single bars, the espousal of AAAAAAA form—rondo without digressions, or one-themed sonata of perpetual recapitulation—heightens the ontological dignity of the repeated thing. A thing repeated long enough becomes context for itself, its own environment, its own body of interpretation. At the center of music, there seems to be an object, something with its own inviolability, its own weight—something of quality, worth looping. For Satie, the loop existed for the pleasure of rotation, and the master bar, the looped event, was more or less arbitrary; but for Antheil (as Pound described him), the loop existed in order to fasten attention upon, even to glorify, a discrete bit of music, the marvelous A.

Occasionally Antheil referred to his work in Poundian language: "One must begin with hard musical objects, perhaps simple banalities, so fast and unalterable that they are born hard as stone, indestructible fragments for all ages." But typically, Antheil conceived himself less as a physicist of music than as a painter in sound. He repeatedly referred to his score as a "time canvas," and in a 1936 letter to Slonimsky, he pursued the analogy between the musical and the pictorial:

> I personally consider that the *Ballet Mécanique* was important in one particular and this is that it was conceived in a new form, that form specifically being the filling out of a certain time canvas with musical abstractions and sound material composed and contrasted against one another with the thought of time values rather than tonal values. . . . Now in order to paint musical pictures one must admit right at the outset that the only canvas of music can be time. Music does not exist all at once like a painting but it unrolls itself. Nevertheless, we must consider it in the terms of painting as something that exists all at once. In other words, time is our musical canvas, not the notes and timbres of the orchestra or the melodies and tunes or the tonal forms handed down to us by the great masters. In the *Ballet Mécanique* I used time as Picasso might have used the blank spaces of his canvas. I did not hesitate, for instance, to repeat one measure one hundred times; I did not hesitate to have absolutely nothing on my pianola rolls for sixty-two bars; I did not hesitate to ring a bell against a certain given section of time or indeed to do whatever I pleased to do with the time canvas as long as each part of it stood up against the other. My ideas were the most abstract of the abstract.

Pound conceived Antheil as a discoverer of unsplittable musical atoms; but Antheil conceived himself as an artful arranger of tiny hard musical objects against long silences, blank space. A blank pianola roll looked like a coagulation of time itself, a tabula rasa waiting for music-paint.

Antheil regarded the Laocoön problem as negligible: he could simply choose to regard a musical composition as "something that exists all at once," as if music's temporal extension were more accidental than essential. He insisted that he could understand the forward flow of time as a sort of billboard on which music-icons could be attached; and so he wrote music in which repetitiousness disabled any sense of vicissitude or mutability of an acoustic object in time. And he wrote music in which spatial metaphors seemed overwhelmingly salient— metaphors such as *figure* and *background*. The irony of all this pictorializing of music—as we'll see when we come to the film of the *Ballet Mécanique*—lies in how strongly Antheil's score resists any actual accompaniment by the visual arts.

As a *Gestalt* psychologist of music, studying how figures achieve themselves and melt away, Antheil was extraordinarily resourceful. His sort of musical *découpage* depends on new strategies for nontonal discriminations of figure from ground. In commonplace tonal music, how do we know what is figure and what is ground?—or, to put it another way, what is theme and what is accompaniment? The theme tends to be linear (sinuous or angular), while the accompaniment tends to be chordal and repetitive; this simple formula can be restated in a number of ways, all of which finally reduce to the statement that the accompaniment is more boring than the theme—a monotonous sort of theme-flattery derived by extracting crucial notes from the theme and making explicit the implied harmonic underpinning, selected from the possibilities available in the system of tonality. The accompaniment, in this sense, doesn't usually provide a strong contrast to the theme: it is a harmonic abstraction of the theme, overstressed in order to mark rungs on a tone ladder against which the theme's flight can be measured accurately. On occasion, as in *Jingle Bells,* the theme is so weakly contrasted with the accompaniment that the theme itself looks like the accompaniment figure for some unknown, more active theme.

But a composer who wishes to write music that, in effect, superimposes fire-engine-red designs upon chartreuse must use different procedures for differentiating figure from background. One strategy might be to use different keys for theme and for accompaniment; but this bitonal procedure provides contrasts only within the fixed and limited circuit of the standard harmonic relationships in two different keys—bitonality provides only a narrow sort of adventurousness, for the composer must be careful to avoid chords that might fit into both keys and therefore weaken the oppositional tension between the two. To provide pigment contrasts across an infinitely graduated spectrum of musical possibilities, one must enter the world of the nontonal.

But in this excitingly disoriented domain, all seems figure and nothing seems ground—at least, nothing can be called a harmonic abstraction of anything else, since there exists no harmony to abstract, as harmony is normally understood. (Schoenberg tried to solve this difficulty by writing on some of his scores *Hauptthema* [principal theme] or *Nebenthema* [secondary theme], since the music itself could in no way specify its own level of subordination, its own parentheticality.) On the other hand, the possibility for boredom is just as open in nontonal music as in tonal music: insofar as certain musical events can be deprived of acoustic salience, made into a yawn, those events can be demoted to a kind of background.

Also, there exist two kinds of default backgrounds, backgrounds always available to music: silence, and noise.

Antheil considered himself a nontonal composer, a kind of painter-in-sound who referred the individual notes in his compositions not to a tonic, but to silence itself. The note A means one thing if it is juxtaposed against C; but it means something entirely different, something purer, more autonomous, if it is juxtaposed against silence. It is no longer part of a system of sound-relations, but a thing liberated from submediancy, triumphant. In this sense the work of Antheil anticipates that of John Cage, a painter-in-sound who could refigure a Japanese garden as a trombone piece—or take the outline of Marcel Duchamp's profile, turn it ninety degrees, and instruct a performer to interpret the profile as a continuously varying musical line. Antheil, of course, was a far more brutal composer, but equally committed to the pictorial emancipation of music, as he explained in his 1953 preface to the score of the revised, shortened version (1952–53) of the *Ballet Mécanique*:

Strawinsky attempted to move away from [tonality's] iron grip by making his music "super-tonal" so to speak. Schoenberg, going to the opposite pole, destroyed tonality entirely by removing all tonal centers in the 12 tone system. BALLET MECANIQUE, while utilizing (subconsciously, for at the time this work was written, 12 tone-ism was unknown as such) both systems, concentrated on what I then called "the time canvas". Rather than to consider musical form as a series of tonalities, atonalities with a tonal center, or a tonal center at all, it supposed that music actually takes place in time; and that, therefore, time is the real construction principle, "stuff of music," as it unreels. It is the musician's "canvas". The tones which he uses, therefore, are merely his crayons, his colors. The "Time-Space" principle, therefore, is an aesthetic of "looking", so to speak, at a piece of music "all at once". One might propose, therefore, that it is a sort of "Fourth Dimension"-al way of looking at music; its constructive principles may, or may not have been touched in this work, but they have been attempted.

By the end of this paragraph, the musical time canvas has leaped from two dimensions to four, as if it were a kind of sounding mobile that not only spins but reshapes itself as it spins. It is not enough that music simply take place in time: the listener must *hear* time. Time is not a passive medium but a vivid, kinetic background against which the sound-events register.

Potentially, time is even a kind of figure, and the music a kind of background: there are places in the third roll of the *Ballet Mécanique* and in Antheil's first violin sonata (1923) where the silences become so long that the gaps threaten to overwhelm the hard bits of sound that punctuate them. Inoperancy is part of the program that governs the machine. It contains its own sixty-two-bar chunks of silence. Just as painters are sometimes trained to contemplate the shape that air makes around the objects to be depicted, so Antheil devised a method for palpating the shape of time around certain phonic objects. Despite his boisterousness, Antheil was the Mallarmé of music, the master of the blank page. He achieved a sense of time so decelerated that it nearly stops and transforms itself into space.

But noise, as well as silence, can make time audible. Antheil conceived that beneath the music, there was a steady unreeling of the "stuff of music," time itself; and, just as a film projector makes a clatter as the sprockets unwind the film-rolls past the beam of light, so time is imaged in passages of the *Ballet Mécanique* as a continuous, fluttery roar. The scoring of the music is significant: Antheil originally hoped to have sixteen pianolas—player pianos—linked together mechanically, to be monitored by (of all people) Virgil Thomson; but as the instrumentarium slowly took shape during 1925–26, Antheil settled for one pianola, several pianos (ranging from two to ten), three xylophones, four bass drums, tam-tam, siren, electric bells, and airplane propellers. (It will be noted that the screaming siren is the closest thing to a melody instrument in this orchestra of percussion.) The airplane propellers were simulated in various ways, such as by tying leather strips to the blades of an open fan and letting them slap rapidly against a thin board.

In a sense, the whole of the *Ballet Mécanique* consists of various decelerations and decompositions of the airplane propellers, the root time-noise. This constant whap-whap-whap undergirds much of the score, a rhythm so fast it is a blur of sound, a wash on the canvas. In front of this, at the beginning, there pound the rigid chords—great thick clots that might be understood as combinations of $E\flat$ and $B\flat^7$ chords if there were any conceivable incentive to construe them as harmonic entities; at other times, the pianists simply press clumps of white or black notes with the palms of their hands, in a fashion that Antheil borrowed (as he acknowledged) from Henry Cowell. These piano hammerings have little harmonic definition, and while they are certainly highly rhythmic, the rhythm is difficult to grasp; they inhabit a space midway between the foreground and the background of noise.

But Antheil's fascinating experiments with the background of his time canvas can't elucidate the composition's purpose; the meaning (if the *Ballet Mécanique* has a meaning) must be generated in the foreground. What, in the midst of time's tumult, can the ear grasp as a definite figure? Perhaps the first foregrounded,

EX. 9.4. Antheil, *Ballet Mécanique:* opening

EX. 9.5. Antheil, *Ballet Mécanique: Oh My Baby*

EX. 9.6. Antheil, *Ballet Mécanique*: 2+3+4+5+6+7+8

figurally confident moment in the piece occurs when a snatch of American popular song (*Oh My Baby,* according to Benjamin Lees) suddenly disengages itself
and sets up a little ostinato. This perhaps sounds to us today more like Al Jolson
in blackface than like the African roots of American jazz, but Antheil evidently
considered it an authentic evocation of primitive rite, as he noted in the 1953
score:

> I always hesitate to give any "program" to any piece of music, preferring to
> have it speak for itself. However, and if this piece had any program . . . it
> would be towards the barbaric and mystic splendor of modern civilization;
> mathematics of the universe in which the abstraction of "the human soul"
> lives. More locally, the first "theme" may be considered that of mechanical
> scientific civilization; the second and third barbaric ones, not unrelated to the
> American continent, Indian, Negro.

Antheil, in the normal Modernist way, considered that Modernist art represented
a convergence of the mathematical-technological and the savage. And so the
whole *Ballet Mécanique* is a complicated sonata—in any sense except the ordinary musical one—for mediating between these extremes: a device for pasting
various emblems of the barbaric and the cerebral onto a background that is
simply a faster version of both, the motor hum of the twentieth century itself,
impersonated by the propeller. The emblems of the cerebral include such arithmetical abstractions as the invariant 2+3+4+5+6+7+8 drum figure in the
third roll; the emblems of the primitive include not only the chewed-up ragtime
fragments, but also the strikingly pentatonic passages near the beginning of the
first roll, derived, like the cadenzas in the second tableau of *Petrushka* (1911),
from separating the pianist's hands into a black-note plane and a white-note
plane.

The importance of the mathematical-technological aspects of the score is
obvious—to hear it is to enter a boiler factory; but one should also give the
"Indian, Negro" figures their due. When the *Ballet Mécanique* had its American
première, in 1927 at Carnegie Hall, the stage designer, Joe Mullens, suspended a
cyclorama of futuristic skyscrapers at the back of the stage—and for the first half
of the concert, during which Antheil's *A Jazz Symphony* was played, he created

EX. 9.7. Antheil, *Ballet Mécanique:* white keys vs. black keys

EX. 9.8. Stravinsky, *Petrushka:* white keys vs. black keys

a backdrop of "a gigantic Negro couple dancing the Charleston, the girl holding an American flag in her left hand, while the man clasped her ecstatically around the buttocks." A combination of both backdrops would have been appropriate for the *Ballet Mécanique,* since Antheil's semantic discriminations between the primitive and the futuristic are somewhat frail: the unsuspecting listener to Antheil's *Airplane Sonata* (1921)—an evocation of machines—and his *Sonata Sauvage* (1922)—an evocation of *négritude*—might have trouble guessing which was which. The savage is simply the mechanical with a certain lilt or twang added on.

In the first roll of the *Ballet Mécanique,* a figure becomes salient through rhythmic deviation: a moment of syncopation or dotted rhythm registers as an unsteady pounding, opposed to the steadier pounding in the background. In the second half of the third roll—the composition is divided not into movements but into three "rolls," onto which the pianola part is punched—a figure becomes salient simply from isolation: silence abuts it from both directions. (The great, much-repeated pattern-unit of the third roll consists of a violent trill followed by a leap to a complicated chord.) These two rolls demonstrate two different techniques for *découpage*-with-sound: in the third roll, the same squiggle is glued all over a nearly empty background; in the first roll, however, the figures register far more dimly against a busy, oversaturated background.

Antheil seems to have taken special pride in having invented the technique (long periods of silence) for the third roll, but I'm inclined to think that the technique for the first roll was equally important and possibly more consequential in the history of music: here Antheil devised a method for establishing a *continuum between noise and pitched sound,* the futurist equivalent of the continuum between consonance and dissonance in conventional music. Much of the score of the *Ballet Mécanique* consists of pitched sounds, but they are treated in ways that suggest that any audible pattern is simply what noise sounds like in slow motion, an engine's lethargy. (It should be noted that the antitheses between sound and silence and between technology and savagery are far weaker in the 1952–53 revised version—the only version published; it has no explicit popular-song episode near the beginning, nor any large trills or long silences near the end.)

What does the *Ballet Mécanique* mean? Antheil greatly disliked the obvious inference that his music was the representation of the interior of a factory—like Mosolov's *Iron Foundry* (1926–28), or like Prokofiev's *Pas d'acier* (1927), in which dancers operate gigantic machines as they dance, or like the 1920 Concert of Factory Whistles performed in the early days of the Soviet Union, to illustrate the aesthetic pleasures of heavy industry. In his note to the 1953 score, Antheil explained:

BALLET MECANIQUE was never intended to demonstrate (as has been erroneously said) "the beauty and precision of machines". Rather it was to experiment with and thus, to demonstrate a new principle in music construction, that of "Time-Space", or in which the time principle, rather than the tonal principle, is held to be of main importance.

Elsewhere Antheil insisted that the title was intended to be abstract, disconnected from the music, and he claimed that he couldn't remember why he called the piece *Ballet Mécanique.* These disclaimers have a certain disingenuousness, since Antheil himself declared loudly, in 1925, that "My *Ballet Mécanique* is the first piece of music that has been composed *out of* and *for* machines, *on earth*" (what does it mean to write a piece of music *for* machines?). But soon afterward Antheil seems to have decided that if he aspired to an audience of people, rather than an audience of robots with iron transducers for ears, he'd better find a more humanly agreeable defense of his art. His original title for the *Ballet Mécanique* is also of interest in assessing his intentions:

> My original title for the work (given on the manuscript in Germany) was "Message to Mars." . . . it had nothing whatsoever to do with the actual description of factories, machinery—and if this has been misunderstood by others, Honegger, Mosolov included, it is not my fault; had they considered it purely as music (as, being musicians, they should have), they might have found it rather a "mechanistic" dance of life, or even a signal of these troubled and war-potential 1924 times placed in a rocket and shot to Mars.

Antheil wanted the *Ballet Mécanique* considered "purely as music"—as a disengaged aesthetic construct; again, this is disingenuous, for he himself didn't consider it a disengaged aesthetic construct, but instead an expression of the mental condition of the year 1924 sealed in a spaceship or a time capsule: "The words 'Ballet Mécanique' were brutal, contemporary, hard-boiled, symbolic of the spiritual exhaustion, the superathletic, non-sentimental period commencing 'The Long Armistice.'" So, even if the *Ballet Mécanique* isn't directly concerned with machines, it is intended to be a "'mechanistic' dance of life," life as it is felt in a state of postwar frenzy, hyperstimulated fatigue. It would scarcely be surprising if the residents of Mars, investigating the score of the *Ballet Mécanique* in the ruins of the rocket's nose cone, might think the music an act of aggression, if not a declaration of war.

And yet, Antheil's vitalistic, sociopolitical reading of his music may be no more convincing than the Honegger-Mosolov workman's-compensation reading. Either as a dance of life or as a dance of locomotives, the *Ballet Mécanique* doesn't set toe or piston tapping. This is due partly to the complexities of the rhythm and partly to the long cardiac arrhythmias, the blocks of silence in the third roll; but mostly it is due to the fact that violent rhythms, when sustained for too long a time, suffer a kind of kinesthetic erosion, and become interpreted not as fury but as an increasingly listless confusion of sound. Stravinsky's *Danse des adolescentes, Danse de la terre,* and *Danse sacrale* from *The Rite of Spring* (1913)—the models for much of Antheil's rhythmic practice—retain their vehemence because they are fairly brief episodes set among more relaxed episodes, rhythmically speaking. But Antheil, with his hoarse insistence on the AAAAAAA, on perpetual urgency of expression, often simply levels down the thing that he wishes to intensify.

A case in point is the central figure that interrupts the silences in the second half of the third roll—the loud trill that bounds into a thick piano-clot. Mechanistically, this might be interpreted as the vibrating of something stuck that at last lurches into a sudden spasm of motion: the listener has a strong impression of frustration followed by futile release: clicklicklick-*sproing*. But Antheil's trill progressively dissipates its semantic energy: as Saussure taught, where there is no differentiation, there is no language. We recall that Antheil congratulated himself for his non-contrastive AAAAAAA musical forms, for his ability to portray a large foot without worrying about a complete human image. But one may ask whether the continual reiteration of a foot increases the podal intensity of a composition. I remember a game I played as a boy in which we used to say a word over and over again in order to listen to a word unword itself; in fact, *foot* was a word we especially liked:

foot foot foot foot foot foot foot foot footfootfootfoot

It doesn't take long for the word *foot* to become mere undenoting sound, the noise of an outboard motor; and after a little more time, the noise doesn't represent an outboard motor either, but is simply a sort of autistic convulsion of the mouth. To a certain point, repetition can be a mode of emphasis; but once that point is past, all emphasis collapses into a sonorous puddle. By the end of the *Ballet Mécanique,* all the representative potential of the trill has drained away; what might have been the seizing of a misaligned gear has become a pseudo-pictorial unit in an abstract composition. Antheil, then, was wrong to believe that he'd written a message to Mars, but right when he emphasized the painterly, aesthetic, disengaged quality of his work.

There is a strange chastity to the *Ballet Mécanique:* Antheil noted that during the long silences in the third roll, *"time itself acts as music;* here was the ultimate fulfillment of my poetry; here I had time moving *without touching it"*—as if sound were a kind of stain, a violation of time's whiteness, candor. The notion of untouched time, virgin time, is worthy of John Cage. The toccata for percussion dismantles itself into a *tempo non toccato.* Antheil insisted that the spaces of a painting already exist on the blank canvas: "the forms come out of the canvas, and not the crayon. . . . the crayon is merely a human means for indicating the spaces *existing only upon the canvas.*" Similarly, the heavily blackened pages of the score to the *Ballet Mécanique* serve to frame preexisting surfaces of blank time, silences made hard by the deafening noises that chop them up, appoint their duration.

The Léger-Murphy Film of Ballet Mécanique: *Cinematic Abstraction*

The film *BALLET MECHANIQUE* (in the misspelled French of the title shot) claims to have a *synchronisme musical* by George Antheil; but since the idea of the music predates the idea of the film, it might be better to call the film a *syn-*

chronisme visuel to the music. In any case, the concept of *synchronisme* is more wishful than real, since in 1924 the technology for close coordination of sound and picture didn't exist—and the music is almost twice as long as the film. Fernand Léger and Dudley Murphy worked independently of Antheil, and though Antheil tried to time the repetitions in his score to match the loops in the film, the pianola and the film projector were doomed to operate out of phase. (In 1935, for a performance at the Museum of Modern Art, Antheil prepared a one-pianola version of the score suitable for simultaneous presentation with the film.) The eye is engrossed in mechanical whorls, and the ear is engrossed in mechanical whorls, but these loopinesses inhabit different planes of reality, and there is some queasiness in their discord.

The chief elements of the music are (1) insistent futuristic rhythm, (2) allusion to popular song, and (3) silence. The chief elements of the film are (1) images of the repetitive motion of machines, (2) images of the repetitive motion of people, and (3) abstract figures and letters. It is easy to find congruences between these two trios, and it is easy to analyze both film and music as a dialectic of the mechanical and the human, and as a dialectic of the figurative and the abstract. But in fact, in each case the dialectical potential so quickly loses salience that the most striking point of comparison between film and music is erosion of meaning.

Watching the film is an experience very little like hearing the music. (Today, prints can be seen in a number of film libraries; or the reader can examine the many stills reproduced in *Fernand Léger, 1911–1924: The Rhythm of Modern Life,* edited by Dorothy Kosinski.) There is nothing threatening, nothing like an *allegro feroce;* the film begins sweetly, and stays sweet. The first thing we see after the title is the legend "Charlot présente": and, sure enough, Charlie Chaplin appears, in the form of paper cutouts of various body parts of the Little Tramp, disassembling and reassembling in a fashion that anticipates Monty Python. Chaplin will also bid us farewell at the film's end; and he is the proper host for this "first abstract motion picture," as Antheil called it in the note to the 1953 score. Chaplin is of course a man often threatened by machines, most famously in *Modern Times;* but there is some irony in the theme of Chaplin-as-schlemiel, a victim of the inanimate, since Chaplin himself often seems to be bolted together. He has a trick of loosely swinging his forearm from his elbow, and his lower leg from his knee, as if he were a puppet with a 360-degree range of swivel in his joints. In a sense, the whole film *Ballet Mécanique* is a conscious extrapolation of the abstract, anti-theatrical visual rhythms of Chaplin's cinematic art, his machine-extracted pathos. Chaplin hated talkies, he told Gertrude Stein, because in the silent films "they could do something the theatre had not done they could change the rhythm but if you had a voice accompanying naturally after that you could never change the rhythm you were always held by the rhythm that the

FIG. 22. Fernand Léger, *Ballet Mécanique*, film stills, 1924 (© 1999 ARS, New York/ADAGP, Paris; reprinted from Kosinski, *Fernand Léger*, pp. 192–93)

voice gave them." (The rhythm of Stein's summary sentence nicely denaturalizes Chaplin's speech, creates something of the liberation from narrative and dramatic conventions in which Chaplin delighted.)

The film *Ballet Mécanique* has no characters, only *femmes-décor;* it tells no story; it has no structure except the structure of music. Unfortunately, the musical structure of the film has little to do with the musical structure of Antheil's score: instead of Antheil's maniacally insistent experimentation with more or less non-contrastive, large-scale form, Léger and Murphy offer a conventional rondo, in which a regular refrain is interrupted by contrasting episodes: ABACADA, except that the refrain is compound and the episodes numerous. The most important elements of the visual refrain are a rapid alternation of a triangle and a circle, and a rapid alternation of a smiling mouth and an unsmiling mouth, a perfect Cupid's bow. The latter element is disconcerting, in that such an interrupted, flickery smile loses all normal sense of friendliness, or intimacy, or even human expression; it becomes an arbitrary grimace, as formal as a triangle or circle. And yet, the effect is too playful to seem dehumanizing or cold: it serves not to destroy the concept of a smile, but to extend smiliness into an unusually broad domain—like the waves of fog in Eliot's "Morning at the Window" (1916) that

> tear from a passer-by with muddy skirts
> An aimless smile that hovers in the air
> And vanishes along the level of the roofs.

Perhaps circles and triangles, as well as human faces, can smile. Elsewhere in the film, the screen is filled by a great blinking upside-down eye; such decontextualization and inversion tend to estrange any sympathy or sense of familiarity with the blinker, but on the other hand the concept of wink has instantly become a property available to cake tins, straw hats, eccentric gears, and other rapidly intercut circular objects. The film discovers (or imposes) such uniform rhythms in the world of machines and the world of human beings that it tends to flatten any distinction between them. Attractive women and piston engines seem two species of the same genus—or, as Marinetti put it, the heat of iron is just as interesting as the smile of a woman. Both machines and persons seem equally urbane, compelling, witty.

The episodes between the refrains tend to make the same point. The first episode shows a happy young woman on a swing; later episodes show various clock pendulums, and swinging balls, and an older woman climbing up the same few stone steps over and over, and locomotive-like pistons, and other sorts of back-and-forth and in-and-out. The young woman on the swing is perhaps the key episode, in that it contains both a human being and a (very simple) machine, cohabiting quite amiably. In D. H. Lawrence's novel *Women in Love* (1920), the sculptor Loerke is in love with the "extremely, maddeningly beautiful" machinery of the modern factory: he has been hired to produce a great granite frieze for a factory in Cologne, which depicts ordinary people at a fair with merry-go-rounds, swing-boats, and other carnival rides. As Loerke explains, "What is man doing, when he is at a fair like this? He is fulfilling the counterpart of labour—the machine works him, instead of he the machine. He enjoys the mechanical motion, in his own body." Loerke, by Lawrence's standards a monster of depravity, is by Léger's standards a hero: *Ballet Mécanique* is an étude in the delight of feeling the mechanicalness of your own body; the film even seems to ascribe to iron gadgets a kind of erotic pleasure in their own frictionless operation. Similarly, in Léger's oil paintings, the shiny cylinders, the spiffy, sinuously bent tubes, all suggest that machines take pride in their gleaming, efficient surfaces.

To Léger and Murphy, the notion of a *Ballet Mécanique* implied a dance of machines; whereas Antheil insisted that "I had no idea . . . of *copying* a machine

FIG. 23. Fernand Léger, *La partie de cartes,* 1917 ()119© 1999 ARS, New York/ADAGP, Paris; in the collection of the Kröller-Müller Museum, Otterlo)

directly down into music," Léger and Murphy seemed to dote on representations of machines, to the point of turning the film into a kind of machine itself, with slow chugging sections (such as the leisurely shots of the young woman on the swing or the old woman climbing stairs) followed by dizzyingly rapid cuts, as the cinema-machine entered overdrive. As Léger noted, "Contrasting objects, slow and rapid passages, rest and intensity—the whole film was constructed on that." During one of these exercises in velocity, we see outlines of a woman's upside-down legs unfurling into a kind of rosette—as if a ballerina could herself become a rotary machine. The film is abstract in that it concerns movement for movement's sake: human movement, mechanical movement, it is all the same. The boundaries between leg and wheel, wheel and piston, are called into question; as André Breton put it (explicitly remembering and modifying a passage from Apollinaire's preface to *Les mamelles de Tirésias*), "The idea of the human leg, lost in the wheel, was found again only by chance in the locomotive's connecting rod"—or, as Antheil put it in 1922, "machines which are new arms and legs of steel."

But in the last part of the film—the part that would correspond to the third roll of Antheil's score—the ballet of dancing machines is superseded by a ballet of dancing letters. An O appears on the screen, which turns out to be part of a sign: ON A VOLÉ UN COLLIER DE PERLES DE 5 MILLIONS—"they've stolen a pearl necklace worth 5 million." But, just as the human limbs and chuffing cylinders were prized not for the work they could perform but as pure isolates of rhythm—rat-tat or tick-tock or kick-kick—so the headline about the necklace is prized not for the implicit narrative behind it but as a heap of abstract letter-shapes. The O is sometimes multiplied into OOO; the 5 is turned backward, so that we may admire it from another angle. This pulling-apart of an intelligible sentence into alphabet soup is the final stage in the destruction of the normal syntax of films about machines. The *Ballet Mécanique* is the exact opposite of the sort of documentary in which we learn, say, how an automobile is made, through watching a careful sequence of lathe work, sheet-metal-cutting, and so forth, until the finished Ford is presented for our delight: instead, Léger and Murphy make the functions—even the scale—of the machines wholly obscure, so that it is hard to tell whether we are seeing a fragment of a sewing machine or the boiler room of an ocean liner. (Sometimes, indeed, the mechanical operations are multiplied by prismatic mirrors, further to aestheticize the acts and bewilder the spectator; this effect may owe something to Ezra Pound, for Dudley Murphy worked with the vorticist photographer Alvin Coburn, who used Pound's shaving mirror to rig up a "vortoscope"—a device "that lets one take Picassos directly from nature.") Normal understandings of cause and effect must be disabled if the machines are to be felt as elements of a ballet; and this disabling terminates, appropriately enough, in a general assault on language—not only the language of the legend about the necklace, but also the language of music, since Antheil regarded the score (especially the third roll) as the abolishing of the tonal system in favor of the time-canvas system. Just as Picasso and Braque used printed alphabet letters—which the eye interprets as flat—to flatten early cubist canvases, so Léger and Murphy used letter-play to flatten the preceding images of people and machines, to render them useless, innocuous, a disembodied fluency of movement. Instead of futurist insistence on the heady brutality and danger of airplanes, Bessemer converters, and sports cars, Léger, Murphy, and Antheil offer a kind of valentine to the neutered machine.

Surrealism (Literature and Art)

Q For a long time we have been exploring the domain of the surreal: the giddiness of automatism, the disequilibrating of the senses. And now it is time to reorient our discussion, our concussion, in terms of the classical surrealist theory of the 1920s—for surrealism is the movement that most explicitly prized dissonance among competing planes of attention within the art work. It may seem odd to treat surreal works of art before treating surrealism itself; but this method is faithful to the dynamic that brought surrealism into being, since the thing to be classified invariably precedes the classification. Satie, Picasso, and Cocteau conceived *Parade* according to the art movements with which they were familiar, principally cubism and futurism; but *Parade* inspired the coinage of a new term, *surrealism,* which led to a new art movement. This new movement achieved a kind of institutionalizing of the strangeness of *Parade,* a codifying of hostility among competing artistic media. Surrealism soon developed its own vocabulary of themes and its own cultural and political stances; but what concerns us here is the way in which surrealism gave explicit license to certain figures of dissonance, and created an audience that could savor such figures.

Apollinaire's Coining of the Word Surrealism

The term *surrealism* was invented by Guillaume Apollinaire, in a note concerning the ballet *Parade* that was published in a newspaper on 11 May 1917 and reprinted the following week in the program note for the ballet:

> The cubist painter Picasso and the boldest of choreographers, Léonide Massine, have effected it, consummating for

the first time the alliance of painting and dance, of plastic and mime, which is the sign of the advent of a more complete art.

Let no one cry paradox! The Ancients, in whose life music held such a great place, knew absolutely nothing of harmony, which is almost everything in modern music.

From this new alliance, for until now stage sets and costumes on one side and choreography on the other had only a sham bond between them, there has come about, in *Parade,* a kind of super-realism *[sur-réalisme],* in which I see the starting point of a series of manifestations of this new spirit *[esprit nouveau],* which, finding today the opportunity to reveal itself, will not fail to seduce the elite, and which promises to modify arts and manners from top to bottom for the world's delight, since it is only common sense to wish that arts and manners reach at least to the same height as scientific and industrial progress.

Breaking with tradition . . . Massine has kept himself from falling into pantomime. He has effected this thing entirely new, marvelously seductive, with a truth so lyrical, so human, so joyous, that it might well be capable of illuminating, if it were worth the trouble, the frightening black sun of Dürer's *Melancolia*—what Jean Cocteau calls a realistic ballet. Picasso's cubist stage sets and costumes bear witness to the realism of his art.

This realism, or this cubism, if you like, is what has most deeply stirred the arts during the last ten years.

The stage sets and costumes of *Parade* clearly demonstrate his preoccupation with extracting from an object all the aesthetic emotion that it can give. Quite often, they have sought to bring painting back to its strictly necessary elements *[stricts éléments].* . . .

Picasso goes much further than all of them. . . . Above all it's a question of translating reality. However, the motif is no longer reproduced but only represented, and rather than being represented it would like to be suggested by a kind of analysis-synthesis embracing all its visible elements and something more, if possible: an integral schematization that would seek to reconcile contradictions while sometimes deliberately renouncing any rendering of the immediate outward aspect of the object.

The intellectual tension level of this passage is high, but its clarity is perhaps low—the text itself, if it is to be understood, demands a kind of analysis-synthesis. On the one hand, Apollinaire seems to say that the arts need to be combined in order to produce the full excitement of Greek theatre and in order to conform to the high expectations of progress achieved by modern science; on the other hand, he especially prizes Picasso for having reduced painting to its sparest elements, for having accomplished pure painting, painting for painting's

sake, without extraneous narrative—just as he congratulates Massine for strip-
ping dance of pantomime elements. It is difficult to tell, then, whether Apollinaire
likes his arts separated, or all balled up together.

But, even as Picasso's art manages to "reconcile contradictions," so it may be
possible to reconcile Apollinaire's contradictions. Apollinaire dreamed of a new
kind of theatre, in which the arts were *coextensive but multiplanar:* in which
music, dance, and painting coexisted in a condition of inter-regarding independence, without leakage among artistic media, without deformity of one artistic
medium through attempts to imitate an alien medium. Each medium should pursue its own way of seizing the world, its private apprehension of reality; then the
combination of these media will reveal a complete, multidimensional grasp of
truth. This is a major Modernist form of *Gesamtkunst:* pursued not as Wagner
pursued it, through music that sags into the shape of a text, a polychrome blast,
a general convulsion of property trees, but through a counterpoint of hard-edged,
distinct, impermeable media.

Apollinaire's Les mamelles de Tirésias

In 1917, Apollinaire was making extensive revisions in his 1903 skit *Les mamelles de Tirésias,* preparing it for its first production, which was to take place
one month after the première of *Parade;* and in the new prologue (written in
1916), he defined more exactly the *esprit nouveau* of the Modernist theatre:

> We're trying here to infuse a new spirit into the theatre
> A joy a voluptuousness a virtue
> In order to replace this pessimism more than a century old
> Which is quite old for a thing so boring
> This play has been made for an old stage
> For they won't have built for us a new theatre
> A theatre in the round, with two stages,
> One at the center the other forming a sort of ring
> Around the audience and which will permit
> The grand deployment of our modern art
> Marrying often without apparent bond as in life
> The sounds the gestures the colors the cries the noises
> The music the dance the acrobatics the poetry the painting
> The choruses the actions and the multiple décors
>
> You will find here some actions
> Which are added to the main drama and adorn it
> The changings of tone from pathos to burlesque

And the reasonable use of improbabilities
As in the case of the actors collective or not
Who aren't forcibly extracted from humanity
But from the entire universe

For the theatre must not be an art to fool the eye

It is right that the dramatist feel free to use
Every sort of available mirage
As Morgana did on Mount Etna
It is right that he compel the crowds the inanimate objects to speak
If he please
And that he take no more account of time
Than of space

His universe is his play
Inside of which he is the creator god
Who arranges to his liking
The sounds the gestures the steps the masses the colors
Not for the mere goal
Of photographing what you call a slice of life
But in order to make life itself arise in all its truth
For the play must be a complete universe

This is, I believe, the crucial passage in Apollinaire's theory of surrealism, although the word *surrealism* nowhere appears here. Aristotle taught, in the eighth chapter of the *Poetics,* that a probable impossibility was far preferable, in the art of the playwright, to a possible improbability; but for Apollinaire the art of the improbable, the uncaused, the inexplicable, has its own prestige. The mind, with its logical analyses of chains of motivation and consequence, is no longer the central organ for judging the success of a drama: instead, a drama appeals to the whole sensorium of the spectator, who must *feel* the realness of the experience.

Surrealism, as Apollinaire defined it in the *Parade* note, arises from the non-superficial union of a variety of artistic media; and in the prologue to *Les mamelles,* Apollinaire gave a firmer definition of his meaning: the virtual reality created by an art that gives intensely discrepant versions of experience to several sense organs at the same time. Surreality is hyperreality, sesquireality, an aesthetic experience that gives a stronger feeling of the weight and thoroughness of reality than life itself can give. This is why Apollinaire wanted a peculiar sort of theatre building, in which the spectators were crammed into an annular space with stages both in front of them and behind them: he hankered after a theatrical effect in which stage data were assaulting the spectators from all sides at once—like real life, in which percepts pour in from all directions, except that the stage data are louder, stranger, more glaring. A surreal experience is a model of the joyous freshness of apprehension, as if we had stepped into a newly created world in which the relations of sight to sound, sound to touch, were not yet established. *Les mamelles de Tirésias* is a play that urges the French to conceive multitudes of babies; and it makes infants of us all, in that every spectator must cope with a funhouse universe, in which all conventional bindings have been loosened.

The key line of the prologue is *Mariant souvent sans lien apparent comme dans la vie*—"Marrying often without apparent bond as in life." What makes life lively? To Apollinaire, it is the lack of intelligible correlation between sounds, gestures, colors, acrobatics. Life is a kind of shotgun marriage between unrelated sensory phenomena.

In scholastic philosophy, there exists a sense that is not seeing nor hearing nor touching nor tasting nor smelling, but a guarantee of the connectedness of all five: the *sensus communis*. This is the sense that bundles up the eye's world, the ear's world, the nose's world, into a single objective reality. According to the *sensus communis*, if I see a cow, and hear a moo, and smell manure, these perceptions all point to the same unrelenting truth: that behind the image of a cow, and the sound of a cow, and the odor of a cow, there is a cow.

But, of course, the actual modality of being human doesn't always conform to this intellectually satisfying scheme. I may walk through a field and watch a distant cow open its mouth, and hear, at that very instant, the tweet of a bird. And the twittering cow is, I take it, the primary surrealist act: the simulation of the normal discords that exist in our negotiation of felt life. From Aeschylus to Ibsen, the theatre mostly followed an abstracted propriety of event, according to which a horse could be counted on to whinny; but Apollinaire substituted a surreal theatre, in which a horse might be just as likely to hiss. A surreal theatre is at once more-than-real and more-real: more-than-real in that such absurdities seem to belong to a fictitious, looking-glass world, Fata Morgana's mirages; but more-real in that the more closely we attend to the minutiae of perception, the more often we notice mismatches between ear and eye, cricket-chirps that come from empty expanses of floor, unplayed pianos that seem to make noises like defective plumbing. The coherent lives we pretend we live—in which drips from ice cream cones are always cold, and green Jell-O tastes like lime—are largely a result of distraction and inattentiveness, since we do our living inside crude mental constructs, prefabricated interpretations of reality. Surrealism reminds us of the suppressed dissonances of our commonplace sensory existence.

Surrealism, then, is a natural evolution of realism. Indeed, many of the most radical artistic movements of the late 1910s defended themselves in the most old-fashioned manner possible, as pure forms of mimesis of reality. Tristan Tzara conceived dadaism, for example, as an imitation of the randomness, the absurdity, the unintelligibility of nature itself:

> We [dadaists] are often told that we are incoherent, but into this word people try to put an insult that it is rather hard for me to fathom. Everything is incoherent. . . . There is no logic. . . . The acts of life have no beginning and no end. Everything happens in a completely idiotic way. That is why everything is alike. Simplicity is Dada.

For Tzara, logic, system, science, are merely illusions fostered by the foolish belief that we know something about the world around us; and art that aspires to beauty, clarity, precision, is a kind of offense to reality, an act of dishonesty, insincereness. Apollinaire's surrealism—like Tzara's dadaism but far more hedonistic—is a technique for imitating aspects of the world of experience that can't easily be assimilated into models of experience, abstractions of experience. Apollinaire's surrealism, in this sense, is extremely concrete. Alfred Jarry—Apollinaire's predecessor in the theatre of the absurd—invented the term *pataphysics,* that is, the science of exceptions to rules; and surrealism is an extremely pataphysical movement, in that it denies every sort of rule, scheme, or generalization, in favor of the arresting instant of felt life. Cocteau thought that the scar on Apollinaire's head, a result of his severe wounding in the Great War, was "a microphone, thanks to which he heard what others cannot hear"—as if he had an access to reality through a direct hole to his brain, without the usual mediation of the senses. Surrealism aspires to a similar state of supersensible insight, a kind of trepanned gnosis.

But the realism at the heart of surrealism does not imply any sort of comfortable or easy relation between the spectator and the art work. In a preface written for the published version of *Les mamelles de Tirésias*—this prose preface shouldn't be confused with the *vers libre* prologue, which is part of the play—Apollinaire noted:

> In order to characterize my drama, I've made use of a neologism (for which you will pardon me, for that happens rarely with me) and I've coined the adjective surrealist, which in no way means symbolic. . . .
>
> In order to attempt if not a renovation of the theatre, at least a personal effort, I thought it necessary to go back to nature itself, but without imitating it in the manner of photographs.
>
> When man wanted to imitate walking, he created the wheel, which doesn't look like a leg. He made surrealism without knowing it.

A wheel isn't a symbol of a leg or an abstraction of a leg; instead, it is a functional equivalent of a leg, an analogue. Biologists distinguish homologues from analogues in the following way: a homologue is a structural equivalent, while an analogue is a functional equivalent—an elephant's trunk is a homologue of my nose, but an analogue of my arm. For Apollinaire, traditional art has dealt, far too long, far too laboriously, in the world of homologues, in which human beings are represented by actors, or puppets, or shadows, or other simulacra of human bodies. But instead of a theatre of stilts, Apollinaire supplied a theatre of wheels, a vitally metaphorical domain in which human beings are represented by various inhuman or semihuman objects, in which a kiosk can talk, and human beings seem to be made largely of rubber. The surrealist theatre is a continual displacement of homologues by analogues, in which the principle of equivalence is switched from the level of structure to the level of function—likeness pertains to what things do, not to how things look. For Apollinaire, there is much less resemblance among the universe's constituents than we've been taught to believe: the field of likenesses is unstable, a kind of quicksand.

* * *

Les mamelles de Tirésias is a play with a moral, a distinct thesis: women must bear many children, in order to repopulate France after the devastation of the Great War. And it represents a society in which selfish women seem to have decided to seek personal fulfillment outside of traditional maternal roles. But in Apollinaire's theatre of non-homologous analogues, his land of unlikenesses, this situation and this exhortation are recast as a series of discords among the various components of the theatrical experience, discords that imitate both the inevitable skewedness of all sensory processing of reality, and the special distortions of wartime Modernist France.

It is morning in a marketplace in Zanzibar. Thérèse, the protagonist, announces to her husband that she's a feminist, determined to join the army, because she wants to make war, not babies—and after becoming a soldier, she intends to become an artist, a senator, a mathematician, a telegrapher, and so forth; her husband's only response to her tirade is, "Give me some bacon, I tell you, give me some bacon." But she fixes him: she instantly grows a beard, opens up her blouse, detaches her breasts—which turn out to be rubber balloons—jerks them around by their strings, and finally pops them. The husband has trouble accepting this, but Thérèse decisively abandons him, marking her desertion by flinging out of the window a chamber pot, a basin, and a urinal. She undresses her husband and switches clothes with him; but while she's engaged in this pantomime, two men armed with rifles, Presto and Lacouf, old friends, quarrel bitterly concerning the outcome of a dice game called Zanzibar: Presto

JEAN THILLOIS   HOWARD EDMOND VALLÉE   J. NORVILLE

FIG. 24. Photograph of the cast of *Les mamelles de Tirésias,* 1917

says that he has lost everything, while Lacouf says that he's won nothing; and furthermore, Presto claims that this whole scene is taking place in Paris, while Lacouf insists that they are all actually in Zanzibar. They fight a duel; but as they confront each other, the People of Zanzibar (the name of a single male character, in charge of all sound effects) takes out a revolver and shoots them both—they fall. But they quickly get bored by being dead, and from time to time throughout the rest of the act, they resume their duel, only to fall dead again. A policeman comes by to drag the corpses off stage and notices the husband, in women's clothes, all tied up: overcome with desire for this beautiful creature, the policeman tickles him and flirts, and the husband plays along with the game in order to get untied. The husband explains that he's been feminized through a kind of symmetry:

> Because my woman is man
> It is proper that I be woman
> > *to the policeman, modestly*
> I am an honest woman-mister
> My wife is a man-madam

The policeman isn't much troubled to learn that the husband is a man, and still hopes to marry him, by proxy. And the first act ends amid happy shouts from the chorus of "Vive le Général Tirésias"—celebrating the exploits of the renamed Thérèse—as the husband deplores, in classic alexandrine verse, Zanzibar's hatred of children:

Zanzibar women are in a political phase
And renounce all at once the prolific embrace
You hear them cry No more babies No more babies
To populate the land you only need monkeys
Snakes ostriches elephants mosquitoes these thrive
But our women are sterile as drones in the hive

But the husband grandly announces that he will solve the problem: he will contrive to have children without the assistance of a wife.

In the second act, the husband has made this boast good: in fact, he has given birth to 40,049 children in a single day, who make a considerable racket despite his repeated cry "Silence." A journalist comes by to note this marvel, and asks the husband how he can afford so many offspring—but the husband replies that children are themselves the wealth of a household, far more than money. And the husband proves this point by proudly displaying Arthur, who, though only a few hours old, has already made a million by hoarding the curdled-milk supply; and precocious Joseph, who has already written a prize-winning novel; and a daughter, already divorced from the potato king with a huge alimony. The journalist is so impressed that he asks for a small loan, but the husband angrily kicks him out. But of course, such a prolific husband needn't lack a journalist long: he immediately synthesizes a 40,050th child, a baby journalist, from old newspaper clippings, scissors, and glue, with ink for blood and a pen for a spine. This newborn chatterbox immediately tries to blackmail the husband, his father, by threatening to print sexual scandal concerning the husband unless he's given five hundred francs—"Bravo there's a mastersinger," the husband responds—and instantly the baby journalist is busy spouting all sorts of exciting news: "A great fire has destroyed Niagara Falls"; "Monsieur Picasso is making a picture that moves"; he also promises to make up tomorrow's news as well. Soon the overwhelmed husband regrets having made a journalist. The policeman tells the husband that something needs to be done: the whole populace will die of starvation with all these new mouths to feed; the husband replies that cards will substitute nicely for food—and where there is a fortune-teller, there will be cards. The fortune-teller arrives, to offer eloquent prophecies of luck to those who make babies:

Know that fortune and glory
Forests of pineapples herds of elephants
Belong by right

In the near future
To those who will take them by making children

But to the childless policeman she foretells fearful poverty; the policeman tries to arrest her, but she strangles him to death. Then she throws off her fortune-telling disguise: she is Thérèse/Tirésias. The policeman comes back to life; husband and wife reconcile, though the husband seems a bit disturbed that she's "flat as a bug," and he offers her some new balloons—but instead of stuffing two of them into her blouse, she pushes the whole bunch into the audience: "Fly away birds of my weakness Go feed all the children Of the repopulation." And so the play ends in a galaxy of rubber breasts, and some general advice from the cast to the audience: love well, and scratch yourself wherever you itch.

Les mamelles de Tirésias is the ideal Saussurean drama, in that it shows a domain of arbitrary names, indeed a whole world of misnomers. The central principle of its theatrical evolution is the revolt against old errors of caption, thereby creating new errors of caption.

The most notable such revolt occurs, of course, when Thérèse unwomans herself by casting off her name and flinging away her balloon-breasts, those flimsy markers, airy and empty, that establish her gender. But her beard can never be more than a prop beard, an obvious fake; the new labels of masculinity are just as tentative and removable as the old feminine ones. People are simply tailor's dummies madly affixing and tearing off various badges of identification: while the husband engages in his crazy parthenogenesis, populating Zanzibar with a city's worth of residents in a day, Thérèse/Tirésias engages in a crazy re-population of her own body with new selves—general, fortune-teller, and wife again. The mime theatre and the speech theatre are strangely disjunct: the actors propose a limited spectacle of gesticulating bodies, while the words propose an endlessly fluid, billowing spectacle that occasionally condescends to connect itself with the physical events on stage. Instead of a theatre predicated on human characters, Apollinaire offers a theatre predicated on nouns, in which a generalization (the People of Zanzibar) and an inanimate object (the kiosk—a minor character) jostle for discursive space with the normal Dramatis Personae, the Proper Nouns that make up the cast of traditional plays.

But captioning errors determine other aspects of the drama as well. When Lacouf and Presto stage their duel, they are shot dead not by each other, as one might expect, but by the People of Zanzibar, as if the duel were suddenly demoted to a kind of sub-theatre while a more dramatically (even ontologically) ambitious character takes over the burden of action. The sound of fatal bullets comes from the wrong gun—another aspect of the oddly contrived mismatchings within Apollinaire's dismembered staging. A still more provocative example occurs in the scene where Thérèse unhouseholds herself by throwing out of the window various lavatory objects: the husband examines each in turn, exclaiming "The piano" as he picks up the chamber pot, "The violin" as he picks up the urinal—perhaps suggesting the profound truth of Freud's theory that art is excrement—and again exclaiming, as he picks up the washbasin, "the butter plate the situation is becoming grave." This scene anticipates René Magritte's *The Key of Dreams* (1930), a painting divided into six panels, each showing a common object with a caption in flowing script, as if part of a lesson: a picture of an egg is labeled "The Acacia," a picture of a high-heeled shoe "The Moon," and so forth. Samuel Beckett was to imagine a literature in which "there could be no things but nameless things, no names but thingless names"; and *Les mamelles de Tirésias* depicts a condition in which names are starting to exuberate away from the finite objects on the stage, just as Thérèse's breasts float away from her body. The denotations of words are nicely popped, exploded. Apollinaire is Humpty-Dumpty, insisting that words mean just what he wants them to mean, no more, no less—Apollinaire's face, in Picasso's caricatures, even looks like an egg, or perhaps I should say that his face looks like an acacia.

The verbalness of Apollinaire's stage art is also enforced by his remarkable reliance on placards and playing cards. After the first fatal duel, the People of Zanzibar sets up placards on opposite sides of the stage:

Pancarte pour Presto	*Placard for Presto*
Comme il perdait au Zanzibar	As he lost at Zanzibar
Monsieur Pres[t]o a perdu son pari	Mister Presto has lost his wager
Puisque nous sommes à Paris	Since we are in Paris

Pancarte pour Lacouf	*Placard for Lacouf*
Monsieur Lacouf n'a rien gagné	Mister Lacouf has won nothing
Puisque la scène se passe à Zanzibar	Since the scene takes place in Zanzibar
Autant que la Seine passe à Paris	Inasmuch as the Seine passes through Paris

After this pithy visual summary of the quarrel is displayed to the audience, Presto and Lacouf resurrect themselves, fight another duel, and die once more—not for the last time. The point of this peculiar correlation of a gambling dispute and an argument over the location of the whole *mise-en-Seine* is difficult to suggest in English, since it depends on a series of French puns: Zanzibar is both an African spice island and the name of a dice game, and *Paris* is a homonym of *pari*, "wager." So the dissension over the outcome of the dice game starts to acquire a secondary meaning in the field of geography—and in this theatrical universe where words can't restrict themselves to a finite area of meaning, the absurd geographical discourse starts to overwhelm the familiar gambling discourse. It must also be noted that the *zibar* of *Zanzibar* is a sort of mushy anagram of *Paris,* as if the whole Zanzibarian scene were a distorted metamorphosis of the Parisian scene. *Les mamelles de Tirésias* is not only a theatre of analogues, but a theatre of anagrams—as the protagonist's two names, Thérèse and Tirésias, might suggest. Zanzibar is both a displacement of Paris and a defamiliarization of it, a recombination of its elements in a dice game the size of the whole stage, where nothing is ventured and nothing is gained. In Apollinaire's theatre, just as homologues are displaced by analogues, so objects are displaced by homonyms.

In addition to placards, Apollinaire gives us cards, and keeps shuffling his deck. Thérèse is disguised not as just any kind of fortune-teller, but as a *cartomancienne,* a woman who divines by means of cards—as in the tarot pack. (In this way she anticipates Madame Sosostris in Eliot's 1922 poem *The Waste Land*—in 1921 Eliot was reading Apollinaire, and finding him "a little disappointing"; but themes dear to Eliot such as card divination, Tiresian sex change, and fecundity and sterility are so prominent in *Les mamelles de Tirésias* that *The Waste Land* seems almost a grumpy parody of the earlier work.) The cartomancer appears just as the policeman is complaining that Zanzibar's uncontrolled population growth threatens mass starvation, to which the husband replies, *Donnez-lui des cartes ça remplace tout* [Give it some cards *they* substitute for everything]. This might refer to ration cards for food in wartime Paris, but the notion that images and texts might become surrogates for physical objects has far wider application in the world of this play. It appears that it is possible to nourish oneself by eating pieces of paper inscribed with the names of things: the word *pineapple* has plenty of food value, and spares one the expense of procuring a real fruit.

How does the husband create 40,050 children in one day?—evidently, by naming them. To say "Arthur" or "Joseph" is enough to produce a child. In the scene where we witness an act of male birth, the husband accomplishes this feat purely through textual manipulation, by synthesizing a baby journalist out of old clippings and writing implements. Parturition is publication: the children seem generated en masse by a sort of printing press. Human beings arise out of words, and sink back into words. The loquacious characters in the play exist mostly as images of discourse, and so the stage is cluttered with megaphones, placards, and enormous books: Apollinaire erases all the boundaries between speaker and speech. As the Director says in the prologue, "the actors . . . aren't forcibly extracted from humanity / But from the entire universe": the arbitrary division between man and woman, between sentient and insentient, between noun and thing, between subject and predicate, vanishes into a uniform field of infinitely invertible actions. Dead characters effortlessly revivify, because life and death exist in a continuous loop; speaker and speech effortlessly switch places, because the play posits a continuous textual loop in which words embody themselves in characters and then disembody themselves. *Les mamelles de Tirésias* is a play about the delight of verbal creativity, which seems absolutely indistinguishable from sexual procreation.

Calligrams

Les mamelles de Tirésias is a kind of card game, in which strips of text experiment with possible (and impossible) referents in the physical phenomena on the stage. It is the work of a card-driven author: with the possible exception of Alban Berg (in his *Altenberg-Lieder*), Apollinaire used picture postcards as a basis for radical art more successfully than any other Modernist artist.

Sometimes it is possible to see the whole Modernist movement as a passing-around of cards with doodles scribbled on them. An entire division of cubist art (such as Picasso's 1914 *Bouteille de Bass, verre, paquet de tabac et carte de visite 'André Level'*) consists of glued assemblages of cards, labels, and so forth—some real, some faked; but this is only one of the more obvious appropriations of the picture card, the vagrant design, into modern art. The stray diagram can become an image of power. Yeats and his astrologer uncle, George Pollexfen, spent endless hours trying to make telepathic signals to each other by means of concentrating on abstract printed symbols. In *Concerning the Spiritual in Art* (1911), Kandinsky—an artist strongly influenced by theosophy, as Yeats was—figures his text with circles and lines in order to explain the complicated spinnings and borings suggested by various pigments; these diagrams are meta-abstractions, icons of abstractivity. For Kandinsky, an abstract painting is a hieroglyph, not legible in the sense that the spectator can reduce it to words, but legible in the sense that the spectator can decode the image kinesthetically, into a set of implied vectors, implied recessions into and bulgings out of the picture-plane. Every Kandinsky painting is an occult set of instructions for a vibrating, a whirling, an

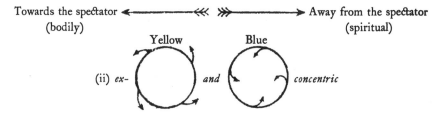

FIG. 25. Wassily Kandinsky: how blue spots recede, how yellow spots bulge, 1911 (*Concerning the Spiritual in Art,* trans. M. T. H. Sadler [New York: Dover Publications, 1977], fig. 1, opposite p. 36)

FIG. 26. Michel Fokine, *Schéhérazade: Notations for Finale Floor Pattern* (detail), 1910 (Institute of Contemporary Art, *Art and Dance*, p. 38)

opening-out, a cosmos of movement temporarily stunned into two dimensions. To some extent, the choreography of the Ballets Russes was simply a reification with human bodies of the abstract schemata of Kandinsky—as the extraordinary similarity of Fokine's dance-doodles and Kandinsky's doodles of color-spins may suggest.

But it is important to distinguish casual diagrams fraught with metaphysical significance—such as those of Yeats and Kandinsky, who belong to a symbolist tradition—from casual diagrams that make sport of metaphysical significance. Picasso's collages often isolate sexually charged linguistic and pictorial elements (as in his 1913 *Nature morte 'Au Bon Marché,'* which juxtaposes the syllable *trou* [hole], cut out of a newspaper headline, with a drawing of a demure woman in a slip, cut out of a lingerie advertisement), thereby constructing an ideogram of sexual arousal—a hieroglyph as a dirty joke. The cubist theft of text into painting stirred up Apollinaire's competitive instincts, and the poet found a way of twisting his texts into the playful semblance of pictures: one could doodle with words as well as with line drawings.

One of Apollinaire's crucial contributions was what he called the *calligramme,* a shaped poem in which the layout of the words makes visual images that reinforce, or provide a counterpoint to, the meanings of the words—and so provide either a figure of consonance or a figure of dissonance. Thus the calligram *Paysage* (Landscape) contains four separate phrase-icons, including a cigar-shaped word *cigar,* off the end of which snake upward the words *which smokes;* and a tree-shaped sentence, "This shrub that is preparing to bear fruit resembles you"—a richer, more complex version of Baudelaire's line about the *pays qui te ressemble* [country that looks like you], from *L'invitation au voyage* (1857). Ordinarily, the act of reading involves three carefully discriminated planes: the reader sitting with the book, the text sitting on the page, and the referent of the text, the sum of bodies sitting in the world of fictitious experience, toward which the text points. But the calligram *Paysage* is monoplanar: the text is shaped like its referent, a shrub; and furthermore, the text-shrub resembles *you,* the reader. To read this poem properly is to imagine oneself made of alphabet letters that

CET
ARBRISSEAU
QUI SE PRÉPARE
A FRUCTIFIER
TE
RES
SEM
BLE

FIG. 27. Guillaume Apollinaire, *Paysage* (detail), 1917 (Guillaume Apollinaire, *Calligrammes: Poèmes de la paix et de la guerre* [Paris: Éditions Gallimard, 1925], p. 27)

hunch themselves into a trunk, ramify, prepare to flower: Apollinaire's relation to the reader is that of Apollo to Daphne. But the violent distortion of the usual model for interpreting a text may only serve to arouse skepticism about the possibilities for annihilating the boundaries between poem and painting. In *Les mamelles de Tirésias,* there was too much unlikeness between word and thing for us to feel comfortable; in the more consonant of the calligrams, there is too much likeness.

It is possible that these arrogations across media thresholds will emphasize the dissimilarities of the arts. A bird-shaped way of intertwining the letters B I R D may aspire to be an intensification, a cutting-deeper of the meaning of the word; but since we are aware that the same letters could just as easily be deformed into a little picture of a rabbit, or a cow, or a house, this word-icon in no way overcomes the arbitrariness of captions. Magritte, in *The Wind and the Song* (1928–29), painted a picture of a pipe labeled "This is not a pipe"; but if he had deleted the negative, it would not have brought the image of the pipe and the word *pipe* into closer relation—either with each other or with the actual physical object, the tubed cup. Apollinaire could achieve a similar effect both by arranging a sentence about a bird into a bird shape (as in the calligram *Voyage*) and by having a character hold up a urinal and cry "The violin." The simpler calligrams are experiments in unison among media, while *Les mamelles de Tirésias* is an experiment in dissonance; but there's a certain desperation behind the act of calligramming, even a sort of condescension to language, as if denotation is so fragile that the word *bird* won't mean anything unless the reader can actually see the feathered tail. The overdetermined semiosis of the calligrams is as much of a threat to language as the wrong-direction semiosis of the play.

Paysage, with its chunky architecture of house and shrub, is a somewhat commonplace experiment in producing shape-rhymes between text and referent. The shrub is *rhopalique,* to use the term of S. I. Lockerbie: a clubbed typographic mass that lies inert on the page, demanding to be seen as a picture only by virtue of its strangely enforced margins. More typical of Apollinaire's best calligrammatic work is a fluid, ultracursive sort of writing, sensitive to currents of energy, indeed conforming itself to patterns of radiation. A calligram, it turned out, had more excitement as a tracing of an oscilloscope or a spectrometer than as a Kodak snapshot of the poet's back yard.

Apollinaire generated the first calligram, *Lettre-Océan* (1914), by a simple but daring strategy: he imagined a postcard ("Bonjour mon frère Albert à Mexico") in which the obverse and the reverse were conflated into a single verbal-pictorial plane. We are used to postcards in which the front has a pictured landscape and the back contains a personal message: but Apollinaire conceived a postcard in which the words of the message are arrayed into a kind of textual landscape. The letter is not *about* the ocean—it *is* the ocean. Long squiggly horizontal lines drawn across the page seem to suggest a calm sea, or radio waves beaming across the earth, or the decorative border for an area of the postcard, or the cancellation marks for the stamps ("Republica Mexicana Tarjeta Postal . . . U. S. Postage 2 cents 2"); and the radial arrangement of a section of the text might suggest rays proceeding from the sun, or streets proceeding from a Parisian traffic circle (the center of the design reads "On the left bank in front of the Pont d'Iéna"), or a voice or voices broadcasting messages in 360 degrees ("Long live the King . . . Down with the priesthood . . . Long live the Pope . . . Shut up"). The notion of *antithesis* has been translated from a syntactical structure into a visual structure: contradictory messages radiate from opposite sides of a center point. In a sense the characters of *Les mamelles de Tirésias* are only stage enactments of such shaped voices, as if pieces of paper inscribed with texts were crumpled into expressive human bodies.

A calligram, then, is an imaginative reconstruction of a telegram, in which the text-strips have been unglued and bizarrely reglued in order to defeat rectilinear logic and create a pictorial instantaneity of apprehension. Apollinaire saw himself as the enemy of the discursive:

> It doesn't matter *psychologically* that this image be composed of fragments of spoken language, for the bond between these fragments is no longer that of grammatical logic, but that of an ideographic logic ending in an order of spatial disposition totally contrary to the order of discursive juxtaposition. . . . *[Lettre-Océan]* is the opposite of narration, since narration is of all literary genres the one that requires the greatest share of discursive logic.

Apollinaire understood the calligram as a complement to the cubist collages of Braque and Picasso: just as they deformed the outward visual aspect of a thing in order to seize a higher reality, a sur-reality, an integrity that comprises a thing's extensions of itself along several axes of perception, so Apollinaire wished to deform the print appearance of his poem in order to embody aspects of his sub-

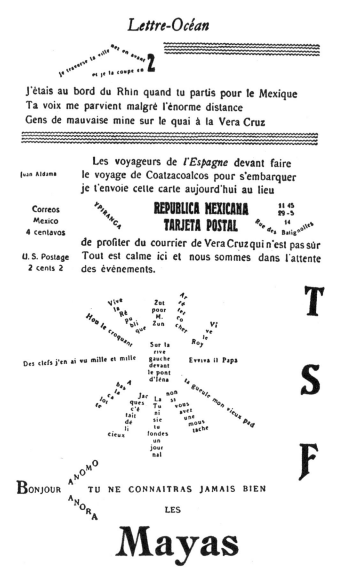

FIG. 28. Guillaume Apollinaire, *Lettre-Océan* (first page), 1917 (Apollinaire, *Calligrammes,* p. 43)

ject that exist only in the domain of the visual, not the linguistic. He offered, in effect, re-parsings, new diagrams of sentences created not to illustrate patterns of subordination in grammar, but to illustrate asyntactic, atemporal connections among linguistic elements. Language unlanguages itself, loses itself in the pictorial.

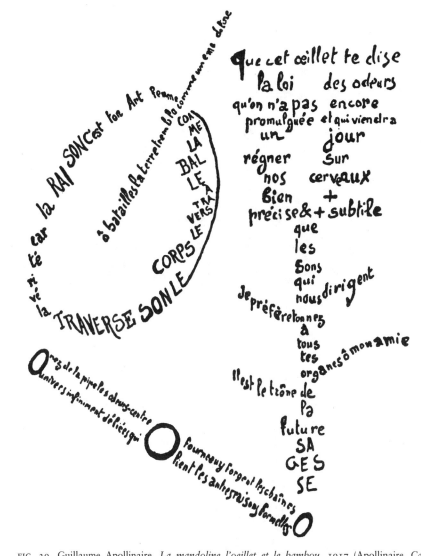

FIG. 29. Guillaume Apollinaire, *La mandoline l'oeillet et le bambou*, 1917 (Apollinaire, *Calligrammes*, p. 70)

Some of his calligrams follow Picasso and Braque quite closely. For instance, in *La mandoline l'oeillet et le bambou* (Mandolin Carnation and Bamboo), the three objects of the title are clearly outlined by the contours of the words, and make up a clear visual allusion to the set formulae of the cubist still life; indeed, in 1914 Apollinaire intended to publish his first five calligrams—then known as

FIG. 30. Guillaume Apollinaire, *Venu de Dieuze*, 1917 (Apollinaire, *Calligrammes*, p. 106)

idéogrammes lyriques—in a small book (abandoned when the war broke out) to be called *Me, I'm a Painter Too*. And Apollinaire had some ambition, it seems, to be considered a musician as well: in *Venu de Dieuze*, he included snatches of musical notation, perhaps representing discordant trumpet blasts that might accompany the emphatic military challenges ("Who goes there?"), passwords, grumblings, and patriotic catchphrases that make up the text—just as Picasso included snippets of printed scores in several of his cubist collages. Here we see Apollinaire struggling to make a sort of *Gesamtkunst*-gram, a whole opera that can be apprehended in a moment. If enough torsion can be exerted on the shapes of the letters, normal French, it seems, can realize the old dream of a hieroglyph or an ideogram, an entity that embodies meaning in a flash, without the slow and studied protocols of grammar.

A calligram has ambitions beyond those of an ideogram: an ideogram is a picture of meaning, but a calligram intends to provide a picture of experience as it impinges on the whole sensorium. An ideogram is centripetal, convergent, a focusing of meaning; a calligram (I speak here of the more complicated calligrams, not the bird of *Voyage*) is centrifugal, divergent, scattery—an embodiment of dissonance among media, in that language seems to yelp as Apollinaire tortures it into foreign shapes. *Le mandoline l'oeillet et le bambou* is a hymn to the liberating powers of certain odors, such as opium and perfume, an attempt to shape words into the sinuosity of fragrance, a dispersal of discourse into thin air. And the largest phrase-icon in *Lettre-Océan* depicts a phonograph record, in which the grooves seem to fling out a spatter of detached syllables—*cré, Hou, ting,* an outspewing onomatopoeia of bus horns, sirens, and the squeak of the poet's new shoes. *Lettre-Océan* is both a radio transmission from the Eiffel Tower (the height of which, three hundred meters, appears in the center of the record disc) and an acoustic storage device: it simultaneously emits random noise and retains it, a singing telegram. In 1912 Apollinaire made a recording of his poem *Le pont Mirabeau*—one can listen today to his heavily sonorous, wistful baritone; and *Lettre-Océan* attempts to phonogrammatize the street noises of Paris.

Simultanism: Verbal Polyphony

Toward the bottom of *Venu de Dieuze,* Apollinaire wrote *Cantato* to the left of a large brace, bringing together four fragments of slang exclamations by (I suppose) randy soldiers: and I assume that this is a kind of performance instruction to indicate that the four fragments are to be "sung" simultaneously. Apollinaire was much intrigued by a movement called *simultanisme,* and he often recalled with pleasure Jules Romains's experiment in 1909 with the simultaneous recitation of different texts by several speakers—verbal polyphony. This is a potent method for shortening the temporal span of discourse, for rendering discourse anti-discursive; in a sense, *verbal polyphony is to speech what the calligram is to writing*—a device for achieving planar juxtaposition of words, instead of logical development of words. (A musical analogue can be found in certain versions of the *missa brevis,* where the mass is amazingly abbreviated by the simple means of singing several different passages of the text at the same time—Haydn once wrote a whole *Gloria* [Hob. 22:7] that lasts about fifty seconds.) Apollinaire also noted that Blaise Cendrars and other poets had experimented with lines printed in inks of different colors—another means for increasing the visuality of poetry, for translating the act of reading into an instantaneous pictorial apprehension:

> if people have tried . . . to accustom the mind to conceiving a poem simultaneously like a scene in life, Blaise Cendrars and Mme. Delaunay-Turk have made a first attempt at written simultaneity, in which the contrasts of colors accustomed the eye to reading in only one glance, as an orchestra conductor reads in only one glance the superimposed notes in the score, as one sees in only one glance the plastic and printed elements of a billboard. . . .
>
> The idea of simultaneity has long preoccupied artists; already in 1907 it was preoccupying a Picasso, a Braque, who strove to represent figures and objects with several faces at the same time. Since then it has preoccupied all the cubists, and you can ask Léger what delight he felt in fixing a face seen at once in full face and profile.

This is from Apollinaire's 1914 essay "Simultanisme-Librettisme." Cubism is a kind of visual polyphony, in which the information of several different perceivers, scrutinizing an object from various angles, is conflated into a single cunning, synthetic image. Just as the ear can co-process different verbal messages, so the eye can co-process different points of view.

And surrealism itself, as Apollinaire understood it, is only an extension of simultanism from one medium to several media at once: it is a method for engaging the eye and the ear simultaneously with discrepant versions of reality, so that the mind is forced to engage itself in primary mental acts, trying to piece together a universe by means of the *sensus communis* into common sense. It is well known that the eye sees an upside-down world—that is, the lens registers on the retina an image in which the sky is on the bottom and the grass is on the top. Now, no one can remember a stage in childhood in which Mother's feet walked across the ceiling, because the mind automatically inverts the retinal image. Psychologists have studied this phenomenon by providing subjects with inverting eyeglasses, so that they behold the universe upside down—that is, right side up; and the mind soon compensates for this reinversion, too. The world quickly asserts its proper, conservative orientation, in which smoke rises and lead balls sink, no matter what optical tricks are played.

But simultanism and surrealism attempt to offer mentally unprocessed sensory experience, so that we can feel the topsy-turvy, the tohu-bohu, at the center of all cognition. Apollinaire disliked art that appeals to conventional, easily cognizable images of reality; as he wrote in his famous book *Les peintres cubistes* (1913),

You don't have to lug your father's cadaver on your back wherever you go. . . .

One will never discover reality once and for all. Truth will always be new. Otherwise, it is only a system more miserable than nature.

In this case, the deplorable truth, more distant, less distinct, less real each day, will reduce painting to the state of plastic scripture *[écriture plastique]* merely destined to facilitate relations among people of the same kind.

In our day, they would quickly invent a machine to reproduce such signs, without understanding.

Imitating planes in order to represent volumes, Picasso gives the diverse elements that compose objects an enumeration so complete and so acute that they *don't take the shape of an object,* thanks to the work of the spectators, who are forced to perceive the simultaneity of the elements, but in consideration of their arrangement [that is, in consideration of their aesthetic juxtaposition, not of the ways in which the elements add up to a standard pictorial figure for the intended object].

Is this art more profound than exalted? It doesn't dispense with the observation of nature and acts on us as familiarly as nature itself.

We live our lives inside a stale, eroded reality, in which all sharp edges have been filed away; and our art usually tends to reinforce this mollified, macerated, C-major world. Painting has declined into a lazy mechanical semiosis, in which we applaud ourselves for recognizing images that have been placed before us precisely for the sake of maximum ease of recognition. But Picasso acts as a corrective, in that Picasso's paintings are so overloaded with data that the spectator can't complete the little trick of reducing the image to a sign: there are too many elements for the spectator to be able to efface their clamor of conspicuousness into a commonplace picture of an object. The spectator can go a little way toward resolving the dissonances of the implied spaces into the consonance of a visible body; but, just as the great musical dissonances, such as the minor second and the major seventh, are the intervals only slightly removed from unison or octave, so the half-apprehended picture in the cubist construction serves to emphasize the dissonances that outrage the eye. Picasso forces us to study the world with new eyes, by providing paintings that model the endless novelty of the world around us. The perceptual discords in the painting are images of the perceptual discords that lurk everywhere in the sensory universe, if we take the trouble to live in the world rather than in Wurld-Whiz, a mental construct, the packaged aerosol version of reality.

The danger, of course, is that cubism itself will soon petrify into a mannerism, an old deplorable truth. Apollinaire was sensitive to this danger: he wrote, in an unpublished 1917 piece that seems to be a draft for the program note on *Parade,* of

> cubism, which has after all nothing to do with this hybrid tendency of the painters who cut up their boring academic figures, indeed their landscapes, into facets that recall those of the pendants of those crystal chandeliers that adorned salons when I was a child.

Even by 1917, certain cubists were starting to lug father Picasso's corpse on their backs; and *Parade* itself was, to Apollinaire, a device for refreshing the slightly arthritic cubist vision of reality—a vision that now seems refracted through the antique glass of a chandelier, ceremonious and deadening. Only by a steady invention of new styles, new apprehensions, new isms, can art hope to avoid hardening into a means for suppressing reality.

Surrealism as a Codified Style: Breton's Land of Unlikeness

It is probable that Apollinaire, in the postwar years, would not have developed surrealism into an official theory and a codified practice—more likely he would have outgrown the word, as he outgrew other movements that he devised or helped to spread. But Apollinaire died in the great influenza epidemic of 1918, two days before Armistice Day itself (some of his friends noted that the cries on November 11 of *À bas Guillaume* [Down with Kaiser Wilhelm] seemed oddly to recall the name Guillaume Apollinaire). His term *surrealism* turned out to have an astonishingly active afterlife. As the dadaists of the later 1910s and very early 1920s settled into a less productive nihilism and a less impudent espousal of randomness—or simply quarreled over politics—it became convenient to find a less nonsensical-sounding name for radical art; and that name was to be surrealism. And the name itself seemed to open new energies.

The most vociferous surrealist was André Breton, a talented writer and a provocative ideologist who regarded himself, with some justification, as the central figure and chief instigator of the surrealism of the 1920s and 1930s. Not surprisingly, Breton's version of surrealism owed something to Apollinaire's, and, also not surprisingly, it had many striking divergences as well.

There are passages in Breton's early writings that recall the surrealist doctrine we've been examining:

> Doesn't the mediocrity of our universe depend essentially on our power of wording *[énonciation]*? Poetry, in its most dead seasons, has often furnished

us with proof of this: what a debauch of starry skies, precious stones, dead leaves. Thank God, a slow but sure reaction has at last taken place in the mind. Things said and said again meet a solid barrier today. These are the things that have riveted us to this commonplace *[commun]* universe. These are the things from which we've got this taste for money, these limiting fears, this sentiment for the "fatherland," this horror of our destiny. I believe it is not too late to wake up from this deception, inherent in the words of which we've so far made such bad use. What holds me back from jumbling the order of words, from trying to kill the visible manner of existence of things? Language can be and must be torn from this slavery. No more descriptions from nature. . . . I don't see why people should protest when they hear me affirm that the most satisfying image of the earth I can make at this moment is that of a paper hoop. If such an ineptitude has never been proclaimed before me, it is obviously not an ineptitude. . . . One day a rather dishonest person [Remy de Gourmont], in a note in an anthology, happened to draw up a table of some of the images found in the work of one of our greatest living poets. It read:

Next day of the caterpillar dressed for the ball means: butterfly.

Breast of crystal means: a carafe.

Etc. No, sir, *does not mean that.* Put your butterfly back in your carafe. Be certain: what Saint-Pol-Roux meant was what he said.

This is from Breton's "Introduction to the Discourse on the Paucity *[peu]* of Reality," published in 1924, just before the *Surrealist Manifesto.* It will be noticed that, just as Apollinaire condemned an art based on commonplace models of reality and applauded an art in which the mind couldn't easily reassemble the constituents into recognizable objects, so Breton condemns an art enslaved to reality and applauds an art of novel arrangements and untranslatable images.

But there is a vast difference: for Breton, the ennui lies not in models of the universe, but in the universe itself. For Apollinaire, nature is endlessly fecund, inexhaustible; but for Breton, nature—at least the nature apparent to our waking senses—is a vulgarity and an impoverishment and a yawn. Breton advocates a deliberately unnatural art, an art of delirious juxtapositions, liberated from mimesis or any other form of reliance on the sensible world. Apollinaire's surrealism is a method for exploring the realness of reality; Breton's surrealism is a method for escaping from the oppressiveness of reality—a sort of irrealism. When Samuel Beckett, in his "Three Dialogues" of 1949, applauded an art faithful to the incoercible absence of relation between the art object and the world of experience, he followed good surrealist practice—and indeed, Beckett translated several of Breton's essays into English.

Breton believed that creativity resulted simply from turning attention away from the outer world and attending instead to the perpetual, spastic recombinings of sense data that occur in the unconscious mind. As Breton defined his term in the *Surrealist Manifesto:*

> SURREALISM, n. Pure psychic automatism, by which one proposes to express, either verbally, or in writing, or by any other manner, the real functioning of thought. Dictation of thought in the absence of all control exercised by reason, outside of all aesthetic and moral preoccupation.

Breton came to think that perhaps he should have inserted the word *conscious* before *aesthetic* in the final clause, but—dogmatist of the irrational that he was—he often insisted on the correctness of this definition. He understood surrealism as an instinctual, even mechanical process of inventing new realities:

> The idea of a bed of stone is just as intolerable to me as a bed of feathers. What do you expect, I can sleep only on a bed made of the pith of the elder tree. Take a turn sleeping there yourself. Very comfortable, isn't it? . . . *In reality,* do I sleep on a bed of elder pith? Enough! I don't know. It must be true in some way, because I say it.

Beckett, in his novel *Watt* (1953), described a fish that keeps rising to the surface and falling to the ocean bed, in order to learn to endure the middle depths: "But do such fish exist? Yes, such fish exist, now." The surrealist, according to Breton, continues the work of creating the universe, by positing entities that evidently taxed the resources of God's imagination: "The God that dwells within us is nowhere near ready to rest on the seventh day. We have yet to read the first pages of Genesis." To speak of the earth as an oblate spheroid is to be prosaic, boring, enslaved; to speak of the earth as a paper hoop is to be interesting—as long as no one has thought of this image before.

For Breton, an image is attractive as long as it resists becoming an interpretative metaphor: he likes the phrase "breast of crystal" until someone comes along to decipher it as a carafe. And for Breton, a simile is attractive as long as it fails to display much likeness between its two parts. The earth and a paper hoop are both round, but it would be difficult to find two round entities that less resembled one another. In 1929 Breton attacked Baudelaire's *Correspondances* (1857), the famous symbolist sonnet that posits occult transsensual harmonies—perfumes fresh as child's flesh, sweet as oboes, green as meadows: "A tomato is also a child's balloon, surrealism, I repeat, having suppressed the word *like.*" Surrealism suppresses the word *comme*—a rationalistic, proportion-determining sort of word, a word that presupposes some rule of resemblance—because in a fully concrete and alogical universe, there exists no criterion for determining similarity and difference: such ascertainments as *like* and *unlike* (or *is equal to* and *is not equal to*) are interchangeable and meaningless. As Breton noted in the discourse on paucity, "two leaves of the same tree are exactly alike: it's even the same leaf. I have only one word. I insist that if two drops of water resemble each other, it is because there is only one drop of water. One thread, repeating itself and crossing over itself, makes silk. The staircase up which I walk has only one step. There is only one color: white." It would be equally true, and equally unhelpful, to say that the universe is such a unity that any object is identical to any other object, or that the universe is such a diversity, such a heap of disparatenesses, that no object is similar to any other object. As another surrealist, Georges Bataille, wrote, reality is above all else *informe,* a kind of squish: "the universe resembles nothing . . . the universe is something like a spider or a gob of spit."

Impossible equations, such as *earth is hoop* or *tomato is balloon,* are potent tools for dismantling our illusions of order, our false belief that we can make classifications and discriminations of the entities we observe; to exhaust the permutations of verbal propositions in the form $x = y$ is to reduce the universe to its essential blobbiness. In this way, concepts such as *equals* or *is like* vanish into a general, overwhelming incomparability, or excess of comparability. Apollinaire believed in analogies but not in homologies; but for the puritanical Breton, analogies don't exist, either. Breton's art is an art without relations, as if relations between artistic constituents, or relations between the art work and the real world, would tend to spoil the purity of the imaginary object. One of Beckett's heroes remarks, "here I come again, just when most needed, like the square root of minus one, having terminated my humanities"; and Breton's artifices also seem to dwell on the plane of complex numbers, in an imaginary dimension where normal arithmetic doesn't work. I should point out that the older Breton of 1947 reinstated the word *like,* and the usefulness of the concept of similarity, in order to be able to explain his hatred for certain far-fetched metaphors (such as Cocteau's "Guitar bidet that sings")—but even here he cited with approval Reverdy's principle that the greater the distance between two juxtaposed realities, the stronger will be the image. In general, Breton kept faith with his definition of *image* in the *Abridged Dictionary of Surrealism* (1938): "The strongest surrealist image is that which presents the highest degree of arbitrariness. . . . it may look feebly untied." The weaker the connections among its parts, the more surreal the image.

Breton experimented with a number of different strategies for investigating aesthetics as it constitutes itself without any principle of choice or feeling for propriety: the aesthetics of convulsion, for the constituents of an art work must be determined not by logical analysis, but by a sort of epileptic seizure. It is not easy to make art in a world without analogy, where nothing is like anything else: not only is mimetic art obviously impossible or foolish, but many kinds of non-mimetic art are also disabled—though there seems to be a faint persistence of valid geometrical categories, such as *roundness,* amid the general loss of relation. In order to avoid selection, preference, and sense of similitude, Breton famously recommended automatic writing and automatic drawing—that is, art within a state of trance, as if the mind liberated from its endless vigilance, its daily tedium of making logically consistent maps of the universe, might be able to come up with something interesting, a serious *unlikeness* to reality.

But Breton was also intrigued by certain conscious or semiconscious strategies for producing art works: in 1933, he compared the act of writing to "*photographic* development," as if a text precipitated on the page out of some hazy pretextual blank, and he remembered that "Leonardo da Vinci recommended to his students, in quest of an original subject that suited them, to look for a long time at an old decrepit wall. 'You will not wait long,' he told them, 'before you notice, little by little, forms and scenes that will become more and more precise.'" The surrealist, confronted with the teasing disorder of the stars in the sky, or of random marks on an old wall, generates mental patterns, but without the assimilation of those patterns to conventional designs that Leonardo undertook. There is some distance between Leonardo, seeing the Battle of Anghiari taking shape on the surface of the wall he's about to paint, and John Cage, blackening small imperfections in his music paper in order to generate a composition: both allow accidental flaws in the medium to determine the art to be imposed on the medium, but Cage is far more chaste, in that he refuses to connect the dots, to organize the fortuities according to normal principles of intelligibility. The surrealist likes patterns that allude to patternlessness: by misconnecting the elements of our perceptual field, the surrealist generates all sorts of intellectual monsters, teratologies that make us confront the weakness and futility of our constructions of reality. We necessarily live in a chimerical world, and so the proper objects of our scrutiny are chimeras.

Lautréamont's Tryst of Sewing Machine and Umbrella

To an extent, the existence of a human artist is an embarrassment to surrealism. On the one hand, Breton's surrealism aspires to a pure manifestation of psychic processes; but on the other hand, the mind is always in danger of pulling the art work back into commonplace shapes, familiarizing it faster than inspiration can defamiliarize it. If one could persuade an elephant to paint, or a computer to write music, one might be jolted by something really startling. But alas, the elephant must select from pigments given to it by human keepers, who will also decide when the painting is "finished"; and the computer had to be programmed by a human intelligence—it is extremely difficult to rid the art work of contamination by human subjectivity. Dehumanization is more a theoretical ideal than an attainable goal.

Nevertheless, surrealism has always been fascinated by technology, as if, by engaging our imaginations with mechanical simulacra, we could dream the dreams of machines—the purest of all psychic automatisms. Breton considered that the first authentic passage of modern surrealism appeared in the sixth chapter of *Les chants de Maldoror* (1868–69), by Lautréamont (Isidore Ducasse):

> He is as beautiful as the retractability of the claws of birds of prey; or again, as the uncertainty of the muscular movements in the wounds of soft parts of the posterior cervical region; or rather, as the perpetual rat-trap, re-engaged each time by the trapped animal, that can catch rodents indefinitely and can function even hidden under straw; and above all, as the chance meeting *[rencontre fortuite]* on a dissection table of a sewing machine and an umbrella!

It will be noted that this bizarre chain of similes proceeds from organic convulsions (grasping claws, spasms in the back of the neck) to inorganic convulsions (the unstoppable rat-trap) to a tryst between a feminine machine and a masculine

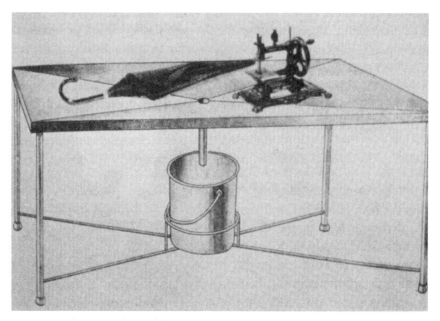

FIG. 31. Man Ray, *The Image of Isidore Ducasse* (© 2000 Man Ray Trust/ARS, New York/ADAGP, Paris)

one. The encounter between the sewing machine and the umbrella haunts the surrealist movement: Man Ray illustrated it, and Max Ernst spent endless hours arranging various quasi-sexual acts among pictures of machines and other bric-a-brac copied out of catalogues. The erotic power of the machine is a primary tenet of surrealism, since it assaults our normal map of the borders between the human and the nonhuman, between the animate and the inanimate. When Breton tried in 1937 to show what he meant by his catchphrase for the surrealist aesthetic, "convulsive beauty," he asked the reader to imagine the spontaneous growth of crystals, and bouquets of "halcyonoids and madrepores" from the bottom of the sea: "Here the inanimate so closely touches on the animate that the imagination is free to frolic to infinity concerning these forms completely mineral in appearance, and to reproduce along these lines the procedure by which one recognizes a nest or a bunch of grapes taken out of a petrifying fountain." Surrealism is most comfortable in the limbo between death and life, where coral is a living parody of rock, and crystals sprout and ramify as if they were alive. Surrealism posits a kind of reverse fetishism, in which human genitals are the dildos that preoccupy the fantasies of tumescent furniture. Surrealism concerns the thinking of dead heads.

One of the basic surrealist constructions is the displacement of the human mind, the human body, by inorganic surrogates: the flattening of the human and the nonhuman onto a single involuntary plane of action. The surrealists revel in an undistinguished reality where mental operations exist only as the swarmings of physical objects, and vice versa. This is how life feels in a world without relations, a world without the word *like,* a world where, in Breton's fine phrase, opposites are not perceived as contradictions.

Headlessness

Apollinaire conceived surrealism as a phenomenon of mixed media, but Breton did not. It is true that Breton used metaphors derived from the visual arts (such as the photographic negative) to describe his writing; that he paid close attention to psychological experiments with invertible afterimages; that he wrote at length about art exhibitions; that he even experimented with "poem-objects," photographic conflations of things and words. Nevertheless, Breton considered that literature is a nobler, more competent art than any other, and requires little supplementation from other media. As he wrote in 1933, "I always hold, and here is the essential point, that verbal inspiration is infinitely richer in visual meaning... than visual images properly so called. From this comes the protest that I've never stopped uttering against the 'visionary' power claimed for the poet. No, Lautréamont, Rimbaud did not *see* ... what they described." After this assertion, Breton challenged painters to contradict him. Inspiration, according to Breton, occurs when you hear a voice in your head, speaking mysterious words. In the *Surrealist Manifesto*, he gave a famous example of words that *"knocked at the window"* of his mind: " 'There is a man cut in two by the window' . . . it was accompanied by a feeble visual representation of a walking man sliced halfway up by a window perpendicular to this axis of his body." It is easy to find similar examples of voice mail from the unconscious in the works of Rilke and Yeats. But such logocentric notions of inspiration aren't conducive to the easy interchange or counterpointing of media that we find in *Parade* or *Les mamelles de Tirésias*. If the other artistic media are derivations from the verbal, they are ancillae, mood-auxiliaries to literature, incapable of finding a private access to reality. To Breton, pictures are essentially illustrations of words.

It might be argued that the surrealism of the 1920s and 1930s attempts to realize discords across media boundaries within the domain of a single medium. The shock of seeing a picture in which a slab of wood rises from the neck hole of a dinner jacket (as in Magritte's *The Conqueror,* 1925) doesn't arise merely from the visual impropriety: it is an affront to our whole sensory network, insofar as it

FIG. 32. René Magritte, *The Conqueror,* 1925 (© 1999 C. Herscovici, Brussels/ARS, New York; reprinted from Stich, *Anxious Visions,* p. 47)

suggests that a plank might have a point of view, a code of etiquette for dress. (The flying tree in the background suggests another form of giddy liberation for wood.) The painter arouses certain coenesthetic anxieties: how would I feel if I touched my head and felt something striated, dry, splintery—felt a two-by-four, with engraved scrolling instead of a face? The very textures of surrealist paint, such as the frottages and decalcomanias of Dominguez and Ernst, sometimes make a strong appeal to the sense of touch, as if a painting could assume a sort of mineral nubbliness or metal scarification. Bataille edited, from 1936 to 1939, a surrealist magazine called *Acéphale* (Headless), and some surrealist works struggle to provide an ingress into reality as it would appear to a torso groping with flailing arms—to provide complicated simulations of the vertigo and density of an eyeless, earless, brainless apprehension of the world. Adorno conceived Stravinsky exactly according to this model, as if Stravinsky were simply Magritte's conqueror turned musician: "The completely shrewd, illusionless *I* exalts the *Not-I* as an idol"; a work by Stravinsky "maliciously bows to the public, takes off its mask, and shows that there is no face under it, only a knob."

But this sort of sensorium-less surrealism isn't the same as the polysensual surrealism promoted in *Les mamelles de Tirésias*. I believe that the death of Apollinaire may have aborted certain promising possibilities for a surrealism of mixed media—the disabling of the *sensus communis* through the dissonance of *lexis, opsis, melos, mythos*. Breton and the official surrealists had a narrower view of art, and were more restricted to a single medium. The turning point of the movement might be seen in the première of *Les mamelles de Tirésias* in 1917, disrupted when a friend of Breton's, Jacques Vaché, brandished a pistol and threatened to shoot into the audience. This aggression prefigured a good deal of the calculatedly pointless hostility of later surrealism—as Breton was to claim in the *Second Surrealist Manifesto* (1930), "the simplest surrealist act consists of going out into the street, revolvers in fist, and firing at random, as fast as possible, into a crowd." Instead of the elegant epistemological violence of Apollinaire, surrealism tended to evolve toward a blunter violence, a more commonplace terror.

One reason for the absence of successful transmedia spectacles among the formal surrealists was quite simple: ignorance of music. Breton admitted candidly that he knew nothing about music, and Francis Poulenc, a composer strongly attracted to surrealist poetry, repeatedly deplored the utter indifference to music among all the surrealists except Paul Éluard. But Poulenc managed to create, long after the death of Apollinaire, when the anguish of the First World War had been replaced by the anguish of the Second, the spectacle of Apollinaire's surrealist dreams—the operatic version of *Les mamelles de Tirésias*.

Surrealism (Music)

ELEVEN

What is surrealist music? To my knowledge, the composers involved with surrealist texts left behind no theory of musical surrealism; and Breton and his fellow writers were in no position to provide one. But from our vantage point at the end of the twentieth century, we can perhaps see the outlines of such a theory.

There is a substantial body of music that might be called surrealist: settings by Poulenc and Honegger of poems by surrealist writers; Milhaud's *Le boeuf sur le toit* (1920), a ballet to a scenario by Cocteau; the collaboration by five of the composers known as Les Six on Cocteau's *Les mariés de la Tour Eiffel* (1921); Schulhoff's *Bassnachtigall* for contrabassoon (1922), complete with a preface denouncing "withered expressionists"; Ravel's *L'enfant et les sortilèges* (1925), with a cuddly-nightmare text by Colette; operas by Martinů based on plays by Georges Neveux *(Julietta, Ariane)*, along with Martinů's ballet *The Revolt* (1925), in which dancers costumed as musical notes rebel against their abuse by musicians—eventually Igor Stravinsky is forced to seek refuge on a Pacific island; (conceivably) Stravinsky's own *Oedipus Rex* (1927), also to a scenario by Cocteau; Antheil's set of piano preludes (1933) for Ernst's *La femme 100 têtes*. This is only the beginning of a catalogue.

In studying this list, one first notices the overwhelming presence of Jean Cocteau, whom the official surrealists often despised, partly because he seemed a fatuous, flighty, effeminate man, partly because of his notorious conversion to Roman Catholicism, and partly because he spent a great deal of time with duchesses and other not very surreal, or all too surreal, people. (Cocteau, however, sometimes had occasion to regret consorting with rich ladies, as when one of them warned her lapdog not to nuzzle Cocteau lest it get makeup all over its face.) Indeed, as far as Breton was concerned, the whole art of music was contaminated by Cocteau's interest in it: "If only a few writers show themselves violently hostile to music, displaying signs of aggressiveness, many others only feel indifference to it . . . this disfavor was perhaps accentuated in the last twenty years by the fact that in Paris the cause of modern music acknowledged as its champion a notorious *false poet* [Cocteau], a versifier who happens to *debase* rather than to *elevate* everything he touches." This is from an essay of 1946, with a title that clearly asserts the surrealist attitude toward music: "Silence is Golden."

But the world of surrealist art, as opposed to surrealist artists, was extremely congenial to Cocteau, and again and again in his works we find passages that sound like surrealist paintings come to life: for example, in *Orpheus* (1926), Orpheus ponders the panic that a block of marble feels while a sculptor chisels its veins; and in *The Knights of the Round Table* (1937) a cactus becomes a living gramophone, able to record messages and, if you tear off one of its leaves, play them back; and in his film *Beauty and the Beast* (1946) human arms emerge from the wall, holding lighted candelabra. The old myth that meant the most to Cocteau was the story of Pygmalion: his statues are never long able to resist the temptation to come to life—as in *Beauty and the Beast*, when a statue of Diana in the Beast's garden shoots the fatal arrow at Avenant. Pygmalion's statue is not the only active sculpture of antiquity, however: there is also the colossus of Memnon, reputed to sing when struck by the first rays of the sun; and both Stravinsky and Cocteau conceived *Oedipus Rex* as an opera of singing statues—in a poem to Stravinsky, Cocteau wrote, "Je sculpte en rêve Igor ton audible statue" [Dreaming I sculpt Igor your audible statue]. This continual equivocation between real human beings and images of human beings, between real voices and technological images of voices, strongly links Cocteau to the surrealist movement.

The Cocteau-Milhaud Le boeuf sur le toit: *Nothing Happens*

Cocteau's surrealist music skits, from *Parade* on, pay close attention to musical forms: for Cocteau, a drama organized like (for example) a rondo could escape from conventional dramatic proprieties and be faithful to the peculiar rhythms of invertible recurrence that seemed to him a feature of human life—Cocteau tended to conceive the succession of events as a system of infernal machines in which one act unwinds what another act has wound, and to conceive memory as a kind of running-backward of a filmstrip. We've seen, in *Parade,* how the concept of loop dominates the whole work, from the Chinese Conjuror's pantomime to Satie's music. Cocteau's next important collaboration with a musician was *Le boeuf sur le toit*. In this case Milhaud had already written the music, based on his experience in Brazil, where he'd gone in 1917 as a secretary to his friend Paul

Claudel, the French ambassador. Milhaud had no notion of linking the music to a drama—but he did think his score (subtitled *Cinéma-fantaisie sur des airs sud-américains*) might work as an accompaniment to a Chaplin silent film. And the whole score can be construed as a single giant film loop: the famous bitonal refrain is repeated twelve times; and the keys of the carioca-tapioca tunes that make up the filling move upward three times by minor thirds (from C to E♭, G♭, A), then the key moves down a major second (to G), and the whole harmonic procedure is repeated, until the piece has run the gamut of all twelve keys: what starts in C ends in C. It is an exciting piece, but there's something deliberately factitious about its excitement: at its heart is a kind of stasis, a mechanical rotation rather than a progression.

Cocteau, devising a scenario to fit the music for performance at the Comédie des Champs-Élysées, was extremely sensitive to its combination of energy and sloth, so characteristic of Modernist music loops. He set the ballet-pantomime in a Manhattan bar during Prohibition and populated it with a variety of striking types, including a black boxer, a black dwarf, a transvestite, and a gorgeous, Antinous-like bartender; they are busy drinking illegal alcohol, until a policeman comes—at which point the speakeasy is converted into a milk bar. The bartender tickles the policeman; a red-haired woman dances on her hands before the policeman, "like the Salomé in Rouen Cathedral," in the phrase that Milhaud used in his memoirs. But the bartender turns on a giant electric fan, which decapitates the policeman; then the red-haired woman dances, Salomé-fashion, with the severed head. The characters leave one by one; the policeman revives, and the bartender presents him with an enormously long bill.

Milhaud's score was soon known, in English, as *The Nothing-Doing Bar*—a good name, for nothing is done there. Indeed, Cocteau stressed the absolute lack of event during his spectacle: "*Parade* still had a literary content, a message. . . . Here I avoid subject and symbol. Nothing happens, or what does happen is so crude, so ridiculous, that it is as though nothing happens. Look for no double meaning." Evidently one shouldn't look for a single meaning, either: it is an exercise in pure inconsequentiality of gesture. The policeman's harmless decapitation was borrowed from an unused idea for *Parade*— there was a stage direction for the Chinese Conjuror at the end of his turn: "he cuts off his head and bows." One of the barflies is a transvestite, and Cocteau may have conceived the policeman as a kind of transvestite between the quick and the dead. Being alive is a matter of preference, or a mere social construct, like class or gender: just as a broken statue can easily be glued back together, so can a broken man.

But this headlessness also provides a certain quality of symbolist acephalism— recalling the dreamy severed Baptist-heads, liberated from the inconveniences of the sensuous world, so dear to Flaubert, Moreau, Wilde, Beardsley, Strauss, Florent Schmitt, Yeats. (Wilde even imagined a sequel to his *Salomé*, in which

Salomé survived her crushing by the soldiers' shields and became an ascetic in the desert, living like the prophet on locusts and honey, becoming a missionary for Christ, until she was finally decapitated in a fall through the thin ice of the river Rhone—an extremely Coctelian plot of transvestism, surrogation, empty and tantalizing symmetry.) Perhaps, in a sense, symbolism is to surrealism as tragedy is to farce: their bizarreries are often identical, but the symbolist dotes on occult relations, whereas the surrealist dotes on non-relation. The policeman's ability to lose his head and regain it has no special metaphysical import; it is simply a way of demonstrating that the events of the drama are only parodies of events, frenzies of non-events. The policeman is a John the Baptist for the flapper era, trying to enforce a moral code, though the sin here isn't the incest of Herod but bathtub booze—a vapid sin for a disconnected age, an illusion of a theme produced in order to disguise a general themelessness.

The alcohol police versus the alcohol drinkers—Cocteau's plot is a simple dialectic of restraint and indulgence, appropriate for a musical composition in which the indulgences of the dances can never stray far from the control of the refrain, and in which the indulgences of remote keys can never stray far from the control of C major. Just when you think that a remote key has murdered C and trampled on its corpse, C comes back to life, an unkillable tonic. As in *Parade,* the stage doings have only the faintest connections with the implied semantic content of the music; but they have strong connections with the form of the music. The Brazilian aspect of the music of *Le boeuf sur le toit* is irrelevant to Cocteau's scheme, except insofar as it reflects various *absences*—absence of edifying Germanic grimness, absence of concert-hall hush, absence of cultural pretension of any sort. But the formal aspects of Milhaud's music—the obstinacy and tonal ambiguity of the refrain, the harmonic arch—are quite relevant. As a phrase-by-phrase translation of music into gesture, in the normal fashion of ballet, *Le boeuf sur le toit* is a deliberate failure: indeed, the physical movement is completely dissonant with the tempo of the music, because Cocteau instructed his players to move very slowly, in contradiction to the peppiness of Milhaud's score; but as a simile for the whole experience of the music, its fun vanity, its self-cheapening thrills, its iridescence of boredom, Cocteau's scenario is effective.

The Cocteau–Les Six Les mariés de la Tour Eiffel

Cocteau's next large experiment in cross-media surrealism, *Les mariés de la Tour Eiffel* (The Eiffel Tower Wedding Party), was in some ways the most ambitious of all. There is a method of surrealist art-making known as *cadavre exquis,* in which several artists draw a single picture, or write a poem, on paper folded or blocked in such a way that they can't coordinate their efforts: a technique that enforces the ideal of incongruity on many levels, from subject matter to style.

Les mariés de la Tour Eiffel seems an application of *cadavre exquis* to the field of music, in that five different composers (Auric, Milhaud, Poulenc, Tailleferre, Honegger) contributed the score to Cocteau's skit—but it is a timid application, in that the composers were aware of the whole scenario, and were so stylistically similar to one another, at least superficially, that the listener marvels at the musical coherence, not the scatteredness. Honegger's funeral march borrows a violin line from Milhaud's wedding march—the composers themselves had little interest in incongruity for incongruity's sake.

But if the relations among the individual musical movements aren't especially surreal, the ballet as a whole is a pure surreality. The painted backdrop, by Irène Lagut, resembles a kind of tent, a tall trapezoid framed by flat, cross-hatched wings like an abstraction of the base of the tower; in the middle area the two halves of a central street seem to tilt upward, so that the rows of buildings on the two sides of the street rise quickly together to form a single apex—it is as if the Eiffel Tower were nothing more than a vision in iron of the vanishing point of all Paris's perspectives. (It is possible that Lagut was inspired by Delaunay's well-known painting, circa 1911, of the Eiffel Tower as a crazed, splayed, striding, dislocated thing.) In his preface to the published text, Cocteau congratulated

FIG. 33. Irène Lagut, set for *Les mariés de la Tour Eiffel*, 1921 (© 1999 ARS, New York/ADAGP, Paris)

Lagut for evoking "postcards of Paris over which I've seen little Arabs sighing, in Africa": it is Paris at once overfamiliar and defamiliarized, as if seen from the point of view of Zanzibar, or from some extraterrestrial vantage point.

But the major theme of Cocteau's preface is not the strangeness of the spectacle, but its ordinariness:

> The poet must extricate objects and feelings from their veils and their mists, to show them suddenly, so naked and so alive that a man can scarcely recognize them. They strike him then with their youth, as if they had never become old, official things.
>
> This is the case with commonplaces, old, powerful, and universally admitted, in the way that masterpieces are, but whose beauty and originality no longer surprise us, because we are used to them.
>
> In our spectacle, I rehabilitate the commonplace.

The costume designer, Jean Hugo, was so struck by the force of the last sentence—Cocteau must have uttered it often during the early stages of the production—that he devised the costumes after the little pictures that accompany the entries for *bather, lion, cyclist, bride,* and so forth in the Larousse dictionary. *Les mariés de la Tour Eiffel* is an exercise in the decontextualization of stock figures. It is, finally, less a *cadavre exquis* than a snipping-out and repasting-together of stereotyped images, from postcards or department-store catalogues or kitsch engravings—a theatrical anticipation of Max Ernst's surrealist "collage novels," or comic books, such as *La femme 100 têtes* (1929). The bather, the lion, the cyclist, the bride, all seem to belong to different orders of pop art, ranging from pinup pictures to safari adventure tales to sporting magazines to figures on top of wedding cakes; but Cocteau juxtaposed these jarring images to study their discord, the shock that arises when beloved icons desecrate one another.

Another surrealist aspect of the scenario can be seen in Cocteau's amazing simulations of the technology of mechanical reproduction: *Les mariés de la Tour Eiffel* is George Eastman's and Thomas Edison's dream play. On each side of the stage, enormous acoustic horns poke out; on one side there is a huge camera, large enough that the characters can pass through its "lens" and enter or exit the stage down its vast bellows. Cocteau does everything in his power to destabilize the boundary between image and imaged object.

The setting of the skit is the first platform of the Eiffel Tower; the two gramophones, Cocteau's parody of a Greek chorus, speak loudly and very fast, both narrating the action and reciting all the dialogue. Auric's overture, called *Le quatorze juillet,* evokes "crossing regiments, marching troops, whose music brightens a corner of a street and grows distant, evokes also the powerful charm of the sidewalk, of the popular festival, of the streetside stands made up like guillotines,

FIG. 34. Illustrations of general and lion from the Larousse dictionary, paired with Jean Hugo's costume designs for *Les mariés de la Tour Eiffel*, 1921 (*Nouveau Larousse illustré; dictionnaire universel encyclopédique* [Librairie Larousse, 1898–1904])

around which the drums and cornets compel the stenographers, the sailors, the clerks to dance." The stage business begins when we see an ostrich running around, chased by a hunter; the hunter shoots, and a large blue telegram floats down from the sky—a dead (that is, out-of-date) letter, evidently killed by the hunter in lieu of the ostrich. The director of the Eiffel Tower reads the telegram and learns that there's to be a wedding party this very day—just enough time to set the table if everyone hurries. The exasperated photographer explains that his camera is broken: this morning, when he cried Watch the birdie! and activated the little toy that focuses the attention of his subjects for the photograph, an ostrich popped out; the photographer is determined to recover the birdie and cram it back into the camera.

To the strains of Milhaud's *Marche nuptiale*, the wedding party enters, "walking like dogs in plays for dogs." Lunch is served, and the general gives a speech—on what topic we know not, since his words are represented not by one of the gramophones but by Poulenc's *Discours du général*, a polka for two cornets; but the music suggests that it is platitudinous and mercifully brief. When his official discourse is over, the general starts to describe mirages in Africa, how a piece of pie only *seemed* to be covered with wasps, for the wasps were actually distant tigers. A female cyclist rides up, asking directions to Chatou—but the party decides that she too is a mirage, that she was never up in the Eiffel Tower, but on the road to Chatou all along. The photographer tries to take a group shot: but when he cries Watch the birdie! a bathing beauty steps out of the camera—"Oh! a pretty postcard!"—and dances a little dance, accompanied by a number in Poulenc's best pseudo-vulgar *ooh-la-la!* manner. The photographer persuades the bathing beauty that his camera is a cabana, and so she prances back into it, blowing kisses. The photographer is discombobulated by all this: "Alas! I tremble each time I say the accursed words. Who knows what will come out? Since these mysteries are beyond me, let's pretend that I've organized them." This last sentence, according to Cocteau's preface, should serve as the epigraph for the whole spectacle.

The photographer hopes that he'll have better luck with a snapshot than with a posed picture—but the camera rebels, and spurts eau de cologne instead of taking a picture. So the photographer tries again to organize a posed picture, and once again pronounces the accursed words: this time there appears not an ostrich, not a bathing beauty, but a big boy—in fact, the largest physical presence on the stage—carrying a basket of balls. As in *Les mamelles de Tirésias,* the boy seems to have been conceived, born, and raised in the space of a minute: the whole wedding party croons over his resemblance to mother or father or grandmother or grandfather, and predicts a bright future for him as captain, architect, boxer, poet, president; but the child seems unimpressed with their sentimental drivel and decides to slaughter the wedding party by bombarding them with balls, so that he can have all the macaroons for himself; as he hurls the balls he screams, "I want to live my own life!" (Milhaud wrote a *Fugue du massacre* for this scene, alas lost, but reconstructed by the composer in 1971 for the first publication of the score.)

The director of the Eiffel Tower asks the party to be less noisy: the wireless telegrams might be frightened away. A flock of these timid telegrams arrive from New York and dance, to Tailleferre's *Valse des dépêches.* The big boy asks the photographer to take a picture of him posed with the general, reading Jules Verne together. The photographer says, once again, the damned words Watch the birdie!—and a lion comes out of the camera. The whole party hides except the general, who calmly announces the lion is a mere mirage, just like the cyclist; in fact the whole scene is a phenomenon of *intermirage,* since the lion in Africa can see the Eiffel Tower, just as the Parisians can see the lion. But the lion, unimpressed with this theory of optics, eats up the general, leaving only a boot behind, and strolls back into the camera. The wedding party becomes a funeral procession, to Honegger's *Marche funèbre*—a remarkably black piece, given the context of farce. Just as the mirage lion turns out to be real, so the spoof-music threatens for a moment to grow dense, *pathétique*.

The father-in-law delivers a eulogy for the general: "We have seen you confront the wild beast, careless of danger, not understanding it, not fleeing when you did understand it. . . . your type will last as long as there are men on the earth." The Garde républicaine marches up and dances to Tailleferre's *Quadrille*. The big boy wishes to feed some bread to the Eiffel Tower, but is informed that it can only be fed at certain hours—that's why they keep an iron railing around it. The ostrich is found hiding in the elevator; the photographer puts a hat on the ostrich, thus rendering it invisible, and escorts it safely past the hunter and back into the camera. Now the camera is fixed: the photograph can at last be taken. A dealer in modern art and a collector appear, and discuss the wedding party as if it were a painting ("a little like the Mona Lisa . . . a masterpiece . . . look at this style, this nobility, this *joie de vivre!* . . . It's more than a wedding. It's all weddings"). The collector decides to buy it, for a million francs, and the dealer puts a placard saying "Sold" next to the wedding party. The collector wants the "Sold" sign included in the photograph of the wedding party, so that he can make an impressive show of his masterpiece in American magazines.

At last all is ready for the photograph—but no, the camera itself speaks: "I'd like . . . I'd like . . . I'd like to give back the general." And indeed the general reappears, minus a boot and half his mustache. The collector notes this as an unexpected detail, of the sort that one keeps discovering in masterpieces. The photographer starts to count: at the cry of One, the bride and groom walk over and disappear into the camera; and at each subsequent count (as the orchestra plays *Ritournelles* by Auric), more members of the wedding party enter the camera, lastly the general and the big boy—no one is left but the director, the hunter, and the photographer. The director announces that it's closing time; but they've missed the last train, so the camera turns into a train and chugs off stage, as we see the legs of the wedding party sticking out from the bottom and their arms waving handkerchiefs, to the tune of Milhaud's wedding march.

I understand Cocteau's farce as a meditation on the phrase *take a photograph*—the French *prendre une photographie* has a range of meanings similar to those of the English phrase. What is taken when you take a photograph? Some tribes far from Europe are said to believe that a camera, when it takes a picture, captures the soul of the person photographed, as if photography were a means for generating voodoo dolls; and the notion of photography as a kind of theft is everywhere behind Cocteau's plot. A camera is a ravenous stomach that consumes the visible world: a lion may leap out of it and gobble up anything that stands before it. By the end, the camera has swallowed the whole wedding party—instead of distinct individuals staring at a lens, we have a monstrous jumble, a hybrid of apparatus and human being, a thrashing centipede. Not only are the bride and groom married, but the human race and the machine are intermarried, intermiraged, a remarkable experiment in recombinant genetics. Cocteau specified that his photographer should be a hunchback, as if he were half-slumped into his apparatus, an extension or parasite of the machine, even before the bizarre events begin. A camera is dangerous, a threat to the integrity of the photographer and of the thing he photographs. Behind *Les mariés de la Tour Eiffel* is an anxiety about photography—in some ways similar to that in Kurt Weill's farce *Der Zar läßt sich photographieren* (1928), to a text by Georg Kaiser, in which terrorists have rigged a camera with a gun to shoot the Tsar when he has his picture taken.

But what the camera takes, the camera can give; it can vomit as well as swallow. I assume that when the photographer says Watch the birdie! *[un petit oiseau va sortir]*, he has a sort of toy bird that extends itself from the camera when he presses a button or moves a switch. A stuffed canary, however, is the least of the things that a camera can emit: it can give forth ostriches, bathing beauties, lions, whole worlds. The Modernists lived in an age of an astonishing proliferation of images, when streets could be so covered with show posters, advertising billboards, shop signs, and so forth that the eye might tend to lose itself in the torsions of specious realities, more vibrant, more engaging than the physical objects they were glued onto. The surrealist Remedios Varo painted a picture, *Embroidering the Terrestrial Mantle,* that showed "a number of frail girls with heart-shaped faces, huge eyes, spun-gold hair, prisoners in the top room of a circular tower, embroidering a kind of tapestry which spilled out the slit windows and into a void, seeking hopelessly to fill the void: for all the other buildings and creatures, all the waves, ships and forests of the earth were contained in the tapestry, and the tapestry was the world." But photography can accomplish the same thing, in a far less labor-intensive manner than tapestry-weaving: it can generate an infinite stream of affordable images, drowning reality in copies of itself. From the art dealer's point of view, the wedding is already a Mona Lisa, even before a picture of it is made; we've learned to eliminate the asperities of a real world, and to live in an inescapably imagistic state of being.

Images, of course, are subject to manipulation in ways that physical objects are not. A photograph can be enlarged, or overexposed, or double-exposed; and one of the jokes of *Les mariés de la Tour Eiffel* is that the objects on stage can behave in exactly this manner. A canary can be enlarged into an ostrich; an ostrich can white out into pure invisibility; a cyclist on the road to Chatou can cohabit with a wedding party on the first platform of the tower. In *Parade*, Cocteau experimented with the possibility of having the American Girl tremble as if she were a film image shown on a shaky projector; here, Cocteau experiments with a far more thorough confusion of stage personages with reproduced images.

Just as the stage set looks like Paris reconstructed with mirrors, so the stage events are representations of mirages—mirages so impossible to confine to a merely illusory plane that a mirage of a lion in Africa can devour a general. In some sense the whole skit takes place inside the camera: what we see is a realization of cinematic trickery by means of live actors—an enactment on stage of the derangements that we would observe if we could live inside double exposures, inside film loops. Cocteau has extrapolated our suspicion that we dwell in a technological simulacrum of a world—that we are just the stand-ins, the much-battered stunt doubles, for the leading men and women who will enact our lives in the way that they should be led, with a far more experienced, more handsome, more endearing, better-equipped cast. If I think to myself, How much better Dustin Hoffman could play the role of a professor writing a book on Modernist collaborations, amid cute telephone interruptions from a madwoman determined to inform him about the playing conditions at a tennis court he's never seen—split screen, professor right, talking cautiously, tweed jacket, book-lined study, madwoman left, voluble, sweat clothes, running in place—then I'm in the right frame of mind to see a Cocteau farce.

But the confusion of a photograph with an object photographed is only one of several confusions between image and imaged. Cocteau is equally insistent on destabilizing the boundary between text and spectacle, *lexis* and *opsis*—in this he follows the example of Apollinaire's *Les mamelles de Tirésias,* though in his preface Cocteau scoffs at this work for developing "a boring thesis about repopulation." Just as mirages are characters in *Les mariés de la Tour Eiffel,* so words are characters, too: a gang of telegrams can descend on the stage to dance a waltz. Breton believed that he could create new objects, such as a bed of elder pith, simply by saying the words; Cocteau illustrates on stage this easy commerce between noun and physical thing. The play is the hallucination of camera and gramophone, a *folie à deux.*

The presence of the gramophones is crucial. Cocteau hid himself in the box of one gramophone for some of the performances, and it must have delighted him to think that his voice seemed able to improvise new realities out of thin air—if the play has no thesis, it might nonetheless be regarded as a rehearsal of pure creativity by means of technological simulations of the faculty of imagination itself. The text of the play consists of a mélange of stage directions, plot summary, and dialogue: the need for conversations between characters explains the presence of *two* gramophones. The notion of a narrated opera is very old: Monteverdi, at the dawn of the genre, devised his *Il combattimento di Tancredi e Clorinda* (1624) as a spectacle in which a narrator, or *testo,* sang stanzas from an epic poem, interrupted by brief passages in which Tancredi and Clorinda sang their own direct discourse, all the while miming the events of the poem—

Monteverdi even had his Tancredi enter on a real horse, if a *cavallo mariano* is a real horse. But Cocteau's talking texts are far more aggressive: not only do they insist on speaking all the dialogue, but they seem less to be quoting already-written words than to be making the words up as they go along. Words seem to shift endlessly between invisible radiation in the air at one extreme—the Eiffel Tower was used as an antenna for wireless telegraphy—and physical objects at the other: the words of the gramophone keep liquefying and hardening before our eyes and ears, metamorphosing into written formulae (such as "Vendu," Sold) or into music *(Discours du général)*. Even in his preface, Cocteau found it hard to maintain a clear distinction between speaking and writing when he considered the gramophones: he complimented two of his reciters for their diction "black as ink, as big and clear as capital letters."

The disconcerting slipperiness of images and imaged things also extends to the music. Much of the music consists of, so to speak, images of preexisting music. When we hear Auric's overture, we are supposed to hear not actual marching bands on Bastille Day, but an evocation of such bands: just as the stage set shows Paris broken up by mirrors, so the music is a refraction of popular music. But as the play proceeds, it becomes increasingly difficult to distinguish "real" music from "imaginary" music, that is, self-sufficient music from music that alludes to or founds itself upon familiar music. This difficulty is especially noticeable in the one movement in the score that seems sober, stylistically uncompromised: Honegger's *Marche funèbre*. This was the movement that most pleased critics made uneasy by the self-conscious japes of popular style elsewhere; but the creators of *Les mariés de la Tour Eiffel* had the last laugh on these critics. As Cocteau recalled in his preface:

> In the *Funeral March,* Arthur Honegger has fun parodying the *grande musique,* or, better, what our writers on music gravely call: *la Musique. . . .* Scarcely were the first strains of the march heard before the big ears prick up and recognize their stable. No one advised them that this march was beautiful in the manner of a sarcasm, written with taste, with a feeling for an extraordinary opportunity. None of those critics, all agreeing in their praise of the piece, recognized in its bass line the waltz of *Faust!*

Just as Saint-Saëns amused himself, in his *Carnival of the Animals* (1886—but not published until 1922, the year after *Les mariés de la Tour Eiffel*), by transposing Offenbach's famous can-can to the low bass and slowing it down until it became almost unrecognizably ponderous, dim, lacking in kick, so Honegger buried Gounod's waltz from *Faust* deep within a funeral march for a marionette, or, even less than a marionette, a mirage. To hear the whole score is to hear a constant stream of acoustic mirages, reflections of everything from parades and ballroom dances to operatic hit tunes, echoes that dislocate any notion of original voice.

Poulenc's *Discours du général*—the most surrealistically far-reaching piece of the score—presents us with a different kind of musical unreliability, imaginariness. The first theme is clear enough: it is musical cliché, designed to imitate verbal cliché, in exactly the same manner as Sancho Panza's proverbs in Strauss's *Don Quixote* (1898). But the second theme is a quotation, from the opening bars of the first scene of *Rigoletto* (1851)—what we hear just as the curtain rises, after the malediction-prelude. This is an odd passage to quote. It's extremely familiar, but not an easily placed hit tune, like the Gounod waltz. Furthermore, there would seem to be little point in spoofing it: whereas Gounod's tune is a corpulent, delightful thing, plausibly symbolic of complacent taste and vain cultural pretension in the audience that adores it, the lean figure played by Verdi's onstage band is already a kind of spoof, since it images the hollowness, the blare and glare, of the Duke's toying with human love, his court-theatre of rape. It is possible to construct an argument that Poulenc quotes this theme in order to show the frenetic emptiness of Cocteau's general, a kind of duke without a duchy, even without an appetite. But I understand Poulenc's manner of quotation—and he was a music thief of amazing flagrancy—not as a technique for making pointed semantic allusions, but as a technique for disabling the normal semantic procedures of music. Poulenc was, at times, almost aggressively retro in his taste: as a French critic noted in 1922, "M. Poulenc, 'advanced' as he is, declares that nothing pleases him like *Rigoletto*." The hunchbacked tragicomic figure of Verdi has been demoted to a Punch, popping out of the jack-in-the-box of *Les mariés de la tour Eiffel*. Poulenc is a composer of surrealizing misquotations.

EX. 11.1. Poulenc, *Les mariés de la Tour Eiffel: Discours du général*

EX. 11.2. Verdi, *Rigoletto*: opening of first act

Dadaist Music: Schwitters and Duchamp

When we look at musical compositions that might be called surreal—works by Poulenc, Martinů, Ravel, and so forth from the 1920s—and compare them with Schoenberg's early twelve-tone compositions, also from the 1920s, we notice that the surrealist works seem strikingly conservative in certain ways. Melodies tend to move in a conjunct, singable manner; harmonies rarely grate; structures are often easily assimilated and full of predictable recurrences. But it is a mistake to think of Schoenberg as a more modern or venturesome sort of composer than Poulenc, because *Poulenc attacked musical conventions as fiercely as Schoenberg, not on the level of harmonic syntax, but on the level of semantics.* As a harmonist, Poulenc was, compared to Schoenberg, a child; but Schoenberg's *Moses und Aron* (1930–32) depends on interpretative cues every bit as simple and rigid as those of Saint-Saëns's *Samson and Delilah* (1875)—as soon as the spectator learns that triadic figures, instead of chromatic figures, represent evil. Poulenc was original not in the way that his music sounds, but in the way that his music means.

Why does surrealist music sound fairly normal, when surrealist painting seems to outrage the eye so flagrantly? In order to answer this, it is helpful to study the most playfully outrageous music of the 1920s, which arose not among the surrealists but among the dadaists. The contrast between dadaist and surrealist music is striking. The dadaists produced little that could be called music—but what there is challenges the very definition of music. Perhaps the best-known piece of music-dada is Kurt Schwitters's *Ursonate* (1921–32), a composition for solo spoken voice. Schwitters based it on a poem by Raoul Hausmann: where Hausmann wrote *fmsbwtözäu*, Schwitters devised a pronunciation guide *(fümms bö wö tää zää Uu)*, called the pronunciation guide the first theme of a rondo, and added three other themes *(Dedesnn nn rrrrrr; Rinnzekete bee bee nnz krr müü?; Rrummpff tillff toooo?)*; the reciter reads these lines according to the strict recurrence rules that govern the musical form of the rondo. (Not all the thematic material is of equal merit, but the listener soon begins to look forward to hearing the angular and explosive *Rinnzekete bee bee* theme.) At the end of the last of the four movements, the *Presto-Kadenz-Schluss*, the reciter begins to chant the letters of the German alphabet—a crystallizing of nonsense into the basis for sense comparable to the moment in the film *2001* where an australopithecine tosses a bone into the air and the twirling bone melts into a twirling space station. Those who prefer English nonsense to German nonsense—or who wish to ponder the issue of whether distinctions among languages still exist amid bombed-out phonetic rubble—may turn to Schwitters's musical compositions written during his sojourn in England as a refugee during the Second World War, such as *RIBBLE BOBBLE PIMLICO.*

Schwitters's music is an exercise in the counterpoint between total destruction of some rules and total submission to other rules, such as the digression pattern of the rondo. Another dadaist, Marcel Duchamp, devised a more abject, a more will-less manner of writing music: his "musical erratum" to *The Bride Stripped Bare by Her Bachelors, Even* (1915–23) asks the performer to compose his own music by running a toy train with open boxcars directly beneath a funnel; various balls, with numbers representing musical notes, are crammed into the funnel; the note-balls fall into the boxcars, and their sequence, from engine to caboose, determines the music. In this manner, music is stripped bare by her baccalaureates: we have entered a state of pure anomie and apathy, without melody or harmony or meaning, a kind of heat-death in sound. The funnel ejaculates music into the void.

Allusion in the Music of Les mariés de la Tour Eiffel

Surrealist music, however, is recognizably music, often of a quite familiar style. When Cocteau listened to the music for *Les mariés de la Tour Eiffel,* he was reminded of music heard on other occasions, such as Bastille Day parades— he even thought that the composers had done for France what Stravinsky, in *Petrushka,* had done for Russia: provide a complete and sophisticated evocation of a child's delight in popular music. Obviously, the music of Schwitters or Duchamp reminds nobody of parades, or funerals, or weddings, or any other event at which music is commonly heard—it is, or at least aspires to be, almost perfectly asemantic. Dada is a phenomenon of semantic destruction; but surrealism is a phenomenon of semantic dislocation and fissure. It is impossible to disorient unless some principle of orientation has been established in the first place; it is impossible to open abysses of meaning without first securing a semantic space in which such concepts as *top, bottom,* and *bottomless* can register.

In other words, you can't provide music that means wrong unless you provide music that means something. The 1920s saw an astonishing number of experiments in increasing the expressive possibilities of music—not only the experiments that are now an integral part of our musical world, such as those of the second Viennese school, but also several that seemed abortive or premature, such as Alois Hába's microtonal chamber music, leading up to his quarter-tone opera *Mother* (1931)—an opera so shocked by its own daring that it often sticks to simple ascending and descending scalar figures, as if Hába were more fascinated by the scale itself than by anything that could be played on the scale. But the surrealism of Poulenc and his fellows didn't try to create a new language of music—it simply tilted the semantic planes of the old language of music. Just as surrealist paintings often have a horizon line and a highly developed sense of perspective, in order that the falseness of the space and the errors of scale

among the painted entities can register their various outrages to normal decorum, so surrealist music provides an intelligible context of familiar sounds in
order to develop a system of meanings that can assault or discredit other systems
of meanings.

If Webern or Hába had written the music for *Les mariés de la Tour Eiffel*—
not an easy thing to imagine—the funeral march would have had no striking
musical relation to the sort of music by Handel or Chopin that we associate
with dead marches. Its interpretation would have been controlled entirely by the
events on stage; except for a vague sense of extraterrestriality, it could have contributed no semantic content of its own. But the very ordinariness of the music
that Les Six provided for Cocteau's spectacle allowed it to have precise, powerfully determined meanings of its own: meanings that counterpoint or undercut
the things we see on stage or hear from the reciters. It is homely music, with a
stiffness, an inertia, capable of resisting meanings applied to it from outside. It
is canned music, with a definite taste of tin, appropriate for a play that takes
us inside a camera, inside a gramophone. When an anthropologist visited New
Guinea, he filmed the sacred rituals of a primitive tribe there; after he had finished, he explained what he'd done to the chief, who asked him if the tribe could
have a copy of the film so that its members wouldn't have to go to the inconvenience of performing their rituals every year—they could propitiate their gods
by playing the film. I feel that *Les mariés de la Tour Eiffel* is the equivalent for a

FIG. 35. Max Ernst, *Third Visible
Poem, no. 2,* 1934 (© 1999 ARS, New
York/ADAGP, Paris; reprinted from
John Russell, *Max Ernst: Life and
Work* [New York: Harry N. Abrams,
1967], p. 202)

Parisian wedding: it illustrates the swallowing of a human spectacle by the means for the technical reproduction of that spectacle. But the camera, the gramophone, and the orchestra have competing versions of the spectacle—and it is the excitement of the discords among them that make the excitement of the whole.

As we've seen, Honegger's funeral march is incongruously serious against the spectacle of a funeral for a cartoonish general wearing a big plaster head who's just been eaten by the mirage of a lion. This incongruity exists only because the music has a semantic weight of its own—because it sounds like other funeral marches we've heard. But the march is incongruous not just with respect to the visual aspects of the theatre, but within itself as well: partly because of the submerged allusion to Gounod's *Faust,* but also in much more obvious ways—for example, the main theme is a slow cascade of falling chromatic three-note figures, with a built-in excess of *boo-hoo-hoo,* a caricature of lamentation, like the crocodile tears shed in the funereal opening of Dvořák's *The Wood Dove* (1896). Auden once wrote that music cannot lie—but I think these passages are evidence that music *can* lie. Indeed, surrealist music is about the possibilities for lying, for self-incongruity, for calculated inauthenticity of being. It isn't expressionistic, but *about* expression: it takes expressionistic devices and arrays them into odd aesthetic constructs. It inspects the musical signs for joy, sorrow, languor, and so forth, and twists them into exotic curlicues. It cultivates a semantic vertigo, since the signs it uses both mean and do not mean what they seem to mean. Surrealist music is a far more wide-awake business than the surrealist writing of Breton; but it remains close to the surrealism of Apollinaire, in that it drives wedges into our normal way of assembling sense data into a big, consistent world.

Honegger's funeral march is a parody—and parody, in the sense of burlesque or derisive aping, is not an important feature of the surrealist movement, in that surrealism calls into question the distinction between the serious and the playful. It is possible to write music that incorporates the textures, the sign systems, even the actual melodies of prior music entirely without parody. And for non-parodic musical embezzlement, we turn again to Poulenc, who was a kind of human gramophone, a device for recording old music and playing it back with a heightened artificiality.

Stravinsky as Fagin

Poulenc cheerfully confessed, to anyone who would listen, his extraordinary dependence on other composers. In a series of radio broadcasts, the transcripts of which were published in 1954 as *Entretiens avec Claude Rostand,* Poulenc suggested that he was a sort of secondary limb or organ of Stravinsky:

> In my music, you hear constantly the presence of the great Igor. In Stravinsky's protean canon *[oeuvre-Protée],* each of us has found the leavening for his per-

sonality, in the most opposite scores. If Honegger and Milhaud are in debt to *The Rite of Spring,* if Messiaen can refer himself to *The Nightingale,* it's from *Pulcinella, Mavra, Apollo,* and *Le baiser de la fée* that I've pilfered my honey.

C. R. It seems, in effect, rather natural, given your melodic temperament, that you've chosen works of an especially singing nature, and in which certain themes are themselves borrowed, from Pergolesi and Tchaikovsky.

F. P. A point well taken. And besides, you can find the rhythmic echo of *Les noces,* very Frenchified to be sure, in the songs for dancing in *Les biches.* But it's evident that there's much more of *Le baiser de la fée* and *Apollo* in *Aubade,* for example, and of *Pulcinella* in *Les biches* and the *Concert champêtre.*

I will never minimize these influences, since I don't want to be the son of an unknown father. . . . Chabrier is my grandfather, and Musorgsky remains my master in the domain of melody.

As Rostand noticed, Poulenc likes to steal from thieves—what a thief steals, you can steal from the thief, as Loge put it in *Das Rheingold.* Just as Pound translated his Canto 1 not from Homer's *Odyssey* but from a Renaissance Latin translation of the *Odyssey,* so the ownership of musical themes seems to be vanishing into a delirium of quotation: Poulenc borrows from Stravinsky, who borrows from Pergolesi—but "Pergolesi" is himself largely a publisher's fraud, since many of the works attributed to Pergolesi (dead at the age of twenty-six), including a good number of the works quoted in *Pulcinella,* were written by Gallo or by Unico van Wassenaer or by nobody in particular. Here we have the equivalent in music of that transcendental anonymity so beloved by Roland Barthes and other critics. And here we have Stravinsky as Fagin, teaching his younger colleagues how to pick pockets—except that many of Poulenc's thefts are so gross that they seem more like outright robbery than theft by stealth. (Stravinsky was also a pioneer in the world of surrealist mismatch between text and music, though in ways in- telligible only to Russian speakers: Taruskin notes that the first of the *Pribaoutki* sets the text of a "carousing jingle" to stately music appropriate to a bridal shower.)

The Jacob-Poulenc Le bal masqué

Poulenc confessed a number of his crimes: for example, he not only told Rostand that the adagietto from *Les biches* was heisted from Tchaikovsky's *Sleeping Beauty,* but he played both passages on the radio so that the listener could savor the misdemeanor. But the borrowings that he never (as far as I know) confessed are more relevant to his role as a surrealist.

In the *Discours du général,* as we've seen, there is an odd intrusion of *Rigo- letto* into the calculated musical banalities. Eleven years later, in 1932, Poulenc set some surrealist poems by Max Jacob in a "profane cantata" for baritone and chamber orchestra, *Le bal masqué*—commissioned by the Vicomtesse de Noailles for a "spectacle-concert," an almost official surrealist gathering in that the director Buñuel was present. Poulenc said that he wanted "to create a vocal style that would be both hallucinatory—something like photographs of crimes or vulgar, popular magazines—and full of jarring ideas, mixing vulgar harmonies with refined ones, deforming words and sounds." Some idea of Jacob's text can be gained by a translation of the finale:

> Crippled repairman of old automobiles
> the hermit has returned to his lair
> by my beard I'm getting too old for Paris
> the angle of your houses runs into my ankles
> they say my checkered vest looks Etruscan
> and my duds go badly with my purple hat
> warning! they've put a poster on my entrance
> the whole place smells like the skin of dead goat.

Poulenc thought that these lines seemed a self-portrait of Max Jacob—a clumsy, endearing man, so Apollinaire-besotted (as Poulenc told Stéphane Audel) that he even treated his mother exactly the way Apollinaire treated *his* mother. Jacob kept a large glassed armoire without a back in the middle of his apartment, and pretended that it was a doorway in a partition. And for Poulenc, Jacob's text was like the looking-glass through which Alice traveled to Wonderland, a place where Poulenc found "a sort of carnival from Nogent with pictures of monsters, from my childhood at the edge of the Marne."

EX. 11.3. Poulenc, *Le bal masqué,* finale: flute swirl

EX. 11.4. Tchaikovsky, *The Nutcracker, Waltz of the Snowflakes:* flute swirl

Poulenc's music for this finale, in C major, begins with an orchestral evocation of music-hall frivolity, marked *frénétique;* but its frenzy is qualified by several

strange features. At one point *(subito più lento)* a slinky dance starts tangoing out of nowhere, most disconcertingly; but before that, in the frenetic part, a flute intrudes with a chromatic swirl right out of the *Waltz of the Snowflakes* from Tchaikovsky's *Nutcracker* (1892), with its rhythm slightly regularized. Here is the purest possible juxtaposition of the refined and the vulgar—a graceful sprinkling of talcum powder onto the sweaty pop show—but what makes it *really* hallucinatory is that Tchaikovsky, in this context, sounds as vulgar and impudent as the music hall or the tango—or the orchestral simulations of automobile horns, perhaps sounded in honor of the crippled repairman. Poulenc seems to be disabling the sign system that distinguishes vulgar from refined. High culture has dwindled to a cellophane preciosity. Both here and in the *Discours du général,* Poulenc has used music history to produce an acoustic collage in which classical grotesques—a hunchbacked jester, a fairy-tale prince who is only an enchanted gimmick for shelling walnuts—consort with the clichés of popular music. When Poulenc described *Le bal masqué* as the musical equivalent of crime photographs and jarring visual juxtapositions, he seemed to be imagining his composition along the lines of those Max Ernst pictures in which icky stuff from the inside of

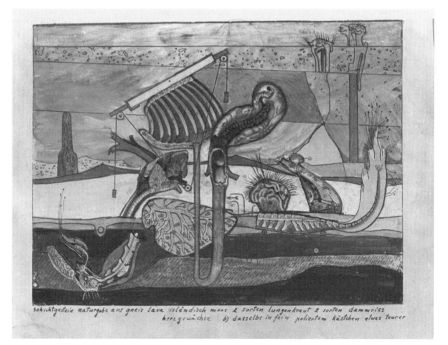

FIG. 36. Max Ernst, *Stratified Rocks, Nature's Gift of Gneiss Iceland Moss 2 Kinds of Lungwort 2 Kinds of Ruptures of the Perineum Growths of the Heart (b) The Same Thing in a Well-Polished Box Somewhat More Expensive,* ca. 1920 (© 1999 ARS, New York/ADAGP, Paris)

mammals develops into a whimsical landscape—as in *Stratified Rocks, Nature's Gift of Gneiss Iceland Moss 2 Kinds of Lungwort 2 Kinds of Ruptures of the Perineum Growths of the Heart (b) The Same Thing in a Well-Polished Box Somewhat More Expensive* (ca. 1920). Breton's assault on the basic dichotomies of reality, such as organic/inorganic, found visible form in Ernst, and audible form in Poulenc's vivisection of the semantic tropes of music.

During the late 1930s and the 1940s, Poulenc was still profoundly involved with surrealism. But he was sobered by war and by personal tragedy, such as the death of his friend Pierre-Octave Ferroud in a car wreck in 1936. In 1942 Max Jacob, the author of the *Le bal masqué* poems, a pious convert to Roman Catholicism, insisted on wearing the yellow star that the Nazis assigned to the Jews, and was seized by the Gestapo. Poulenc's surrealist projects of these years seldom have a carnival air: instead of frivolity, Poulenc offered, in *Sécheresses* (1937), to a text by Edward James, a wasteland, locust-ridden, in which even the sea has been reduced to its skeleton; in *Figure humaine* (written in 1943), to a text by Éluard, a desperate hymn to liberty, especially the liberation of France—far from the athematic surrealism of Cocteau, this is a piece with a clear thesis; and in *Les mamelles de Tirésias* itself (1944; 1947), a strange rhyme of the century's two great world wars—though here, at last, the carnival returns, only to find itself shivering in the cold.

The *Éluard-Poulenc* Un soir de neige: *Theft from Ravel*

The new features of Poulenc's later surrealist style are easily seen in a somewhat less ambitious piece, *Un soir de neige* (Snowy Evening), a set of four part-songs to texts by Éluard, written at Christmas 1944. The third piece, *Bois meurtri* (Bruised Forest), is stark and somber:

> Bruised forest forest lost of a winter journey
> Ship where the snow takes footing
> Forest of refuge dead forest where hopeless I dream
> Of the sea of broken mirrors . . .

The first six syllables *(Bois meurtri bois perdu)* are set to a strikingly desolate theme in simple root-position triads: F♯ minor *(Bois meur-)*, C minor *(tri)*; E minor *(bois per-)*, B♭ minor *(du)*. The two triads in each pair are related by that disturbing interval, the tritone; and the slippage of a whole tone between the first pair and the second seems a further development of a swooning, a sob. And yet this idea is stolen baldly, shamelessly, from Ravel's and Colette's *L'enfant et les sortilèges*—and in fact from a scene concerning an injured tree, a tree that moans *Ma blessure, ma blessure* [My wound, my wound] as he remembers what the child did to his bark with a stolen knife; it's a nice literalization of Satie's quip about the Wagnerian music drama in which the property trees go into convulsions. Here is the same sequence of tritonally related chords in pairs, D *(Ma bles-)*, G♯ *(sure)*; C *(ma bles-)*, F♯ *(sure)*—the only difference, besides the transposition, is that Ravel's theme has no thirds, whereas Poulenc has filled out Ravel's spare fourths and fifths.

EX. 11.5. Poulenc, *Un soir de neige: Bois meurtri bois perdu*

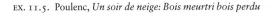
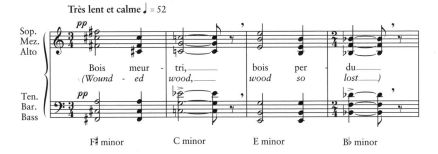

EX. 11.6. Ravel, *L'enfant et les sortilèges: Ma blessure, ma blessure*

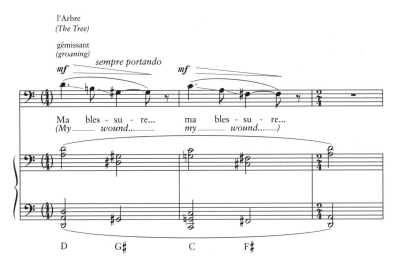

Theft is understandable when it is affable and easygoing, as in *Pulcinella* or *Les biches*. And the theft in *Un soir de neige* ought to be funny, in that Ravel's comical tree, complaining over a slight breach of its bark, has been promoted to a whole ruined forest. But no one, I think, is tempted to laugh. Poulenc has achieved something remarkable: backward parody, in which a burlesque has been twisted into something profoundly earnest. In early music we find this all the time, as in Lassus's mass *Entre vous filles* (1581), based on an indecent *chanson* (by Clemens). But in the twentieth century it seems a strong violation of musical protocol—indeed, an attack on the viability of the funny/serious distinction. The *bois meurtri* theme has a strong semantic content—it straightforwardly means *sadness*—but this content hovers over the text without adhering intimately to it, since it inhabits two contexts at the same time, Colette's as well as Éluard's. This sort of bi-spatial meaning is analogous to the spatial outrages of surrealist painting.

Poulenc's Setting of Les mamelles de Tirésias

In his masterpiece of surrealism, *Les mamelles de Tirésias,* Poulenc investigated the far reaches of semantic dissonance without parody. Above all, Poulenc was determined to avoid parody—to avoid a sense of the farcical, the fantastic, the unreal. Given Apollinaire's text, this was no easy matter: but Poulenc had a number of strategies for *grounding* his opera, for placing it on such concrete foundations that sheer comedy and sheer tragedy could confront each other.

Poulenc's vision of the opera differed in several ways from anything that could have occurred to Apollinaire; but Poulenc was extremely well informed about Apollinaire's aesthetic, especially concerning *Les mamelles de Tirésias*. Poulenc, at eighteen years of age, had attended the first performance of the play, and in later life he clearly recalled the original music (by an amateur, one Germaine Albert-Birot—Satie had refused Apollinaire's pleas to write the score) and the original décor and costumes, in the cubist style, by Serge Ferat. When he became interested in writing the opera, in the early 1940s, Poulenc visited Apollinaire's widow—who lived only six kilometers from his house in Touraine—and asked for permission to cut the text and to move the action back from 1917 to 1912. The cutting wasn't particularly significant, except for part of the extraordinary discussion of the ideal theatre from the prologue; few spectators will regret, for example, the loss of one of the repetitions of Presto's and Lacouf's duel to the death (in Poulenc they keep killing each other without involving the People of Zanzibar). But the change in time is quite significant. For one thing, Poulenc has erased the Great War from the opera, by setting it in a generic prewar France: perhaps in order to make its repopulation thesis pertinent to the Second World War, and perhaps in order to represent a kind of peacetime exuberance of the French imagination, from which most of the horrors of wartime have been dispelled. For another thing, Poulenc has resituated the action "in an atmosphere, if I dare to say it, decubified *[decubifiée]*"—before the war, cubism was less a general aspect of public style than an area of exclusive research in advanced art. And

Poulenc wanted his opera to look not at all cubist, not like an abstraction from experience but like an embodiment of experience, as down-to-earth as possible. Poulenc changed the place as well as the time:

> I've substituted Monte Carlo for Zanzibar in order to avoid exoticism, and because Monte Carlo (which I adore, and where Apollinaire spent the first fifteen years of his life) is plenty tropical for a Parisian like me.
> The ravishing décors that Erté made for the Opéra-Comique, with, for the finale, these lamp standards in the style of a dining car in 1914, were exactly what I wanted.
> As for the women's costumes, they were exact replicas of the dresses (back then you said *toilettes*) that Erté had designed for Poiret's 1912 collection.

By having the almost physically immortal Erté re-create in 1947 the clothes and interior design that he'd made fashionable some thirty-five years before, Poulenc achieved a remarkable verisimilitude. In all his talk concerning the opera, Poulenc's motto is always the same: *nothing exotic*. The first page of the score prints this same warning, and is quite firm that the place must be southern France, and the time must be 1910 (Poulenc evidently vacillated between 1910 and 1912— 1910 was the better choice, for by 1912 cubist design was spreading to popular culture); to explain the name Zanzibar, Poulenc claims that it's an imaginary town between Monte Carlo and Nice. Not a preposterous African island, but familiar Monte Carlo, where the opera's dice games seem quite nonchalant; not cubist décor, but décor lifted directly from the museum of haute couture; not a year of wartime disruption, but a year of opulence.

Furthermore, Poulenc's music is intended to be equally non-exotic, earth-bound. When Rostand commented on the discord between the *bouffonnerie sans limites* of Apollinaire's text and the unextravagant style of Poulenc's music, Poulenc replied: "I'm always suspicious of orchestral bizarreness, and besides, since I don't have, like Ravel . . . the sense of the fairy-like that ennobles the unusual, I've preferred to hold myself to an orchestration that has its feet solidly on the ground." Poulenc's dislike of the fanciful and trivial in music is also shown by his vehement resistance to all suggestions that his music was operetta-like: "operetta amuses me, but I've no gift for writing one. . . . the finale to the second act of *Mamelles*, which has a false look of operetta, isn't an operetta finale. It's too dry, too affected *[grimaçant]*, and not so gay as that." *Les mamelles de Tirésias,* then, is a pseudo-operetta, an opera that only pretends to frivolity, that feigns feigning. It attempts to unclown a clownish text, to find gravity amid a delirium of figments. I wonder whether Mozart, had he been given to radio broadcasts, might not have described his music to *The Magic Flute* in somewhat similar terms.

It is clear that Poulenc was attracted to Apollinaire's text not because it was absurd, but because it was freakish:

> People have often asked me: "Why have you been able to write music to a text like that?"
>
> Now, it's just like love: it's impossible to explain your choice. The one-legged lady with a ravishing face who used to stroll down the Boulevard de la Madeleine didn't lack for admirers, as far as I know.

In Poulenc's music for *Les mariés de la Tour Eiffel,* a postcard bathing beauty comes to life; but by the 1940s she seems to have lost a leg—actually, of course, Thérèse inflicts on herself a double mastectomy, as opposed to the original Tiresias, who was merely blinded. Poulenc's surrealism, from the crippled repairman in *Le bal masqué* on, has a strong tendency to mutilation: he constructs musical equivalents to those crutches that prop up sheets of skin or pale protuberances in the paintings of Dalí. In the Breton-Éluard *Abridged Dictionary of Surrealism,* Dalí wrote the entry for *béquille,* crutch: "Wooden prop deriving from Cartesian philosophy. Generally used to support the tenderness of *soft structures.*" In the prosthetic erotics of surrealism, the crutch takes the place of the crotch, and the peg leg intensifies desire, or is itself the object of desire. The human body, hollow and droopy, deskeletonized, lacks sufficient rigor. *Les mamelles de Tirésias* investigates the *cantabile* of rubber breasts—here music itself is fetishized, made a kind of support for limp human tissue. This is another aspect of the solidity of the music, its unfantastical, down-to-earth quality: the amputated Thérèse and her castrated husband need the music's vehicular security in order to move, in order to save themselves from utter inanity. An eerie, tintinnabulatory sort of music would be too insubstantial for Poulenc's purposes: a fetish must have a certain hardness, a certain heft.

Poulenc's music may sound strange, gross, almost sordid; it sometimes seems completely obvious, and yet its very obviousness has a sort of subtlety behind it. Poulenc described his compositional procedure as if he responded to the text in the most blatant way imaginable:

> I only had to follow Apollinaire's text strictly in order to find the musical tone. *Les mamelles* dates from 1903. . . . In reworking *Les mamelles* in 1916, Apollinaire made a prologue in which the stage director explains what the play will be.
>
> This prologue is grave and melancholy. Naturally, the fragments that I've set to music reflect the same tone.
>
> In the same way, knowing the secret meaning that Apollinaire attributed to

certain words, concerning Paris and the Seine, you'll note that the music becomes aroused [*s'émeut*].

When, in the middle of the worst buffoonery, a phrase could give rise to a lyrical and melancholy change of perspective [*optique*], I didn't hesitate to modify the tone, knowing what sadness Apollinaire's smile hid.

Poulenc makes it sound as if his music had the instantaneity of semantic response that has been such an important aspect of music drama from Monteverdi's *Orfeo* to Schoenberg's *Erwartung*. But in fact, Poulenc's practice has little to do with Monteverdi's or Schoenberg's—unless one can imagine Monteverdi's Orpheus playing patty-cake with Charon by the banks of the Styx, or Schoenberg's woman singing *This little piggy went to market* as she counted her dead lover's toes. Affect lacks its proper inertia in *Les mamelles de Tirésias*—clowning and weeping switch back and forth too quickly to be pertinent to any human subject, even to an insane one. Poulenc's music follows not the trajectory of the presumed emotions of the characters, but the trajectory of the words of the text, in a bizarrely dogged, earthbound manner. It is a conscious violation of music-dramatic propriety, as flagrant in its way as Schoenberg's violations of harmonic propriety. The music's tendency to prop up the wrong or the half-right leads to an erosion of all semantic elements, sordid and sacred alike, into a general tease of meaning.

In a curious manual of advice for writing a bad opera, *Il teatro alla moda* (ca. 1720), Benedetto Marcello informs the apprentice hack how to organize his arias:

> The ariettas should have no relation whatever to the recitative, but the poet should do his best to introduce into them . . . the terms "butterfly," "mosquito," "nightingale," "quail," "bark," "canoe," "jessamine," "gillyflower," "saucepan," "cooking pot," "tiger" . . . etc., for in this way he reveals himself as a good philosopher, distinguishing the properties of animals, plants, flowers, etc., in his similes.

> Let [the composer] see to it that the arias, to the very end of the opera, are alternatively a lively one and a pathetic one, without regard to the words, the modes, or the proprieties of the scene. If substantive nouns, e.g., *padre, impero* [empire], *amore, arena, beltà* [beauty], *lena* [vigor], *core* [heart], etc., etc., or adverbs, as *no, senza* [without], *già* [already], and others, should occur in the arias, the modern composer should base upon them a long passage; e.g., *pa . . . impeeee . . . amoooo . . . areeee . . . reeee . . . beltàaaaa . . . lenaaaaa* [. . .] The object is to get away from the ancient style, which did not use passages on substantive nouns or on adverbs, but only on words signifying some pas-

sion or movement; e.g., *tormento, affanno* [breathlessness], *canto, volar* [to fly], *cader* [to fall], etc.

To Marcello, the proper style for an opera is an elevated, impassioned style that rarely descends into the boring, prosaic world of object-nouns, but remains in a realm of hovering verbs, a continual gliding and rising and sinking on the wings of feeling: the coloratura runs in the singer's throat trace the exact contours of the arc of the emotion. But Poulenc delights in transgressing these rules. He alternates the lively and the pathetic in a mechanical, indeed a maniacal manner, and not just from one set piece to the next, but even within a single musical phrase. Not only is he happy to set to music words like "mosquito"—this is one of the very words that Marcello thought derived from the librettist's encyclopedia of laborious tropes—but he is also eager to respond more closely to the accidents of the figures of speech than to the feelings that the similes attempt to image. Where Marcello's ideal opera writer flies, Poulenc stubbornly insists on sinking. To some extent, what the twentieth century calls surreal is simply what earlier ages called bad.

A example of Poulenc's treatment of Apollinaire's figures of speech comes in the crucial scene where Thérèse unbreasts herself and becomes a man:

> I'm feeling virile as the devil
> I'm a stallion
> From head to foot
> Watch me be bull
> I'll make myself toreador

In Apollinaire's text, the metaphor of the bull is no more important than the metaphor of the stallion; and Thérèse's fantasy of herself as a bullfighter has little more prestige than any other item in her immense repertory of imaginary male futures, from mathematician to senator. But Poulenc seizes on the bull and the bullfighter as the basis for the abrupt insplice of a bit of flamenco, complete with a new stage direction, "She dances a Spanish dance," and a new fragment of a text, an *Olé* sung by a chorus of baritones to a Spanish-sounding snap to a root-position C♯ chord (act 1, seven bars after rehearsal figure 32). Nothing here is particularly inappropriate—the Escamillo music seems masculine enough to serve as an illustration for a sex-change scene—and yet the spectator may feel that the composer has got lost for a minute inside a figure of speech, that he's more interested in the trope than in the feeling of exultant liberation intended by the trope. The bull has crashed out of the text and begun to prance in the orchestra as a quasi-autonomous being; in Marcello's terms, the composer has started snorting about animals, attending to nouns instead of verbs. The texture of the music keeps undergoing concrete metamorphoses far more radical and conspicuous than those of the transsexual hero/ine. It's all she can do to keep up with the music, which seems to lead her by the nose.

EX. 11.7. Poulenc, *Les mamelles de Tirésias: Olé*

Surrealist music rarely neglects the text entirely, but it tends to pay attention to false, misleading, or irrelevant aspects of the text—as if the most opaque, least legible aspects of the text were most worthy of close musical attention. In this sense, the greatest surrealist scene in all opera is from *Cardillac* (1926), written by a composer not usually associated with the surrealist movement, Paul Hindemith. At the end of the first act, there is a long pantomime during which a man quietly opens a woman's bedroom door, awakens her (with a hushing finger on his lips), and presents her with a magnificent belt of gold; delighted, she tries it on, then takes it off and starts to kiss and fondle the man; at the end, a masked figure dressed in black climbs in through the bedroom window, crawls toward the bed like an animal, and suddenly interrupts the lovers: he stabs the man in the neck, steals the gold belt, and flees. It is easy to imagine the sort of music that a film composer (Bernard Hermann, say) would supply for this scene; but Hindemith, radically contravening expectations, supplied a neo-Baroque duet for two flutes. Nothing in the music expresses the slumber or the passionate kiss, and certainly not the stealthy murderer just outside the window, about to crawl in at the instant the duet ends—the flutes remain tranquil, self-possessed, rhythmically even, tootling along oblivious to sex and death alike. The only aspect of the text that Hindemith wished to notice was the idea of pairing: two entwined lovers equal two entwined flutes. But by allowing the concept of *duet* to dominate the musical proceedings, Hindemith flouted normal notions of what's important and what's trivial in the domain of musical expression, and thereby produced a kind of music-dramatic gargoyle. He noted the noun *pair* instead of such verbs or movement-figures as *desire you*, or *what's that noise?* or *aaarggh*.

Poulenc also finds ways of erecting imaginary planes of meaning, set at odd angles to the literal meaning of the text—of course, in a text as polytextual as *Les mamelles de Tirésias*, Poulenc didn't have to look far to find odd angles. Poulenc once remarked of *Le bal masqué* that Jacob's words were full of unexpected ricochets; and Poulenc's surrealist practice consists of writing music that glances away from the primary denotation of the text, that follows semantic ricochets.

Poulenc thought that the heart of *Les mamelles de Tirésias* lay in its soberer passages; and sometimes they are so very sober that they threaten to tear apart the gauzy fabric of Apollinaire's farce. Consider, for example, the music that Poulenc wrote for the funeral of Presto and Lacouf. A less surrealist composer would have written music that somehow acknowledged the fact that this is a funeral for two extremely resilient corpses—*poussahs,* clowns that pop right back up whenever you strike them down. Honegger's funeral march in *Les mariés de la Tour Eiffel*—or Mendelssohn's quickstep toy funeral march for Pyramus and Thisbe in *A Midsummer Night's Dream* (1843)—represents just the sort of conventionally witty response a composer might make to the death of Presto and Lacouf: music that winks at its own grimness. But Poulenc's music does not connive, does not parody: "I consider *Les mamelles* as my most authentic work, along with *Figure humaine* and the *Stabat*. . . . Look, for example, at the funeral scene, where Denise Duval [who played Thérèse] reads in the newspaper *Le petit Zanzibar* of the death of the two drunkards Lacouf and Presto, you could very easily replace the words with a liturgical text, without great scandal, I think. Listen." And he then played, for his radio audience, the Cluytens recording of the funeral music in *Les mamelles de Tirésias,* which would indeed feel perfectly appropriate in Poulenc's *Stabat Mater* (1950), describing Mary's grief at the death of Jesus Christ.

But of course Christ, like Presto and Lacouf, was a corpse that refused to stay dead. By following a peculiar ricochet from Apollinaire's text, Poulenc has converted a surrealist truth—that opposites aren't contradictions—into a Christian truth concerning the hilarity at the heart of grief, the grief at the heart of hilarity. *Les mamelles de Tirésias* is "authentic" in that there is not one moment of our lives in which there isn't a funeral march playing somewhere in the back of our skulls—and yet these corpses always resurrect themselves, at least in our dreams. Poulenc's authenticity lies in his faithfulness to the coextension of tragedy and farce, dissonant yet inextricable, throughout human life. Musical semantics, like all semantics, depends on differentiation; and by extensive development of frivolous music-hall numbers (such as the policeman's catchy *Dites ma belle enfant,* a tune all twinkly eyes and winkly elbows, very suitable for Maurice Chevalier, if one can imagine Chevalier trying to seduce a tied-up husband wearing a dress), Poulenc created exactly that clear system of differentiation that permits the funeral music to register as funereal. Indeed, it is arguable that the funeral in *Les mamelles de Tirésias* is graver, more anguished, than anything in the *Stabat Mater,* simply because the *Stabat Mater* is so thoroughgoingly sad that its wrenching chromaticisms lose force, lacking much contrasting material to wrench away from. The very disorientation of *Les mamelles de Tirésias* permits, paradoxically, extreme clarity of organization—just as its farfetchedness, its inauthenticity, permits an unusually authentic response to certain aspects of our emotional lives. The opera is a kind of laboratory for investigating the semantics of music in a petri dish, without prior audience expectation—since no audience could imagine how to respond to the death of two such galoots as Presto and Lacouf until the music told them how. The text is too strange, too much-meaning, too little-meaning, to resist any construal that the music might choose to make of it.

To understand musical meanings as an arbitrary system of differentiations may seem to be an assault on the dignity of music. For those composers who feel that falling minor seconds are *naturally* sad, or that a hornpipe rhythm is *naturally* cheerful, the cultivation of semantic distinctions in a farce—that is, in a vacuum—will seem an outrage or a fraud. Schoenberg, for example, strongly believed in natural meanings: even near the end of his life, in 1949, he was capable of writing, "The greatest incongruity with what the text expresses is its contrary.... Why not play a boogie-woogie when Wotan walks across a rainbow to Valhalla?" To Schoenberg, nothing could seem a greater affront to the sanctity of music than Wotan boogieing up the rainbow bridge. But for Poulenc, a true Saussurean (surely without knowing it), incongruities—whether between spectacle and music or between one aspect of music and another—are the prime generators of musical excitement, musical significance. In the theatre, every reinforcement of meaning leads, paradoxically, to overdetermination, to weakening of meaning; every awareness of incongruity leads, at least potentially, to a strengthening of meaning. Poulenc's "grandfather" Chabrier, who in his *Souvenir of Munich* (1885–86) treated Isolde's *Liebestod* as a peppy little ditty suitable for a quadrille, heard aspects of Wagner's tune to which Schoenberg wished to be deaf. But the stateliness of Wotan's ascent, or the dignity of Isolde's death, exists only by virtue of an array of semantic antitheses: without the latency of a woo-hoo quadrille, there is no possibility for transfiguration. And furthermore, there could exist a system of differentiations in which a boogie-woogie could be a perfectly sober and appropriate dance for a triumphant god entering his new home. Duke Ellington wrote incidental music for *Timon of Athens:* if the system of meaning is adjusted properly, (almost) any musical phenomenon can develop any meaning. The charm of Poulenc arises from his unusual adeptness at working out fluid systems of musical meaning while bobbling along on rivers of disabled textual systems.

Schoenberg worked to emancipate harmonic dissonance; Poulenc worked to emancipate semantic dissonance, to draw power from the inconsequentiality of musical events.

The funeral music for Presto and Lacouf shows Poulenc's skill at using obvious cues for grief, in a situation where the obvious is completely unexpected. The funeral music, however, is atypical for this score in that it is a rather extended passage: most of the other "serious" music (except in the prologue) consists of brief and sudden seizures, as if the music hall had a trapdoor that opened from time to time, deleting a dancer or two from the frolic. Sometimes these serious moments call into question not only the surrounding vaudeville, but also their own seriousness, as when the husband makes his comic threat to kill his male wife—"What have you done with my little Thérèse, you vile personage?"—and Thérèse replies, decisively, gravely, "And yet I am Thérèse" (act 1, two bars after rehearsal figure 37). She says these words to four startling chords, A♭ minor, D minor, G♭ minor, C minor—and we recognize this figure as yet another transposition of the *bois meurtri* tritonal sequence, for Thérèse borrows once again the voice of Ravel's wounded tree in order to insist on her injured dignity. Perhaps by now the quotation has almost entirely cleansed itself of its quotedness.

EX. 11.8. Poulenc, *Les mamelles de Tirésias:* return of the bruised wood

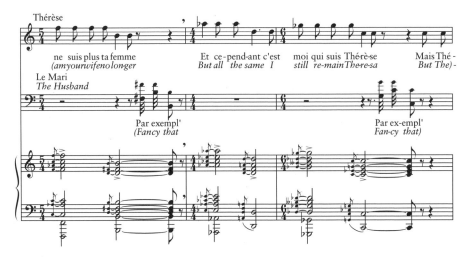

Les mamelles de Tirésias is packed with quotations, especially from Stravinsky: in the prologue, a figure in the fourth and fifth bars proposes a little harmonic riddle, not too challenging, concerning the propriety of a C♯ in a G-minor triad, exactly in the way that Stravinsky put the question (concerning an F♮ in a B-minor triad) in the *accelerando* of the *Naissance d'Apollon* from *Apollo* (1928). Stravinsky noted that *Apollo* was a ballet about iambic prosody, and even provided an epigraph from Boileau about the position of caesuras—it is as if Poulenc conceived the stage director who speaks the prologue as a new Boileau, legislating verse forms for the Modernist age; possibly, too, these bars serve to encrypt the pen name of the author, Guillaume de Kostrowitzky, who published much of his work under one of his middle names, Apollinaire.

EX. 11.9. Poulenc, *Les mamelles de Tirésias:* beginning

Stravinsky steps forward from time to time throughout the first act: at the end of the funeral music, the entry of the policeman on his hobbyhorse is signaled (four bars after rehearsal figure 56) by a soft, ominous, widely spread,

EX. 11.10. Stravinsky, *Apollo:* moment of Apollo's birth

unprepared seventh chord, which I hear—perhaps not everyone will agree—as a simplification of the famous chord in the "Kiss of the Earth" scene in *The Rite of Spring;* and to introduce the husband's speech about the sterility of Zanzibar's women, Poulenc provided (at rehearsal figure 70) something similar to the song of the real nightingale from *The Nightingale* (1914). It isn't easy to imagine explanations for all these borrowings and quasi-borrowings: they seem designed less to appeal to the vocabulary of Modernist semantics than to dismember it. The stolen phrases seem part of a musical discourse so thickly borrowed that it has lost all sense of allusiveness. Poulenc became "authentic" simply by piling on inauthenticities in such quantity that they anesthetize one another. (Just after the *Apollo* citation in the prologue, as the stage director prepares to speak, we hear [at rehearsal figure 1] the main theme of the *allegro malinconico* of Poulenc's famous flute sonata [1958]—and so this part of the prologue has, for the listener today, the eerie feel of a theft from a work not yet written.) It is as if *Les mamelles de Tirésias* were a *cadavre exquis,* but performed single-handedly, for Poulenc has managed to become a whole assortment of composers bundled up into one person.

Most of the serious moments, the gulfs that open beneath the cute patter and silly antics, occur at the mention of the opera's code words. Poulenc told Rostand that his music roused itself when Apollinaire mentioned words, such as *Paris* and *Seine,* which had secret significance to him; and in a letter written during the composition of the opera, Poulenc also noted that the word *Paris,* cropping up over and over in the text, inspired him with nostalgia and enabled him to capture something moving in the midst of Apollinaire's larks. The opera's gravity indeed may grow stronger when the text mentions *Paris;* but I think that a sudden increase in semantic weight is still more strongly felt when the text mentions the word *children.*

When the husband tells the journalist, in the second act, that men are able to make babies, Poulenc wrote a lovely quiet phrase beginning in D♭ major, marked *très doux* (two bars before rehearsal figure 18); the phrase recurs several times in this scene—for example, to depict a father's delight in showing off his newborn daughter (three bars after rehearsal figure 22). It is by no means clear that there is any aspect of this broadly farcical scene, with its 40,049 yowling infants and the synthesis of yet another out of printroom junk, that calls for subdued, elegant music, but Poulenc provided it nevertheless. And it is by no means clear that a composer ought to interrupt the pseudo-operetta finale of this act, with its amorous snuggling and loud recommendations to scratch anything that itches, with sudden moments of hush, reserved for the words *des enfants*—but that is exactly what Poulenc did. The word *children* seems to belong to a different musical plane from the rest of the opera. Instead of trying to assimilate the opera of the *children* and the opera of the zany cross-sexual spoofing into one consistent work, Poulenc allowed them to remain radically inconsistent, staring at one another across a wide semantic fissure.

Voice-Training Lessons

One typical musical style of the adult, burlesque action of the opera is the vocal exercise: when the journalist reads aloud a few words ("A lady named Cambron") from baby Joseph's prize-winning novel, it seems a rudimentary voice lesson in mastering the interval of the minor third (act 2, rehearsal figure 21); and later, when Thérèse appears as the fortune-teller, she announces her presence with a far more advanced vocal étude, all roulades, runs, and trills (rehearsal figure 43). Thérèse, who dreamed of being a mathematician, a senator, a toreador, has at last shown her true identity: a coloratura soprano. There is a rich Modernist tradition of operatic characters who confess their status as singers by performing warm-up exercises on stage—for example, the bearded lady Baba the Turk in Stravinsky's *The Rake's Progress* (1951), a work that seems indebted

EX. 11.11. Poulenc, *Les mamelles de Tirésias:* a lady named Cambron

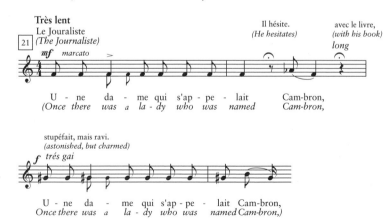

to *Les mamelles de Tirésias.* Such voice exercises enforce dissonance among the component media of a stage work: when a soprano sings meaningless simplicities, such as scales and triads, she is enclosing herself in music, instead of using music as a vehicle for expressing a text. Like Baba, Thérèse is a walking epitome of the extravagance and folly and polymorphous perversity of opera itself. But her flamboyance, her *niaiserie,* makes itself felt against the quiet, sober music reserved to the unborn children.

Why children possess such *gravitas* amid all the adult high jinks is a matter of conjecture. It is not likely that Poulenc, a homosexual, thought that he would personally be contributing to the postwar baby boom that Apollinaire's text so strenuously commands. But we may note that Poulenc habitually spoke of childhood when he considered his surrealist work, particularly *Le bal masqué,* which he saw as a rehearsal of the carnivals he knew as a child; surrealism is a style for recovering the delight of early childhood, when even the most familiar things are strange. What adults call wonder may be nothing but an echo of infantile amnesia, where all experience is novel, because our brains haven't yet learned to retrieve and compare experiences by encoding them in language.

Perhaps the moment in the score to *Les mamelles de Tirésias* of the sheerest wonder occurs at the end of the prologue, where the director earnestly pleads, "Make babies": after saying the key word *enfants,* he slowly descends through a trapdoor, while bells and high woodwinds play absolutely static and even figures, built exotically around fourths and fifths (act 1, two bars after rehearsal figure 18). The interval of a tritone is also prominent, but there is no suggestion of evil or suffering: instead, for the only time in the opera, we seem to have abandoned Monte Carlo and terra firma for someplace distant and ravishing, perhaps African—or, more exactly, Balinese, since this passage strongly recalls the end of the first movement of Poulenc's concerto for two pianos (1932), a conscious evocation of the gamelan music that Poulenc heard in the Colonial Exposition in Paris in 1931. For a moment the opera, just about to begin its main intrigue, swerves upward, almost out of the range of semiosis, pre-dismissing itself. Beyond the codes that govern sadness and happiness, or excitement and calm, or vulgarity and *hauteur,* there is a child beating something metal with a stick. And that is what music is. I think that Poulenc set his opera in 1910 or 1912 in order to recover the child Poulenc, aged eleven or thirteen, marveling on the threshold of puberty at a world not yet sick but about to go to war, not yet sexual but about to become sexual—a world that hadn't quite worlded itself.

In *Les mamelles de Tirésias,* we see that the most serious matters can attain a remarkable gravity of presentation in the interstices between a literary farce and a musical farce. The sheer dissonance of the media leads to a kind of self-canceling of frivolities; the collapse of inauthenticities leads to an unusually intense seizure of the fact of pain.

Heaven

And now we come to a final exercise in multimedia semantics, concerning *Four Saints in Three Acts,* by Gertrude Stein and Virgil Thomson. As an object of contemplation, this opera is so benign that it even criticizes itself: all that later critics can do is to rehearse the collaborative story that Stein and Thomson (both superbly articulate critics) have already told, at length and in detail. Their opera embodies its own interpretation, keeps a continual tally of its own elements; and criticism of the opera is a matter of listening to those self-explicating voices that chant from the rising of the curtain onward.

In this work the component media attain such a state of perfect disregard for one another that dissonance itself is superseded, and a new consonance is achieved, in a sort of afterlife of the dream of total theatre. On the far side of surrealism lies a kind of stressless grace, where the *Gesamtkunstwerk* abandons its struggle for integrity, liquidates its internal tensions, goes to heaven.

Temporal Images of the Timeless

I don't have confidence in visions, and I don't believe in heaven, but, when completely sober, I once had a vision of heaven. It consisted of two parts, a sentence and a picture, a picture that kept changing. This was the sentence:

> In heaven, when a bird flies from a bush to a tree, the bird is on the bush and on the tree and everywhere in between.

The picture showed a bush and a tree, both consisting of puffy scrawls carelessly colored with green and brown crayon, in the way that a happy child draws such things. But the bird, a combination of quetzal and macaw, seemed to be painted in oils, with a kind of Day-Glo sheen. The left half of the bird sat on a branch of the bush; the right half sat on a branch of the tree; and between the two halves was a polychrome streak, which shimmered and twisted as I watched. Then the bird flew away to some other heavenly destination, leaving another track of iris on the air behind it; and soon the crisscross of bird-tubes covered my whole field of vision.

Like many visions of heaven, my vision represented a struggle to imagine the ways in which eternity alters the human perceptual field. What kind of event can take place in a condition of total achronicity? What kind of spatial placement can exist in a condition of total ubiquity? Just as the Father, in Milton's *Paradise Lost* (1674), is perfectly omniscient but chooses to unfurl his rigid foreknowledge slowly, in order to provide a semblance of suspense to the plot, and just as He occupies and controls all space except for a tiny envelope around human beings, permitting them some scope for free action, so the notion of a *nunc stans,* or Standing Now, the eternal present of scholastic philosophy, tends to derange and vitiate all the normal means of narrative and drama, unless somehow concealed. A heavenly mind, an intellect that comprehends past, present, and future all at once, will understand the figure of my life as a simultaneous growth and decay, a blooming withering, in which I am at once baby, corpse, and everything in between, with a thousand versions of my limbs sprouting from my trunk, in every conceivable position that their range of motion allows. Imagine the fast-motion photography of the Reggio-Glass film *Koyaanisqatsi* (1982), in which automobiles leave whizz-traces of their passage through the air, speeded up still further, until all motion attenuates into a ghostly stasis, wisps, curlicues of pedestrians and vehicles washed over the buildings of a city, buildings themselves translucent from their not-yet-having-been, from their being-no-more: that would be a heaven's-eye view of earth.

Heaven, then, is the limit point of the convergence of the temporal and the spatial; as Wagner's Gurnemanz says, *Zum Raum wird hier die Zeit,* Here time becomes space. Heaven is attained, in art, by an absolute refusal to distinguish *nacheinander* from *nebeneinander:* where the juxtapositive and the sequential are one, there we have an intuition of a life disencumbered from the usual fictions of space and time.

There have always been literary works that attempted to show how people conduct their lives after death, from Gilgamesh's visit to the house where everything is dust, to Homer's Hades where souls gibber like bats, to Dante's *Paradiso,* and beyond. There have even been a few attempts to make a multimedia theatre of the afterlife, such as the Metastasio-Mozart *Il sogno di Scipione* (1771). But for the most part the depiction of excessive, overwhelming, unrelieved beatitude has been left to painters, more adept than poets and composers at presenting attractive stasis: there is no equivalent to gold foil in the domains of literature and music. When Liszt wanted to write a third part, a *paradiso,* to his *Dante Symphony* (1857), Wagner talked him out of it: Liszt was asking music to do more than music could. And Wagner was right, in that composers have traditionally been reluctant to tackle heaven. Only in recent times, I believe, have composers attempted to write music faithful to heaven's immobility—though I could understand an argument that passages in the old religious music, such as parts of Josquin's mass *Mater patris* (1514), were experiments in celestial harmonic lethargy.

Transfiguration in Strauss, Fauré, and Elgar

In late-nineteenth-century music, there are several strategies for attaining a kind of paralysis of the sublime. Strauss, in *Death and Transfiguration* (1889), devised the huge transfiguration coda as a set of gorgeous consonant modulations of a short motive with a big leap (scale degrees $\hat{5}$–$\hat{1}$–$\hat{2}$–$\hat{3}$–$\hat{3}'$–$\hat{2}'$ in C major), as if heaven were an endless recession of haloes, slowly losing contour until they were lost in white light. A perhaps more daring strategy was that of Fauré, in the *In paradisum* (and elsewhere) of the *Requiem* (1888), where he constructs passages around surges and withdrawals of emphasis within long, repetitive melodic lines, lines fairly uniform in color and texture, emphases unpredictable and yet never startling, a subdued flamboyance. The music doesn't seem to evolve: some element simply intensifies its there-ness for a moment amid the undulations of melody, like adjustments of focal distance within an unchanging field. There is often little consciousness of meter, as if the music had reached a state of divine rhythmlessness. In both pieces, the constant elements are a little too constant, and the variable elements a little too variable: heaven is a place where absolute invariability is imagined through a displacement of the normal patterns of variation, or through such a surfeit and exhaustion of variation that there is nothing left to vary. And heaven is a place where all boxes are open, all springs sprung: this is why Schoenberg would later (in *Moses und Aron*) find it right to depict God through a simultaneous speaking and singing and playing of all twelve notes of the scale.

In *The Dream of Gerontius* (1900), Elgar inaugurated a certain strain of the celestial in music by setting Cardinal Newman's lines about the newly dead soul in heaven:

I went to sleep; and now I am refreshed.
A strange refreshment: for I feel in me
An inexpressive lightness, and a sense

Of freedom, as I were at length myself,
And ne'er had been before. How still it is!
I hear no more the busy beat of time,
No, nor my fluttering breath, nor struggling pulse;
Nor does one moment differ from the next.

Like Fauré, Elgar imagined the breathlessness, the pulselessness of heaven as an ebbing and flowing of a long, repetitious melodic line, like the beating of a heart so slow that it must belong to a creature much larger than a human being. But, of course, it is not literally true that "one moment" does not "differ from the next": Elgar and Newman offer only an artful simulation of monotony, not the endless sustaining of a single note, in the manner of La Monte Young, or an endless repetition of a single figure, in the manner of Philip Glass.

But it was not long after *The Dream of Gerontius* that composers and poets found some truly extraordinary techniques for defeating the sequentiality of their sequential art. In fact, we have been dwelling in heaven ever since we began discussing Satie, long ago.

Pieces like *Parade, Les mariés de la Tour Eiffel,* and *Les mamelles de Tirésias* fail to present an orthodox conception of heaven—unless your orthodoxy permits a heaven like a freak show with acrobats and a suggestion of backstage torture, or a heaven like a giant camera and gramophone, or a heaven of transsexual conniving. And yet, none of these things is wholly alien to traditional conceptions of heaven. As to the carnival sideshow: heaven has often been conceived as a condition of pure play, winged flight—and, as the parable of Dives and Lazarus suggests, the blest souls evidently like to contemplate the spectacle of the damned in hell. As to the giant camera: the mind of God is an infallible and omnipresent recording instrument that numbers every sparrow that falls. As to the destabilizing of gender: in heaven there is neither marrying nor giving in marriage—as Britten put it in his *Hymn of St. Columba,* the love of women will cease *(cessabit mulierum amor);* in heaven the categories of male and female are superseded, as are perhaps all categories whatsoever. *Parade, Les mariés de la Tour Eiffel,* and *Les mamelles de Tirésias* all investigate procedures for disabling the consequential, developmental aspect of music: and anything that flattens time tends to pertain to eternity. All these works are constructed with loops, and the ultimate loop is the resurrection of the body. Heaven is a place where the loose film of our life is rewound tight onto the one reel.

It is fitting, then, to conclude this study with the most intently focused vision of heaven in the collaborative art projects of the twentieth century, *Four Saints in Three Acts.* Both writer and composer arrived, from very different origins, at a language with an amazing power to empty itself in a full aesthetic kenosis, to arrest itself into a likeness of the cheerful catatonia of heaven.

Stein, Automatic Writing, and Dalí

Gertrude Stein was, in a sense, trained to be a surrealist, though she revolted against her training. As a student at Harvard she assisted her professor, William James, in a series of experiments on automatic writing. As she recalled it much later:

> Gertrude Stein never had subconscious reactions, nor was she a successful subject for automatic writing. . . . When [another student] read his paper upon the result of his experiments, he began by explaining that one of the subjects gave absolutely no results and as this much lowered the average and made the conclusion of his experiments false he wished to be allowed to cut this record out. Whose record is it, said James. Miss Stein's, said the student. Ah, said James, if Miss Stein gave no response I should say that it was as normal not to give a response as to give one and decidedly the result must not be cut out.

Like Poe, a writer she liked, Stein insisted that her art was a purely conscious act of craft. Her dislike of the subconscious, the abnormal, the inexplicable also entailed a distinct preference for the visual over the auditory:

> Music she [Stein, writing in the third person] cared for only in her adolescence. She finds it difficult to listen to it, it does not hold her attention. All of which of course may seem strange because it has been so often said that the appeal of her work is to the ear and to the subconscious. Actually it is her eyes and mind that are active and important and concerned in choosing.

> I write with my eyes, not with my ears or mouth. . . . The words as seen by my eyes are the important words, and the ears and mouth do not count. I said to Picasso, "When you were young you never looked at things." He seemed to swallow the things he saw, but he never looked. . . . A writer should write with his eyes, and a painter paint with his ears.

Whereas Yeats, Rilke, and Breton waited for the inner voice to speak, Stein heard no inner voices: indeed, she became rather deaf in her later years, as if to emphasize the unimportance of things heard.

Furthermore, she tended to be hostile to all "inspired" art, art that claimed a sanction from the subconscious. "Surrealism never did interest me," she reported, and she remembered that when she and Dalí talked, "neither of us listened very much to one another." If Dalí was a bore, Tzara seemed "like a pleasant and not very exciting cousin." But even in her expressions of distaste for surrealists and surrealism and automatic writing, it is possible to notice certain surrealist habits of thought. The notion that poetry is addressed to the eye and painting to the ear is exactly the sort of sensory switching that the surrealists cultivated. If her jingles are eye jingles, if her repetitions are to be enjoyed as recurrences in a visual schema on the page, if her anti-linear, sometimes asyntactic sentences force the eye to keep doubling back on words already read but not yet construed—then Stein might say, in the words of the discarded title for the calligrams, *Me, I'm a painter too.* Stein is a surrealist not in the Breton or Dalí tradition, but in the Apollinaire tradition—except that some of Stein's experiments in shaped verbal textures predated Apollinaire's.

Stein's Early *"Psychological"* Style: The Making of Americans

Stein's story of her stylistic evolution was as follows: she considered that she wrote her first works in an expansive, inward style, faithful to the convolutions of psychological processes; and that later, around 1913, she turned outward, toward an increasingly objective, elliptical, painter-like presentation of things. This may be so, but her notions of subjectivity and objectivity deviate from our normal sense of these words. Here is a fairly typical sample of her early, "psychological" manner, taken from her immensely long novel *The Making of Americans* (1903–11; 1925):

> There are then two kinds of women, those who have dependent independence in them, those who have in them independent dependence inside them; the one of the first of them always somehow own the ones they need to love them, the second kind of them have it in them to love only those who need them, such of them have it in them to have power in them over others only when these others have begun already a little to love them, others loving them give to such of them strength in domination. . . . There are then two kinds of women, there are those who have in them resisting and attacking, and a bottom weakness in them, women with independent dependence in them, women who are strong in attacking, women who sometimes have not bottom weakness in them, some who have in them bottom weakness in them and this inside is a strength in them when they have children.

This has little resemblance to the interior style of the later Henry James, or of Joyce. It is too general and abstract, making distinctions, grand and vague, in the absence of finite behavior to be distinguished. The calmness of language, the air of poised philosophical disquisition ("There are then two kinds of women"), belie a strange impotence and fury of thought: such categories as *dependent independence,* as opposed to *independent dependence,* are such oxymoronic and self-tortured instruments of intellectual navigation that the reader can't possibly come to any conclusion, or even to insight in the usual sense, concerning human psychology; the reader can only read in the hope that this interminable grappling with antitheses will provide a certain mimetic pleasure, since it imitates the normal failure of our minds to come to grips with the social realities around us. The usual Modernist method of psychological realism—that of *Ulysses,* or Woolf's *The Waves*—is deliquescence: it provides a texture rich in concrete nouns, but these nouns lack the connective tissue that could provide a sense of hardness and spatial orientation. Stein's method, however, is not deliquescence but evacuation: Stein evidently believed that mental operations could be isolated and purified by depriving them of a physical world.

Stein's Objective Style: Tender Buttons

Just before the Great War, Stein's style, and her notion of her artistic purpose, shifted completely, toward what she called "still life": "she [Stein, writing in the third person] had been interested only in the insides of people, their character and what went on inside them, it was during that summer [in Spain] that she first felt a desire to express the rhythm of the visible world." The result of this was *Tender Buttons* (1913; 1914), a book that offers none of the usual consolations of objectivity:

A DOG

A little monkey goes like a donkey that means to say that means to say that more sighs last goes. Leave with it. A little monkey goes like a donkey.

This is the entire text of one of the entries in the "Objects" section of the book. But the questions arise: What is the object? And what do the three sentences of the text have to do with the object? One answer to the first question is (for those readers who have paid attention to the title), A dog. But that is probably, alas, an oversimplification. For Stein said (as Virgil Thomson remembered) that *Tender Buttons* was "'an effort to describe something without naming it,' which is what the cubist painters were doing with still life": Stein provided not the visible world, but the *rhythm* of the visible world.

Rhythm is the dominant idea of *Tender Buttons,* though Stein's notions of the role of rhythm kept changing. Her affirmation that *Tender Buttons* expressed the rhythm of the visible world wasn't written until 1933; and an earlier comment on the book, from 1923, seems to contradict it: "It was my first conscious struggle with the problem of correlating sight, sound, and sense, and eliminating rhythm." But perhaps by that she meant that she was eliminating the word-rhythm of the English language in order to capture the thing-rhythm of the outer world. The peculiar stutters and gaps and short circuits in Stein's text attempt to

present the jerkinesses and continuities of movement in the world around us—
and also the erratic flow of our perceptions of those movements. In the last year
of her life, 1946, Stein tried to tell an interviewer what she meant by "A Dog":
"'A little monkey goes like a donkey . . .' That was an effort to illustrate the
movement of a donkey going up a hill, you can see it plainly. 'A little monkey
goes like a donkey.' An effort to make the movement of the donkey, and so the
picture hangs complete." So Stein's "object" seems to be a climbing donkey—it
is difficult for the reader to know how to know why the donkey should have
priority over the dog, or the monkey, or the sighs; but evidently the reader's mistake is to *read* the text, instead of *seeing* the picture of the motion implied by the
text. The text embodies a halting, patient, one-foot-at-a-time gait—not through
the meaning of the words, not through the sound of the words, but through the
look of the words. The onkey advances from point m to point d, up the rugged
terrain of a simile. "A Dog" is a calligram of a movement, in which the normal-
ness of the typographical layout tends to conceal the fact that it is a shaped text,
directed primarily to the eye.

A much easier example of an action-calligram—easier, that is, for the reader
who knows that Stein's nickname for her Ford was Aunt Pauline—can be found
in a Tender Button entitled "A Little Girl Called Pauline"; Stein glossed a line
from it as follows: "'A little called anything shows shudders.' This was another
attempt to have only enough to describe the movement of one of those old-
fashioned automobiles, an old Ford, that movement is like that automobile." But
the denotation of the word *shudders* is so close to the movement-effect intended
by the line that it's almost cheating—Stein thought it better sport to try to reify
the rhythm of the thing without naming either the thing or the rhythm. As Stein
noted, "in Tender Buttons . . . I struggled with the ridding myself of nouns, I knew
nouns must go." Of course there are plenty of nouns in *Tender Buttons,* but
they are misleading nouns, denominalized nouns—in effect, they are highly colored pronouns that operate as surrogates for concealed objects, somewhat as the
cubes in a cubist painting are surrogates for the volumes of objects.

Stein tended to resist any facile comparisons between her writing and the
painting of her close friend Picasso, but she cheerfully admitted that Cézanne was
all-important as an influence in her art: "Cézanne conceived the idea that in composition one thing was as important as another thing. Each part is as important
as the whole, and that impressed me enormously." This decentered aspect of
Modernist painting, this all-overness, has a close analogue in the unsubordinated
texture of Stein's prose, in which it is impossible to distinguish subject from predicate. Thus, in "A Dog," the dog in the title and the monkey at the beginning of
the first sentence, which seem so central to the text's enterprise, are evidently false
subjects; the true subject, buried in a prepositional phrase as the second term of
a comparison, is the donkey, or, more exactly, the way the donkey moves. Stein

marveled at Cézanne's realness: "The apples looked like apples the chairs looked like chairs. . . . They were so entirely these things that they were not an oil painting and yet that is just what the Cezannes were they were an oil painting." Stein saw a Cézanne painting in exactly the way that Cézanne wanted it to be seen: Cézanne regarded his work as a "réalisation sur nature," a making-real of an apple or a chair in an art universe parallel to (but not contingent upon or mimetic of) the natural universe. Similarly, the text-objects in *Tender Buttons* aspire not to be *about* things in the real world, but to *be* things, in a different mode of extension from the usual; they aspire to seize the heft of actual things, unnamed things that the words at once conceal and thrust out.

Stein's An Elucidation: *Discourse Vanishing into Visual Pattern*

To destroy the prestige of the noun helps to destroy the whole capitalist-colonialist enterprise of the sentence, in which a gubernator, a key word (the grammatical subject), assumes ownership of the other words in the sentence. Stein wished to liberate other parts of speech, so long enslaved to nouns and to nouns' running dogs, adjectives:

> I say it again more and more one does not use nouns. . . . Verbs and adverbs are more interesting. In the first place they have one very nice quality and that is that they can be so mistaken. It is wonderful the number of mistakes a verb can make and that is equally true of its adverb. Nouns and adjectives never can make mistakes can never be mistaken but verbs can be so endlessly. . . . Articles please, a and an and the please as the name that follows cannot please. They the names that is the nouns cannot please, because after all you know well after all that is what Shakespeare meant when he talked about a rose by any other name.

Nouns are boring, listless, inert, because they are labels glued tight onto physical objects; they never make mistakes, and so they can't rise to the creative potential of non-denoting parts of speech: nounless articles or verbless adverbs or co-ordinating conjunctions vainly searching for something to coordinate—all these free linguistic radicals so useful for building in the void Stein's hypertexts, or hypotexts. A rose by any other name would smell as sweet: the word *rose* gropes at the actual flower, in a simple-minded, monomaniacal fashion, but the flower always escapes the noun's clutch—the flower's sweetness always exceeds the power of any mere deodorized noun. "Rose is a rose is a rose is a rose," Stein wrote in *Sacred Emily* (1913), and quoted in *Lifting Belly* (1915–17) and elsewhere: her most famous line, engraved in a ring on her stationery. This line simultaneously shows the sullen obstinacy of a noun—a noun, once it has performed

its little trick of denotation, has exhausted its repertoire of artistic possibility—
and shows how repetition can designify the noun, un-noun the noun, render it
innocuous, demote it to a pattern-unit, like the AAAAAAA music-construct that
Antheil compared to a single giant foot.

In *An Elucidation* (1923)—one of the most dazzling ventures of the Modernist movement in erasing the boundary between critical prose and literature—
Stein wrote "Suppose, to suppose, suppose a rose is a rose is a rose is a rose," and
went on to suggest that in this line, "there arose an instance of knowing." And
yet we don't usually consider a tautology a species of knowing; we seem to be
learning not something about botany, but something about the placement of the
long *o* vowel, and other phonemes. Elsewhere in this text she wrote a passage
that becomes a fantasia on five words, a specimen of the nounlessness Stein so
heartily recommended:

> I know the difference between white marble and black marble. White and
> black marble make a checker board and I never mention either.
> Either of them you know very well that I may have said no.
>
> Now to explain.
>
> Did I say explanations mean across and across and carry. Carry me across.
>
> Another Example.

I think I won't
I think I will
I think I will
I think I won't.
I think I won't
I think I will
I think I will
I think I won't.
I think I won't
I think I will
I think I will
I think I won't
I think I will
I think I won't
I think I will
I think I won't.
I think I will

> I think I won't
> I think I won't
> I think I won't
> I think I won't
> I think I will
> I think I won't
> Of course

This passage begins with an assertion of knowledge of a distinction, between white and black marble, and an awareness of the pattern that white and black squares make. Then she seems to offer to explain what she means; but instead of explaining, she seems stuck on the word *explain*, which she pretends to define as "carry across," which is actually the definition of the word *translate*. Byron once wrote, "I wish he would explain his Explanation"—but Stein goes still further, by trying to explain the word *explain*. Now, the word *explain* comes from a Latin root that could also mean "flatten"—and Stein indeed seems to be flattening the distinction between an explanation and the thing explained. The reader feels caught inside a linguistic system that keeps closing in on itself, like the ring design on Stein's stationery, instead of opening outward onto a world of reference; Stein, like Poulenc, was a Saussurean by instinct. *An Elucidation* keeps shining inward, a sort of colonoscopy of language.

In the section marked "Another Example," Stein seems to be pondering whether to provide an example or not ("I think I will / I think I won't"), as if she were plucking the petals of the rose that is a rose, trying to come to a decision. But soon the reader realizes that the long section of willing and won'ting *is* the example. This is in fact perhaps the clearest example in all of Stein's work of the anti-discursive quality of her language, its addressing itself to the eye. This passage is itself a checkerboard, a design in black and white squares, represented by positive and negative propositions: the pattern slowly shifts from a two-by-two layout to a one-by-one layout, until the end, where Stein experiments with an almost all-black segment.

But despite Stein's insistence that her work was to be seen by the eye, not heard with the ear, her techniques have irresistible analogues with the musical as well as with the pictorial. George Bernard Shaw once offered a spoof of musicological analysis by describing Hamlet's "To be or not to be: that is the question" in the manner of the music academy:

> Shakespeare, dispensing with his customary exordium, announces his subject at once in the infinitive, in which mood it is presently repeated after a short connecting passage in which, brief as it is, we recognize the alternative and negative forms on which so much of the significance of repetition depends.

Here we reach a colon; and a pointed prepository phrase, in which the accent falls decisively on the relative pronoun, brings us to the first full stop.

Shaw considered this silly, and yet it anticipates the sort of analysis that seems suitable, perhaps even necessary, for Stein's prose: the alternation of positive and negative ("I think I will / I think I won't") has an extreme thematic concentration more typical of music than of verbal language. And indeed, Stein made explicit textual experiments in musical form, such as *A Sonatina Followed by Another* (1921), in which I fancy it is possible to distinguish a first thematic group (declamatory and formal) from a second thematic group (intimate and lyrical)—though it must be remembered that Stein's knowledge of music was rudimentary and her manner of engaging herself with music was bizarre: "I like to improvise on a piano I like to play sonatinas followed by another always on the white keys I do not like black keys and never two notes struck by the same hand at the same time because I do not like chords." It is not surprising, then, that when Stein heard Virgil Thomson playing *Socrate*, a piece of the greatest diatonic chastity, she became "a Satie enthusiast"; presumably she would have liked Cage's recasting of *Socrate* for piano-one-finger even better. In many ways, the extraordinary difficulty of much of Stein's writing reflects the recalcitrance of language at being treated according to patterning principles which, applied to painting or music, would seem quite simple and ingratiating. Surely no principle is simpler than an alternation of two opposites, such as black and white; and yet a text patterned in that way has a hallucinatory look to it.

Stein's textures are also musical through avoidance (or misplacement) of nouns. Nounless strings of words tend to move quickly, since there's little to detain the mind, as in this passage from *Patriarchal Poetry* (1927): "For before let it before to be before spell to be before to be before to have to be to be for before to be tell to be to having held to be to be for before"—I quote only the first sixth or so of this sentence (which Virgil Thomson extravagantly praised), but the reader can easily imagine the rest. Pre-Modernist literature written without nouns is quite scanty, but I know one example:

So notwithstanding heretofore
Strait forward by and by
Now everlastingly therefore
Too low and eke too high.

Then for almost and also why
Not thus when less so near
Oh! for hereafter quite so nigh
But greatly ever here.

This is Richard Steele's "Lyric for Italian Music" (1720), a witty cringe at the stupidity of the Italian opera. It is an odd stringing-out of adjectives and adverbs of approximation, lack, or superfluity—*by, too, near, nigh*—as if imitating the singers' swoopings at pitches that are never quite reached; it is a discourse all sharps and flats and flutters, accidentals and ornaments without steady notes. One way of rendering a text musical is simply to empty it of substantives. In a bizarre way, Steele's parody exactly meets the requirements that his contemporary Marcello proposed for an ideally singable text.

The Land of Unlikeness, Revisited

Stein's writings sometimes seem to consist of differentiations in the absence of any finite things to differentiate. The cited passage from *An Elucidation* begins with "I know the difference between"—a typical Steinian phrase. Stein is always claiming to know a difference, or not to know a difference:

Night is different from bright.

There is no difference between a white carnation and a white lily both are white.

Water does not resemble water at all.

Another man, a don, next to him jumped up and asked something else. They did this several times, the two of them, jumping up one after the other. Then the first man jumped up and said, you say that everything being the same everything is always different, how can that be so. Consider, she replied, the two of you, you jump up one after the other, that is the same thing and surely you admit that the two of you are always different. Touché, he said.

To say that two things are different is not to say much, if the two things could just as accurately be called the same. Therefore Stein's endless labor in making pronouncements of exact discrimination is futile, a fetching of water by pouring it into a sieve; the whole linguistic mechanism of qualification, comparison, and equation is trivial, for the universe consists of neutral elements, indifferently like or unlike one another, as you please. We've seen the surrealist attack on the word *like;* and Stein also worked to destroy its power of assimilation: "There is the likeliness lying in liking likely likeliness"; "To be liking liked like it like if like like to like like and often often where where is it. It is there just there where I am looking. Very clearly expressed." Stein liked *like,* but we may feel that *like* suffered horrible abuse at her hands. *Like* as the preposition that governs a simile, *like* as the verb of affection, *likely* as the adjective of probability, all are balled up into a bloody grammatical mess, a *comme*Merz of several parts of speech in one. I wonder whether Stein remembered that in Middle English there is a word *lyke,* meaning "corpse."

Of all the rhythms of the visible world, the rhythm that most intrigued Stein was the simplest: the mere extancy, the *Dasein* of things. Stein often attempted to find words that imitated not objects, but the persistence of objects in time. This is the source of her famous repetitiveness. Stein, however, denied that she was ever strictly repetitive: she kept introducing small variations in her verbal strings in order to display the vivacity of settled objects, the way they shift their emphases as the angle of light changes, or doors open, or a cloud passes over the sun:

> every time one of the hundreds of times a newspaper man makes fun of my writing and of my repetition he always has the same theme, always having the same theme, that is, if you like, repetition, that is if you like the repeating that is the same thing, but once started expressing this thing, expressing any thing there can be no repetition because the essence of that expression is insistence, and if you insist you must each time use emphasis and if you use emphasis it is not possible while anybody is alive that they should use exactly the same emphasis. . . . there was no repetition. In a cinema picture no two pictures are exactly alike one is just that much different from the one before.

Andy Warhol once made a film by fixing a camera on the Empire State Building and letting it run for several hours. I take it that Stein kept striving for a similar effect, an expression of the sheer stamina of people, places, and things—with the difference that it's sometimes impossible to know exactly what object she's describing the stamina of. If my calendar is absolutely empty, I can take great pleasure in reading even second-rate texts by Stein, in watching the slow writhe of familiar sentences altering and re-knotting, in listening to the counterpoint that a phrase makes with the sound-residues of previous versions of itself in my memory. But even the faintest urging of other responsibility—say, an appointment to get my hair cut a week from Wednesday—can sometimes make me feel the same exasperation that Leo Stein felt when he read his sister's work:

> Gertrude knows that everything changes and that the more it changes the more it's the same thing. Also that people repeat to insist. . . . When Jesus said Verily Verily, he was insisting, but if he had said Verily Verily, Verily, verily, verily, verily, verily, verily, verily, verily, some one in the audience would have yelled, 'Say Mr Jesus you said that already.'

Most writing is *about* change; Stein instead tries to *embody* change by making gross or infinitesimal mutations of some textual element that can identify itself as the thing-to-be-changed only by strong repetition. She had to create the verbal equivalent of an object, before she could write about an object.

Stein's Landscape Style: Drama without a Story

Tender Buttons, written just before the Great War, depicts, according to the titles of its three sections, objects, food, and rooms. But Stein tried, then and later, to widen the field of her literary depiction, first to people, then to landscapes. One of her portraits of Picasso, "If I Told Him," reads in part, "Would he like it would Napoleon would Napoleon would would he like it. . . . Shutters shut and open so do queens. Shutters shut and shutters and so shutters shut and shutters and so and so shutters and so and so shutters shut." It is easy to understand what character traits might be indicated by an apposition of Picasso and Napoleon; the rest is more difficult, but possibly the shutters that seem to shut so much more frequently than they open have something to do with the faceted surfaces of cubist painting, imaged as a network of closed windows at once hiding and bodying forth the subject—just as Stein's portrait at once hides and bodies forth Picasso. It is also possible that the compulsive sentence structure verbalizes the obsessive rhythm of Picasso's work habits, or the rhythm of brush on canvas. Just as *Tender Buttons* provides action-calligrams of things, so Stein's portraits provide action-calligrams of people.

But perhaps Stein found landscape even more fruitful than objects or portraits. Stein considered that her career as a playwright began through the conjunction of her responses to advanced music theatre and to landscape:

> Strauss' Electra made me realize that in a kind of a way there could be a solution of the problem of conversation on the stage. . . . I settled down to Paris life and I forgot about the theatre and almost forgot opera. There was of course Isadora Duncan and then the Russian ballet and in between Spain and the Argentine and bullfights and I began once more to feel something going on at a theatre. . . .
>
> And so one day all of a sudden I began to write Plays. . . .
>
> I had just come home from a pleasant dinner party and I realized then as anybody can know that something is always happening. . . . Everyone knows so many stories and what is the use of telling another story. . . . I concluded that anything that was not a story could be a play and I even made plays in letters and advertisements.

For most writers, a play is an enactment of a story, but for Stein a play is an enactment of what is not a story: drama is the opposite of narrative. A play omits any expression of what happened, in favor of expressing "the essence of what happened." It is an abstract inenarrability, a garrulous pantomime, a Diaghilev dance translated into the medium of words. It concerns familiar things—from pleasant dinner parties to billboard advertisements—just as Picasso took inspiration for the Managers in *Parade* from the *hommes-sandwich,* the human advertising displays that tramped along the streets of Paris. But Stein achieved an extraordinary defamiliarization of these familiar things, first by making the boundaries between one character and another difficult to ascertain, and second by paralyzing any sense of plot development: Stein's plays demonstrate the Cézanne principle of decentered composition, in which each area is of equal importance, thereby allowing no suspense, no climax, no dénouement.

There can be no untying of a knot where nothing is tied up in the first place; Stein's plays are astonishingly tensionless:

MARIUS. I am very pleased I am indeed very pleased that it is a great pleasure.
MARTHA. If four are sitting at a table and one of them is lying upon it it does not make any difference. If bread and pomegranates are on a table and four are sitting at the table and one of them is leaning upon it it does not make any difference.
MARTHA. It does not make any difference if four are seated at a table and one is leaning upon it.
MARYAS. If five are seated at a table and there is bread on it and there are pomegranates on it and one of the five is leaning on the table it does not make any difference.

This passage comes from one of Stein's first plays, *A List* (ca. 1922). This play, unlike some, has speech prefixes, but the fact that all the names begin with the letter *M* and the fact that the characters say approximately the same thing tend to defeat any sense of individuation. Also, it isn't clear whether there are two (or more) characters named Martha, or just one Martha who likes to interrupt herself from time to time. To imagine a staging of *A List* is to imagine a painter's still life given the power of speech, and enough intellect to ponder alternative constructions of itself—various arrangements of bread and pomegranates, various dispositions of the spectators who contemplate the arrangements.

Stein herself cited this passage from *A List* as a typical specimen of her dramatic art, and provided a commentary on how this play came into being:

I found that since the landscape was the thing, a play was a thing and I went on writing plays a great many plays. The landscape at Bilignin so completely made a play that I wrote quantities of plays.

I felt that if a play was exactly like a landscape then there would be no difficulty about the emotion of the person looking on at the play being behind or ahead of the play because the landscape does not have to make acquaintance. You may have to make acquaintance with it, but it does not with you, it is there and so the play being written the relation between you at any time is so exactly that that it is of no importance unless you look at it.

Stein believed that the trouble with most plays was that the scene on the stage was "almost always in syncopated time in relation to the emotion of anybody in the audience"—that is, the emotion of the audience either lags behind or anticipates the emotion being expressed by the actors, an effect of nervous asynchronicity that Stein disliked. But a play that represents the experience not of viscid human interactions, but of lucid being-in-a-landscape, can overcome this difficulty: there is only a single temporal plane, not a thick texture of reminiscence and foreshadowing. Most plays sound heavy chords; but a Stein play is simply one white note at a time, a sonatina. *A List* in no way describes a landscape—indeed, it seems to take place indoors; but it embodies a feeling of perfect ease, the ease one feels in those landscapes in southern Europe that seem to accommodate the human presence without any effort, as if sunlight and grass and the other soft clarities needed only a watching eye to finish themselves. Stein thought that "The business of Art . . . is to live in the actual present, that is the complete actual present, and to completely express that complete actual present"; and a play such as *A List* seems to remember nothing, to wish for nothing, merely to notate the pleasant presentness of the present instant. Stein's art has crossed the river Lethe and entered a realm where nothing makes any difference, because notions of similarity and difference no longer obtain.

Landscape Grammar

The further Stein investigated the artistic possibilities of landscape, the more she found herself inclined to manipulate the landscape that she tried to capture in writing:

> Bravig Imbs . . . once came upon her doing this. The scene took place in a field, its enactors being Gertrude, Alice [B. Toklas, Stein's companion], and a cow. Alice, by means of a stick, would drive the cow around the field. Then, at a sign from Gertrude, the cow would be stopped, and Gertrude would write in her copybook. After a bit, she would pick up her folding stool and progress to another spot, whereupon Alice would again start the cow moving around the field till Gertrude signaled she was ready to write again. Though Alice now says that Gertrude drove the cow, she waiting in the car.

Doubtless if Stein had been Cézanne, she would have asked Mont Sainte-Victoire to move a little to the left, please, and to flatten itself a bit. She treated the whole countryside as the elements of a giant still life, as if a *tableau vivant* were just a *tableau mort* in a state of partial locomotion, but nonetheless subject to auto-cratic rule by the artist. Stein's later landscapes are to some extent generated by preexisting aesthetic principles; and in the greatest of all her landscapes, *Four Saints in Three Acts* (1929), Stein managed to find, or create, landscape derived from her peculiar notions of grammar.

Four Saints in Three Acts differs from the earlier landscape pieces in that it contemplates a vacuum—an empty canvas, a region of the earth from which all finite objects have been removed:

> there can only be religion and the charm of religion where there is a desert country. That is natural enough. Deserts do not make painters but they make charm and religion, because where there is nothing to do and nothing to see anybody cannot know that time is passing and so naturally there is religion but there is no painting because there is no pleasure in looking. . . .
>
> And so it was natural then when I wanted saints that they should be Spanish saints. There are saints everywhere. There have been saints in Italy and in France and even in Germany and I suppose in Austria. I do not know anything about them, but the important saints have been Spanish and Italian and that is natural enough, there must be really weather to wander in order to be a saint.
>
> A saint a real saint never does anything, a martyr does sometimes but a really good saint does nothing, and so I wanted to have Four Saints who did nothing and I wrote the Four Saints In Three Acts and they did nothing and that was everything.
>
> Generally speaking anybody is more interesting doing nothing than doing something.

Breton approved of Leonardo's advice to his students to stare at a dilapidated wall until they seemed to see pictures; and Stein seems to have devised her opera according to a similar plan. The landscape is a void, and the actors do nothing: it is the ultimate refinement of her anti-narrative model of theatre. Stein thought that all successful plays were plays in which "nothing was happening . . . after all Hamlet Shakespeare's most interesting play has really nothing happening except that they live and die . . . an interesting thing is when there is nothing happening. I said that the moon excited dogs because it did nothing, lights coming and going do not excite them." *Four Saints in Three Acts* is even better than *Hamlet*, in that even less happens—no fuss about living and dying, since saints are beyond that.

(If Stein had lived only a few years longer, she could have seen her dream theatre of acedia realized in the early plays of Samuel Beckett.) Instead of the action-calligrams in *Tender Buttons, Four Saints in Three Acts* presents us with a calligram of pure inaction, an intricate tracing of mental operations in the absence of a world, almost in the absence of a finite mind. Its excitement is the excitement of the moon, indivisible, unassailable, extraterrestrial, complete beyond discourse. Some of the play's techniques, such as the fragility of denotation, or the playing with differentiations in the absence of any solid things to be differentiated, may recall those of Stein's early "psychological" work; but here the text is generated not from meditations on (say) weakness and strength in American women, but from meditations on the tenability and untenability of grammar.

Stein discussed the relation of grammar to landscape in a book called *How to Write* (1927–31):

> Willows a grammar. . . .
> Where there is no more grass to be found pink dahlias can take its place and when the pink dahlias are gone a yellow dahlia can take their place slowly. In spite of a hesitation a yellow dahlia can be consumed after pink dahlias have been absorbed after they have replaced the grass which is no longer a delight.
> Partly a grammar. . . .
> Hills a grammar.
> A hill slopes and there is a long length when there is not a deception.
> Hills a grammar. . . .
> Poplars. Poplars may be they certainly will be cut down and sawn up.

According to Stein, if you want to understand grammar, just look out your window: the whole landscape constitutes itself according to the same principles that determine the shape of a sentence. Stein elaborates, at great length, Fenollosa's (and Pound's) belief that a language—or a prose style—should be judged according to the relevance of its grammar to the grammar of the natural world. The slope of a hill is an embodiment of a grammatical declension; the vegetative cycle, by which a collective entity *(grass)* is replaced by a plural entity *(pink dahlias)* and in turn by a singular entity *(a yellow dahlia),* mirrors exactly the continual surrogation pattern of nouns and pronouns, always standing in place of one another. (Stein's use of such odd verbs as *consumed* and *absorbed* to denote the withering of plants suggests that she's creating a pattern of substitutions for "normal" words within her own text.) Nature is a syntagma, full of appositions and dependent clauses; you can even take a poplar and parse it into a heap of planks. One reason for Stein's love of adverbs, prepositions, and conjunctions seems to be their grammatical vitality, far superior to that of listless nouns—an exuber-ance, a connective energy in the domain of words, comparable to radiation or magnetism in the domain of things.

Certain passages in *How to Write* hint at the algebraic, abstracting power of grammar: "I am a grammarian. . . . I love my love with a b because she is pre-cious. I love her with a c because she is all mine." The *b* and the *c* seem to be sexually charged placeholders in a grammatical calculus—signs not for a par-ticular noun but for a whole range of interesting nouns, nouns all the more inter-esting because not specified. Elsewhere, too, Stein seems to think of grammar as a study that purifies languages, perhaps to the point where English words will have the chaste, cool, empty precision of cardinal numbers: for example, Stein writes a heading, "Grammar. In a breath," after which she lists four numbered items, the last of which is: "4. Four five six seven all good children go to heaven some are good and some are bad one two three four five six seven." This is one of several passages in which grammar seems to have a halo of heavenly glamour (Stein may have known that *grammar* and *glamour* are etymologically related); another occurs when she speaks of "Grammar an angel an angel made of pud-ding a pudding made of angels pudding angel," in order to illustrate the inverti-bility of the elements in dependent prepositional phrases.

Indeed, Stein devised the celestial landscape of *Four Saints in Three Acts* ac-cording to the principle of maximum grammatical plasticity: her heaven is a sort of proto-Chomskian heaven, an infinitely long sentence of infinitely transform-able grammar, a place where anything sayable can be said and be said truly, a place where angels are made of pudding and pudding is made of angels and any other construct involving angels and pudding is valid and any other construct involving two or two million other words is valid. Heaven is a place where rhymes denote real relations among the things that rhyme, where homonyms represent arcane identities, where synonyms represent arcane divisions. The play is an abstraction of human life into a domain of grammatical figments, predicates happy to be free from any subject.

Four Saints in Three Acts takes place in grammatically challenging, logically forbidden areas of human experience. The sentence form "X is trying to prove the existence of God" logically requires that X be a human being; but grammar is satisfied if X is a chicken, or a log, or bobsledding, or there, or even God himself. Similarly, Chomsky noted that such grammatically correct forms as "colorless green ideas" present problems in practical speech. Stein's text is full of grammatically correct but completely puzzling sentences, such as "Saint Ignatius might be very well adapted to plans and a distance." But Stein's linguistic space keeps growing wider, more inclusive, as the words inside it keep undergoing a kind of mutagenesis, until grammar loses its ability to position the sentence elements. "Saint Therese with the land and laid," we are told at one point: the word *land* loses an *n* and sprouts an *i,* therefore generating a floating past participle, *laid,* serenely seeking something to modify, or preening itself as the impossible object of the preposition *with,* or hovering forever in midair, a detached radical, delighting in its irrelevance.

Tiny grammatical fragments can detach themselves from any context and permute themselves into an oversaturated, loopy verbal field: "Letting pin in letting let in let in in in in let in let in wet in wed in dead in dead wed led in led wed dead in dead in led in wed in said in said led wed dead wed dead said led led said wed dead wed dead led in led." At first Stein seems to be playing with a pun on *let in* and *inlet;* but when the *l* of *let* metamorphoses into a *w,* the *let-wet* rhyme suddenly opens up some new potentials: change the *t*'s to *d*'s, and a wedding procession starts to wend its way: *led-wed.* With one more mutation of the syllable the wedding procession becomes a funeral march, or some heavenly ceremony that might be imagined indifferently as wedding or funeral, since the categories of life and death no longer apply: *dead-wed.* And then the light iambs turns into heavy spondees, for a while, though the unstressed syllable *in* doesn't stray far, and returns to leaven the texture and to provide a ghost of prepositional force. It is as if rhyming can generate new sorts of sentence structures, on an axis at right angles to the axis of normal subject-predicate formations. The opera seems to explore dimensions of syntax little known on earth. On earth, rose is a rose is a rose; but in the heaven of music (as Stein noted in *A Sonatina Followed by Another*), "rose is a nose."

Four Saints in Three Acts: *An Opera with No Acts*

Four Saints in Three Acts provides derangements of theatrical grammar as well as English grammar. We expect a play to begin with a list of dramatis personae and some indication of their relations with one another; the playbill tells us that Lear is king of Britain and has three daughters, Goneril, Regan, and Cordelia, and that the Duke of Cornwall is Regan's husband. But Stein's opera puts the cast list well into the text: a long list of saints, some of whom are familiar, such as Saint Therese, Saint Ignatius, and Saint Paul, others of whom are doubtful, such as Saint Settlement, Saint Electra, and Saint Plan. Also, we expect speech prefixes to assign words to particular characters; but huge chunks of Stein's opera appear on the page in normal prose paragraphs, without any indications of speaker or spoken-to. The numerical specificity of the title is everywhere belied by the astonishing indeterminacy of the text—a more accurate title would have been *Lots of Saints in at Least Four Acts.* Since the headline "Repeat First Act" appears just after the first act has begun, even the number of acts is hard to count; and the division into scenes is irregular and impossible to follow, as if the author kept losing her place.

Indeterminacy is perhaps necessary in a play that embodies an unfigured desert landscape, a play in which nothing happens. It is hard to make accurate computations in the void; as mathematicians like to say, you can prove any theorem on the null set, the set with no elements in it. In an early section of the text before the headline "Act One," Stein writes:

> A narrative of prepare for saints in narrative prepare for saints. . . .
> A narrative who do who does.
> A narrative to plan an opera.
> Four saints in three acts.
> A croquet scene and when they made their habits.

It is as if Stein were not so much writing a play as making a preliminary sketch for a play; and in a sense the whole text seems to dwell in some pre-textual limbo, in which the narrative never gets told and the play never gets played. A narrative is indeed an account of Who do? and Who does?, but we never learn who does anything, and by Stein's own admission we cannot, since saints are too busy being saintly to do anything. Stein pretends to be observing the decorum of a prologue: first we will present the opera's narrative plan, and then we will present the opera. But it seems that instead of a plan, we get Saint Plan, who is, disturbingly enough, a character in the drama: it is as if Mr. Plot walked on stage in order to stir up a dangerously drooping play, except that Saint Plan seems as inactive and unobtrusive as the rest of the cast. Similarly, instead of specifying a setting for the opera, Stein offers no hint of locale (except insofar as places such as Barcelona and Avila are mentioned in the text), but does provide a character named Saint Settlement. If Stein had traveled a little further down this road, we might have had Saint Prompter, Saint Spotlight, and Saint Prop Guitar. The normal ingredients of a play—plot, character, and setting—are all smeared together, doubtful inferences from a monoplanar text that resembles a drama squashed against a windshield.

In the pseudo-prologue, Stein suggests that the opera will show "A croquet scene and when they made their habits." This seems to be bluff or prevarication or the dramatic equivalent of an amputee's phantom limb: if the croquet scene is ever played, the text makes no mention of it; on the other hand, we do hear, a little later, about the nuns' habits: "Saint Therese could be photographed having been dressed like a lady and then they taking out her head changed it to a nun and a nun a saint and a saint so." This sentence alludes to an important element of the opera's composition history—let me cite Stein's important statement of her intentions at some length:

In Four Saints I made the Saints the landscape. All the saints that I made and I made a number of them because after all a great many pieces of things are in a landscape all these saints together made my landscape. These attendant saints were the landscape and it the play really is a landscape.

A landscape does not move nothing really moves in a landscape but things are there, and I put into the play the things that were there.

Magpies are in the landscape that is they are in the sky of a landscape, they are black and white and they are in the sky of the landscape in Bilignin and in Spain, especially in Avila. When they are in the sky they do something that I have never seen any other bird do they hold themselves up and down and look flat against the sky.

A very famous French inventor of things that have to do with stabilization in aviation told me that what I told him magpies did could not be done by any bird but anyway whether the magpies at Avila do do it or do not at least they look as if they do do it. They look exactly like the birds in the Annunciation pictures the bird which is the Holy Ghost and rests flat against the side sky very high. . . .

The scarecrows on the ground are the same thing as the magpies in the sky, they are a part of the landscape.

They the magpies may tell their story if they and you like or even if I like but stories are only stories but that they stay in the air is not a story but a landscape. . . .

While I was writing the Four Saints I wanted one always does want the saints to be actually saints before them as well as inside them, I had to see them as well as feel them. As it happened there is on the Boulevard Raspail a place where they make photographs that have always held my attention. They take a photograph of a young girl dressed in the costume of her ordinary life and little by little in successive photographs they change it into a nun. These photographs are small and the thing takes four or five changes but at the end it is a nun and this is done for the family when the nun is dead and in memoriam. . . . I saw how Saint Therese existed from the life of an ordinary young lady to that of the nun. . . .

All these things might have been a story but as a landscape they were just there and a play is just there. . . .

Anyway I did write Four Saints . . . it made a landscape and the movement in it was like a movement in and out with which anybody looking on can keep in time. I also wanted it to have the movement of nuns very busy and in continuous movement but placid as a landscape has to be because after all the life in a convent is the life of a landscape, it may look excited but its quality is that of a landscape if it ever did go away would have to go away to stay.

The notion of eternity as an unrolled filmstrip, a simultaneous presentation of an image in all its possible projections into time, from little girl to nun to saint in heaven, governs many aspects of the opera. It not only explains the leisurely, stressless, unclimaxing dramatic rhythm—everything that has been and will be is *there,* and merely needs to display various angles of itself—but even explains the diction of the sentences, their rhythm of perpetual word-substitution, as if the sentences were trying on different costumes.

And just as time loses its sense of duration, space loses its sense of extension. The magpies have learned to move in a dimension unavailable to normal birds: they go directly up and down, with wings outspread, as if they were raised and lowered on wires. The orthogonalities of conventional space have been rotated or bent or simply abolished. Space has deflated into a fresco-like flatness ("birds in the Annunciation pictures"), yet retains a disturbing freedom for movement in impossible directions.

Stein's strange boast "I made the Saints the landscape" also tends to vitiate the solid orientation of our sense of space. The saints don't inhabit a landscape; they *are* the landscape. All the saints, so to speak, are Saint Settlement: they exist in the way that rock and sand exist, they talk in the way that rock and sand would talk if given a voice. They interact not as human beings, but as diuturnities. When Stein thought of Spain, she often thought of distance and abstraction—indeed, she considered that Picasso's cubist landscapes were "realistic" transcriptions of the look of Spanish landscapes: "too photographic a copy of nature. . . . americans can understand spaniards. . . . they are the only two western nations that can realise abstraction." The saints in Stein's opera are like people beheld at such a remote distance that they have receded into an abstract landscape, a landscape that they constitute. When Stein took her first airplane ride, in America, following her successes with *The Autobiography of Alice B. Toklas* and *Four Saints in Three Acts,* she looked down at the countryside and noted that it was all "postcubist painting": "The wandering line of Masson was there the mixed line of Picasso coming and coming again and following itself into a beginning was there, the simple solution of Braque was there." When I read *Four Saints in Three Acts,* I can similarly make out the wandering lines and loops and grids of advanced Modernist painting—not from the sky looking down, but from the ground looking up, into amiable abstractions of language.

Heavenly Reconfigurings of Position

What thoughts would occupy the mind of a thinking landscape? The evidence of the text suggests that the distribution of its elements is its main preoccupation:

Saint Therese seated and not surrounded. There are a great many persons and places near together. . . .

Saint Therese very nearly half inside and half outside the house and not surrounded. . . .

The garden inside and outside outside and inside of the wall.

Nobody visits more than they do visits them. . . .

How many saints can sit around. A great many saints can sit around with one standing. . . .

How many saints can remember a house which was built before they can remember.

Ten saints can.

How many saints can be and land be and sand be and on a high plateau there is no sand there is snow.

Virgil Thomson noted that in setting the text to music, he set the stage directions as well as the speeches; but I wonder how he knew which was which, since the stage directions and the speeches inhabit the same equable and placid textual space. Some of the sentences cited here seem to be more stage directions than speeches, but there is a continuum between announcements of distribution (stage directions) and discussions of distribution (speeches). Saint Therese is seated; one saint is standing; a great many saints are seated, but not seated in such a manner that Saint Therese would look surrounded; Saint Therese is very nearly (but not quite) half inside and half outside the house; the garden is inside and outside of the wall, or perhaps it would be more accurate to say that the garden is outside and inside of the wall. The basic Sesame Street categories that orient us in the world, such as *in* and *out,* have lost focus, lost prepositional force: Saint Therese isn't exactly outside the house, and isn't exactly inside the house, and isn't exactly half inside and half outside the house. This is a troublesome answer to the question, Where is Saint Therese?—but in heaven questions of geography are hard to answer. Stein has provided here a verbal equivalent to the spatial outrages of cubist and post-cubist painting, by staring beyond the vanishing point of earth's horizon.

In heaven, nothing can happen any more; therefore, instead of events, there can only be reconfigurings of position. All writers who write about heaven sooner or later find themselves studying the placement of the inhabitants, for topography is a kind of default mode when narrative movement tends toward absolute zero. The Bible mentions ranks of angels—thrones, dominions, principalities, and powers; Dante first arranges the blessed according to the circles of Ptolemaic astronomy, as he passes through the great frictionless blobs of light that make up the moon and the other planets—but finally Dante passes to the universe's other side, and sees the residents of heaven making up the petals of a single rose; Milton dramatizes a God whose first concern, after the angels vanquish the devils, is to preserve the symmetrical distribution of the celestial spaces: "inhabit lax, ye Powers of Heav'n," He commands, instructing the angels to move further apart from one another in order to fill the void left by the defection of Lucifer's gang. Heaven may have two dimensions, and it may have four dimensions, but it rarely has a conventional three dimensions; and those whose artistic speciality is heaven tend to trace intricate designs in a dizzying space where down is only one of many directions in which it's possible to fall.

Stein makes use of several strategies to create verbal vertigo. One is the strange defunction of meaning in such placement-words as *inside* and *outside;* another is her denial of the paradoxicality of paradoxes: "How many saints can remember a house which was built before they can remember." Logically, the answer is No saints—that is, if the question implies, How many saints can remember *the building of* a house; but Stein instead answers, "Ten saints can." When I was a child, someone asked me whether God could create a stone so heavy that He couldn't lift it—a theological tease, since God's omnipotence is threatened whether the answer is Yes, in which case there's a sort of stone that God can't lift, or No, in which case there's a sort of stone that God can't create. Perhaps Stein had heard this same riddle, and echoed it in her formulation of the question about the saints remembering the unrememberable house. Where chronology has no forward motion, where the timeline is knotted and looped, the logic of sequence has no meaning; and where there is little distinction between one saint and another saint, or between one number and another number, the answer to the question How many? can be chosen on the grounds of euphony rather than mathematics. Somewhere behind all the How many? questions in the opera lies the scholastic head-scratcher, How many angels can dance on the head of a pin? And since saints, like angels, are incorporeal and alogical, the answer is always along the lines of A whole bunch, or As many as you like.

Counting for Counting's Sake

Numbers are arbitrary, divinely arbitrary. *Four Saints in Three Acts* is, as the title implies, an opera about numbers, numbers emancipated from the usual constraints of arithmetic—not only in the unconsecutive scene and act enumerations, but even in the texts of the speeches themselves, for the saints love to count for the sheer joy of counting: "One two three four five six seven all good children go to heaven some are good and some are bad." This is the same nursery rhyme quoted in Stein's book about grammar, *How to Write,* and again in a portrait, *To Virgil and Eugene.* Stein conceived heaven as an endless game of skiprope or hopscotch; you can either note the arrangements of the elements that occupy the

Elysian fields, or you can engage in an eternal tallying of them. Most thinkers discriminate human beings from animals on the basis of thinking or speaking; but for Stein the principal human attribute is the ability to count:

> There is no difference between men and animals except that they can count and never has there been so much counting as is going on at present. Everybody is counting, counting is everybody's occupation. . . . I always liked counting but I liked counting one two three four five six seven, or one little Indian two little Indians three little Indian boys counting more than ten is not interesting at least not to me because the numbers higher than ten unless they are fifty-five or something like that do not look interesting.

In heaven you don't have to concern yourself with paying the rent, or making dinner plans, or going to sleep; you can simply count to your heart's content.

One of the largest numbers mentioned appears in an odd ethical tease in the first Act One: "If it were possible to kill five thousand chinamen by pressing a button would it be done. Saint Therese not interested." This is an allusion to a problem posed by Stein's friend Hutchins Hapgood, who "liked to think of the number of angels on the point of a needle. . . . one day he gave me a test question. Would I if I could by pushing a button would I kill five thousand Chinamen if I could save my brother from anything. Well I was very fond of my brother and I could completely imagine his suffering and I replied that five thousand Chinamen were something I could not imagine and so it was not interesting." Saint Therese, however, seems even more indifferent to the sufferings of others, since no brother enters into her moral calculus; she has evidently attained a divine apathy, immunity from pain. According to Lucretius's *De rerum natura,* the gods, looking down at us from the clouds, regard human suffering, human warfare, as an amusing spectator sport; and Stein's saints manifest a certain Lucretian quality, even a sort of autism, in that they seem engrossed with counting on their fingers, with speaking texts to rhythms so perfectly pointless that they seem the verbal equivalent of dangling a bright object in front of one's eyes or rocking endlessly back and forth. Absolute goallessness always seems frightening, pathological, on earth; but in heaven it is a given condition.

Another of Stein's strategies for liquidating language, for rendering the reader giddy or seasick, lies in her perversion of the vocabulary of differentiation. We've already seen that Stein's use of terms such as *like* or *is different from* or *is not different from* or *is the same as* tends to be exceedingly unreliable, a parody of comparison. In *Four Saints in Three Acts* we reach the apotheosis of vain discrimination:

> Is there a difference between a sound a hiss a kiss as well.

Saint Therese can know the difference between singing and women. Saint Therese can know the difference between snow and thirds. Saint Therese can know the difference between when there is a day to-day to-day. To-day.

Was Saint Ignatius able to tell the difference between palms and Eucalyptus trees.

Never to return to distinctions.

He asked for a distant magpie as if they made a difference.

There is a difference between Barcelona and Avila.
There is a difference between Barcelona.

Saint Therese, so unconcerned with the death of five thousand Chinamen, seems to take a good deal of quiet satisfaction from her power to discriminate singing from women, or snow from thirds. And well she might, for she lives in a place in which objects are so subject to random typographical mutation—a *land* is so likely to turn into a *laid,* or a *hiss* into a *kiss*—that even the grossest distinctions are strangely tentative, fragile. The language of confident differentiation ("Saint Therese can know"; "There is a difference between Barcelona and Avila") is everywhere undercut, first by inverting these declarations into questions ("Is there a difference"), second by creating grammatical absurdities through the loss of one of the terms of comparison ("There is a difference between Barcelona"). Perhaps the only viable distinctions are visual, not logical: a word differs from another word insofar as it *looks* different from that word. But even to say this is to assume that the word *difference* has a meaning; and in the imperturbable re-lationlessness of this opera, this may be to assume too much. Some phrases alter, some phrases stay the same, but sameness gives no sense of prestige, and altera-tion imparts no sense of inadequacy. The opera's most famous phrase, "Pigeons in the grass alas," undergoes only slight changes through its frequent repetition— for example, "The pigeon on the grass and alas." But I think it would be wrong to assume that its relative stability is a reflex of its association with the sacred symbol of the Holy Ghost, since the phrase is itself a metamorphosis—I almost wrote a metastasis—of a phrase Stein wrote in 1922, "Chickens made of glass. Alas." In a world made up purely from words, or from the visual apparitions of words, all textual shifting is directionless, neither from nor toward, since there is no underlying substrate of the denotable. Pound noted that "The pseudo Diony-sius mentions that the order of angels called Dominions is 'elevated above simi-larity'"; and Stein's opera also takes place in a region elevated above all judgment of similarity and dissimilarity.

Four Saints in Three Acts erects a little universe manufactured according to the disorienting principles of Stein's literary style. Most of Stein's work is burdened by some notion of agreement between a text and its referent—the face of Picasso, or a stumbling donkey, or the landscape of Bilignin. But here, where there is no referent except desert, or vacuum, her prose could exuberate without constraints.

Thomson's Early Stein Settings: Susie Asado, Capital Capitals

Before 1927, Stein's work was mostly written in an uncompromised Modernist solitude, with little certainty of publication and with no concessions to her audience. But *Four Saints in Three Acts,* begun in March 1927—Stein was fifty-three years old—was a collaborative venture from the start: it was designed as a libretto for Virgil Thomson, and Thomson influenced it in many ways. Stein and Thomson first discussed George Washington as a subject, but Thomson felt that the characters would look too much alike in eighteenth-century costume:

> we gave up history and chose saints. . . . Eventually our saints turned out to be Baroque and Spanish, a solution that delighted Gertrude, for she loved Spain, and that was far from displeasing me, since, as I pointed out, mass-market Catholic art, the basic living art of Christianity, was still Baroque. And Maurice Grosser [the scenarist for the opera] was later to remind us that musical instruments of the violin family still present themselves as functional Baroque forms.

On the one hand, *Four Saints in Three Acts* promotes to a full evening's entertainment the abstract curves of a violin's shape, so dear to Picasso and Braque, just as *Parade* realized on stage a less sinuous, more boxy and awkward cubist style. On the other hand, *Four Saints in Three Acts* is an experiment in Christian kitsch—plastic Jesuses and reliquaries for saints' toenails—comparable to *Parade*'s experimentation with advertising displays and streetwise *réaliste* gestures. Stein also had a certain love of kitsch, as Mabel Dodge remembered: "she didn't care whether a thing was *bon gout* or not. . . . She adored those miniature alabaster fountains, with two tiny white doves poised on the brink that tourists brought and she had a penchant for forget me not mosaic brooches." The peculiar thrill of this opera comes from its simultaneous existence as advanced, sophisticated Modernist art and as a sort of giant magnification of a paperweight shrine in a dome filled with gypsum snow.

Thomson had admired *Tender Buttons* from his college days, but he didn't get to know Stein until late 1925 and 1926, when he was thirty: they "got on like Harvard men," and Thomson took lifelong pride in the fact that Stein admitted him directly to her circle, without the normal screening process through Alice B. Toklas. Thomson soon ingratiated himself by composing a musical setting of her brief *Susie Asado*—when Stein received the manuscript, she immediately wrote back, "I like its looks immensely and want to frame it." It is worth noting that, from the very beginning, Stein responded to the *visual* aspect of Thomson's music, as if a page of score were simply an abstract painting in five-line grids and squiggles and flagged black dots. If Stein saw Thomson as a painter with notes, Thomson saw Stein as a short but monumental statue, "some saint or sibyl sculpted three-fourths life size."

Thomson regarded *Susie Asado* as a breakthrough:

> My hope in putting Gertrude Stein to music had been to break, crack open, and solve for all time . . . English musical declamation. My theory was that if a text is set correctly for the sound of it, the meaning will take care of itself. And the Stein texts, for prosodizing in this way, were manna. With meanings already abstracted, or absent, or so multiplied that choice among them was impossible, there was no temptation toward tonal illustration, say, of birdie babbling by the brook or heavy heavy hangs my heart.

Elsewhere, Thomson insisted that his accompaniment for *Susie Asado* consisted of "musical abstractions only." And yet *Susie Asado* did provide some "temptation toward tonal illustration," and Thomson succumbed: in the first line, "Sweet sweet sweet sweet sweet tea," he set the *sweet*s as detached eighth notes all on the note C, finally leaping to E♭ on *tea*, creating a strong suggestion of cheeping, if not explicitly a "birdie babbling by the brook." But Thomson devised a tonal illustration not for the semantic elements of Stein's text—the word *bird* never appears, nor (until the very end) any word associated with birds—but for the phonic elements: Thomson read Stein's "sweet tea," heard the *sweetie* that is easily derived from the term, then heard the *tweety* that extends out of the text as a phantom orthogonal, and made a bird call in response.

EX. 12.1. Thomson, *Susie Asado:* beginning

But *Susie Asado* is less than two minutes long; Thomson's first ambitious setting of a Stein text was *Capital Capitals* (1927), one of Stein's garrulous landscapes: four local Provençal capitals are impersonated and sung, as Thomson heard it, by two tenors and two baritones. Many aspects of its *Klangfarbe,* its sound-tint, anticipate *Four Saints in Three Acts:* the relaxed vivacity of Provence clearly foreshadows heaven. Thomson was excited by the audience response:

> Not a sacred work but sounds sort of so. Seems to remind everyone of what he heard in childhood.
>
> Fania Marinoff—Jewish synagogue
> Miguel Covarrubias—Mexican church
> Mary Butts—Greek chants
> Jean Cocteau—Catholic liturgy
> Edward Ashcroft—Gilbert and Sullivan patter.

(Whereas Stein looked at *Susie Asado* and saw something worth framing, Cocteau heard *Capital Capitals* and said the music was "'At last a table that stands on four legs'": Thomson's music evidently had a certain plastic solidity as well as a visual impressiveness.) I suspect that this line of praise for *Capital Capitals* strongly informed the kind of music that Thomson would soon write for *Four Saints in Three Acts:* he would go back to the Protestant hymnody of his Kansas City childhood and seek diatonic elements so rudimentary, so universal, that the music would seem part of the general heritage of Western civilization—not just Thomson's earliest memories, but everybody's autobiography. When Thomson played the first act of *Four Saints in Three Acts* for a few friends on Christmas Day 1927, he "wondered whether a piece so drenched in Anglican chant (running from Gilbert and Sullivan to morning prayer and back) could rise and sail. But no one seemed bothered by its origins." The extreme simplicity of Thomson's musical language creates a sort of heuristic opera, in which each listener creates a separate semantic construction out of a private assortment of nursery rhymes, patriotic tunes, and liturgy.

Thomson's Discipline of Spontaneity

Thomson's method of composing *Four Saints in Three Acts* differed from his usual practice: "With the text on my piano's music rack, I would sing and play, improvising melody to fit the words and harmony for underpinning them with shape. I did this every day, wrote down nothing. When the first act would improvise itself every day in the same way, I knew it was set." This method is related to that of Thomson's portraits—musical compositions devised without premeditation in the presence of the sitter:

> an enlightenment had come to me that made portrait writing possible. This was the very simple discovery that the classic masters, in terms of logic and syntax, did not always quite make sense. My sudden awareness of their

liberties in this regard forced me to take up my own freedom. . . . This meant that I could write almost automatically, cultivate the *discipline of spontaneity,* let it flow.

Now the value of spontaneous work is often zero, especially when it merely follows reflexes, as in pianoforte improvisation. But spontaneity can be original also, if it wells up from a state of self-containment. And it was through practicing my spontaneities, at first in a primitive way, and through questioning Gertrude Stein about this method of work, which was her own, that I grew expert at tapping my resources.

Four Saints in Three Acts, then, is a portrait, not of a human being, but of a text. Thomson simply let the music well up from the words, without interposing conscious control, until the music kept welling up in the same way. Stein herself hated automatic writing, and offered only an artful simulation of textual unconsciousnesses; but Thomson's music is derived from the scales, triads, and snatches of simple hymns that constitute the racial unconscious of Western music. D. H. Lawrence despised Freud's notion of the unconscious: what did Freud find in the caves of sleep?—"Nothing but a huge slimy serpent of sex, and heaps of excrement, and a myriad repulsive little horrors spawned between sex and excrement . . . gagged, bound, maniacal repressions"; but Lawrence argued instead that the unconscious mind is clean, sane, lithe, full of forthright nakedness and healthy desire. In the world of music, the Schoenberg of *Erwartung* plays the role of Freud; and Virgil Thomson plays the role of Lawrence.

But just as Lawrence's version of the unconscious, as presented in his novels, is rather more disturbing than his theoretical writings would suggest, so there is something distorted, perverse, in Thomson's boob-simple diatonicism. Just after writing *Four Saints in Three Acts,* Thomson wrote *Commentaire sur Saint Jérome* (1928), in which the piano accompaniment, as Anthony Tommasini has noted, consists entirely of four notes of the B♭-major scale—while the singer sings a text in which the Marquis de Sade remembers that the Scots used to eat the buttocks of young shepherds and the breasts of young girls (Sade speculates that the taste of the flesh of human females, as with all animals, must be inferior to that of males). In the post-*Erwartung* world, nothing but a straight major scale could be shocking enough to match Sade's text; in Thomson's hands, the tetrachord turns urbane and vicious, surreal.

"The discipline of spontaneity"—the method of the musical portraits—is Thomson's catchphrase for the whole surrealist movement: "I got myself into a lovely little—shall we say controversy—with André Breton, by pointing out that the discipline of spontaneity, which he was asking his surrealist neophytes to adopt, was new for language but something that composers had been practicing for centuries." Just as the surrealist paintings often provide many of the entertainments of conventional painting—a plane receding to a horizon, in consistent perspective, on which recognizable objects appear—so Thomson provides many of the entertainments of conventional music; but only because to be recognized as *wrong*, something has to be recognizable in the first place.

Four Saints: *Consonant Harmony, Dissonant Syntax*

The white-note chastity of the music of *Four Saints in Three Acts* conceals a twisted grin: in a musical culture where dissonance is expected as a sign of knowledge and good breeding, a dismembered, deliberately incompetent euphony is the final sophistication:

> Now the *Four Saints* accompaniment is as odd as its text, so odd, indeed, that it has sometimes been taken for childish. In fact, many persons . . . have been worried by my use of what seems to them a backward-looking music idiom in connection with a forward-looking literary one. That worry can only be argued against by denying the assumption that discord is advanced and harmoniousness old-fashioned. . . . In setting Stein texts to music I had in mind the acoustical support of a trajectory, of a verbal volubility that would brook no braking. My skill was to be employed not for protecting such composers as had invested in the dissonant manner but for avoiding all those interval frictions and contrapuntal viscosities which are built into the dissonant style and which if indulged unduly might trip up my verbal speeds. Not to have skirted standard modernism would have been to fall into a booby trap. On the contrary, I built up my accompaniments by selecting chords for their tensile strength and by employing in a vast majority of cases only those melodic elements from the liturgical vernacular of Christendom, both Catholic and Protestant, that had for centuries borne the weight of long prayers.

Thomson wanted his opera to move quickly—it is a Modernist, streamlined opera, like a bullet train.

And, in a sense, the opera is Modernist in its dissonance as well—except that the dissonance exists on the level not of harmony but of syntax. Schoenberg, one might say, wrote the musical equivalent of *fmsbwtözäu*—disruptions of his language on the level of the phoneme; Thomson, by contrast, wrote the musical equivalent of *colorless green ideas*—disruptions on the level of the lexeme. Schoenberg moves slowly, because every strange new chord asks to be pondered both in isolation and in context; it takes up a huge volume of psychoacoustic space. Thomson moves quickly, because the facile, dechromatized sounds are exactly like millions of other sounds you've heard from infancy onward; it is only in retrospect that the opera's unstartlingness seems startling, that its withholding of expressivity, its refusal of salience, its gesturelessness, seem as radical as quar-ter tones or strings of major sevenths. Thomson is Ives backward, experimenting in the too white instead of the too chromatic. And just as extremely dissonant music can lose all sense of progressiveness, unless the composer can devise some nontonal principle of consequence, so extremely consonant music can find its progressiveness dwindling to near zero. But the absence of harmonic motion, as we know it, actually helps the music to develop speed. In most tonal music, the speed of harmonic change acts as a kind of tempo regulator, just as engine com-pression acts as a brake when a car is in gear. But Thomson's music simply rolls down the slopes of the text, so to speak; the music forgets itself almost instantly, as if the chords and melodies that have already sounded have little bearing on the chords and melodies that are sounding now. The music's past doesn't impinge on the music's present. Begin to listen to the opera at any point, and it makes just as much sense as it would if you had begun at the first bar.

The opera is full of musical patterns: repetitions, phrase structures, intelligible changes of key. But these patterns, though they sometimes suggest a direction, never suggest a goal. The harmony changes, but it doesn't *progress,* since it cre-ates no structure of antithesis that requires resolution.

Much of Thomson's method can be understood from the first page of the score, which sets Stein's introductory quatrain:

To know to know to love her so.
Four saints prepare for saints.
It makes it well fish.
Four saints it makes it well fish.

This begins in good iambic tetrameter, but soon loses first a sense of tetrameter, then a sense of iamb. And Thomson's music at first seems to be a clear 3/4 beat, a steady *oom*-pah-pah, in which an *oom*-pah-pah in the tonic (F) alternates strictly with an *oom*-pah-pah in the dominant (C^7). This is normal enough, but there are several disquieting features. For one thing, it is harmonically galumphing: first I, then V, then I, then V, then I, then V—the tonic is overdetermined, overweighted, paralyzed by the dominant chords that monitor it and define it, like rows of guardian angels. We want to cry out (to paraphrase Leo Stein), Say Mr. Thomson you said that already—we *know* the key is F major. Overemphasis leads to a weakening of the thing emphasized, in this case the concept of tonic. Another oddity is the meter. The implied rhythm of the accompaniment is a rigid 3/4; but most of the bars are written in 4/4, with an occasional 5/4 or 3/2 bar thrown in, so that the accent of the passage as a whole is just as likely to fall on the first *pah* or the second *pah* as on the *oom*. Thomson was initially attracted to 4/4, I sup-pose, because of Stein's tetrameter first line, but he must have liked the implied

rhythmic dissonance between the vocal line and the accompaniment, because he kept it up throughout his setting of the quatrain. The accompaniment seems oblivious of the vocal line, as if it inhabited a different precinct of heaven, and yet all is tranquil, euphonious, without false steps. The vocal line places the stress in all the expected places: every bar from bar 6 to bar 14 begins with either the word *saints* or the word *fish*. But the vocal line's stresses fall on the accompaniment in all the wrong places: *oom*-pah-pah is scrutinized under different metric grids, examined in all three permutations of stress—since a whomp from the vocal line gets superimposed on all three beats (*oom*-pah-pah; oom-*pah*-pah; oom-pah-*pah*)—and it is ascertained to be agreeable in each one. Tonic and dominant have been presented and found good: but they don't appear to possess much power of antithesis or tension of opposition; they simply take up acoustic space.

The music of heaven, it seems, is not a choir of harps, but an enormous accordion. The composer Lyapunov thought that the decline in musical taste among the Russian folk could be traced to the concertina, making banal everything that it touched: "With its doubtful intonation and its poverty of chord combinations, consisting exclusively of tonics and dominants, this instrument can deal without strain only with uncomplicated melodies." But Thomson revels in the poverty of endless strings of tonics and dominants: heaven is a state of total simplism, the sort of place where your ignorant grandfather, whose idea of a fine time was to dance the beer-barrel polka, would feel right at home.

Thomson could easily have made different choices, more highbrow or more colorful; but surrealist opera composers (such as Poulenc in *Les mamelles de Tirésias*) tend to ignore the elements of the text to which normal composers would respond, and to respond to elements that normal composers would ignore. Thomson might have filled an opera about Spanish saints with allusions to Victoria masses, to boleros and jotas. (In fact, he went to Spain for the first time *after* writing the vocal score, in order to see whether he wanted to include Spanish instrumental color; but he rejected any other Spanish elements: "Her tunes & her rhythms are too good to be interesting.") Thomson might have filled an opera that seems to take place in heaven with harps and Gregorian chant and pious hymn tunes. A few aspects of the opera show faint tendencies in these directions: as for Hispanicism, Thomson wrote a tango (two bars after rehearsal figure 163), thereby approaching Spain in a roundabout fashion, via Argentina; and as for hymnody, there are many passages that sound as if they're going to turn into familiar hymns, but never quite do.

Thomson composed *Four Saints in Three Acts* just after the first three movements of *Symphony on a Hymn Tune* (1926–28), a work full of unmistakable allusions to *How Firm a Foundation* and *Yes, Jesus Loves Me*, among other tunes—John Cage suggested that the symphony's title should be *Four Adventures* in *Collage:* "Its continuity is not that of narrative. It is related rather to painting, and to painting that substitutes for brush and pigment scissors, paste, and various ready-made materials." But *Four Saints in Three Acts* isn't like a collage at all, for its constituents hover on the brink of recognizability without becoming recognizable. When Thomson's chorus sings "Could all four saints not only be in brief" (one bar before rehearsal figure 52) to a rising perfect triad, it may recall "say can you see" in *The Star-Spangled Banner*—but the chorus avoids the allusion just after having raised its possibility. Thomson concerns himself with musical figures too elementary, too easily intercombined, to terminate in the distinct, hard-edged areas of a collage; the texture is too uniform and aimless to permit the spectator to distinguish between glued-on patch and background canvas. The one clear allusion in Thomson's music follows exactly the one clear allusion in Stein's text: "My country 'tis of thee sweet land of liberty" (three bars after rehearsal figure 19)—as if to say that no semantic direction is excluded from the world of the opera, though none is assigned any special stress, either. Perhaps Stein and Thomson quoted this anthem as a smiling glance back to their initial plan for an opera on George Washington—though when Thomson did write a ballet about Washington (*Parson Weems and the Cherry Tree*, 1975), the predominant tune was not *My Country 'Tis of Thee*, but *Ten Little Indians*—a counting tune, because Thomson, like Stein, enjoyed tallying.

Counting for Counting's Sake, in Music

If Thomson paid little attention to musical conventions for Spain and for heaven, he did pay extremely close attention to one element of Stein's text: counting. Marin Marais wrote a peculiar piece for violin, bass viol, and harpsichord called *La gamme, en forme de petit opéra* (1723), in which the notes of the major scale become the characters in an amusing opera without voices; Thomson reverses Marais's curriculum, by writing an opera in the form of the scale. Much of Stein's text consists of strings of numbers, such as "One two three four five six seven all good children go to heaven some are good and some are bad one two three four five six seven"—a rhyme that we've already had occasion to examine. When Thomson set this to music (three bars after rehearsal figure 82), he simply assigned the eight syllables of "One two three four five six seven" to a descending D-major scale: "One two three four" are undergirded with a root-position tonic chord; the words "five and six" appear over a IV chord; and the word "seven," appropriately enough, seems to provoke a ♮VII chord (C major) in the accompaniment—a bland overstressing of the notion of seven-ness. Then the next phrase skips down another D-major scale; and the next, too—but Stein only provided seven syllables in this phrase, so now Thomson has reached the last word, "bad," on the note E, and still has another note to go before he can finish his scale.

EX. 12.3. Thomson, *Four Saints in Three Acts:* counting aloud

So he steps on the heels of the last phrase, by completing his descending scale with the word "One," then leaping up an octave to set the word "Two," and then merrily tripping down the scale, even though he knows he's going to run out of text and must have his chorus end on a rest instead of singing the conclusive D. The text, by counting, inspires the music to enumerate its fingers, to count along with it—but the music-counting soon gets desynchronized from the text-counting, unobtrusively, without a fuss. In heaven every clock, fast, slow, or stopped, tells the right time.

Thomson amuses himself with little games of music notation that toy with numbers mentioned in the text—the true ancestor of *Four Saints in Three Acts* is Busnoys's tribute to Ockeghem, the motet *In hydraulis* (late fifteenth century), in which the text discusses the division of the monochord into tessaron and penthe and so forth, all these intervals being reflected directly in the music. If Stein provides lines such as "Sound them with the thirds and that" or "Snow third high third there third" (rehearsal figure 55; two bars after 56), the genial Thomson will provide his chorus with descending scales harmonized in thirds. Some of Thomson's games with numbers are motivated not by actual names of numbers, but simply by the fact that the text keeps permuting a small set of nouns: "It is very easy in winter to remember winter spring and summer it is very easy in winter to remember spring and winter and summer it is very easy in winter to remember summer spring and winter" (five bars after rehearsal figure 10). A text like this tends strongly to emphasize the number 3, since three entities keep shifting amid a stable sentence context. Thomson's response is to write a fantasy on three consecutive notes of the scale: first Bb, C, and D, understood as scale degrees $\hat{3}$, $\hat{4}$, and $\hat{5}$ in G minor (the basic key of this whole section); then G, A, and Bb; then D, E, and F#—except that E and F# don't belong in this key, so the final note gets supported by a D-major chord, as the harmony sidles over to the dominant. Thomson's way of thrusting forth the number 3 is different from Stein's, in that Stein permutes the three seasons whereas Thomson keeps the three notes in the same ascending sequence and permutes the harmonic context; but librettist and composer are nonetheless playing similar games, on different planes—games, perhaps, with the notion of *trinity*. Thomson can afford to be diverted by any number game that arises in the text—since he wishes to avoid long-range planning, the sense of a musical destination, these local elucidations of arithmetic help him to disorient the music, to undirect it.

Thomson's most focused and effective application of the technique of counting the permutable elements of Stein's text occurs in his setting of the processional that begins "Letting pin in letting let" (one bar after rehearsal figure 187)—the finest passage in the opera, I think. As we've seen, Stein here juggles four important words ("said led wed dead")—but the numbers *four* and *three* are particularly hard to distinguish in this opera, so Thomson restricts himself to three

EX. 12.4. Thomson, *Four Saints in Three Acts:* said led wed dead

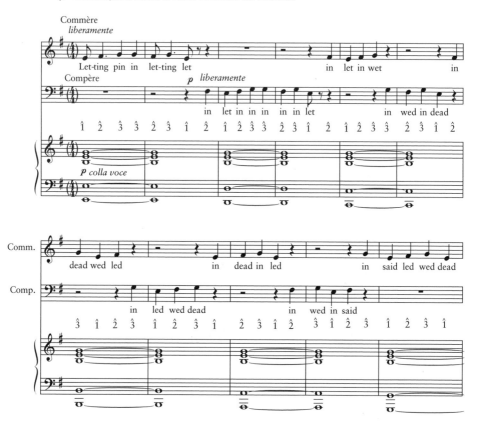

notes, scale degrees î, 2̂, and 3̂, in the key of E minor: Four Words in Three Notes. Just as the opening of the opera is in F major to an excessive, almost intolerable degree, so this scene is almost punishingly devoted to E minor—not because the dominant keeps clicking it into place, but because the accompaniment consists of absolutely nothing except E-minor triads, sustained for twenty-one slow bars—except that beneath the triads, the bass creeps down from E to D to C and so forth, until it's spanned a tenth, and can stop on a very low C. (A tenth, of course, is an amplified third—the bass line, like everything else in this passage, obeys the rule of three.) Meanwhile, the vocal line is examining those scale degrees î, 2̂, and 3̂, with astonishing persistence.

Thomson set this "Saints' procession" as a duet for the Commère and the Compère—two characters of his own invention, the masters of ceremonies in the opera's vaudeville, especially useful for those prologue- and stage-direction-like

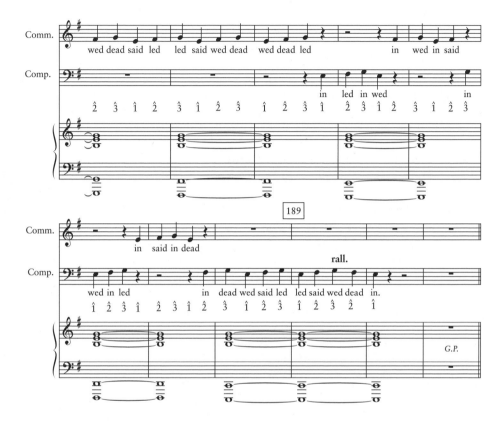

passages that don't seem easily affiliated with any of the saints; they are, in effect, bridges between the nondramatic and the pseudo-dramatic aspects of Stein's text, in that they can make the text talk without being part of the "story." (Thomson's other major innovation in the dramatis personae was the splitting of St. Teresa—whose name Thomson, unlike Stein, always spelled in the Spanish fashion—into a St. Teresa I and a St. Teresa II: another sign of the precariousness of human identity in a heaven where *all* talking is talking to oneself.) In "Letting pin in letting let," Thomson distributed the text randomly between the two—there being no principle other than randomness that Thomson could possibly have used. And just as Stein at first seems stuck on the word *in*—"in let in in in in in let in let in wet"—so the Commère and Compère seem uncertain in what order to sing their three notes: the Commère sings the first seven syllables to scale degrees $\hat{1}$, $\hat{2}$, $\hat{3}$, $\hat{3}$, $\hat{2}$, $\hat{3}$, $\hat{1}$, then the Compère replies with $\hat{2}$, $\hat{1}$, $\hat{2}$, $\hat{3}$, $\hat{3}$, $\hat{2}$, $\hat{3}$, $\hat{1}$, then she with $\hat{2}$, $\hat{1}$, $\hat{2}$, $\hat{3}$, then he with $\hat{3}$, $\hat{2}$, $\hat{3}$, $\hat{1}$—but by now they've entered the long "in wed in dead" section, and the vocal line starts to lock into place at the moment when the text discovers the four key words "said led wed dead." From here on, instead of groping for an ordering of scale degrees $\hat{1}$, $\hat{2}$, and $\hat{3}$, the Commère and Compère have found it: they sing in strict scalar order, $\hat{1}$, $\hat{2}$, $\hat{3}$, $\hat{1}$, $\hat{2}$, $\hat{3}$, over and over, until the last two notes, which gracefully terminate the count with a $\hat{2}$ and a $\hat{1}$. Thomson skillfully avoids monotony by grouping the three degrees in units of four, so that the Compère sings "in led in wed" ($\hat{1}$, $\hat{2}$, $\hat{3}$, $\hat{1}$), and the Commère adds "in wed in said" ($\hat{2}$, $\hat{3}$, $\hat{1}$, $\hat{2}$), to which the Compère can only respond "in wed in led" ($\hat{3}$, $\hat{1}$, $\hat{2}$, $\hat{3}$), which prompts the Commère to the natural rejoinder "in said in dead" ($\hat{1}$, $\hat{2}$, $\hat{3}$, $\hat{1}$). This is a simple ostinato—an oversimple ostinato, a naked obstinacy deprived of any other musical line to push against; given Thomson's extraordinary preoccupation with arithmetic, we might describe him as a sort of parody serialist, manipulating one of the shortest tone rows ever devised, a row of only three notes, not even capable of transposition, inversion, or (except for the last bar) retrograde. Schoenberg, in *Moses und Aron,* found music for God by sounding all twelve notes; Thomson does something similar, but in a bizarrely narrow bandwidth instead of the whole spectrum of colors. Instead of a magic square with 144 notes, a twelve-tone row that can be spun out into a whole galaxy of pitch possibilities, we have three, and only three, proud little notes. Thomson was sufficiently intrigued with Schoenberg's methods that in later life (in *Wheat Field at Noon,* 1948) he was to try his hand at twelve-tone canons; and in *Four Saints in Three Acts,* odd traces of Schoenbergian rigor can be found, reduced to a giggle. The diatonic God is a limit of contraction, not a limit of expansion.

Thomson counters Schoenberg through a diatonicism as flagrant, thorough, and arithmetically dogged as any chromatic procedure of the second Viennese school. He composes according to a principle that might be called diatonic overdetermination, comparable to the overdetermination that Freud found in the interpretation of dreams. After writing twenty-one consecutive bars in which the vocal line is restricted to three notes, Thomson followed it with a setting of the line "That makes they have might kind find fined when this arbitrarily makes it" (three bars after rehearsal figure 189) in which the orchestra insists mightily on three root-position triads, D, G, and C. Thomson implies that if you can learn enough about these rudimentary things, $\hat{1}$, $\hat{2}$, $\hat{3}$, or I–IV–V, you will know everything. *Four Saints in Three Acts* often resembles a kind of dream-liquid textbook of harmony, a manual and a model of the whole diatonic system.

Elsewhere Thomson tries to fill out his operatic textbook with more advanced lessons in the theory of tonality. The opera's best-known passage, St. Ignatius's urbane and mellifluous aria *Pigeons on the grass alas* (rehearsal figure 146, marked *Vision of the Holy Ghost*), provides an example of diatonic saturation: it starts out in the simplest possible harmony, but eventually proceeds to fill in the harmonic interstices of the scale. Like the very opening of the opera, it starts with an ordinary-seeming but actually somewhat eccentric thumpy-thump accompaniment, here in 3/2 meter: *oom*-pah-[rest]-*pah*-oom-pah, in which the first four beats of the measure display tonic chords (in G major) and the last two beats move to the subdominant. This pious harmony accompanies St. Ignatius through a lot of pigeons before it comes to rest on a half-cadence; then St. Ignatius's field of vision shifts upward, to the magpies in the sky, over similar I–IV bars in 3/2 time. The Holy Ghost seems to want to be plagal, but can't quite terminate in a cadence.

In due course this aria ends, and Thomson suddenly cuts to an *allegro marziale* for the chorus, first in A major ("There might be very well") and then in B major ("Let Lucy Lily Lily Lucy"); and the harmony gets so excited that it adds the dominant to the stressless I–IV–I–IV of the opening section: I–V–I–IV–I–V–I–IV, and so forth. As St. Ignatius's vision fades, the chords start slipping down by semitones, to prepare a modulation from the key of B to A♭. It is as if some after-iridescence from the Holy Ghost opens up fields of heaven far beyond the white expanses of most of the opera. Soon we find ourselves in A major ("Might they be with they be with"—four bars after rehearsal figure 150), though the key signature has no sharps or flats. Here is a forthright, active series of chords, I–I⁶–vi–V; but the voice-leading is crude, consisting primarily of parallel fifths in the lower two voices. When St. Chavez sings "Never to return to distinctions," the E-major chord creates tension with his long high A, and the tonality seems then to shift to D major, only to shift right back again to A major—Thomson seems to provide a slightly incoherent tonality as a musical icon of Stein's message concerning the untenability of distinctions. Parallel fifths (as at the beginning of the *Symphony on a Hymn Tune*) tend to push the music backward into the world of medieval organum, something disestablished and primeval. Here, as in several other passages in the opera, elementary compositional "errors" act as a kind of punctuation: in this case, the parallel fifths and octaves mark the shift from St. Ignatius's set-piece aria to a more fluid musical discourse—in terms of the late-nineteenth-century opera that Thomson here parodies, they mark the shift from *pezzo* to *scena*.

Despite St. Chavez's pronouncement about never returning to distinctions, Thomson *will* return to tonal distinctions—but these distinctions are arbitrary, just as (to quote a favorite motto of Auden's) heaven's grace is arbitrary. Because of the key changes through this scene, we've heard by this point most of the major triads of the chromatic scale, triads that become increasingly destabilized by fast modulations and other shifty procedures. Heaven is the calm coexistence of all

EX. 12.5. Thomson, *Four Saints in Three Acts:* compositional "errors"

triads at the same time, without rank or precedence, without jostling for position; the dominant *seemed* to dominate, but its authority is fragile. Similarly, all tonics are local tonics; key changes are felt as changes but not as deviations, according to the opera's pan-diatonic method of construction. There's a short organ piece attributed to Bach, *Kleines harmonisches Labyrinth* (Little Harmonic Labyrinth), circumnavigating the circle of fifths; and *Four Saints in Three Acts* is a big harmonic labyrinth, in which the spectator is at all points equally lost, equally found.

Grosser's Scenario for Four Saints: Imposing Narrative on the Inenarrable

Stein and Thomson decided that *Four Saints in Three Acts* might benefit from having a story and a stage set. Thomson's companion, Maurice Grosser, provided the scenario, after both music and text were complete. Stein, of course, thought that a play could be defined as a literary act that is not a story, so no conceivable story could be appropriate. On the other hand, no conceivable story could be inappropriate: Stein's text is an open, denarratized field of words, incapable of resisting any story imposed on it. This explains her extreme equanimity concerning Grosser's scenario.

Grosser's hunt through the text for narrative cues is amusing to follow, and it is possible in places to admire his ingenuity. Stein provided him with two hints, concerning, as it happens, the two most elaborate scenes, both musically and textually: as Grosser noted in the preface to the 1948 vocal score, "The present scenario . . . is to a large extent my invention. . . . Gertrude Stein . . . did intend Saint Ignatius's aria *Pigeons on the Grass Alas* to represent a vision of the Holy Ghost and . . . *Letting Pin In Letting Let,* to represent a religious procession." Stein didn't specify the exact nature of this procession, but Grosser must have noted that Thomson's peculiarly fixed E-minor tonality, and the repeated word *dead,* lent a plausibly dark character to the scene; furthermore, he chose to interpret the word *sound* in the preceding scene (St. Ignatius sings "Once in a while and where and where around around is as a sound and around is a sound") as a reference to Gabriel's trumpet—he captioned this passage *St. Ignatius predicts the Last Judgment* (four bars before rehearsal figure 180). Putting these two observations together, Grosser had his scenario for the procession: "Saint Ignatius . . . predicts the Last Judgment. It gets dark. . . . Everyone is a little frightened. Men and women saints together form a devotional and expiatory procession." And Grosser was right: this is the only passage where the music seems, through sheer harmonic inertia, to suggest awe or majesty—even though, as we've seen, the music is based on the same sort of arithmetical tomfoolery as the rest of the opera.

In other parts of the opera, Grosser had to do a little more work. Sometimes the text or the music was so specific that it almost emitted its own scenario: for example, when Thomson wrote a tango, or when Stein wrote "How many windows and doors and floors are there in it" (Grosser took the latter as a *Vision of a Heavenly Mansion,* one bar after rehearsal figure 124, and had St. Plan enter with a telescope, passed around to other saints in order for them to inspect the mansion). Similarly, Stein's allusion to the photographs of the girl changing into a nun led Grosser to imagine a scene in which St. Settlement photographs St. Teresa II with a dove (rehearsal figure 37); and Stein's line "Leave later gaily the troubadour plays his guitar" inspired a scene in which St. Ignatius serenades St. Teresa II with a guitar (four bars after rehearsal figure 42). But sometimes Stein's text was so barren of visual elements that Grosser had to depend on a single word to generate a scene: for example, the word *nestle* (which Thomson set, invitingly, as a tiny duet of the two St. Teresas in tender thirds) was the flimsy pretext for a love scene between the Commère and Compère (two bars after rehearsal figure 109)—perhaps on the theory that every opera needs a love scene, even if it must be between two fringe figures, since saints can't be romantically attached. And sometimes Grosser had no help whatsoever from text or music, as in the opening of Act One, where Grosser instructs "Saint Teresa II is seated under a tree painting flowers on giant Easter eggs." Stein's text for this scene provides neither trees nor flowers nor eggs—only five thousand dead Chinamen, and a good deal of sitting and surrounding; and yet the homely harmlessness of painting Easter eggs, the evocation of a Christian ritual that's more aesthetic than sacred—more like a silly game than like an inquiry into the mysteries of the Resurrection—seems exactly right for the opera.

Grosser, born in Alabama, was a painter specializing in landscapes and still lifes, and he understood a scenario as a series of pictures—appropriately enough, given Stein's anti-narrative stance. His ideas for the scenario were often derived from old paintings and sculptures: as when St. Teresa II and St. Ignatius admire a model of a large house, the Heavenly Mansion (five bars after rehearsal figure 58); or when an angel stands over St. Teresa II and she "is shown in an attitude of ecstasy" (rehearsal figure 67). Grosser may have been thinking of Bernini's statue of St. Teresa in orgasmic swoon, the angel's dart in her breast; but Stein's text ("A scene and withers. Scene three and scene two. How can a sister see Saint Teresa suitably") and Thomson's spare, low-profile, wholly unecstatic music, all low bells with broken D-major scales in the vocal line, so contradict the scenario that I wonder whether Grosser made a mistake: the dissonance between the visual element and the other elements seems too strenuous for the smooth surfaces and untroubled concords of the opera. The historical Teresa and Ignatius have undergone considerable erosion in the course of becoming fined down into these nearly anonymous saints: St. Teresa possesses only the ghost of her old ecstasy, St. Ignatius only the ghost of his old militancy. (At one point Thomson thought Teresa and Ignatius should be given "fictitious names.") The opera has marches and dances, but no ferocity, no sharpness, no anticipation, no resolution.

But Grosser might have made a case that the audience needed to remember that Teresa of Avila was the most erotically intense of saints—"our Lord was pleased, that I should see an Angell. . . . His face was . . . inflamed . . . he had a long Dart of gold in his hand; and at the end of the iron below, me thought, there was a little fire; and I conceaued, that he thrust it, some seuerall times, through my verie Hart, after such a manner, as that it passed the verie inwards, of my Bowells." Perhaps we can only measure the pixilation of the St. Teresas in the opera ("Not April fool's day a pleasure . . . April fool's day as not as pleasure. . . . There are a great many persons and places near together" [after rehearsal figure 26]) against the background of the desperate frenzy of the historical Teresa's vision. The saltpeter, bleached, unstrung quality of the opera needs to register against some residue of vivid feeling.

Grosser set most of the opera in Barcelona or Avila—the places mentioned in the text—and he asked the background saints to do such innocuous Spanishy things as mending fishnets. But the brief last act was set in heaven, as the preface to the vocal score explains: "the Compère and Commère, in front of the house curtain, discuss whether there is to be a fourth act. When they finally agree, the curtain rises, revealing all the saints reassembled in heaven. They sing their happy memories of life on earth and join at the last in a hymn of communion, 'When this you see remember me.'" But the music and the text know what the scenario doesn't know, that the opera has been taking place in heaven all along—only dead people get to be saints. Thomson set the final "When this you see" chorus to the same music as the opening of the prologue: the last act isn't an ascent, or a fulfillment, or even a progression, for the saints have gone nowhere, accomplished nothing—as Stein said, her text is about not doing anything.

There is one fascinating difference, however, between the last page of the score and the first page: "When this you see" begins with the same melody, the same waltz-in-4/4-time, F and C^7, as the beginning; but soon we hear F-minor and Bb^7-minor chords taking their place, in the same pattern—and the last chord to be heard in the opera is F minor. It's as if there's a huge span, from F major to F minor, across the opera. But I regard this as a parody of grand tonal architecture. Thomson's joke is that the music seems just the same in the minor as in the major—the same tensionless pomp, the same easy self-display. Thomson has neutralized the distinction between major and minor, between dominant and subdominant: I and V (at the beginning) or i and iv (at the end), what does it matter? Thomson dismisses the great musical polarities with a shrug: both are equally celestial, equally all-meaning, equally unmeaning. What began in clunky alternations of tonic and dominant ends on a note of resolute cadencelessness, all spotlights glaring on the lack of conclusion. Thomson's music works down to the same sort of shimmering pointlessness as Stein's text. This is a different surrealism from that of *Les mariés de la Tour Eiffel* or *Les mamelles de Tirésias*: instead of a developed plane of textual meaning juxtaposed against a developed plane of musical meaning, so that the spectator can relish the dissonance between them, Stein and Thomson provide a double inconsequence. Neither text nor music is capable of putting up much resistance against one another; the music sags into a text that is itself one long sag. The text doesn't present salient features, doesn't develop, doesn't conclude—it just *is,* in the same way that an empty landscape just *is.* And Thomson's music is also more a being than a becoming, a state so rare in music that it's difficult to recognize it when we hear it. The musical setting is neither consonant nor dissonant with the text—except insofar as, in a state of pure asemiosis, one zero is consonant with another zero.

Stettheimer's Stage Set: The Knickknack Shelf Enlarged

What sort of stage set would be appropriate for such a theatre piece? The obvious answer is, Completely bare, since Stein thought of the piece as a featureless landscape. But there is another, equally attractive possibility: absurdly overfilled. Dante points out that heaven is a place where every itch is scratched; and sheer itchlessness, absence of desire, is so little known on earth that it's hard to imagine what it would look like, what it would sound like, except as something too static or too quick, too empty or too full. And, in the event, the stage designer chose the path of fullness, happy clutter.

Stein offered Thomson Picasso's services as set designer, but Thomson refused, for the odd reason that he wanted everyone associated with the opera, except Stein, to be approximately his own age. I consider it more likely that Thomson suspected that Picasso's "harsher and more calculated spontaneities" would clash with the opera's tone. For the première, in Hartford in 1934, the designer turned out to be Florine Stettheimer, whose sets, according to Thomson,

> are of a beauty incredible, with trees made out of feathers and a sea-wall at Barcelona made out of shells and for the procession a baldachino of black chiffon & branches of black ostrich plumes just like a Spanish funeral. St. Teresa comes to the picnic in the 2nd act on a cart drawn by a real white donkey & brings her tent with her and sets it up & sits in the doorway of it. It is made of white gauze with gold fringe and has a most elegant shape.

When Stein received this letter, she was especially taken with the idea of a real donkey—as if the opera were returning to the simple actualities of landscape that inspired it in the first place. But, of course, this manner of staging, far from evoking a landscape, suggested a complete unnaturalness; the donkey would have been tinselized, Disneyfied, in such surroundings. The décor, with its trees of feathers, walls of shells, chairs of glass beads, great cellophane cyclorama, and double arch composed of "balls of compressed cellophane" (all this cellophane ultimately caused some difficulty with fire inspectors), seems an apotheosis of the little kitschy knickknacks Stein collected, such as the miniature alabaster fountain with two white doves. It is a whole cellophane opera, a theatrical wraith, a flimsy and transparent artifice. Picasso could never have supplied the souvenir-stand *préciosité* that represented the arbitrary whimsy of a competent heaven, where there's nothing to do except keep rearranging the shelves.

The choice of singers also reflected Thomson's predilection for décor. After a visit to a Harlem nightclub, Thomson turned to a friend and said, " 'I think I'll have my operas sung by Negroes.' . . . I was sure, remembering how proudly the Negroes enunciate." But superior diction wasn't Thomson's only reason for this decision: he liked the look of "negro bodies" dancing around Stettheimer's maypole, "divined only vaguely through long dresses. The movements would be sedate and prim, and the transparence is aimed . . . not at titillating the audience . . . but at keeping the texture of the stage as light as possible." In other words, the singers would be *hommes-décor* and *femmes-décor*—I wonder if Thomson knew that the pantomime horse in Satie's *Parade* had originally been

FIG. 37. Florine Stettheimer, set for *Four Saints in Three Acts* in the form of a doll's house, 1934 (Henry McBride, *Florine Stettheimer* [New York: Museum of Modern Art, 1946], p. 30)

a Negro Manager, wearing a sandwich board and smoking a cigar, in Picasso's early sketches. Thomson was pleased with the cast he chose:

> The Negroes proved in every way rewarding. . . . They resisted not at all Stein's obscure language, adopted it for theirs, conversed in quotations from it. They moved, sang, spoke with grace and with alacrity, took on roles without self-consciousness, as if they were the saints they said they were. I often marveled at the miracle whereby slavery (and some cross-breeding) had turned them into Christians of an earlier stamp than ours, not analytical or self-pitying or romantic in the nineteenth-century sense, but robust, outgoing, and even in disaster sustained by inner joy, very much as Saint Teresa had been. . . . If [the lead singers] seemed less intensely Spanish and self-tortured than their prototypes, they were, as Baroque saints, in every way as grandly simple and convincing.

Today, one reads this passage with discomfort, for Thomson seems to be saying that the brainlessness of the singers made them suitable for representing a post-cerebral heaven, a cheerful and childlike playfulness extended to the end of time. Just as Thomson wrote music that attempted to divest itself of semantic coding, so he sought singers who brought no baggage of irony or doubt or nuance—merely healthy lips that pronounced the text with great care.

The début of *Four Saints in Three Acts* was the high point of Thomson's career: special railroad cars were assigned to take glittering New Yorkers to the

Hartford theatre. The only sadness was that during the years between the writing of the opera and its first performance, Stein and Thomson had quarreled: first because Thomson had intervened on behalf of his friend Georges Hugnet when Hugnet and Stein fought over the publishing of her English adaptations of his surrealistic poems, then because, after Thomson had grandly assigned half the profits of the opera to Stein, he'd thought better of it, and decided that his share ought to be greater than hers. It is striking that the collaborators in an opera about numerical sequences, an opera of counting games, should fall out over the arithmetic of money.

Thomson's Theory of Incidental Music

Thomson's later career was full of theatre work, including two other full-length operas: *The Mother of Us All* (1947), to a posthumous libretto by Stein concerning Susan B. Anthony, and *Lord Byron* (1972), to a libretto by Jack Larson—no second Stein, for (as Anthony Tommasini notes) his best-known contribution to American culture was to play the role of Jimmy Olsen, cub reporter, on the *Superman* television series of the 1950s. Thomson also wrote quantities of film music and incidental music to plays; John Cage, in his book on Thomson, remembered Thomson's procedures as follows:

> Explaining his theories about incidental music, Thomson stated that he is primarily concerned with making its function clear. To this end he asks himself first, "Who is the music?" Is it the author, requesting an emotional response to his characters or commenting on the action? Original music is then required. Is it God or fatality? If so, suspense music is indicated. Is it scenery or nature, requiring auditory décor? Something impressionistic would be best. Second, he asks himself, "What is the music?" Is it actor (a brass band going down the street), stage property (a lullaby or spinning song, for example), or the arch (the proscenium) through which the play is seen (curtain-raising drum rolls, fanfares, and finales)? Given a full-length play, Thomson may use all of the functions outlined, feeling no need for unity of view. He enjoys writing music as nature (weather music) and music as props, and he avoids whenever possible writing music as commentary.

This is a passage that suggests many of the qualities of Thomson's mind: logical, task-oriented, highly intelligent. It also suggests an attractive modesty and tact; in this way, as in many others, Thomson's master was Satie, as Thomson admitted:

> My simplicity was arrived at through an elaborate education. . . . I'm not a naive composer, you see, and neither was Satie. . . . He was a man looking for

clarity. . . . Satie warned Debussy against going all Wagnerian. He said, "Look out for this business of developing leitmotifs. Music should stay where it is, not follow the play. It should be like a decor. A property tree doesn't go into convulsion because an actor crosses the stage." (Laughs.)

Satie and Thomson both advocated a certain reticence, a certain propriety: the music should provide all the assistance it can, without calling attention to itself, without scene-stealing. This is, of course, exactly opposed to the music of the epic theatre as recommended by Brecht, in which the music explains, even under-cuts, the text. For Thomson, music assists the text not by reinforcing it, not by expressing it, not by calling it into question, but by providing a pleasant and commodious *environment* in which the words can achieve their maximum intel-ligibility. If this seems to place music in a hopelessly ancillary position, we must note that behind Satie and Thomson alike, there is a stubbornness, an insistence on the dignity of music. It is the dignity of a well-made piece of furniture, but it is still dignity.

Thomson saw the composer as an ideal tool, politic, deferential, meticulous, glad to be of use. *Four Saints in Three Acts* stands out from the rest of his career, because it was the first and only time he was presented with a long dramatic text that demanded that the composer do—nothing whatsoever. Even *The Mother of Us All* seemed to make demands: it wanted music suggestive of political rallies, or the etiquette of old-fashioned courting, or intimate valediction. *The Mother of Us All* has a distinctively Ivesian quality of articulate sound-reminiscence caught in reverberation, instead of the inarticulations of *Four Saints in Three Acts*. The earlier opera gave Thomson, by temperament a servant, a field of words that made no commands; and the music is one long *Largo al factotum* by a Figaro suddenly free to sing anything he pleases, sing *la*, sing *qua*.

Rossini boasted that he could set a laundry list. But the text of *Four Saints in Three Acts* has far less coherence, far less clarity, far less dramatic tension, than a laundry list. And so Thomson found a kind of default strategy for setting a text that didn't ask for weather music, or suspense music, or brass-band music, or anything else; a text in which the music was free to erect any sort of stage it chose. *Who* is music, in this condition of complete plasticity?—music is a singer en-gaged in voice-training.

Voice-Training Lessons, Again

Several passages in the opera are pure exercises in vocal control—warm-ups for the throat. An early example comes two bars before rehearsal figure 48, when the accompaniment plays a chord in E♭ major and St. Teresa I obligingly sings "She is to meet her" as an ascending perfect triad in E♭; four bars later, the

accompaniment plays an E-major chord, and she sings "Very many go out" as an ascending perfect triad in E; and so on, to F and F♯ and G. This sort of étude attracted Thomson for many reasons. First, it is a kind of limit point in the reduction of music to its naked elements—here is the music primer, scarcely even pretending to be an opera. Second, it is a pure pan-diatonicism, in that it assigns no privilege to any tonic: the singer begins at a note chosen arbitrarily, near the bottom of her range, and proceeds upward by semitones until she stops, not for any reason of music syntax, but only because her voice has run out of notes. Third, it is a semantic void: there is no expression of emotion, no subtlety of phrasing, only an attempt to instill an exact memory of pitch in the muscles of the larynx. In heaven, there is nothing to say, so singing becomes an exercise in singing for singing's sake. Heaven is a place like the Eastman School of Music, a conservatory of many mansions, each with its own hosanna.

At the beginning of this book, we studied musical hieroglyphics: strategies for intensifying a bit of music until it had a fixed, secure apprehension of meaning. An exercise in voice-training is the exact opposite of a hieroglyph: a bit of music secure in its meaninglessness. And here we have the last twist of the serpent's coil: the hieroglyph and the vocal étude may turn out to be the same. When Wagner imagined the locus of ultimate musical power in *Das Rheingold*, he heard an E♭-major triad: the diapason at the whole universe's floor. And when Thomson imagined St. Teresa I singing a phrase notable for its heavenly absence of meaning, its pure nonsensicality, he heard an E♭-major triad. In 1918 a German propagandist of radical art, Johannes Baader, wrote an invitation to Club Dada that claims, "People are angels and live in heaven. . . . Everything that people and all other bodies do and do not do is a diversion for heavenly amusement." And if all extremes in art, in life, really do converge, Baader must be right.

Notes

Introduction

6 "To say that a word has meaning": Wittgenstein, *Wittgenstein's Lectures / Cambridge 1930–32*, pp. 45, 59.

6 "Understanding a sentence is much more": Wittgenstein, *Philosophical Investigations*, #527.

9 "The wide naked opening": Lessing, *Laokoon*, ch. 2, p. 21.

9 "this essential difference": Ibid., ch. 15, pp. 114–15.

10 silent symphonies: Babbitt, *The New Laokoon*, p. 55.

10 concert of perfumes: Ibid., p. 182.

10 admires Mozart: Ibid., p. 230.

10 deplores Strauss: Ibid., p. 247.

10 "eleutheromaniacs": Ibid., p. 197.

11 "the sound beneath the note": Greenberg, *Collected Essays* 1, p. 31.

11 "Shelley . . . exalted poetry": Ibid., p. 26.

11 "Poetry subsists no longer": Ibid., p. 33.

11 "Painting and sculpture": Ibid., p. 25.

12 "To restore the identity": Ibid., p. 32.

12 "The history of avant-garde painting": Ibid., p. 34.

13 "the destruction of realistic": Ibid., p. 35.

13 "an art . . . is abstract": Ibid., p. 32.

13 "what is more abstract": Jarrell, in Williams, *Selected Poems*, p. xi.

14 opponent of kitsch: Adorno, *Philosophie der neuen Musik*, p. 17.

15 "Dramatic music . . . from Monteverdi": Ibid., p. 42.

15 "line . . . is never found": Greenberg, *Collected Essays* 1, pp. 34–35.

15 "The completely canny": Adorno, *Philosophie der neuen Musik*, p. 159.

15 "With Stravinsky there is": Ibid., p. 146.

16 thing pulled by wires: Ibid., p. 144.

16 "The effect-connection": Ibid., p. 182.

16 "a monad of conditioned reflexes": Ibid., p. 185.

16 "the decay of experience": Ibid., p. 179.

17 "the spatialization of music": Ibid., p. 176.

17 "The trick that defines": Ibid., p. 180.

17 moving in circles: Ibid., p. 181.

17 "The more dissonant the chord": Ibid., p. 60.

22 "because you can see their joints": Dube, *The Expressionists*, p. 181.

23 "Novalis often repeated": Weininger, *Geschlecht und Charakter*, pp. 333–34.

23 "Women have no existence": Ibid., pp. 388–89.

24 "pneumatic bliss": Eliot, "Whispers of Immortality," *Collected Poems*, p. 45.

25 "sexual love is founded upon spiritual hate": Yeats, *Letters*, p. 758.

25 "ultra-overstressed": *Hindemith-Jahrbuch* 1972/2: 191, cited in Giselher Schubert's notes to Wergo CD WER 60132-50.

27 "Art wants to stop": Mann, *Doktor Faustus*, p. 181.

30 "transform the rhythm of the steppes": T. S. Eliot, "London Letter," *The Dial*, Sept. 1921.

Chapter 1. Hieroglyph

39 "décor is primarily": Schouvaloff, *Theatre on Paper*, p. 227.

39 "the stone thus brought": Plotinus, Ennead 5, tractate 8, section 1, trans. MacKenna, printed in Hofstadter and Kuhns, eds., *Philosophies of Art and Beauty*.

40 "the wise of Egypt": Ibid., section 6.

40 According to Liselotte Dieckmann: Dieckmann, *Hieroglyphics*, p. 17.

40 things found in Eden: Ibid., pp. 22, 113.

41 "In vain did the Persians": Ege, *Pre-Alphabet Days*, p. 13.

41 Estienne: Dieckmann, *Hieroglyphics*, p. 57.

41 "a mute Hieroglyphick": Ibid., pp. 90–91.

41 "hieroglyph is so light": Ibid., p. 135.

46 plucking daisy petals: Goethe, *Faust*, l. 3181.

49 "hieroglyphical formula": Dieckmann, *Hieroglyphics*, pp. 183–84.

50 "Nach Süden wir ziehen": Ernest Newman, *The Life of Richard Wagner* 2, p. 240.

54 "next to the world": Wagner, *Gesammelte Schriften* 8, p. 152.

55 Leo Treitler has argued: in "Homer and Gregory: The Transmission of Epic Poetry and Plainchant," *Musical Quarterly* 60, no. 3 (1974): 333–73.

56 "When Debussy was new": Pound, *Ezra Pound and Music*, p. 71.

58 "the performers, musical and mimetic": Stravinsky and Craft, *Expositions and Developments*, p. 122.

58 Stravinsky admired Larionov's set: Stravinsky and Craft, *Conversations*, p. 99.

58 "who, alas, now plays the guzla?": Stravinsky and Craft, *Expositions and Developments*, p. 120. The *guzla* is a bowed instrument, unlike the *gusli*, which is plucked: see Karlinsky, in Pasler, ed., *Confronting Stravinsky*, p. 15. According to Taruskin, *Stravinsky and the Russian Traditions*, p. 1251, the error was by Ramuz and Craft, not Stravinsky.

58 "the colour contrasts": Garafola, *Diaghilev's Ballets Russes*, p. 85.

59 "No, no, it's not Vassilek": from an unpublished translation by Barbara Tedford.

59 "my text was too short": Stravinsky and Craft, *Expositions and Developments*, p. 119. Taruskin notes in *Stravinsky and the Russian Traditions*, p. 1245, that Stravinsky had misremembered.

59 "banal moral tale": Stravinsky and Craft, *Expositions and Developments*, p. 122.

62 "I had the mirage": Pound, *Ezra Pound and Music*, p. 372.

Chapter 2. Ideogram

63 But since the word *ab:* Ege, *Pre-Alphabet Days*, p. 20.

64 "A true noun": Fenollosa, *The Chinese Written Character*, pp. 10, 18, 19.

65 "no full sentence": Ibid., p. 11.

65 "Three years ago in Paris": Pound, *Ezra Pound and the Visual Arts*, pp. 203–5.

66 "The Jewel Stairs' Grievance" and note: Pound, *Personae*, p. 132.

Chapter 3. Noh

68 "an intellectual and emotional complex": Pound, *Literary Essays*, p. 4.

68 "to convey a novel": Schoenberg, *Style and Idea*, pp. 483–84.

68 "Papyrus": Pound, *Personae*, p. 112.

68 "the verbal and musical stresses": Taruskin, *Stravinsky and the Russian Traditions*, p. 840.

69 "I am often asked": Pound, *Ezra Pound and the Visual Arts*, p. 209.

70 "was the romance par excellence": Pound, *Translations*, p. 213.

71 "The Japanese would be truly grateful": Pound, *"Ezra Pound Speaking,"* p. 385.

71 Michio Ito, Ruth St. Denis: for much of this information concerning Ito, I am indebted to a University of Virginia Ph.D. dissertation by Judith White.

72 "the tragic image that has stirred": Yeats, *Essays and Introductions*, p. 224.

72 glorified marionette show: Ibid., pp. 223, 226.

72 "There never was anybody heard": Pound, *Translations*, p. 286.

75 "the dancing woman . . . *is not a woman who dances"*: Mallarmé, *Oeuvres complètes*, p. 304.

75 a six-part suite: Pound, *Translations*, p. 220.

77 "a playing upon a single metaphor": Yeats, *Essays and Introductions*, p. 234.

77 "When a text seems": Pound, *Translations*, p. 237.

77 what Fenollosa called sculptural: Ibid., p. 273.

78 a performance, conducted by Thomas Beecham: Gallup notes this in Pound, *Plays Modelled on the Noh*, p. 2.

78 "the ghost of youth / At the undertakers' ball": Eliot, *Inventions of the March Hare*, p. 17.

78 "One felt the man": Pound, *Ezra Pound and Music*, p. 64.

78 "Yet sometimes there's a torch": Yeats, *Variorum Plays*, p. 323.

79 Arthur Symons's essay on Wagner: Yeats, *Letters*, p. 460.

79 "Wagner's period more or less": Yeats, *W. B. Yeats and T. Sturge Moore*, p. 7.

79 no winged helmets: Sidnell, Mayhew, and Clark, *Druid Craft*, p. 191.

79 "Gaudier had been through Wales": Pound, *Gaudier-Brzeska*, p. 76.

79 "Your eyes . . .": Pound, *Plays Modelled on the Noh*, p. 36.

80 "Oh, there is too much": Ibid., p. 37.

80 "clinging tenuous ghost": Pound, *Personae*, p. 87.

81 winters from 1913 to 1916: see Longenbach's *Stone Cottage* for a fine account of the Sussex winters.

81 "Crossed fingers there": Yeats, *Variorum Plays*, p. 1003.

82 putrid: Ibid., p. 1310.

83 "Says the Japanese sentry": All citations for the Cantos are given in the text, at the end of the excerpt. The canto number is followed by a slash and the page number from Pound, *Cantos* (1995).

83 "the one truly Homeric passage": Pound, *"Ezra Pound Speaking,"* p. 385.

84 equivalent of the Noh play is the séance: Pound, *Translations*, p. 236.

85 "Janequin's concept takes a third life": Pound, *Guide to Kulchur*, p. 152.

85 "Janequin inherited": Pound, *Ezra Pound and Music*, p. 379.

85 "Qui lara qui lara ferely fy fy": booklet of Harmonica Mundi CD 901099 (1983), p. 19.

86 "ALL typographic disposition": Pound, *Selected Letters*, p. 322.

89 "The ferryman is waiting": Gishford, ed., *Tribute to Benjamin Britten*, p. 61.

89 "a totally new 'operatic' experience": London CD 421 858-2 (1989), p. 4.

90 "the bond of parenthood": Special Noh Committee, *The Noh Drama*, p. 150.

90 " 'O, birds of Miyako' ": Ibid., pp. 151–52; a footnote explains that "Miyako-bird is a poetic name for sea-gull." The quotation is from a ninth-century novel, *Ise monogatari*, by Narihira. For this and much other information, I'm indebted to William Malm's *Six Hidden Views of Japanese Music*, which makes a detailed comparison between Britten's music and the Japanese music for *Sumidagawa*.

92 "spirit unappeased and peregrine": Eliot, *Collected Poems*, p. 204.

92 "Is it a dream": Ibid., p. 134.

92 "The other side of the River": cited in Carpenter, *Benjamin Britten*, pp. 422, 628.

92 "one of the problems": Ibid., p. 423.

93 "Homer is my example": Yeats, *Poems*, p. 303.

93 "also to lares": Pound, *Pavannes and Divagations*, p. 97.

94 Keller's perspicacity: Carpenter, *Benjamin Britten*, pp. 315–16.

95 "There every lover": Yeats, *Variorum Plays*, p. 991.

96 "wind cry and water cry": Ibid., p. 89.

96 "There floats out there": Ibid., pp. 1060–61.

99 "involvement can be shattered": Graham, *Production Notes* for Curlew River, p. 3.

99 "She turns and throws": Ibid., p. 10.

99 "*N.B.* Throughout the work": Ibid., p. 15.

Chapter 4. Gestus

101 girls would be taught to walk: Nijinska, *Early Memoirs*, p. 451.

102 "At a gymnastic fête": Jaques-Dalcroze, *Eurhythmics Art and Education*, p. 41.

102 "a scale of gestures": Ibid., p. 33.

102 legato or staccato: Ibid., p. 74.

102 "Every man should have": Ibid., p. 58.

102 "Christianity broke the unity": Ibid., p. 188.

103 "'Sylvia takes flight'": Ibid., p. 207.

103 "This music will have to be": Ibid., pp. 44–45.

103 "the *mezzopiano*": Ibid., p. 187.

103 "Canons of lines": Ibid., pp. 76–77.

105 "The men in *Sacre* are primitive": Nijinska, *Early Memoirs*, p. 459.

105 "the dancers look to be": Pasler, in *Confronting Stravinsky*, p. 75.

106 "Nijinsky demonstrated": Nijinska, *Early Memoirs*, p. 460.

106 "wanted me to portray": Ibid., p. 461.

106 "The failure consisted": Cocteau, *Le coq et l'arlequin*, p. 65.

106 Stravinsky, however, made some choreographic: see Pasler, in *Confronting Stravinsky*, p. 79.

108 "Nijinsky has given": cited in Nijinska, *Early Memoirs*, p. 469.

109 "We know only very little": Lessing, *Hamburgische Dramaturgie*, pp. 19–20.

109 "Although the language of gesture": Rousseau, *Oeuvres complètes* 5, p. 376.

110 "Substitute a letter": Ibid., p. 377.

111 "prototype *[Urform]* of opera": Weill, *Ausgewählte Schriften*, p. 55.

111 "the task of music": Ibid., p. 41.

111 "Now, as you know": Ibid., p. 42.

112 "standing on the boundary": cited in Kowalke, *Kurt Weill in Europe*, p. 465. This book offers useful translations of most of Weill's writings on his music.

112 "in a new form": cited in Schebera, *Kurt Weill*, p. 133.

113 "Dies Bildnis": Weill, *Ausgewählte Schriften*, p. 42.

114 "Here a fundamental *gestus*": Ibid., p. 43.

114 "In my composition on the same text": Ibid., p. 44.

115 "the same *gestus*": Ibid., p. 43.

117 "whistled things to him": Morley, in Kowalke, ed., *A New Orpheus*, p. 189.

118 "Not so Egyptian": Schebera, *Kurt Weill*, p. 95.

119 "The opera that we have": Brecht, *Gesammelte Werke* 17, pp. 1006–7.

119 sugar . . . vinegar: Here I'm closely following Michael Morley's argument in his essay on *gestus* in Kim Kowalke's *A New Orpheus*.

119 "The invasion of the methods": Brecht, *Gesammelte Werke* 17, pp. 1010–11.

120 "as culinary as ever": Ibid., p. 1016.

120 "Pluck out the eye": Ibid., vol. 19, p. 398.

120 "Not every *gestus* is a social *gestus*": Ibid., vol. 15, p. 483.

121 "the appeal [of the *Zuhälter-Ballade*]": cited in Kim Kowalke, *The Opera Quarterly* 6, no. 3 (spring 1989): 30.

121 "every text I've set": Weill, *Speak Low*, p. 80.

121 "The tenderest and most intimate": Brecht, *Gesammelte Werke* 15, p. 474.

122 "the first surrealist opera": Adorno, in Kowalke, ed., *A New Orpheus*, p. 67.

122 "How distant I at first feel": Ibid., p. 66.

123 "when a character behaves": Brecht, *Brecht on Theatre*, p. 15. This book offers useful translations of many of Brecht's important essays on theatre.

123 "One should never start": cited in Fuegi, *Brecht and Company*, p. 567.

126 "Because a man never believes his own misery": Brecht, *Stücke*, p. 169.

126 "This miserable Brown": Ibid., p. 187.

128 "You are in the end": Goethe, *Faust*, ll. 1806–9.

128 "Of course I want Timbuktu": cited in Fuegi, *Brecht and Company*, p. 77.

128 "if the Chinese peasant": Auden, *The Dyer's Hand*, p. 328.

131 "musical picture-sheet": Weill, *Ausgewählte Schriften*, p. 60.

132 gestic music ought to be "naive": Ibid., p. 42.

133 "*chanson* and funeral march": cited in Schebera, *Kurt Weill*, p. 115.

134 "memorial tablets, epitaphs": Weill, *Ausgewählte Schriften*, p. 141.

135 photograms: for this discussion, I rely on a superb article by Reinhold Grimm, "Marxist Emblems: Bertolt Brecht's *War Primer*," *Comparative Literature Studies* 12, no. 3 (1975): 263–87.

135 "The communication / Of the dead": Eliot, *Collected Poems*, p. 201.

Chapter 5. Villonaud

138 "*Realistic* means: revealing": Brecht, *Gesammelte Werke* 19, p. 326.

139 "there is no there there": Stein, *Everybody's Autobiography*, p. 298.

140 *Nur wer in Wohlstand schwelgt:* I take this example from Daniel Frey's "Les Ballades de Villon et le *Dreigroschenoper*," *Études des Lettres* 4 (1961): 114–36.

140 militarist and anti-semite: Fuegi, *Brecht and Company*, p. 226.

141 "From decaying paper": Brecht, "Sonett zur Neuausgabe des François Villon," from *Gedichte*, p. 331.

142 (fade in church bell . . .): from Yale University YCAL 53, box 32, folder 738.

143 "Given the material means": Pound, *Selected Prose*, p. 53.

143 "Villon . . . represents": Pound, *ABC of Reading*, pp. 104–5.

144 "my two eyes have died": Synge, *Collected Works* 1, p. 80.

146 "in the sequence of the musical phrase": Pound, *Literary Essays*, p. 3.

146 "To break the pentameter": Pound, *Cantos* 81/518.

146 "there is vers libre": Pound, *Literary Essays,* pp. 12–13.

148 "had made a machine": Pound, *Polite Essays,* pp. 129–30.

148 "The HOLE point": Pound, *Selected Letters,* p. 245.

148 *Mr. Bloom and the Cyclops:* for the score, see *This Quarter (Antheil Musical Supplement)* 1, no. 2 (1925): 22–24. I owe this information to Paul Martin.

149 "Schoenberg has escaped": Butler, *Early Modernism,* p. 52.

149 as Carl Dahlhaus has noted: in *Schoenberg and the New Music,* p. 152.

150 "Wagner, in order to make": Schoenberg, *Style and Idea,* p. 129.

151 "next to the world": Wagner, *Gesammelte Schriften* 8, pp. 152–53.

152 following Adorno: Adorno, *Philosophie der neuen Musik,* p. 80.

152 chromatic saturation: Rosen, *Schoenberg,* pp. 43, 58.

154 "The first atonal works are session notes": Adorno, *Philosophie der neuen Musik,* p. 43. The "first book published on Schoenberg" is *Arnold Schönberg* (1912), ed. Alban Berg et al., reprinted in Hahl-Koch, ed., *Schoenberg,* p. 125.

155 "It is necessary that one always sees": Schoenberg, letter of 14 April 1930, *Briefe,* pp. 149, 151.

158 "I have a vague suspicion": cited in Carpenter, *A Serious Character,* p. 387.

158 "encouraged to tear up": Pound, *Selected Letters,* p. 167.

159 Yale University's Pound collection: the holograph of *Le testament* is YCAL MS 43, series V, box 126, folder 5081.

160 "ignorance having no further terrors": Pound, *Selected Letters,* p. 167.

163 "Certain sounds we accept": Pound, *Guide to Kulchur,* p. 73.

163 "The 60, 72": Ibid., pp. 233–34.

163 "the simplest consideration": *The Treatise on Harmony,* in Pound, *Ezra Pound and Music,* p. 296.

164 Cocteau's continual giggling: Steegmuller, *Cocteau,* p. 277.

166 "The strength of Picasso": Pound, *Ezra Pound and the Visual Arts,* p. 214.

166 "showing marvellous technique": Ibid., p. 178.

168 "the ghosts of dead loves everyone": Pound, *Personae,* p. 10.

168 "No man hath dared": Pound, *Collected Early Poems,* p. 71.

168 "It is probably the best": *Letters of Ezra Pound to Alice Corbin Henderson,* p. 224.

168 "AND my doin muzik": Pound, *Pound/Zukofsky,* p. 210.

Chapter 6. Noh, Again

170 "The main character in it is a boy": Weill, *Ausgewählte Schriften,* p. 68.

171 "I'd like no longer": Ibid., pp. 66–67.

172 "strict in simplicity": Ibid., p. 64.

172 "It can be played in the school": Ibid., pp. 68–69.

172 "The 'arguments against the verdict'": Brecht, *Gesammelte Werke* 17, p. 984.

173 "with masks, completely rigid": Weill, *Speak Low,* p. 62.

179 "Weill considered himself": *Frankfurter Rundschein,* 15 April 1950. For a fine discussion of this obituary, see David Drew's article in Kowalke, ed., *A New Orpheus.*

180 "The work of art!": Mann, *Doktor Faustus,* p. 181.

Chapter 7. Loop

187 a mermaid's tail: Rothschild, *Picasso's "Parade,"* p. 200.

188 blue leotard decorated with stars: Ibid., p. 16.

188 One of Cocteau's penises: Ibid., p. 82.

189 "At Country Fairs": trans. Steegmuller, cited in his *Cocteau,* p. 161.

190 "for an advertisement": Joyce, *Ulysses: A Critical and Synoptic Edition,* Episode 12, ll. 1147–48.

190 "Cocteau . . . suggested": Rothschild, *Picasso's "Parade,"* p. 91.

191 "You know, there's a need": cited in Gillmor, *Erik Satie,* p. 232.

192 "Everyone will tell you": cited in Myers, *Erik Satie,* p. 142.

193 "Look, a property tree": Cocteau, *Le coq et l'arlequin,* p. 28.

194 "A—WELL-INFORMED—MAN": Rothschild, *Picasso's "Parade,"* p. 77.

195 *"Ils lui crevèrent les yeux":* Ibid., p. 92.

195 "For most artists, a work wouldn't know": Cocteau, *Le coq et l'arlequin,* pp. 41–42.

196 "a masterpiece of architecture": Ibid., p. 40.

196 individual mini-stage: Stravinsky and Craft, *Dialogues,* p. 23.

Chapter 8. Cube

198 As Jeffrey Weiss has shown: in *The Popular Culture of Modern Art.*

198 Borges's imaginary country: in *Dreamtigers,* p. 90.

199 "IT IS A CRIME": Rothschild, *Picasso's "Parade,"* p. 80.

199 "O the most violent Paradise": Rimbaud, *Complete Works,* p. 224. I have not used Fowlie's translation.

201 "IF you want to be loved!": Rothschild, *Picasso's "Parade,"* p. 69.

201 "Bouillon des 3 dimensions": Weiss, *The Popular Culture of Modern Art,* p. 65.

201 Pikasso . . . Brak: Ibid., p. 203.

202 a piece called *David:* Steegmuller, *Cocteau,* p. 94.

203 "In the first version the Managers": Cocteau, *Le coq et l'arlequin,* p. 71.

203 "visual space": cited by William Rubin in Rubin, ed., *Cézanne,* pp. 169, 198.

203 "find oneself confronted with a sculpture": cited in Cooper, *The Cubist Epoch,* p. 33.

206 "is of such absolute purity": cited in the notes to Vox CDX 5107, pp. 9–10.

207 as Ornella Volta has noticed: cited in Rothschild, *Picasso's "Parade,"* p. 89.

208 "Contrary to what the public imagines": Cocteau, *Le coq et l'arlequin,* p. 73.

208 "The score of *Parade* ought to serve": Ibid., p. 37.

210 "The dominating sensation": cited in Tisdall and Bozzolla, *Futurism,* p. 43.

211 one surviving recording of the original *intonarumori:* Societi Nazionale del Gram-mofono R6919/20, reissued on Sub Rosa SUBCD 012-19—an extraordinary anthol-ogy of futurist sound-texts.

212 "PUT / YOUR / LEGS": Rothschild, *Picasso's "Parade,"* p. 92.

212 "Médrano—Orion—two biplanes": Ibid., pp. 83–85.

214 "To capture the breath": Marinetti, *Selected Writings,* p. 87.

215 "Discussion between a foot": Ibid., p. 136.

Chapter 9. Loop, Again

217 "at a performance of *Dr. Caligari*": Woolf, *Collected Essays* 2, p. 270.

217 "When I went to the film": Lawrence, "When I Went to the Film," *Complete Poems,* pp. 443–44.

218 "riding a horse, jumping": Rothschild, *Picasso's "Parade,"* p. 95.

219 "Opera is falsehood": Taruskin, *Stravinsky and the Russian Traditions,* p. 982.

219 "The little girl . . . vibrates": Cocteau, *Le coq et l'arlequin,* p. 73.

219 "One day they won't believe": Ibid., p. 41.

220 "Rise of the curtain": Häger, *Ballets Suédois,* p. 265.

222 "an unforgettable vision of Satie": Ibid., p. 264.

222 "As for Satie, the old master": Ibid.

224 "from a celebrated mazurka": Gillmor, *Erik Satie,* p. 161.

226 "I announced to the press": Antheil, *Bad Boy,* pp. 134–35.

226 "When I wrote the *Ballet Mécanique*": Whitesitt, *Life and Music of George Antheil,* p. 105.

227 "Strawinsky's merit lies": Pound, *Ezra Pound and Music,* p. 258.

228 "this sonata thinks": Ibid., p. 316.

228 "Musical moralists have damned": Pound, *Guide to Kulchur,* pp. 94–95.

229 "One must begin with hard musical objects": cited by Whitesitt in the notes to Troy CD 146.

229 "I personally consider": Whitesitt, *Life and Music of George Antheil,* pp. 105–6.

234 *Oh My Baby:* cited in notes to Musicmasters CD 01612-67094-2, p. 18.

235 "a gigantic Negro couple": Whitesitt, *Life and Music of George Antheil,* p. 33.

236 he couldn't remember: Antheil, *Bad Boy,* p. 139.

236 "My *Ballet Mécanique* is the first piece": Whitesitt, *Life and Music of George Antheil,* p. 104.

237 "My original title for the work": Antheil, *Bad Boy,* p. 139.

237 "The words 'Ballet Mécanique' were brutal": Ibid.

238 *"time itself acts as music":* Whitesitt, *Life and Music of George Antheil,* p. 105.

238 "the forms come out of the canvas": Ibid., p. 97.

239 "they could do something the theatre": Stein, *Everybody's Autobiography,* p. 291.

241 "tear from a passer-by": Eliot, *Collected Poems,* p. 19.

241 "What is man doing, when he is at a fair": Lawrence, *Women in Love,* p. 483.

241 "I had no idea": Antheil, *Bad Boy,* p. 140.

242 "Contrasting objects, slow and rapid passages": Whitesitt, *Life and Music of George Antheil,* p. 106.

242 "The idea of the human leg": Breton, *Oeuvres complètes* 1, p. 239.

242 "machines which are new arms": Whitesitt, *Life and Music of George Antheil,* p. 69.

243 "vortoscope": Pound, *Ezra Pound and the Visual Arts,* p. 241.

Chapter 10. Surrealism (Literature and Art)

244 "The cubist painter Picasso": Apollinaire, *Oeuvres en prose* 2, pp. 864–65.

246 "We're trying here": Apollinaire, *Les mamelles,* pp. 29–31.

249 "We [dadaists] are often told": Motherwell, *The Dada Painters,* p. 250.

249 "a microphone, thanks to which": Steegmuller, *Cocteau,* p. 213.

249 "In order to characterize": Apollinaire, *Les mamelles,* pp. 9–10.

251 "Because my woman is man": Ibid., p. 52.

252 "Zanzibar women are in a political phase": Ibid., p. 57.

252 "A great fire . . . Monsieur Picasso": Ibid., pp. 75–76.

252 "Know that fortune and glory": Ibid., p. 83.

253 "Fly away birds of my weakness": Ibid., pp. 87–88.

254 "the butter plate the situation": Ibid., p. 42.

254 "there could be no things": Beckett, *Three Novels,* p. 31.

255 "a little disappointing": Eliot, *Letters* 1, p. 470.

257 *Nature morte 'Au Bon Marché':* Francis Frascina carefully explains the sexual suggestiveness of this picture in Harrison, Frascina, and Perry, *Primitivism, Cubism, Abstraction: The Early Twentieth Century,* pp. 88ff.

258 *rhopalique,* to use the term of S. I. Lockerbie: in "Forme graphique et expressivité dans les calligrammes," *Que Vlo-Ve?* 9, nos. 29–30 (1981): 2.

259 "It doesn't matter *psychologically*": Apollinaire, *Les Soirées de Paris* 2, nos. 18–27: 383. Roger Shattuck discusses this interesting passage in *The Banquet Years,* p. 310.

264 "if people have tried": Apollinaire, *Oeuvres en prose* 2, pp. 976–77.

265 "You don't have to lug": Ibid., pp. 6, 8, 23, emphasis and gloss mine.

266 "cubism, which has after all": Ibid., p. 896.

266 "Doesn't the mediocrity": Breton, *Oeuvres complètes* 2, pp. 276–77.

268 "SURREALISM, n.": Ibid., vol. 1, p. 328.

268 *conscious* before *aesthetic:* Ibid., p. 116.

268 "The idea of a bed of stone": Ibid., vol. 2, p. 278.

268 "But do such fish exist?": Beckett, *Watt,* p. 120.

268 "The God that dwells within us": Breton, *Oeuvres complètes* 2, p. 278.

268 "A tomato is also": Ibid., p. 301.

269 "two leaves of the same tree": Ibid., p. 273.

269 "the universe resembles nothing": Stich, *Anxious Visions*, p. 31.

269 "here I come again": Beckett, *Stories and Texts for Nothing*, p. 128.

269 Reverdy's principle: Breton, *Signe ascendant*, pp. 10–12.

269 "The strongest surrealist image": Breton, *Oeuvres complètes* 2, p. 816.

270 "Leonardo da Vinci recommended": Ibid., p. 377.

271 "He is as beautiful as the retractability": Lautréamont, *Oeuvres complètes*, pp. 224–25.

272 "Here the inanimate so closely touches": Breton, *Oeuvres complètes* 2, p. 681.

272 opposites are not perceived as contradictions: Ibid., p. 846.

272 "I always hold": Ibid., p. 389.

273 *"knocked at the window"*: Ibid., vol. 1, pp. 324–35.

274 "The completely shrewd, illusionless *I*": Adorno, *Philosophie der neuen Musik*, p. 159.

274 "the simplest surrealist act": Breton, *Oeuvres complètes* 1, p. 783.

Chapter 11. Surrealism (Music)

276 "If only a few writers": Breton, *La clé des champs*, p. 77.

276 "Je sculpte en rêve": Disques Montaignes CD TCE 8760, p. 23.

277 "like the Salomé": Milhaud, *Notes without Music*, p. 102.

277 "*Parade* still had a literary content": cited in Steegmuller, *Cocteau*, pp. 241–42.

277 "he cuts off his head and bows": Rothschild, *Picasso's "Parade,"* p. 91.

277 sequel to his *Salomé:* Ellmann, *Oscar Wilde*, pp. 342–43.

280 "postcards of Paris": Cocteau, *Les mariés*, p. 360.

280 "The poet must extricate": Ibid., p. 354.

280 Larousse dictionary: Häger, *Ballets Suédois*, p. 150.

280 "crossing regiments": Cocteau, *Les mariés*, p. 361.

282 "Alas! I tremble each time": Ibid., p. 368.

282 the epigraph for the whole spectacle: Ibid., p. 353.

283 "We have seen you confront": Ibid., p. 375.

283 "a little like the Mona Lisa": Ibid., pp. 377–78.

284 "a number of frail girls": Pynchon, *The Crying of Lot 49*, p. 10.

285 "a boring thesis about repopulation": Cocteau, *Les mariés*, p. 357.

286 "black as ink": Ibid.

286 "In the *Funeral March*": Ibid., p. 361.

287 "M. Poulenc, 'advanced'": Maurice Brillat, cited by Taruskin in *Stravinsky and the Russian Traditions*, p. 1595.

289 "musical erratum" to *The Bride Stripped Bare:* a recording exists, on Sub Rosa SUBCD 012-19.

289 what Stravinsky, in *Petrushka:* Cocteau, *Les mariés*, p. 354.

291   music cannot lie: Auden, *Secondary Worlds,* p. 91.

291   "In my music, you hear": Poulenc, *Entretiens,* pp. 180–81.

292   Taruskin notes that the first of the *Pribaoutki:* in *Stravinsky and the Russian Traditions,* p. 1168.

292   played both passages on the radio: Poulenc, *Entretiens,* p. 55.

293   "to create a vocal style": cited in Roger Nichols's notes to *Virgin Classics* 7 59236 2, p. 11.

293   a self-portrait of Max Jacob: Poulenc, *Entretiens,* p. 140.

293   "a sort of carnival from Nogent": Ibid., p. 142.

297   "in an atmosphere": Ibid., p. 148.

298   "I've substituted Monte Carlo": Ibid.

298   "I'm always suspicious": Ibid., p. 150.

298   "operetta amuses me": Ibid., pp. 151–52.

299   "People have often asked me": Ibid., p. 144.

299   "Wooden prop": Breton, *Oeuvres complètes* 2, p. 790.

299   "I only had to follow Apollinaire's": Poulenc, *Entretiens,* pp. 146–47.

300   "The ariettas should have": trans. R. G. Pauly, in Strunk, *Source Readings in Music History,* pp. 522–23, 526–27.

303   "I consider *Les mamelles*": Poulenc, *Entretiens,* pp. 143, 151.

304   "The greatest incongruity": Schoenberg, *Style and Idea,* p. 146.

307   the word *Paris,* cropping up: Poulenc, 'Echo and Source,' p. 142.

Chapter 12. Heaven

315   "Gertrude Stein never had subconscious": Stein, *Selected Writings,* p. 74.

315   "Music she cared for": Ibid., p. 70.

315   "I write with my eyes": Haas, *Gertrude Stein A Primer,* p. 31.

315   "Surrealism never did interest": Stein, *Everybody's Autobiography,* p. 31.

315   "like a pleasant": Stein, *Selected Writings,* p. 185.

316   "There are then two kinds": Stein, *Stein Reader,* pp. 51–52.

317   "she had been interested": Stein, *Selected Writings,* p. 112.

317   "A DOG": Ibid., p. 474.

317   "an effort to describe": Thomson, *Thomson Reader,* p. 548.

317   "It was my first conscious": Haas, *Gertrude Stein A Primer,* p. 63.

318   "A little monkey goes": Ibid., p. 24.

318   "A little called anything": Ibid.

318   "in Tender Buttons": Stein, *Lectures in America,* p. 242.

318   "Cézanne conceived the idea": Haas, *Gertrude Stein A Primer,* p. 15.

319   "The apples looked like apples": Stein, *Lectures in America,* pp. 76–77.

319   "réalisation sur nature": cited by Lawrence Gowing in Rubin, ed., *Cézanne,* p. 63.

319   "I say it again more and more": Stein, *Lectures in America,* pp. 210–13.

320 "Suppose, to suppose": Stein, *Selected Writings,* p. 440.

320 "I know the difference": Ibid., pp. 436–37.

321 "I wish he would explain": Byron, *Don Juan,* "Dedication" 2.8.

321 "Shakespeare, dispensing": Shaw, *Music in London* 2, p. 338.

322 "I like to improvise": Stein, *Everybody's Autobiography,* p. 26.

322 "a Satie enthusiast": Stein, *Stein Reader,* p. 160.

322 "For before let it before": Stein, *Bee Time Vine,* p. 254.

323 "Night is different from bright": Stein, *Stein Reader,* p. 477.

323 "There is no difference between a white carnation": Stein, *Selected Writings,* p. 519.

323 "Water does not resemble water": Stein, *Bee Time Vine,* p. 20.

323 "Another man, a don": Stein, *Selected Writings,* p. 221.

323 "There is the likeliness": Ibid., p. 528.

323 "To be liking liked": Stein, *Stein Reader,* p. 514.

324 "every time one of the hundreds": Stein, *Lectures in America,* pp. 167, 177.

324 "Gertrude knows that everything": letter to Mabel Weeks, cited in Souhami, *Gertrude and Alice,* p. 113.

325 "Would he like it would Napoleon": Stein, *Lectures in America,* pp. 81–82.

325 "Strauss' Electra": Ibid., pp. 117–19.

325 "the essence of what happened": Ibid., p. 119.

326 "*Marius.* I am very pleased": Stein, *Stein Reader,* p. 403.

326 "I found that since the landscape": Stein, *Lectures in America,* p. 122.

327 "almost always in syncopated": Ibid., p. 93.

327 "The business of Art": Ibid., pp. 104–5.

327 "Bravig Imbs": Thomson, *Thomson Reader,* p. 70.

328 "there can only be religion": Stein, *Everybody's Autobiography,* pp. 111–12.

328 "nothing was happening": Ibid., p. 292.

329 "Willows a grammar": Stein, *How to Write,* p. 89.

330 "I am a grammarian": Ibid., p. 105.

330 "Grammar. In a breath": Ibid., p. 69.

330 "Grammar an angel": Ibid., p. 50.

330 "Saint Ignatius might be very well": Stein, *Selected Writings,* p. 594.

331 "Saint Therese with the land": Ibid., p. 593.

331 "Letting pin in letting let": Ibid., p. 609.

331 "rose is a nose": Stein, *Bee Time Vine,* p. 14.

332 "A narrative of prepare for saints": Stein, *Selected Writings,* pp. 581, 584.

332 "Saint Therese could be photographed": Ibid., p. 588.

333 "In Four Saints I made the Saints": Stein, *Lectures in America,* pp. 128–31.

334 "too photographic a copy": Stein, *Selected Writings,* p. 85.

334 "The wandering line of Masson": Stein, *Everybody's Autobiography,* p. 197.

335 "Saint Therese seated and not surrounded": Stein, *Selected Writings,* pp. 587, 588, 590.

335 he set the stage directions: Thomson, *Virgil Thomson,* p. 106.

336 "inhabit lax": Milton, *Paradise Lost* 7.162.

336 "How many saints can remember": Stein, *Selected Writings,* p. 590.

336 "One two three four": Ibid., p. 594.

336 *To Virgil and Eugene:* Stein, *Painted Lace,* p. 311.

337 "There is no difference between men": Stein, *Everybody's Autobiography,* p. 124.

337 "If it were possible to kill five thousand": Stein, *Selected Writings,* p. 586.

337 "liked to think of the number of angels": Stein, *Everybody's Autobiography,* p. 92.

337 "Is there a difference between a sound": Stein, *Selected Writings,* p. 591.

338 "Saint Therese can know the difference between singing": Ibid., p. 593.

338 "Was Saint Ignatius able to tell the difference": Ibid., p. 594.

338 "Never to return to distinctions": Ibid., p. 605.

338 "He asked for a distant magpie": Ibid.

338 "There is a difference between Barcelona": Ibid., p. 607.

338 "Pigeons in the grass alas": Ibid., p. 604.

338 "The pigeon on the grass and alas": Ibid., p. 605.

338 "Chickens made of glass. Alas": Stein, *Stein Reader,* p. 370.

338 "The pseudo Dionysius": Pound, *Literary Essays,* p. 185.

339 "we gave up history": Thomson, *Virgil Thomson,* p. 91.

339 "she didn't care whether": cited in Souhami, *Gertrude and Alice,* p. 64.

339 "got on like Harvard men": Thomson, *Virgil Thomson,* p. 89.

340 "I like its looks immensely": Ibid., p. 90.

340 "some saint or sibyl": Thomson, *Thomson Reader,* p. 69.

340 "My hope in putting Gertrude Stein": Thomson, *Virgil Thomson,* p. 90.

340 "musical abstractions only": Thomson, *Music with Words,* p. 85.

341 "Not a sacred work": Thomson, *Selected Letters,* p. 82.

341 "At last a table": Ibid.

341 "wondered whether a piece": Thomson, *Virgil Thomson,* p. 105.

341 "With the text on my piano's": Ibid., p. 104.

341 "an enlightenment": Ibid., p. 124, my emphasis.

342 "Nothing but a huge slimy serpent": Lawrence, *Psychoanalysis and the Unconscious,* p. 5.

342 "I got myself into a lovely little": Thomson, *Thomson Reader,* p. 548.

343 "Now the *Four Saints* accompaniment": Thomson, *Virgil Thomson,* p. 106.

344 "To know to know to love her so": Stein, *Selected Writings,* p. 581.

346 "With its doubtful intonation": cited in Taruskin, *Stravinsky and the Russian Traditions,* p. 734.

346 "Her tunes & her rhythms": Thomson, *Virgil Thomson,* p. 121.

346 after the first three movements of *Symphony on a Hymn Tune:* see Tommasini, *Virgil Thomson: Composer on the Aisle,* p. 154.

347 "Its continuity is not that of narrative": Cage, in Hoover and Cage, *Virgil Thomson: His Life and Music*, pp. 154–55.

356 "fictitious names": Thomson, *Selected Letters*, p. 77.

356 "our Lord was pleased": a seventeenth-century translation of St. Teresa's *The Flaming Heart*, cited in Louis L. Martz, *The Meditative Poem*, p. 544.

357 every itch is scratched: Dante, *Paradiso* 17.129.

358 approximately his own age: Thomson, *Virgil Thomson*, p. 99.

358 "harsher and more calculated spontaneities": Ibid., p. 92.

358 "are of a beauty incredible": Thomson, *Selected Letters*, p. 113.

358 real donkey: Thomson, *Virgil Thomson*, p. 231.

358 "balls of compressed cellophane": Tyler, *Florine Stettheimer*, p. 65.

358 "I think I'll have my operas sung by Negroes": Thomson, *Virgil Thomson*, p. 217.

358 "divined only vaguely": Ibid., pp. 230–31.

359 "The Negroes proved in every way": Ibid., p. 239.

360 as Anthony Tommasini notes: in *Virgil Thomson: Composer on the Aisle*, p. 477.

360 "Explaining his theories": Hoover and Cage, *Virgil Thomson: His Life and Music*, pp. 233–34.

360 "My simplicity was arrived at": Thomson, *Thomson Reader*, p. 528.

363 "People are angels": Huelsenbeck, ed., *The Dada Almanac*, p. 136.

Works Cited

Adorno, Theodor W. *Philosophie der neuen Musik*. Frankfurt: Europäische Verlagsanstalt, 1966.

Antheil, George. *Bad Boy of Music*. Hollywood: Samuel French, 1990.

Apollinaire, Guillaume. *Les mamelles de Tirésias / Avec six portraits inédits par Picasso*. Paris: Éditions du Bélier, 1946.

———. *Oeuvres en prose complètes*. Paris: Éditions Gallimard, 1991.

———. *Oeuvres poétiques*. Edited by Marcel Adéma and Michel Décaudin. Paris: Librairie Gallimard, 1956.

———. *Les Soirées de Paris*. Vol. 2, nos. 18–27. Geneva: Slatkine Reprints, 1971.

Auden, W. H. *The Dyer's Hand and Other Essays*. New York: Random House, 1962.

———. *Secondary Worlds*. New York: Random House, 1968.

Babbitt, Irving. *The New Laokoon: An Essay on the Confusion of the Arts*. Boston: Houghton Mifflin Company, ca. 1910.

Beckett, Samuel. *Stories and Texts for Nothing*. New York: Grove Press, 1967.

———. *Three Novels*. New York: Grove Press, 1965.

———. *Watt*. New York: Grove Press, 1953.

Borges, Jorge Luis. *Dreamtigers [El Hacedor]*. Translated by Mildred Boyer and Harold Morland. New York: E. P. Dutton, 1970.

Brecht, Bertolt. *Brecht on Brecht*. Edited and translated by John Willett. New York: Hill and Wang, 1964.

———. *Die Gedichte von Bertolt Brecht in einem Band*. Frankfurt: Suhrkamp Verlag, 1993.

———. *Gesammelte Werke*. Frankfurt: Suhrkamp Verlag, 1967.

———. *Die Stücke von Bertolt Brecht in einem Band*. Frankfurt: Suhrkamp Verlag, 1992.

Breton, André. *La clé des champs*. Paris: Éditions du Sagittaire, 1953.

———. *Oeuvres complètes*. Édition établie par Marguerite Bonnet. Paris: Éditions Gallimard, 1988.

———. *Signe ascendant*. Paris: Éditions Gallimard, 1968.

Butler, Christopher. *Early Modernism: Literature, Music, and Painting in Europe, 1900–1916*. Oxford: Clarendon Press, 1994.

Carpenter, Humphrey. *Benjamin Britten: A Biography*. New York: Charles Scribner's Sons, 1992.

———. *A Serious Character: The Life of Ezra Pound*. New York: Dell Publishing, 1990.

Cocteau, Jean. *Le coq et l'arlequin.—Notes autour de la musique / Avec un portrait de l'auteur et deux monogrammes par P. Picasso*. Paris: Éditions de la Sirène, 1918.

————. *Les mariés de la Tour Eiffel*. Les Oeuvres Libres, vol. 21. Paris, 1923.

Cooper, Douglas. *The Cubist Epoch*. London: Phaidon Press, 1970.

Dahlhaus, Carl. *Schoenberg and the New Music*. Translated by Derrick Puffett and Alfred Clayton. Cambridge: Cambridge University Press, 1990.

Dieckmann, Liselotte. *Hieroglyphics: The History of a Literary Symbol*. St. Louis: Washington University Press, 1970.

Dube, Wolf-Dieter. *The Expressionists*. New York: Thames and Hudson, 1985.

Ege, Otto F. *Pre-Alphabet Days*. Baltimore: Norman T. A. Munder and Company, 1923.

Eliot, T. S. *Collected Poems, 1909–1962*. New York: Harcourt, Brace and World, 1963.

————. *Inventions of the March Hare: Poems, 1909–1917*. Edited by Christopher Ricks. New York: Harcourt, Brace and Company, 1996.

————. *The Letters of T.S. Eliot*. Vol. 1, 1898–1922, edited by Valerie Eliot. San Diego: Harcourt Brace Jovanovich, 1988.

Ellmann, Richard. *Oscar Wilde*. New York: Alfred A. Knopf, 1988.

Fenollosa, Ernest. *The Chinese Written Character as a Medium for Poetry*. San Francisco: City Lights Books, 1969.

Fuegi, John. *Brecht and Company: Sex, Politics, and the Making of the Modern Drama*. New York: Grove Press, 1994.

Garafola, Lynn. *Diaghilev's Ballets Russes*. Oxford: Oxford University Press, 1992.

Gillmor, Alan M. *Erik Satie*. New York: W. W. Norton and Company, 1988.

Gishford, Anthony, ed. *Tribute to Benjamin Britten on His Fiftieth Birthday*. London: Faber and Faber, 1963.

Goethe, Johann Wolfgang von. *Faust*. Edited by R-M. S. Heffner et al. Boston: D. C. Heath and Company, 1954.

Greenberg, Clement. *The Collected Essays and Criticism*. Vol. 1, edited by John O'Brien. Chicago: University of Chicago Press, 1986.

Haas, Robert Bartlett, ed. *Gertrude Stein A Primer for the Gradual Understanding of Gertrude Stein*. Los Angeles: Black Sparrow Press, 1971.

Häger, Bengt. *Ballets Suédois* Translated by Ruth Sharman. New York: Harry N. Abrams, 1990.

Hahl-Koch, Jelena. *Arnold Schoenberg / Wassily Kandinsky / Letters, Pictures, and Documents*. Translated by John C. Crawford. London: Faber and Faber, 1986.

Harrison, Charles, Francis Frascina, and Gill Perry. *Primitivism, Cubism, Abstraction: The Early Twentieth Century*. New Haven: Yale University Press, 1993.

Hofstadter, Albert, and Richard Kuhns, eds. *Philosophies of Art and Beauty: Selected Readings in Aesthetics from Plato to Heidegger*. New York: Tile Modern Library, 1964.

Hoover, Kathleen, and John Cage. *Virgil Thomson: His Life and Music*. New York: Thomas Yoseloff, 1959.

Huelsenbeck, Richard, ed. *The Dada Almanac*. Translated by Malcolm Green. Channel Islands: The Guernsey Press, 1993.

Institute of Contemporary Art. *Art and Dance: Images of the Modern Dialogue, 1890–1980*. Boston: Institute of Contemporary Art, 1982.

Jaques-Dalcroze, E. *Eurhythmics Art and Education*. Translated by Frederick Rothwell; edited by Cynthia Cox. London: Chatto and Windus, 1930.

Joyce, James. *Ulysses: A Critical and Synoptic Edition.* Edited by Hans Walter Gabler et al. New York: Garland Publishing, 1986.

Kosinski, Dorothy, ed. *Fernand Léger, 1911–1924: The Rhythm of Modern Life.* New York: Prestel, 1994.

Kowalke, Kim H. *Kurt Weill in Europe.* Ann Arbor: UMI Research Press, 1979.

———, ed. *A New Orpheus: Essays on Kurt Weill.* New Haven: Yale University Press, 1986.

Lautréamont, Comte de [Isidore Ducasse]. *Oeuvres complètes.* Paris: Gallimard, 1938.

Lawrence, D. H. *The Complete Poems of D. H. Lawrence.* Edited by Vivian de Sola Pinto and Warren Roberts. New York: Viking Press, 1964.

———. *Psychoanalysis and the Unconscious and Fantasia of the Unconscious.* New York: Viking Press, 1960.

———. *Women in Love.* New York: Modern Library, 1950.

Lessing, Gotthold Ephraim. *Hamburgische Dramaturgie.* Edited by Otto Mann. Stuttgart: A. Kroner, ca. 1963.

———. *Lessing's Laokoon.* Edited by A. Hamann. Oxford: Oxford at the Clarendon Press, 1901.

Longenbach, James. *Stone Cottage: Pound, Yeats, and Modernism.* New York: Oxford University Press, 1988.

Mallarmé, Stéphane. *Oeuvres complètes.* Tours: Bibliothèque de la Pléiade, Éditions Gallimard, 1950.

Malm, William P. *Six Hidden Views of Japanese Music.* Berkeley and Los Angeles: University of California Press, 1986.

Mann, Thomas. *Doktor Faustus: Das Leben des deutschen Tonsetzers Adrian Leverkühn erzählt von einem Freunde.* Frankfurt: Fischer Taschenbuch Verlag, 1973.

Marinetti, Filippo Tommaso. *Selected Writings.* Edited and translated by R. W. Flint and Arthur A. Coppotelli. New York: Farrar, Straus and Giroux, 1972.

Martz, Louis L. *The Meditative Poem: An Anthology of Seventeenth-Century Verse.* New York: New York University Press, 1963.

Milhaud, Darius. *Notes without Music: An Autobiography.* New York: Alfred A. Knopf, 1953.

Motherwell, Robert, ed. *The Dada Painters and Poets: An Anthology.* 2d ed. Cambridge: The Belknap Press of Harvard University Press, 1981.

Myers, Rollo H. *Erik Satie.* New York: Dover Publications, 1968.

Newman, Ernest. *The Life of Richard Wagner.* Vol. 2, 1848–1860. New York: Alfred A. Knopf, 1937.

Nijinska, Bronislava. *Early Memoirs.* Translated and edited by Irina Nijinska and Jean Rawlinson. Durham: Duke University Press, 1992.

Pasler, Jann, ed. *Confronting Stravinsky: Man, Musician, and Modernist.* Berkeley and Los Angeles: University of California Press, 1986.

Poulenc, Francis. *'Echo and Source': Selected Correspondence, 1915–1963.* Translated and edited by Sidney Buckland. London: Victor Gollancz, 1991.

———. *Entretiens avec Claude Rostand.* Paris: René Juilliard, 1954.

Pound, Ezra. *ABC of Reading.* New York: New Directions, 1960.

———. *The Cantos of Ezra Pound.* New York: New Directions, 1995.

———. *Collected Early Poems of Ezra Pound.* Edited by Michael John King, with an introduction by Louis L. Martz. New York: New Directions, 1976.

———. *Ezra Pound and Music.* Edited by R. Murray Schafer. New York: New Directions, 1977.

———. *Ezra Pound and the Visual Arts.* Edited by Harriet Zinnes. New York: New Directions, 1980.

———. *"Ezra Pound Speaking": Radio Speeches of World War II.* Edited by Leonard Doob. Westport, Conn.: Greenwood Press, 1978.

———. *Gaudier-Brzeska: A Memoir.* New York: New Directions, 1970.

———. *Guide to Kulchur.* New York: New Directions, 1970.

———. *The Letters of Ezra Pound to Alice Corbin Henderson.* Edited by Ira B. Nadel. Austin: University of Texas Press, 1993.

———. *Literary Essays of Ezra Pound.* Edited by T. S. Eliot. New York: New Directions, 1968.

———. *Pavannes and Divagations.* New York: New Directions, 1958.

———. *Personae: The Collected Shorter Poems of Ezra Pound.* New York: New Directions, 1926.

———. *Plays Modelled on the Noh (1916).* Edited by Donald C. Gallup. Toledo: Friends of the University of Toledo Libraries, 1987.

———. *Polite Essays.* London: Faber and Faber, 1937.

———. *Pound/Zukofsky: Selected Letters of Ezra Pound and Louis Zukofsky.* Edited by Barry Ahearn. New York: New Directions, 1987.

———. *The Selected Letters of Ezra Pound, 1907–1941.* Edited by D. D. Paige. New York: New Directions, 1971.

———. *Selected Prose, 1909–1965.* Edited by William Cookson. New York: New Directions, 1973.

———. *Translations.* With an introduction by Hugh Kenner. New York: New Directions, 1963.

Pynchon, Thomas. *The Crying of Lot 49.* New York: Bantam Books, 1967.

Rapée, Erno. *Motion Picture Moods for Pianists and Organists.* New York: Arno Press, 1974.

Rimbaud, Arthur. *Rimbaud: Complete Works, Selected Letters / French-English.* Translated by Wallace Fowlie. Chicago: University of Chicago Press, 1966.

Rosen, Charles. *Arnold Schoenberg.* New York: Viking Press, 1975.

Rothschild, Deborah Menaker. *Picasso's "Parade": From Street to Stage.* London: Sotheby's Publications, 1991.

Rousseau, Jean-Jacques. *Oeuvres complètes.* Vol. 5, *Écrits sur la musique, la langue et le théâtre.* Paris: Gallimard, 1995.

Rubin, William, ed. *Cézanne: The Late Work.* New York: Museum of Modern Art, 1977.

Schebera, Jürgen. *Kurt Weill: An Illustrated Life.* Translated by Caroline Murphy. New Haven: Yale University Press, 1995.

Schoenberg, Arnold. *Briefe / Ausgewählt und herausgegeben von Erwin Stein.* Mainz: B. Schott's Söhne, 1958.

———. *Style and Idea: Selected Writings of Arnold Schoenberg.* Edited by Leonard Stein;

translated by Leo Black. Berkeley and Los Angeles: University of California Press, 1984.

Schouvaloff, Alexander. *Theatre on Paper*. London: Sotheby's Publications, 1990.

Sekine, Masaru, and Christopher Murray. *Yeats and the Noh: A Comparative Study*. Gerrards Cross, England: Colin Smythe, 1990.

Shattuck, Roger. *The Banquet Years: The Origins of the Avant Garde in France*. New York: Vintage Books, 1968.

Shaw, George Bernard. *Music in London, 1890–94: Criticism Contributed Week by Week to the World*, vol. 2. Vol. 27 of *Major Critical Essays*. New York: Wm. H. Wise and Company, 1931.

Sidnell, Michael J., George P. Mayhew, and David R. Clark. *Druid Craft: The Writing of "The Shadowy Waters."* Amherst: University of Massachusetts Press, 1971.

Souhami, Diana. *Gertrude and Alice*. San Francisco: Pandora, 1991.

Special Noh Committee. *The Noh Drama: Ten Plays from the Japanese Selected and Translated by the Special Noh Committee, Japanese Translation Committee, Nippon Gakujutsi Shinkōkai*. Rutland, Vt.: Charles E. Tuttle Company, 1955.

Steegmuller, Francis. *Cocteau: A Biography*. Boston: Nonpareil Books, 1986.

Stein, Gertrude. *Bee Time Vine and Other Pieces [1913–1927]*. New Haven: Yale University Press, 1953.

———. *Everybody's Autobiography*. Cambridge: Exact Change, 1993.

———. *How to Write*. New York: Dover Publications, 1975.

———. *Lectures in America*. New York: Vintage Books, 1975.

———. *Painted Lace and Other Pieces [1914–1937]*. New Haven: Yale University Press, 1955.

———. *Selected Writings of Gertrude Stein*. Edited by Carl van Vechten. New York: Vintage Books, 1990.

———. *A Stein Reader*. Edited by Ulla E. Dydo. Evanston, Ill.: Northwestern University Press, 1993.

Stich, Sidra. *Anxious Visions: Surrealist Art*. New York: Abbeville Press, 1990.

Stravinsky, Igor, and Robert Craft. *Conversations with Igor Stravinsky*. Berkeley and Los Angeles: University of California Press, 1980.

———. *Dialogues*. Berkeley and Los Angeles: University of California Press, 1982.

———. *Expositions and Developments*. Berkeley and Los Angeles: University of California Press, 1981.

Strunk, Oliver, ed. *Source Readings in Music History: From Classical Antiquity through the Romantic Era*. New York: W. W. Norton and Company, 1950.

Synge, John Millington. *Collected Works*. Vol. 1, edited by Robin Skelton. Gerrards Cross: Colin Smythe, 1982.

Taruskin, Richard. *Stravinsky and the Russian Traditions: A Biography of the Works through Mavra*. Berkeley and Los Angeles: University of California Press, 1996.

Thomson, Virgil. *Music with Words: A Composer's View*. New Haven: Yale University Press, 1989.

———. *Selected Letters of Virgil Thomson*. Edited by Tim Page and Vanessa Weeks Page. New York: Summit Books, 1988.

———. *Virgil Thomson.* New York: Alfred A. Knopf, 1966.

———. *A Virgil Thomson Reader.* New York: E. P. Dutton, 1981.

Tisdall, Caroline, and Angelo Bozzolla. *Futurism.* London: Thames and Hudson, 1977.

Tommasini, Anthony. *Virgil Thomson: Composer on the Aisle.* New York: W. W. Norton and Company, 1997.

Tyler, Parker. *Florine Stettheimer: A Life in Art.* New York: Farrar, Straus and Company, 1963.

Wagner, Richard. *Gesammelte Schriften.* Edited by Julius Kapp. Leipzig: Hesse and Becker, ca. 1914.

Weill, Kurt. *Ausgewählte Schriften.* Edited by David Drew. Frankfurt: Suhrkamp Verlag, 1975.

———. *Speak Low (When You Speak Love): The Letters of Kurt Weill and Lotte Lenya.* Translated by Lys Symonette and Kim H. Kowalke. Berkeley and Los Angeles: University of California Press, 1996.

Weininger, Otto. *Geschlecht und Charakter: Eine prinzipielle Untersuchung.* Vienna: W. Braunmuller, 1903.

Weiss, Jeffrey. *The Popular Culture of Modern Art: Picasso, Duchamp, and Avant-Gardism.* New Haven: Yale University Press, 1994.

Whitesitt, Linda. *The Life and Music of George Antheil, 1900–1959.* Ann Arbor: University of Michigan Research Press, 1983.

Williams, William Carlos. *Selected Poems.* New York: New Directions, 1963.

Wittgenstein, Ludwig. *Philosophical Investigations.* 3d ed. Translated by G. E. M. Anscombe. New York: Macmillan, 1958.

———. *Wittgenstein's Lectures / Cambridge, 1930–32.* From the notes of John King and Desmond Lee. Edited by Desmond Lee. Chicago: University of Chicago Press, 1980.

Woolf, Virginia. *Collected Essays.* Vol. 2. New York: Harcourt, Brace and World, 1967.

Yeats, William Butler. *Essays and Introductions.* New York: Macmillan, 1961.

———. *The Letters of W. B. Yeats.* Edited by Allan Wade. London: Rupert Hart-Davis, 1954.

———. *The Poems of W. B. Yeats.* Edited by Daniel Albright. London: J. M. Dent, 1990.

———. *The Variorum Edition of the Plays of W. B. Yeats.* Edited by Russell K. Alspach. New York: Macmillan, 1966.

———. *W. B. Yeats and T. Sturge Moore: Their Correspondence, 1901–37.* Edited by Ursula Bridge. New York: Oxford University Press, 1953.

Yip, Wai-lim. *Ezra Pound's Cathay.* Princeton: Princeton University Press, 1969.

Photo Credits

Figures

1: Private collection; 4, 7: Theatre Museum Picture Library, the Victoria and Albert Museum, London; 9, 11: Giraudon/Art Resource, NY; 19, 20, 33, 34c: The Dance Museum, Stockholm; 21: Joan Miró, *Person Throwing a Stone at a Bird*. 1926. Oil on canvasm 29 × 36½″ (73.7 × 92.1 cm). The Museum of Modern Art, New York. Purchase. Photograph © 1999 The Museum of Modern Art, New York; 23: Tom Haartsen, Kerkstraat 42, 1191 JD Guderkerk a/d Amstel; 24: © Photo RMN; 31: Telimage, Paris; 36: Max Ernst, *Stratified rocks, nature's gift of gneiss iceland moss 2 kinds of lungwort, 2 kinds of ruptures of the perineum growths of the heart (b) the same thing in a well-polished box somewhat more expensive* (1920). Anatomical engraving altered with gouache and pencil on paper, 6 × 8⅛″ (15.2 × 20.6 cm). The Museum of Modern Art, New York. Purchase. Photograph © 1999 The Museum of Modern Art, New York.

Examples

5.1, 5.2, 5.7, 5.8, 5.9, 5.10: The Beinecke Rare Book and Manuscript Library, New Haven, CT.

Index